WINGS of the DAWNING

THE BATTLE FOR THE INDIAN OCEAN
1939 – 1945

Another book by the same author
(with Dr. T.A.N. Waller)
Drug Misuse. A Pratical Handbook for G.P.s

WINGS of the DAWNING

THE BATTLE FOR THE INDIAN OCEAN
1939 - 1945

ARTHUR BANKS

FOREWORD BY
AIR VICE MARSHAL J.N.STACEY CBE DSO DFC

THE MALVERN PUBLISHING COMPANY

First published in Great Britain 1996 by Images
This edition, 1998
The Malvern Publishing Company Limited,
32, Old Street,
Upton-upon-Severn,
Worcestershire,
WR8 0HW
England.

British Library Cataloguing in Publication Data

A catalogue record for this book is available
from the British Library

ISBN 0 947993 74 6

Printed and bound in Great Britian

CONTENTS

ACKNOWLEGEMENTS

I have had so much help over the past eight years in compiling this history that an alphabetical list seems the only way of recording the people I am indebted to directly, though there are many others who helped indirectly.

Some RAF veterans wrote me pages of reminiscences, with many literary gems, for which there is not enough room. Nevertheless I have benefited from their wisdom, and I will leave much information with the archives at the RAF Museum, Hendon. Others, especially in the Indian Ocean Flying Boat Association which Geoff Guy and I founded in 1988, have given or lent valuable material, both written and photographic. Several busy authors and experts have freely given advice when asked.

No one can be busier than a retired Air Marshal, yet five of them who served 'out there' have given time to my problems and provided their memoirs. I am indebted to Air Vice Marshal John Stacey for his foreword; to Air Chief Marshal Sir John Barraclough for his encouragement; to Air Vice Marshal Avian Case for his insights; to Air Vice Marshal Ted Hawkins for his epilogue, and to Air Marshal Sir Charles Broughton for other help.

Several former members of U-boat crews have proffered memoirs and rare photographs illustrating life 'on the Axis side' and Herr Horst Bredow of the Cuxhaven Museum, the Stifftung Traditionsarchiv Unterseeboote, has been of particular assistance even when rushed off his feet as he always is. The same goes for Herr Walter Schöppe, ex-War correspondent on U-178.

Museums and libraries; staff of the RAF Museum, Hendon; art and archive departments, particularly Miss Christina Tomas, Curator of the Visual Arts; the Imperial War Museum and staff of the Dome library; the Submarine Museum, Gosport, with Gus Britton; the Royal Navy Museum, Portsmouth; the Public Record Office at Kew; the Air Historical Branch, Ministry of Defence, with Air Commodore Henry Probert, Director; and the Naval Historical Branch, MOD, with Robert Coppock; the RAF Staff College library at Bracknell; all of them have always given courteous attention to my needs.

Chelmsford Public Library's access to the wide computer network has unearthed many old books. Its generous staff have supplied many obscure facts. The ladies of Great Baddow Post Office have eased the task of sending hundreds of letters and packages to faraway places with romantic names.

Many individuals have financed different parts of the research needed, in greater or lesser degree, and to all I am grateful. I apologise to some in the book whose names or details may be wrong or even omitted; also to the majority in this list on whose final rank in the forces there has not been time to check. It is safer just to add RAF.

The phrase 'Retd' (retired) is omitted, as Flight Lieutenant Andy Thomas, Aviation Historian, is my only RAF adviser on active service. To him and to R.C.B. 'Chris' Ashworth, also Aviation Historian, my debt is huge. My thanks also to Michael Turner, President of the Guild of Aviation Artists, for permission to use his magnificent painting and to his predecessor Frank Wootton OBE PPGAvA for his encouragement. I cannot thank enough my son John and his friends and Richard Pearson for providing the word-processor which revolutionises the writing of books; also Dr H.J. Missen and his staff at Beauchamp House Surgery, Chelmsford, for photocopier and other assistance. In the following list I have omitted many of those who are already acknowledged in the text.

Ken Arblaster RAF. Ken Ashworth RAF. Ron Anstey RAF. Keith Atterbury, Chelmsford. Captain Oscar Barnett DFC RAF BOAC. Norman Belcher RAF. Les Bennett RAAF. Damien Bhanji, computer expert, with Hywel Chivers of Chelmsford. George Bennett RAF. Aubrey Bradford RAF.

John Bishop RAF. Corporal Gifford Blamey RNZAF. Wing Commander Don Bleach RAF. Andrew Boggon RAF. Miss Danielle Buck. Collin Botham RAF. Frank Borrill, Suffolk. Dr Robert Bower RCAF. My late parents, Canon Ralph and Mrs Dora Banks who preserved my wartime sketches which started off the idea of the book. Arran Buck, Danbury. Miss Ethel Banks, Withington, Manchester. My nephew Philip Budden and his wife Kathy of Bremen, for German Introductions.

Mrs Cornelia Bradford, née van Gennep, Slough. Ron C. Bradford. RAF. Gus (submarine) Britton MBE RN for his special help. Mrs Joan Bryer. Bob Bush RAF. Roger Ballantyne RNZAF.

Flight Lieutenant K.V.S. Caligari DFM. Lt B.G.M. Cangley RN. Ken Churchill RAF. Ian Clyde RCAF. Peter Colyer RAF. Raymond Cox RAF. Mrs Sarah Clayton.

Brian Cull, Author. Ewan Cameron RNZAF. Erin Costello RNZAF. The

10

late Bob Chapman, Hon Sec JAVA FEPOW CLUB 1942. Steve Cairns MBE, Welfare Officer JAVA FEPOW CLUB 1942.

Jack Davies RAF. Len Davis RAF. Dudley T. Dresch RAF. Jim Drew RAF. S/Ldr R.A.P.H. Dutton DFC CPM. Mrs Pam Dutton, Newark. Robert Delpech RAF, UK High Commissioner for the Seychelles. Frank Elliott RAF. Peter Esling RAF. John Evans, Author, Pembroke Dock. Ken Emmott RAF. Joe Edis RAF. The Elim Church, Chelmsford. Mrs Talitha Eck-Constantinescu, Hamburg.

Bob Ferguson RAF. Captain P.D. Fleet RCAF, Squadron Historian, 413 Squadron. The late Flying Officer John Foxon RAF. Mrs Mary Foxon, Great Baddow, Essex. Keith Fitton, Weybridge. Doug Forty RAF. Miss Eunice Frankland, Audenshaw, Manchester.

Nico Geldhof, Historian, Netherlands. Les George RAF. W.J. Ginn RAF. 'Rock' Gunesekare, J.P, Royal Ceylon Naval Volunteer Reserve. Karl Günther U/861 Bremen. R. Gurney RCAF, Hon Secretary of the Canadian Aircrew Association. Geoff Guy RAF, Hon Treasurer of the Indian Ocean Flying Boat Association.

Allan Gee RAF. J. Groves RAF. J. Gibbs RAF. Captain Johnny Hackett RAF BOAC. Tony Harold, Curator of Art, RAF Museum, Hendon. Sid Haskell RAF. Brian Heathorn, my tutor in German, Chelmsford. E. Hopkinson RAF, Hon Secretary IOFBA. Harry Hughes RAF. Harry Hutson, Marine Author, Cleethorpes. Andrew Hendrie, Aviation Historian. Lt/Cdr Arnold Hague (RNR Retd)

Frau Olive Hinz, Dortmund. Herr Friedrich Hafer, U/195. Mrs Helen Haylett, Maldon, Essex. Mike Hughes, Oban. Frank Holland RAF. Arthur Jennings RAF. Wing Commander A.D. Jillings RAF. Lyn Jones, Artist, RAF. Don James RAF.

Geoff Kirkland RAF. Mrs Patricia Kennedy (née Foster) WAAF, Nairobi. John Lang RAF. Jim Lawlor RAF. Alex Lowe RAF. Christopher Lowe, U-boat Adviser, Nottingham. Steve Linsley RAF. W. 'Paddy' Macklin RAF. Mrs Halcion May 'Popsy' Marsh (née Falconer-Taylor) WAAF, Barton-on-Sea. Roy Marshall RAF. Tom McKirdy RAF. Geoff Mobley RAF.

Captain K-F Merten, Knights Cross, with Oak Leaves, Commandant U/68, Waldshut, Germany. Squadron Leader Dudley Martin OBE RAF. R.W. Moorwood RAF. Rear Admiral Mario Maguolo It.N. (Italian Defence and Naval Attaché) London, and the Italian Navy authorities in Rome.

Roy C. Nesbit, Author. Hal New RAF. Capt. Jürgen Oesten, Knight's Cross, Commandant U/861, Bremen. Stanley Overend RAF. Stan Oxley MID, RAF. Herbert Panknin, Knight's Cross, Chief Engineer, U/861, Langen-Sievern. Captain John Petschi, Royal Netherlands Naval Air Service. Brian Philpott, Historian. Air Commodore Henry Probert RAF.

Gus Platts RAF. Doktor (med) Hans Possin, Medical Officer, U/861, Bremen. Don Purdon RAAF. Cecil Philcox, Royal Artillery. Captain Helmuth Pich of U/168. Howard Price RAAF. Air Commodore G.R. Pitchfork MBE.

Dennis Reed RAF. Albert Ridder U/862, Denbigh. Les Ridgeway RAF. Bert Rivers RAF. Mrs Dorothy Robotham, Leamington Spa. The family of Flight Lieutenant Fred Roddick DFC RCAF of Alberta. Wing Commander W.W. Russell RAF. Karl Rode, U/504, Hon Secretary U-Boot-Kameradschaft, Bremen. D.D. Rolph RAF. Ron Rockett RAF.

Len Sales, Merchant Marine. Desmond Scherr RAF. Walter Schöppe, Author (U/178), Wilhelmshaven. The late Doktor (med) Robert Schridde, Charlotte Schliemann, Osterholz-Scharmbeck. Keith Scott RAAF. Miss Samantha Skingley BA, German translator, Terling. Basil Smith RAF. Joe Spencer RAF. Clive Spratt, Chelmsford.

The late Air Commodore Peter Seymour. Mrs Eleanor (Liz) Seymour, Tunbridge Wells. Ronald W. Smith RAF. Lt Andrew Stewart RNVR, Tanganyika Naval Volunteer Force. Keith Scott RAAF. Herr Albert Schirrmann U/862, Bochum-Stiefel. Richard Smith, Boat of Garten, Inverness.

Group Captain C. Rupert Taylor OBE RAF, Durban. Peter Tebbitt RAF. Mrs Pat Thomas, formerly Section Officer Patricia Roberts WAAF. Dr Margaret Thiemeier, German translator, Soest, Germany. Miss Eleanor Taux, German translator, North London.

Mrs Chris Todd, née Lough, Sunderland. Michael Tomlinson, Author RAF. Henry Tomlinson, Television Producer. John Y. Torrie RAF. E.M. Thomas, Rondebosch, South Africa. W/Cdr L.G.R. Virr RCAF

Karl Wahnig, U/802, U-boat Museum, London. John G. Walker JP RAF. Tom Weaving RAF. John Whitaker RAF. Allan Whiting RAF. Karl-Heinz Wiebe, Knights Cross, Chief Engineer, U/178 Bremen. Josef Wieser, Steersman U/532, Wargrave. Syd Wood RAF. L.N. Worth RAF. William H. Wright RCAF. Andrew Wright, Chelmsford.

My publisher has been very tolerant of the mass of statistics and illustrations and I would like to thank the team.

*This book is dedicated with love to Doris, my wife;
to the aircrews who took part in operations in the
Indian Ocean in World War Two and to the ground staff
who supported them; remembering all on the opposing
sides, with the neutrals, who died there, and those
who grieved for them.*

Air Vice Marshal John N. Stacey, CBE DSO DFC

The war in the Far East was in many ways very different from those in Europe and the Middle East and from that of the Americans in the Pacific. These differences affected all three services, and the maritime element of the Royal Air Force no less than others. However, little has been written of maritime operations in the Far East and many will therefore welcome this valuable contribution from Dr Arthur Banks. I am certainly honoured that he invited me to write this foreword and am delighted to do so.

It is difficult to be precise in defining WW2 operational theatres for maritime operations but a broad description of the Far East might be the sea areas west of Africa and Arabia to the west coasts of Burma, Thailand, Malaysia and Sumatra and south of Java. The principal enemies were of course Germany, Italy and Japan, and it was therefore natural that the Far East attracted considerably lower priority than the other theatres which were closer to them.

We in the Far East readily accepted that Europe and the Middle East had first call on all resources, including manpower, the latest aircraft and all such supporting services as radio aids, spares and maintenance equipment. Admittedly the scale and strength of the air and maritime threats were less than in other theatres; even so, commitments were often met only by constant improvisation, ingenuity and accepting standards more appropriate to the pioneer days of aviation than those of the 1940's. A few examples follow.

On arrival in Ceylon with other Catalinas in early 1942, no charts were available and we had to produce our own before we could operate. When detached to Cape Town, a part on my Catalina broke and no replacement could be found. My engineer, Flight Sergeant Baird, fortunately one of Halton's best pre-war engineer products, found a blacksmith and repaired the offending part by delicate and highly skilled welding. The method of assessing technical tradesmen for advancement had to be changed because, instead of giving textbook answers to questions, they explained how to do the job without proper tools! I could quote many more examples and others could match or better each one.

The lack of resources also resulted in less sophisticated command and control methods than elsewhere; consequently, relatively junior officers were allowed greater discretion, right up to VJ Day, than was normal in other theatres. To my mind, proper credit for this has never been given to the senior officers who readily gave such discretion but who nonetheless bore ultimate responsibility.

Those who were there will need no reminding of the 'making do' which accompanied so many activities, nor of the discretion given to, indeed expected, of junior ranks. I stress these matters, however, so that others may be aware of them when enjoying the incidents recorded in this book.

We should all be grateful to Dr Banks for the great pains he has taken to research this individualism which makes his book more readable and interesting than most. For myself, and I'm sure on behalf of others who 'were there', I thank him warmly for reminding me of stressful but stimulating times.

It began one morning in the RAF Museum, Hendon, which even if you know nothing of aeroplanes is a fascinating place to visit. Having myself served in RAF East Africa from 1943 to 1945 as a Meteorological Observer, and done much sketching in my spare time there, I was coming to present to the Museum a collection of these sketches and cartoons, carefully preserved by my parents and two sisters. The previous Curator of Art there, Tony Harold, a pilot-painter himself, was saying that there was little in the museum to represent the RAF East of Suez, at least in 1986.

People knew little enough about the Pacific War, never mind the Indian Ocean. Aircraft had been disposed of abroad so what could one show? We needed background information about it all. That thought started me off on a seven-year quest for knowledge about this area. My wife has seen our leisurely retirement constantly receding into the distance and family has often taken second place.

To have lived in East Africa, my birthplace, and in India (where Doris and I, as medical missionaries, lived with our two sons and our daughter) was a plus; and visiting Germany, where U-boat veterans of that campaign were more than helpful, gave me a wider perspective. Nevertheless I discovered that this war was, as history goes, a dead duck.

The public hadn't heard about it and the historians and most publishers were dubious. The Canadian official historian, T.W. Melnyk, in his excellent overview[1] *Canadian Flying Operations in South East Asia,* has this to say:

'The anti-submarine war in the Indian Ocean has been generally neglected by military historians. Indeed, there are no books which deal solely with the subject, and only a few which include it as part of a larger story.'

This small effort hopes to correct at least that situation. Now, fifty years after WW2, I still have enough participants in the Indian Ocean campaign to put together a mainly oral history. Partly through the formation of an Indian Ocean Flying Boat Association in 1988 with Geoff Guy as one official and myself the other, I received, over seven years, more material than I could hope to handle.

I am sorry there is not much about certain squadrons like 200, 203, 217, 354 and 628 Squadrons. Other RAF colleagues will be unsatisfied, I fear, but even more so the historian fraternity who see an opportunity for a definitive history going to waste. I challenge them, then, to write such a tome.

Seeing that so many folk think that nothing much happened in the Indian Ocean between 1939 and 1945, my first aim is to show that it most certainly did. A few of the stories may appear trivial or irrelevant, but my second aim has been to give a flavour of what it was like to be in that ocean at that time and to balance the many tragedies one has to describe, in sinkings and battles. While RAF readers might like to see more about the host of operations that went on, for the general reader I have picked out the highlights and the sidelights.

However, a third aim would be to show, for those who live around the Indian Ocean and those tourists who sample its delights on holiday, that the war history of the place is worth reading about.

Not being a trained historian, I have left the analyses and delineation of broader issues which Terry Melnyk would like to see, to the wiser and younger minds of the future. Certain surprising factors, however, have struck me.

The wealth of German and other material; the part played by the American naval-air groups in the Atlantic; the interplay, not to say tussles, between the Prime Minister, Sir Winston Churchill, and the Admiralty[2]; the staggering impact of the ULTRA decoding network; and the influence of the IOGROPS (Indian Ocean General Reconnaissance Operations) unified control centre, along with the Royal Navy submarines, and the RAF squadrons (especially mine-laying Liberators) in winding up the Axis depredations – all these have emerged during seven years study.

Apart from some incidental events and the fate of some RAF crews as Japanese Prisoners of War, I have stuck to the anti-submarine work and have not attempted to include the invasion of South East Asia about which many books have been written. Especially recommended on the RAF side are the two volumes of *Bloody Shambles,* and *The Forgotten Air Force* mentioned in my bibliography. In such a wide field of history, though I have tried to name where possible the participants on the scene, I am bound to have made mistakes and omissions for which I apologise.

Since I have no secretary or full-time researcher I am responsible for anything amiss. Mind you, squadron records are not always reliable, if you check with aircrew logbooks and still-sharp memories. As you will see, any literary merit in this book has been due to the many folk who contributed; some sent even richer memoirs, and superb poems which still could not be included in one volume. Regarding quotations from other's writings, great efforts have been made to trace the origins. Where these have been unsuccessful in the time available, I apologise, but am grateful to include what seems vital to record in this history.

Japanese or some German readers may regret that I have included negative-sounding material about some of the naval activities or prisoner-of-war camps in the Far East. One cannot say that those countries who observed the Geneva Convention never faltered, but Indian Ocean examples were not in evidence. I am sorry the grimmer facts of war cannot be excluded but, as with the Madagascar Japanese midget submarines, courage also needs applauding.

The photographs are a mere fraction of those provided by generous participants. One difference from Europe is that tropical squadrons scattered so often on detachment, and then changed personnel, that crew photos and correct names were not often easy to arrange. The author apologises to those whose photographs he has not credited to them owing to mislaid details. You may see "authors collection" or it could be someone else has sent the same photograph. DFC and DFM awards were fewer, though recommendations from the field were not lacking. Picking out those who won medals may seem invidious but they do provide inspiration. So many acts of bravery or endurance in wartime just went unrecorded. I realise that most of the Indian Ocean campaign seemed dull routine.

The cartoons I did in WW2 were kindly supplemented from Sid Scales' astonishing Far East drawings, copies of which can now be seen in both the Imperial War Museum and the RAF Museum, Hendon, for the benefit of JAVA FEPOWS and others. 'And some there be,' says the Apocrypha, 'which have no memorial'. This tribute may go a little way to fill that void. The quest for history has been long but fascinating. I hope you will enjoy sharing it with me.

N O T E S

1   *Canadian Flying Operatioms in South East Asia* T.W. Melnyk. (Ministry of
    Supply and Services, Canada) Ottawa 1976 (only found in museums or military
    libraries).

2   Well illustrated in Captain Roskill's volumes, *The War at Sea,* mentioned later,
    and Sir Winston Churchill's own six-volume masterpiece, *The Second World
    War.*

"One of Ark Royal's Swordfish", as in the Bismarck chase. "Stringbags" played a vital part in the
Indian Ocean. *(Charles E. Brown via Tanqanika Government)*

LET BATTLE COMMENCE

Colossus astride both East and West,
Judge impassive, over friend or foe,
Great Table Mountain yet brings hope
To boats that past the shipwrecks go.

Near the Cape of Good Hope, once fearfully called by sailors the Cape of Storms, the long plateau of Table Mountain, rising behind Cape Town, looks over its shoulder to the Roaring Forties and the South Pole. In the 'warring forties' of the Second World War the great eminence gazed across a vital hunting ground for Germany's submarines, the U-boats, stalking their prey among the scattered herds of shipping which rounded the southernmost part of Africa.

These brave transports were carrying basic supplies, personnel or war materials for the Middle East and Asia. An example may be given from the end of 1942 when the first German U-boats, The *Eisbär* (Icebear) Group, arrived at the Cape, having replaced other merchant ship raiders.

The morning of 10 October 1942 dawned cold and showery 250 miles south-west of Cape Point. Heading from Egypt back to England, the Orient Line's 23,000-ton passenger liner *Orcades* ploughed steadily on through a rough sea. Her captain would have preferred to be nearer the coast. She was a fine ship, used as a troopship with some civilians, having a good supply of lifeboats. The 1,300 passengers were used to lifeboat drills and blackout was observed at night. With women and children among them, they were glad to be leaving the heat and dust of Egypt for Britain, even wartime Britain with its blackout, its rationing and the bombs.

Captain C. Fox, according to the ship's account he has left us, was well aware of reports of U-boats in his vicinity. He had left Cape Town the day before, and at about 11 a.m. went down from the bridge to his cabin for a snooze and a quiet smoke of his pipe. Fox had not long dropped off when at 11.28 he was wakened, he says, by a loud explosion.[1]

'It was the sound I had been dreading throughout the war,' he said later. 'We had been struck by a torpedo.' Back on the bridge Fox ordered the alarm to be sounded, calling passengers and crew to emergency stations. Two more loud explosions followed, as further torpedoes struck the vessel. She lost way, and did not respond to the helm but fortunately remained on an even keel, so the ship was quickly evacuated. From the gaping hole in the bows poured thousand of oranges, the cargo in No. 1 hold, bobbing everywhere on the tossing waves. Sadly one of the lifeboats carrying 38 people, capsized in the stormy waves, drowning all its occupants. The rest of the 1,300 souls aboard were rescued, including the captain.

The previous night *Kapitänleutnant* (Lieutenant Commander) Carl Emmermann, in his long IXC U-boat, U/172, had noted that it was dark and stormy. He was already experienced in the Caribbean Sea where he had sunk nine merchantmen. He was now to sink six more and win the Knights Cross, no easy medal. The dawn had come with rain squalls and at 10.10 a.m., out of one of these, surrounded by a rainbow, he saw emerging the huge grey shape of a liner, the *Orcades*. He found great difficulty getting into position,[2] 'losing his quarry in another squall, picking up her engines again on his hydrophones when submerged, and finally closing at high speed because he could not maintain periscope depth in the heavy sea.' His three torpedoes stopped her, but after the lifeboats had departed a crew of 52 volunteers got her going again at six knots. *Orcades* was keeping up a stream of messages to Cape Town.

Emmermann, with oranges bumping against his periscope, put another three torpedoes into her and the great ship turned on her side. Captain Fox, last off the ship, had to swim for it. As he swam up the crest of a wave he looked back. The *Orcades* lay with her mast and funnels under water. 'It seemed like a scene out of a film and yet it was reality', he writes, continuing:[3]

'War is a dreadful thing. And to see how so beautiful a ship as the Orcades should be destroyed, with no chance to hit back, seemed to crush everything in me. Slowly she sank deeper and deeper. Then she vanished beneath the waves, with her Red Ensign still fluttering.'

The U-boat captain submerged quickly and made off, under the impression that an air attack was beginning.

The Cape's forces were indeed gathered in strength at this time. Another Polar Bear, U/179 under *Korvettenkapitän* (Commander) Sobe, had been sunk by the RN destroyer, HMS *Active* only on 8 October 1942.

Other destroyers and many anti-submarine vessels were moving about everywhere. 23 Squadron of the South African Air Force was equipped with the Lockheed Ventura (B 34) medium bomber, slightly longer than its older sister the cigar-shaped Hudson, and with two more powerful 2,000 hp engines.[4] The range of this aircraft was a useful 1,660 miles, according to the book.

25 Squadron SAAF was also active with Venturas on the day *Orcades* was sunk, and that of Captain Gray was deputed to find the liner. He did not see her or the submarine, but Emmermann made haste to dive and get away. Gray saw the flotilla of heaving lifeboats, however, before they were picked up by the Swedish freighter *Narvik*. The concentration of Allied units forced the *Eisbär* group to abandon the Cape Town area and scatter.

Going back to the years 1939 to 1942, the hunters then were German warships or Disguised Merchant Raiders. In 1939 the first battleship to arrive was the *Admiral Graf Spee*, commanded by *Kapitän zur See* (Captain) Hans Langsdorff. His ship had been attacking British and other freighters in the Atlantic late in the year but when he moved into the Indian Ocean he sank only a small freighter, the *Africa Shell* on 15 November 1939. The *Graf Spee* then returned to the Atlantic but fortunately missed the liner *Arundel Castle* in which I was returning to East Africa, my birthplace, and to the Bulawayo Mining School, Rhodesia (now Zimbabwe) after 13 years schooling in England.

Across the Indian Ocean in the two succeeding years, 1940 and 1941, events unfolded first of all round South Africa. At the beginning of the Second World War that country's coastal Air Force was even more unprepared than Britain's, consisting first of flights of pre-war biplanes, Hawker Furies and Hartebeests at the ports. There were also South African Airways transport 'planes converted as General Reconnaissance aircraft to scour the seas and carry bombs. However, in 1940 and 1941 not even General, later Field Marshal, Jan Smuts, who had become Premier and was a trusted adviser of Churchill, could persuade Britain – with her back against the wall – and America to help him build up a really adequate coastal defence system.

Until 1942, when the long-range Catalina flying boats arrived, South Africa's enormous coastline and sea lanes were watched over by depleted naval forces and a handful of Lockheed Ventura and Lodestar, Martin Maryland, Avro Anson and Bristol Beaufort squadrons of the South African Air Force. These reconnaissance and bomber units were limited in a range of 800 to 1,600 miles, as compared with a Catalina flying boat's range of 3,000-odd miles, as seen in the North Atlantic. Meanwhile what of the enemy? U-boats such as Emmermann's had not reached the Cape.

The more common invader here were those Disguised Merchant Raiders, cunningly camouflaged, which could adopt several roles. Extra funnels and additions to the hull could be put up overnight, to baffle enemy warships or nosy aircraft. If they drew near innocent merchant ships they could fire a hefty broadside from concealed guns and some had two torpedo tubes.

Nine of the raiders were used between the Cape and the Dutch East Indies. The first of them was the *Atlantis* which sailed in 1940 under *Kapitän zur See* (Captain) Bernhardt Rogge. During a one-and-a-half-year cruise in the Indian Ocean she sank or captured 22 ships, of 145,697 nett tons, before being sunk herself, on 21 November 1941, by the cruiser HMS *Devonshire*. She was succeeded between 1940 and 1943, by further raiders: *Orion, Widder, Thor, Pinguin, Kormoran, Komet, Michel* and *Stier*. The *Doggerbank* was mainly used for minelaying.

No German warships nor raiders nor U-boats could have carried out any of this destruction of merchant traffic without supply ships. SKL, or *Seekriegsleitung* – the operational staff of OKM, the *Oberkommando der Kriegsmarine,* which was the German Navy's Supreme Command – allotted three Secret Rendezvous Areas for supplying all their ships in comparative security. One, between Africa and the West Indies, was called *Bayern;* another, in the South Atlantic, was known as *Andalusien;* the third, halfway between South Africa and Australia, bore the name *Siberien*.

These raiders paid off for Germany. Between 1940 and 1943 nine of the Merchant Raiders sank 128 ships totalling 809,611 nett tons. This was about a third of all ships sunk by Axis forces in the five years of war in the Indian Ocean. Britain could only respond by tracking them down with Royal Navy cruisers. The *Kormoran* was sunk by the Australian cruiser HMAS *Sydney* which itself was sunk by the German ship in a long battle.

One further problem for the Allies was that of blockade-runners. Britain's naval blockade of Germany and Italy meant that vital supplies for their war effort were severely restricted. The average German had to put up with ersatz coffee, but substitute rubber had many disadvantages in war. A burst ersatz tyre could wipe out a warplane and its crew; a smudgy eraser on a chart might cause a serious error in operations. Things like tin, manganese, mercury and quinine were impossible to replace but could be brought from the Far East after Japan's entry into the war. In the opposite direction went supplies to Japan of technical material. Later in the war Germany had to use U-boats like U/532 and U/861 for these goods which were stowed in the keel.

At the start of hostilities in 1939 several German and Italian ships were trapped in the harbours of Colonial Italy or in neutral ports like Goa and Lourenço Marques. One such vessel was the Deutsche Ost-Afrika liner *Watussi* of 9,521 tons which was probably not carrying much in the way of goods but was trying to sidle inconspicuously past the Cape of Good Hope. Once back in Germany she would have made a good blockade runner.

She was spotted at 10.15 on 2 December 1939 – a grey merchant ship with two black funnels, 90 miles south of Cape Point, by a South African Junkers reconnaissance aircraft from Wingfield. She was heading west and Captain H.G. Boshoff SAAF, the pilot, correctly identified her in his report to base. To persuade her to head north for Cape Town he fired machine-gun bursts across her bows and dropped a bomb. She obeyed but when Boshoff's petrol ran low and he headed home, the small liner resumed her homeward trek.

When more aircraft and ships encircled her she hove to and lowered her boats, despite machine gun warnings to keep going. Smoke began to pour from the after hatch and once the crew and passengers had pulled away in boats, to be picked up by the cruiser HMS *Sussex,* the ship became a mass of flame. The burning hulk was sunk by gunfire from the battle-cruiser HMS *Renown*. This was a first victory for the South African Air Force and Royal Navy in a maritime war that was just beginning.

So where were the RAF squadrons in all this? Nowhere in the Southern Oceans but keeping watch in the South East Asia region and carrying out patrol routines in the Red Sea. There would be a presence also in East Africa for the campaign to free Abyssinia (Ethiopia) from Italy, and in support of the Mediterranean campaigns and India but the RAF was not engaged in ocean-wide maritime work until later. We will turn first to the Red Sea.

8 Squadron has had a long history dating back to 1915 and was re-formed in 1920 in Egypt. From 1934 the squadron used Vickers Vincents which were dependable biplanes that could carry up to 1,000 pounds of bombs. By 1940 it had some of the 'modern' Blenheim twin-engined bombers, with a top speed of 285 mph, twice that of a Vincent. Later 8 Squadron used Wellington XIIIs, as we shall see when it helped to destroy U/852 in 1944.

Another maritime squadron in the region was 203. It too had been formed during the First World War in 1915, as No. 3 Squadron, Royal Naval Air Service. Again, by 1940, it was flying a variety of tasks in the Red Sea, including anti-submarine work with Blenheim IVs, based on Khormaksar, Aden.

On 10 June 1940 these two squadrons and the Royal Navy were

active just at the time when Mussolini decided to bring Italy into the war on Germany's side and the Abyssinian campaign began. Some of the first Italian vessels to be attacked in World War Two were submarines using Red Sea ports.

Two reports from the Italian Historical Office of the *Marina Militare* or the Navy in Rome, were provided for me through the kindness of Rear Admiral Mario Maguolo, Italian Defence and Naval Attaché at the Embassy in London, along with photographs. Among many movements in the Red Sea in 1941 one report speaks of four submarines leaving Massawa in March; *Perla* on the 1st, *Ferrari* and *Archimede* on the 3rd, and the *Guglielmotti* on the 4th. A paragraph, in a paraphrase of the Italian, continues the story.[5]

> 'As the crossing [into the Atlantic] would be long and difficult, the ships were given orders not to carry out any warlike actions against shipping. If they were to miss any rendezvous with the supply ship for refuelling, they were ordered to head for the nearest neutral port. *Perla* was to proceed to Madagascar. The others should make for Brazil or the Canary Islands or Cadiz, depending on their self- sufficiency in fuel.'

Three submarines, *Archimede, Guglielmotti* and *Brin* later operated in the Atlantic and between them sank or damaged seven merchantmen, totalling 53,200 tons. The *Perla* and the *Ferrari* also reached safety. It was absolutely vital therefore to trap the remaining submarines.

The *Galileo Galilei* was a submarine of the Archimede 1 class, approximately 231 feet long and of 1,016 tons displacement, when surfaced (1,266 tons submerged). Her commander was *Capitano di Corvetta* Nardi, with a crew of approximately fifty on board. On 16 June 1940, patrolling off Aden, she had sunk a Norwegian tanker *James Stove.* We now have to bring in a fighter squadron, Number 94, which was based at RAF Sheikh Othman, just north of Aden.

The squadron flew Gloster Gladiator biplanes with radial engines, like the famous three that were based on Malta, *Faith, Hope* and *Charity.* On 18 June at 1445 Flying Officer Haywood was sent out to locate an Italian submarine believed to be 30 miles away to the south-east. He reported that he had found the sub so a second Gladiator, flown by Sergeant Smith, was sent out to lead a Vickers Vincent biplane, of 8 Squadron, from RAF Khormaksar to the scene.

In the meantime faster Blenheims, also of 8 Squadron, came up and bombed the Italian at 1630, their bombs unfortunately falling 75 yards to one side. Captain Nardi had decided this was too much of an insult and had started to dive. Haywood, following up closely, machine-gunned the conning tower as the craft slid below the limpid waves like a giant shark suddenly disturbed. The Vincent arrived just too late but decided to have a go where the sub had dived. It dropped its depth charges at the site but was flying too low and slow, and nearly blew itself up.[6]

The Navy sent the destroyer HMS *Kandahar* and the sloop HMS *Shoreham* to the area, with the Anti-Submarine Trawler HMS *Moonstone* patrolling another section. It was now dark. Captain Nardi, about 1900 hours brought his submarine to the surface and unwisely broke radio silence with a Morse message. *Kandahar* obtained a good bearing and both ships veered off on the hunt. Nardi saw *Kandahar* heading towards him and dived at 1935. *Shoreham* dropped depth charges, but no satisfying flotsam appeared. The submarine disappeared.

Next day the Navy moved its search to the east when the Anti-Submarine Trawler HMS *Moonstone,* commanded by an RN Boatswain, W.J. Moorman, joined *Shoreham*. The Navy's 'Monthly Anti-Submarine Report'[7] for July/August 1940 states:

'At 1137, H.M.S. *Moonstone* obtained a contact at 5,000 yards and 14 minutes later attacked with one charge set to 150 ft., the depth of water being 37 fathoms.'

Boatswain Moorman made a series of single depth charge attacks, as the sea and swell were slowing him up. After the third charge, *Galileo Galilei* came to the surface 2,000 yards astern and opened fire, somewhat erratically. The Italian tracer flashes made it easy to pinpoint the target and, said Moorman, 'my twin Lewis guns poured a withering fire into the enemy.' He continues:

'Spare hands manned rifles and formed a sniping party keeping slow and deliberate fire, using the gunwale as breastworks. After a hit with my fourth round of 4-inch the range closed rapidly. The submarine appeared to stop. The enemy crew rushed on deck and hauled down their colours and those who had any clothing of a white nature waved it frantically. This was accepted as a token of surrender.'

The captain was killed by a shell. Forty crew members were captured and a prize crew from *Kandahar* put aboard.

Boatswain W.J.H. Moorman was awarded a DSC[8] and his gunlayer, Petty Officer F.G. Quested, the DSM.[9] Midshipman M.J. Hunter received a DSC and DSMs went also to Acting Petty Officer C.R. Ellis and Able Seaman Thomas Brown.

Naval forces, with some air force help, sank the other two escaping

Italian submarines, both on 23 June 1940 and both after a gallant resistance. The first submarine was the *Evangelista Torricelli II* of the Brin class, built by Tosi at the great naval base of Taranto and launched in 1939. Her commander was *Capitano di Corvetta* Salvatore Pelosi and she carried a crew of sixty.

In the Red Sea *Torricelli* was hunted for two days by the naval squadron and finally brought to bay by the destroyers *Kingston, Kandahar* and *Khartoum*. At point-blank range she faced the fire of their formidable guns to which she bravely replied with her one 3.9-inch gun and four 13.2 mm machine-guns. Captain Pelosi later was able to write a report which the Navy forwarded to the Italian Naval Authorities in Rome. In it the Captain wrote:

> 'Started action against 2 gunboats to which 3 other destroyers were added. The fight concluded after 36 minutes at about 400 metres when, with rudder out of action and adversary closing in on submarine I am forced into shallow water. The enemy's manoeuvre aims at capture of unit. I order the sinking of the submarine and "abandon ship". Wounded, I am saved by my crew and picked up by a British destroyer. British naval authorities express their admiration for Torricelli's action, which alone against 5 units, "with a gun and 4 machine-guns against 24 guns and hundreds of machine-guns, accepted and carried on the fight with decision and intensity. "I pay my tribute to the British Naval Authorities for their cordial and sportsman's feelings towards the crew and for the military honour accorded to the dead which, under my wish, were buried at sea. Dead 4, missing 2, survivors 53.'

Salvatore Pelosi Capitano di Corvetta.

Pelosi's defeat was not in vain, however. During the action a round from her deck gun hit the destroyer *Khartoum* causing a fire which led to the loss of the vessel. Pelosi was awarded the gold medal, *Medaglia d'oro al valor militare*.

The third Italian submarine at large in the region, the *Luigi Galvani* (Captain C. Renato Spano) was also hunted down and sunk, after brave resistance, by the destroyer HMS *Falmouth*. Spano received the same medal.

Near the end of the Abyssinian War came the capture, on 8 April 1941, of the Italian port of Massawa on the Red Sea. The defenders scuttled all sixteen of the merchant ships in the harbour. A week prior to this occurred a notable air operation, which prevented Italy from using her destroyers for marauding in the Indian Ocean.

Italian Submarine, The Luigi Galvani (Captain Capitano di Corvetta Renato Spano MDAVM), sunk on 23 June 1940 off Arabia by R.N. *(Courtesy Italian Navy via R. Adml Maguolo)*

It was now the turn of the Fleet Air Arm when the Aircraft Carrier, HMS *Eagle,* was sent to Port Sudan. She left on shore two Fairey Swordfish squadrons, 813 and 824. The Swordfish, another sturdy and incredibly capable, old-fashioned biplane was known affectionately as the 'Stringbag' and carried a crew of three.

Both 813 and 824 Squadrons had taken part in the successful Battle of Taranto and were now poised for another strike.[10] The aircraft carrier HMS *Eagle* disembarked them at the port where the RAF on the airstrip had provided drums of fuel and a stack of 200-pound bombs. Captain C. Keighley-Peach RN led the attack on 3 April 1941 in which several Swordfish bombed the four Italian destroyers in Massawa harbour, one being sunk by Acting Sub-Lieutenant A. Sergeant RNVR and another by Sub-Lieutenant A. Suthers RN. Two others were later run aground in the Red Sea. Indian Ocean shipping was thus spared more Italian surface attacks.

MEN AND WEAPONS

This history now leaves the Arabian area to move eastwards but, before looking at India, there are questions to be asked and one answer that can be given in a practical way. The preface implied the question as to how a 'Battle for the Indian Ocean' could be such a silent struggle. Again one asks: 'Why did no one hear of the Battle? What famous events took place? What films, apart from "The Sea Wolves", with David Niven, were made about it? What novels, even?'

The answers will come later. At least one reason can be given now in brief. War correspondents tended to be sent to land battle zones and few were available for distant naval or air force outposts. Torpedo survivors' stories were plentiful at home. What detail could people possibly give of silent undersea killers in tropical waters? Security clamped down on ships, cargoes and troop movements. So what was available to hit the headlines in Europe or America? The Indian Ocean struggle remained a distant mystery, though to those on the spot it could be painfully real.

To raise another question implied in this book: why were so few 'successes' obtained in the Indian Ocean by RAF and even by naval units against Axis submarines throughout the period 1940 to 1945? The same thing was happening to the Axis forces in the Indian Ocean. Relatively few merchant ships were sunk by them during that whole time.

This was not because the calibre of those who fought the Indian Ocean war was inferior in any way to that of combatants in the Atlantic or the Pacific Oceans. Examples will be seen of many who, like Admiral Sir James Somerville, whose Force H in the Atlantic helped to trap the *Bismarck,* or Vice Admiral Chuichi Nagumo, who directed the attack on Pearl Harbour, had distinguished themselves in other theatres of war.

Wing Commander Dundas Bednall, later Officer Commanding 230 Squadron, played a significant part in the Battle of Cape Matapan,[11] in a 230 Sunderland flying boat. His uncanny observation powers led to the spotting of two sets of Italian cruisers heading for home, which contributed to the British fleet's night victory.[12]

In most accounts of Matapan this patrol on 20 March 1941 by V/230 (N 9029), captained by F/Lt Alan Lywood DFC, has been omitted. However the Sunderland stayed all day moving between both fleets and sending reports to Admiral Cunningham. 'At one stage', writes W/Cdr Tony Jillings who was the Navigator, 'it looked as if they were signalling to us – actually they were firing at us. It was Tony's calculations, including a mistaken one, which led to the chance discovery of the second fleet. Meanwhile the Italian Admiral Iachino was sending urgent signals to the Luftwaffe and the Italian Air Force 'to get this shadowing aircraft off our backs as soon as possible.' Fortunately no aircraft arrived.

Group Captain Jim Louw, affectionately known as Fats Louw, was in 240 Squadron in the Atlantic and India, and later Officer Commanding 265 Squadron in Madagascar. His exploits in the North Sea were recorded in the Rand *Daily Mail* of 27 June 1941. As a South African (educated at King Edward VII School, Johannesburg) 'in April 1941, F/Lt Louw was detailed to search for the survivors of a torpedoed ship.' After a flight of over 500 miles 'the lifeboat was located and its position signalled to base. Louw eventually returned to base after having been in the air for 24 hours.'

Left to right: G/Capt N.L. Smith; G/Capt G.M. Bryer AFC; W/Cdr D.B. Fitzpatrick CB OBE DFC; W/Cdr J.W. Louw DFC OBE. *(Courtesy of G/Capt Louw)*

For this and a convoy defence he was awarded a DFC and Bar, being congratulated by Air Chief Marshal Sir Philip Joubert de la Ferte, head of Coastal Command, in a letter:

> 'You certainly deserved it [the Bar], for the fine show you put up when you saved a convoy from serious damage, first by attacking and probably destroying an enemy submarine and then beating off a heavily armed hostile aircraft [a Condor] after a long battle.'

Later with 202 Catalina Squadron, based on Gibraltar, he was chosen to pick up the Free French General Giraud from the submarime HMS *Seraph* to confer with General Eisenhower prior to the North Africa landings. As will happen again later, I have a school friend from Weymouth College at a crucial point in this history who actually conveyed the General over in his canoe from the sub to the Catalina that day. He is Major J.P. Foot MBE, a commando of the Special Boat Section, and he discovered that the General was too tall to fit into the rear seat of the kayak. He sat behind on the canvas with his legs in the seat thus wobbling and upsetting the centre of gravity. My friend, aware that any accident could mean a court martial and having been told the General knew only French, was swearing away at him in English all the way over trying to get him to move forward or keep very still.

Jim Louw was having to keep the engines of the Catalina going meanwhile, so the slipstream made it hard for Foot to catch up but when they arrived at the flying boat, he shouted up to them that this general was so tall he might have to sit on the back of the Cat. As they parted General Giraud thanked Foot for bringing him safely over – in perfect English!

Years later, at the 21st birthday of the *Seraph*, at the Portsmouth Submarine HQ, HMS *Dolphin*, Major Foot apologised to Giraud's son Leon for swearing at his father. 'Don't worry,' was the answer, 'my father has dined out on that story many a time.' F/Lt Louw, for his part, received the French Legion of Honour Degree of Chevalier and the Croix de Guerre with Palm. Awards for him later in the war were a Mention in Dispatches and an OBE.

Another remarkable person was Commander Wolfgang Lüth, the most highly decorated U-boat captain in the German Navy. He was the only U-boat Commander to be awarded the *Ritterkreuz* (Knights Cross) with Oakleaves, Swords and Diamonds, the highest award in the Navy, the *Kriegsmarine*. He also had one of the highest scores of ships sunk, 46, and sank a French submarine called *Doris* in addition. Many of these sinkings were in the Indian Ocean. Other U-boat captains too, had served elsewhere with distinction.

What about the vessels and aircraft used in the campaign? We have seen that East of Suez the forces had to make do with many vessels that were not front-line. Submarines may be an exception, but Allied aircraft were not always the latest and best for the job. The IX C U-boat was a good long-range vessel and the more powerful IXD2 U-boat will be described later. Regarding flying boats the two aircraft used most in this campaign were the 'Cat' and the 'Sunderland'.

The American Consolidated Company's 'Catalina' (PBY), manufactured at San Diego, California, and the Short Brothers' 'Sunderland' flying boat, made at Chatham and Windermere, along with the land-plane Consolidated 'Liberator' (B24) and Vickers 'Wellington', were the mainstay of the RAF's final push in the Indian Ocean.

The Sunderland was developed for maritime reconnaissance and submarine attack and had about twice the bulk of the Catalina, which from now on will often be spoken of as the Cat, its common name. The Sunderland did have occasional nicknames like 'Sunderpig' and 'Sunderbus', among the Marine Craft fraternity, and the Germans called it

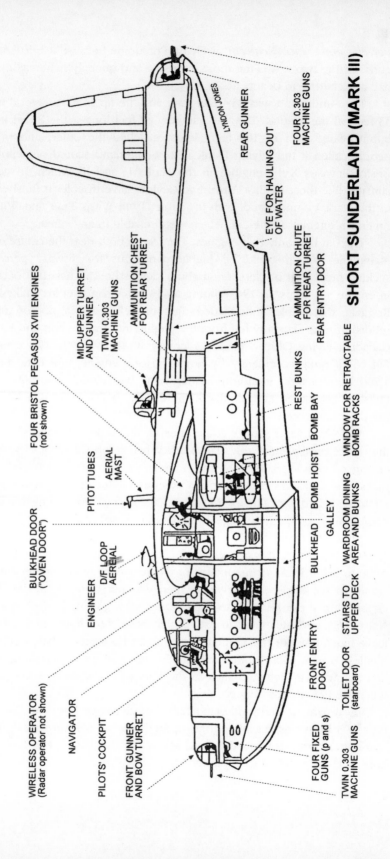

WIRELESS OPERATOR
(Radar operator not shown)

NAVIGATOR

PILOTS' COCKPIT

FRONT GUNNER
AND BOW TURRET

BULKHEAD DOOR
("OVEN DOOR")

FOUR BRISTOL PEGASUS XVIII ENGINES
(not shown)

MID-UPPER TURRET
AND GUNNER

TWIN 0.303
MACHINE GUNS

AMMUNITION CHEST
FOR REAR TURRET

LYNDON JONES

REAR GUNNER

FOUR 0.303
MACHINE GUNS

EYE FOR HAULING OUT
OF WATER

AMMUNITION CHUTE
FOR REAR TURRET

REAR ENTRY DOOR

REST BUNKS

BOMB BAY

WINDOW FOR RETRACTABLE
BOMB RACKS

BOMB HOIST

GALLEY

WARDROOM DINING
AREA AND BUNKS

BULKHEAD

STAIRS TO
UPPER DECK

FRONT ENTRY
DOOR

TOILET DOOR
(starboard)

FOUR FIXED
GUNS (p and s)

TWIN 0.303
MACHINE GUNS

ENGINEER

D/F LOOP
AERIAL

PITOT TUBES

AERIAL
MAST

SHORT SUNDERLAND (MARK III)

der Fliegende Stachelschwein or Flying Porcupine because it bristled with guns. Of the two it was the more imposing and queenly, whereas the Cat had a wicked, lean beauty about it.

The Sunderland was 85.4 feet long and the tip of its tail stood about 33 feet off the ground. The Cat was only 67 feet long with 18 feet height but its wing span of 104 feet almost matched the other, and unkind people called it the 'Flying Plank'. The Sunderland started off with four Bristol Pegasus XVIII engines in the Marks II and III which, in certain climates like those of East Africa and Ceylon, gave trouble. It finished up, in the Mark V Sunderland, with the same 'Twin Wasp' Pratt and Whitney American engines as the Cat, which were reliable in any climate.

The Cat had only two engines. They were both near the centre of the mainplane, which could be highly dangerous for unwary personnel sticking heads out or clambering about carelessly. The risk also occurred in engine accidents. In 1943, during a 413 Squadron Catalina's take-off at Koggala, the whole three-bladed right propeller and a portion of the reduction gear assembly fell from the engine into the cockpit and killed a Canadian Flying Officer, R.S.E. Greenway RCAF (J. 6399). However, the Cat could quite confidently fly home on one engine, which developed 1,200 horsepower. Squadron Leader John Barraclough, later Air Chief Marshal, even tried taking off on one engine in Dar-es-Salaam Harbour, but did not succeed.

The Sunderland Mark V could often fly home on two engines, even if they were on the same side. The Mark V had a top speed of 213 mph, a ceiling of nearly 18,000 feet and a range of between 2,000 and 3,000 miles. The Catalina's cruising speed was often 100 to 120 mph depending on load; it had a ceiling of 24,000 or 28,000 feet, depending on which book you consult; and a range of 3,000 up to 4,000 miles.

Although flying boats, unlike high-level bombers, normally flew at 1,500 to 5,000 feet, it was useful to be able to climb to 15,000 when you came to a hurricane or mountains of dangerous cumulo-nimbus thundercloud. In the tropics, however, oxygen was not brought, neither warm clothing for these heights, so such climbs were avoided when possible. Not even parachutes were in use all that often. Low-flying boats did not leave much time for the 'chute to open and who wants to bale out over a limitless ocean, away from trade routes, into the teeth of waiting sharks and barracudas? 'Better to stick to the kite, son,' the crew would tell us when we flew as passengers.

In armament the Sunderland had the advantage over the Cat. With four .303 Browning machine guns, in the bow and tail turrets, two in the mid-upper turret, four in the nose set in the hull, and even four waist guns, it could repel attackers in the air.

34

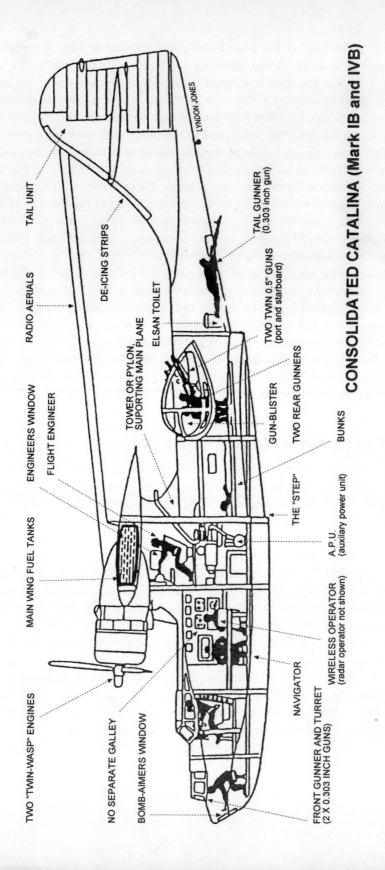

CONSOLIDATED CATALINA (Mark IB and IVB)

TWO "TWIN-WASP" ENGINES

NO SEPARATE GALLEY

BOMB-AIMERS WINDOW

FRONT GUNNER AND TURRET
(2 X 0.303 INCH GUNS)

MAIN WING FUEL TANKS

ENGINEERS WINDOW

FLIGHT ENGINEER

RADIO AERIALS

TAIL UNIT

DE-ICING STRIPS

TAIL GUNNER
(0.303 inch gun)

TOWER OR PYLON,
SUPORTING MAIN PLANE

ELSAN TOILET

TWO TWIN 0.5" GUNS
(port and starboard)

GUN-BLISTER

TWO REAR GUNNERS

BUNKS

THE "STEP"

A.P.U.
(auxiliary power unit)

WIRELESS OPERATOR
(radar operator not shown)

NAVIGATOR

LYNDON JONES

The Catalina, on the other hand, could have done with much better fire-power in front. When attacking a ferocious U-boat which did not intend to dive, the lone bow turret gunner possessed only two .303-inch machine-guns against the fire of a IXD2 sub with a 37 mm Bofors-type gun, four 20 mm Oerlikon-type cannon and occasionally the 10.5 cm big gun on the foredeck, normally used to sink ships. The Cat's waist guns, in a large blister on each side of the aircraft, were a little more powerful. They were twin 0.5-inch Browning machine guns, but they could not fire directly forwards. There was also a single backward-firing 0.303 gun in the hatch underneath, known as the tunnel gun, aft of the blisters, to fire at a U-boat once the Cat had passed over it. By then the Cat or the Sunderland would have used its other armament – usually 6 or 8 Torpex-filled 250-pound depth-charges which could either blow a U-boat to pieces or have no effect at all, depending on just where they exploded. Both aircraft were magnificent for maritime work in their different ways.

So what other factors caused an apparent lack of visible results in this thirteen and a half million square miles of ocean? For the RAF and the Navy the answers will emerge during the ensuing chapters.

For U-boats the haphazard nature of sailings by merchant vessels, the scarcity of bases, the inadequacy of fuel and ammunition stocks along with unreliable torpedoes all helped to limit the tally of sinkings.

FAR EAST TROUBLES

Our story now moves across to India, where again the RAF had no maritime squadrons at the beginning of the war. Singapore had the nearest. The gap was gallantly filled by an unusual force called the Coastal Defence Flights.[13] This force was built up by putting together 'Flights' (units of three aircraft), borrowed from the RAF up on the North-West Frontier and from the Indian Air Force. Then by recruiting British air crews (mostly) with young Indian ground staff to maintain the flights, these were welded into an effective maritime force, limited to the range of the land planes it used. They were at first Westland Wapitis, sturdy old biplanes well proved against Pathan tribesmen. Later some Blenheim bombers were added, with twice the speed, and three times the range of the Wapitis.

All the flights were called upon to do a variety of tasks, such as escorting the Queen Mary in her role as troopship. She was one of the five or six 'Monsters' as they were known, which relied on a speed of 30-odd knots to out-distance U-boats and so could travel alone. The main jobs for the CDF were endless sea patrols, coastal escorts and exercises with the Army and the Navy.

For maritime RAF squadrons in South-East Asia, the Indian Ocean war had officially begun on 3 September 1939 when hostilities broke out in Europe. Initially it was very quiet, and no submarines were involved at that stage between India and Singapore. Potential blockade-runners lurked in some of the neutral ports and 205 Squadron was given the task of keeping an eye on some German freighters in Sabang harbour, at the northern tip of Sumatra.

Flight Lieutenant Alex Jardine, from British Columbia, was the Canadian skipper of a Short Singapore III flying boat with 205 at Seletar, Singapore. He and his crew were given the task of doing reconnaissance over the ports where the Axis ships were confined. Now Group Captain Jardine AFC, he recalls these boats as 'Giant biplanes something like 33,000 lbs all up weight, range of approximately 1,000 miles and a speed in the 90 knots range. The pilot's compartment was singularly bare of instruments, possessing only an altimeter, airspeed indicator, rev counters, turn and bank indicator and a compass on the floor.' The Lewis gunner sat out in the bows, 'facing all the elements'. His boat was FV-J (K/5916), the crew being Williams, Kendall, Popple, Herman and Grant.[14]

Later in 1941 Squadron Leader Jardine did survey flights with a newly acquired Catalina to Mombasa, Dar-es-Salaam and Lindi as well as various Indian Ocean islands and was later awarded the Air Force Cross.

His was the first Catalina into Mauritius. The other flying boat unit at Seletar at the beginning of the war was 230 Squadron. It was the first squadron abroad (and the second anywhere) to be equipped with Short Sunderland aircraft. Wing Commander G.M. Bryer OBE AFC, as Officer Commanding, flew out the first Sunderland in 1938, but by 1940 the Squadron had left for the Middle East. Perhaps not many in 230 Squadron, nor those of us who were privileged to know Peter Bryer and his family in Mombasa later, realised what an early aviation pioneer he was. Born in 1897 and inspired by meeting Cody and Blériot in 1912, he joined the RNAS and helped establish, with Sopwith Pups, the early deck landings on warships. In 1919 he won the AFC for wartime exploits. After years on Wapitis on the North-West Frontier he served with distinction through WW2 in the Mediterranean and Indian Ocean.

En route to the Middle East 230 Squadron stayed at China Bay, near Trincomalee Naval base in northern Ceylon (Sri Lanka). While there Bryer did the first survey for creating a flying boat base on the south coast at Koggala near Galle, which is said to have one of the Top Ten beaches in the tourist world. In 1940 the move towards Egypt was meant to be secret. Group Captain Bryer, who died in 1994 at the age of 97, recalled for me how secret it actually was.

Sunderland Mark GR5, J/209 over the dhow harbour, Mombasa, in 1945.
(Courtesy of W/Cdr Don Bleach)

'We halted at Ceylon on the way, to join in the effort to keep the *Admiral Scheer* away from the convoy bringing the Australians to the Middle East. There were no subs in the area at the time but by chance a ship established moorings at Colombo. It was a freighter from Bombay dockyard piled with buoys, sinkers and chains boldly labelled "OC 230 SQUADRON – MAURITIUS, SEYCHELLES, DIEGO SUAREZ etc." This, within 24 hours, enabled Lord HawHaw[15] on German radio to tell the world that 230 was about to move to Africa.'

205 Squadron continued to carry out uneventful patrols in the Far East. About March 1941 two New Zealanders, Pilot Officers Sid Scales and Ross McHardy were posted to Seletar. They joined the patrols and enjoyed the new Catalinas which were being sent via Manila from San Diego, California. In his spare time, Sid, a professional cartoonist, who has recently retired after 30 years on the *Otago Daily Times* and had been awarded the OBE, acted as squadron artist. He then produced brilliant caricatures as a POW.

The invasion of South-East Asia by the Japanese is not strictly part of the anti-submarine battle in the Indian Ocean itself. The effect on that battle was enormous, not least because it gave Germany such Japan-held

UPPER LEFT: F/Lt A.M. Jardine AFC and his crew of a Singapore III, Nicobar Islands 1941 (Names lost in the Singapore battle).

(Courtesy of A.M. Jardine AFC)

UPPER RIGHT: Short Singapore III of 205 Sq (Chapter 1).

(Courtesy of A.M. Jardine AFC)

LOWER LEFT: New Zealanders in RAF, Singapore, 1941. Left to right: P/O R. Scott, 205 Sq; Sgt Pilot J. Smith 36 Sq; P/O Sid Scales, 205 Sq; Sgt Pilot H.E. Boyes, 36 Sq; P/O E. Garnett, 205 Sq.

(Courtesy of S. Scales OBE)

LOWER RIGHT: 205 Sq Catalina on the slip, with local workers, Seletar, Singapore, 1941.

(Courtesy of Ken Matthews)

Air Vice-Marshal
C. W. H. Pulford, C.B., O.B.E., A.F.C.

Caricature from RAF
Eagle magazine by Sid
Scales. AVM Pulford is
holding a Buffalo plane.

bases as Penang and Sourabaya in which her long-range U-boats could refuel and revictual in peace, with Singapore, renamed Shonan by the Japanese, for major repairs in dry dock.

The two volumes known as *Bloody Shambles* are the most detailed of the books on the RAF aspects of the struggle.[16] A key figure in trying to reduce the shambles was Air Vice Marshal C.W.H. Pulford CB OBE AFC whose likeness Sid Scales has captured here. Instead of the fast modern fighters he had been promised, the AOC had to cope with a force of Brewster Buffaloes, as depicted in Pulford's hand, with various other aircraft, some of the RAAF, RNZAF and Dutch forces. The Buffaloes proved to be obsolete and were in too few numbers to affect the final outcome.

The day before the Japanese extended the war by attacking, it was 7 December 1941, both Pearl Harbour and Singapore, a lone 205 Squadron Catalina, FV-Y, set out on patrol to relieve FV-S, F/Lt Atkinson's Cat in which Sid Scales was Second Pilot. A large Japanese Convoy, with two aircraft carriers and ten cruisers was reported in the Gulf of Siam. FV-Y was captained by Warrant Officer W. E. 'Bill' Webb, a very experienced pilot who came up through the ranks. Most reports assume that because

F/O Pat Bedell was an officer pilot in the crew,[17] he must have been captain, but Sid Scales is concerned that history should have the correct version. Sid's aircraft did not see the convoy, but Webb's Catalina was approaching it, when it was attacked by a patrol of 10st Sentai Ki27's, according to *Bloody Shambles,* led by Lt Toshirou Kubotani. In a brave battle the Cat exploded in the air and, as the book says, 'the crew of FV-Y perished – the first casualties of the Greater Asian War.'

Then came the cataclysmic sinking of Britain's latest battleship HMS *Prince of Wales* (Capt J. C. Leach), with the battlecruiser HMS *Repulse* (Capt W. G. Tennant). These were under the overall command of the C-in-C Eastern Fleet, Admiral Sir Tom S.V. Phillips KCB and their loss by Japanese torpedo aircraft and bombers on 10 December 1941, north-west of Singapore opened the floodgates into the Indian Ocean from the East and proved to be a turning point in naval history. From now on large naval battles would be mainly fought between the aircraft carriers of opposing fleets. The loss of Britain's naval might in the Far East changed the balance of power in the Indian Ocean and the struggle against the submarines began.

Both Jardine and Scales with their Catalinas were involved in the defence of Singapore before being captured. This section ends with one of Sid Scales' sketches in the prison camps. Their Squadron, 205 (later re-formed in Ceylon), played a great part in anti-submarine warfare, while these two, with thousands of others, including the writer Laurens van der Post, faced three years rigour in Japanese prison camps in Java.[18]

Alex Jardine was involved at several stages in the last events surrounding the sinking of the *Prince of Wales.* As the two great ships searched along the east coast of Malaya for the expected Japanese landing fleets at Kuantan or Singora on 9 December, Alex's crew was the one sent out to reconnoitre the coast and report to the battleship any enemy activity. Richard Hough's excellent book *The Hunting of Force Z* states that the Catalina, flying over the *Prince of Wales,* came out of the mist at 1245: 'It came in brave and low over the flagship, flashing by Aldis lamp at the bridge – "Japanese making landing north of Singora".'[19]

I have not yet found the RAF confirmation of this. Group Captain Jardine kindly lent me the original fifty-year-old 205 Squadron records. I have these before me stating, for that patrol, 'No Japanese shipping movements of importance were noticed. Landed 1407.' Jardine's letter of 23 December 1993 to me on this point confirms the record.

'Am quite happy to state categorically we did not see any enemy action during the time we provided anti-submarine patrol for HMS *Prince of Wales* and ships accompanying her.'

In the absence of any note in the squadron record, it is unlikely that another Catalina was out there in the mist flashing a report.

In my own one sortie on a 209 Squadron Catalina convoy patrol for 18 hours out of Mombasa in 1943, acting as Meteorological Observer, two things were clear. One, that you did not fly low suddenly over warships full of eager naval gunners; and two, it was difficult to signal any message by Aldis lamp in Morse to a heaving warship, especially in a mist, except by circling patiently round. Then there would be a risk, in the Far East, of being mistaken for a Jap aircraft by other ships of the group.

When Jardine made his sortie next day, on 10 December, towards the two warships, both had been already sunk in an incredibly brave battle against overwhelming waves of fast, powerful torpedo planes and bombers. He found only the Walrus flying boat from the *Repulse*, floating in a minefield near the coast. Alex dropped them canisters of food and water 'wrapped in Mae Wests'[20] and Petty Officer W. J. Crozer and his crew were picked up by the destroyer HMS *Stronghold,* the aircraft being towed back to Singapore! Alex's aircraft of that occasion was FV/Z-205 (AH 540).[21]

Pilot Officer Sid Scales was less fortunate on Christmas Eve 1941. His Catalina FV/Z, captained by Flight Lieutenant R. A. 'Dickie' Atkinson, was shot down by a large twin-engined aircraft possessing cannon, and they all landed in the water with no rubber dinghy. Some even had no Mae Wests and were supported by others. Two more 205 Squadron aircraft failed to find them but they were eventually picked up on Christmas Day by a Dutch submarine, *K/12.* All were suffering from burns and/or bullet wounds.[22] Sid writes:

'As you know I spent some time in hospital in Singapore with burns. From hospital I was evacuated by sea to Batavia in early February. [205 Squadron had already been transferred to Java to carry on the fight.] My first job after being passed fit for service was to take two trucks with spares across the island to Tjilatjap where the squadron was now operating. On Feb 21 I took off as second pilot to F/O Tucker on Catalina FV/K for a patrol in the area of Billiton Island and the west coast of Borneo.

'Taking off at first light we hit an uncharted reef in Tjilatjap harbour and ripped a 3-foot gash in the hull just as we were becoming airborne. We managed to stay flying and during the patrol we sighted survivors from sunk ships, floating around on wreckage – no lifeboats. We circled and signalled Batavia the position and waited till we had a signal that assistance was coming. There were nearly a hundred people and we could see they were dreadfully sunburnt. They were all picked up by three Dutch flying boats, two Dorniers and a Cat – some had to taxi over a hundred miles back to Batavia because of their load. Fortunately it was a calm sea.'

The main remnants of 205 Squadron were then transferred to Australia, losing the last of their Cats on arrival at Broome when the harbour was shot up by Japanese fighters.[23] A small remainder of the squadron was left in Java under Squadron Leader Jardine which found itself in Japanese prison camps. Sid and Alex fetched up at Bandoeng where camp conditions in the first year were not as bad as elsewhere, nor as harsh as they became after that time in Java.

Their POW experiences and Sid's sketches in Java typify, not the highlights of the Indian Ocean War but the 'sidelights'. RAF personnel shot down and wounded or imprisoned seemed, as it were, chess pieces put aside on the margin of the deadly game. To the author they appear no less of interest than those still battling it out on the chequered board. It has been both moving and fascinating to record their stories for the last chapter.

BRIDGE AT ALL COSTS! — EVENING SCENE IN JAPANESE P.O.W. BILLETS — JAVA.

Sid Scales' first impressions of POW camp, Bandoeng Java.

Regarding Bandoeng, Alex Jardine says: 'We attempted to make life as normal as possible. I know one group of people who played bridge all day.' Sid Scales' cartoons and his sketches later in the book prove this.

The surrender of Singapore to the all-conquering Japanese army took place on 15 February 1942 when 80,000 of the defenders went into a harsh and often terrible captivity. The fall of South East Asia closed a long chapter in British and Dutch imperial history.

NOTES

[1] *U-Boot Gruppe Eisbär* Martin Pfitzmann (Moewig) Munich via Karl Wahnig.

[2] *War in the Southern Oceans,* Turner, Gordon-Cumming and Betzler (Oxford University Press), Cape Town 1961.

[3] *U-boot Gruppe Eisbär* - see no 1.

[4] *WITSO* see no 2.

[5] *La Marina Italiana nella Seconda Guerra Mondiale* Volume X *Le Operazione in Africa Orientale,* Chapter 5 (Italian Navy Historical Office), Rome 1976.

[6] Squadron Records, Public Record Office, Kew.

[7] Royal Navy's *Monthly Antisubmarine Report* July/August 1940 (Naval Historical Branch, Ministry of Defence, London), courtesy Robert Coppock.

[8] DSC - Distinguished Service Cross (Officers).

[9] DSM - Distinguished Service Medal (Other Ranks).

[10] *Squadrons of the Fleet Air Arm,* Ray Sturtivant (Air Britain), Tonbridge 1984.

[11] *Sun on My Wings,* W/Cdr D. Bednall (Paterchurch Publications), Pembroke Dock 1989.

[12] *Salvo!: Classic Big Gun Actions,* Bernard Edwards (Arms and Armour Press), London 1995.

[13] *In Defence of India,* article, S/Ldr D. W. Warne (Air Enthusiast) 7.10.1985.

[14] 205 Squadron Records, via G/Capt A. Jardine AFC RCAF.

[15] Lord HawHaw - the 'aristocratic' braying English voice of an American-born broadcaster, William Joyce, on German Radio. Joyce was hanged after the war.

[16] *Bloody Shambles,* Shores, Cull and Izawa (Grub Street), London 1992.

[17] The crew were: W/O William E. Webb, (Capt), F/O Patrick E. Bedell, 2nd Pilot, Sgt Colin B. Treloar RAAF, Sgt Edward A. Bailey, Fitter 2, Sgt Stanley Abraham and Sgt Peter Eaton, WOP/AGs, LAC Arthur H. Chapman, AG, AC1 William T. D. Burnett, Flt Mechanic (mainly as named in *Bloody Shambles*).

[18] *The Night of the New Moon,* Laurens van der Post (Hogarth Press - London) refers to Scales and other RAF personnel.

[19] *The Hunting of Force Z,* Richard Hough (Collins), London 1963.

[20] Mae West - inflatable yellow life-jacket (named after the famous large-bosomed American actress).

[21] Jardine's crew: P/O McVicker, F/Sgt Miles, Sergeants Tugwell and Morris, Corporals Abbott and Wynant, with LAC Ballard.

[22] Atkinson's crew: Atkinson and Scales Pilots; Babineau, Navigator; Borchers, Observer; Sergeants Smith and Morris; Petty Officer Heath RN; Corporal Wynant; and again LAC Ballard.

[23] In the Broome attack (known as Australia's Pearl Harbour), according to Jim Bowden, a 205 Sq Flight Engineer who was wounded in his Cat there, the Japanese Navy Zeros sank 10 Catalinas, 4 Dutch Dorniers, 2 Short Empire Flying Boats and a seaplane. There were also many casualties. Jim's skipper was shot and the Second Pilot, a Sikh, was drowned on 3 March 1942 in a 10-minute raid.

CEYLON IS SAVED

J apan lost no time in turning her attention to India and Ceylon. Unknown to the Allies, Grand Admiral Raeder, the German Navy's Commander-in-Chief, in a report to Hitler dated 13 February 1942, gave the following information, quoted by the late Michael Tomlinson in the *Most Dangerous Moment*, a brilliant book on this whole period.[1]

> 'Japan plans to protect this front in the Indian Ocean by capturing the key position of Ceylon, and she also plans to gain control of the seas in that area by means of superior naval forces. Fifteen Japanese submarines are at the moment operating in the Bay of Bengal, in the waters off Ceylon and in the straits on both side of Sumatra and Java. Once Japanese battleships, aircraft carriers and submarines and the Japanese Air Force are based on Ceylon, Britain will be forced to resort to heavily escorted convoys if she desires to maintain communications with India and the Far East.'

Tomlinson adds:

> 'Plans to strike westwards into the Indian Ocean and seize Ceylon had been prepared by the staff of the Japanese Combined Fleet. They had gone further and even envisaged taking over Madagascar, then in Vichy French hands, as they had virtually taken over Indo-China.'

In the event, although the Imperial Japanese Navy chiefs favoured the idea of capturing Ceylon by a combined invasion, the Imperial Japanese Army chiefs disagreed and, with their eyes on Australia, refused to commit forces to Ceylon. The Navy, therefore, decided on a two-pronged naval attack, under the overall command of Vice-Admiral Kondo. Vice-Admiral Chuichi Nagumo was to lead the larger force to find and destroy Britain's Eastern Fleet and to smash the naval bases in Ceylon. A second force was to be led by Vice-Admiral Ozawa into the Bay of Bengal to destroy as much shipping as possible there. The stage was now set for a possible Japanese takeover of the Indian Ocean.

Vice Admiral Nagumo had been the leader Japan chose to direct the devastating attack on the American fleet at Pearl Harbour on 7 December 1941 which brought the United States fully into World War Two. Now, at the end of March 1941, Nagumo still had five of the six carriers which he commanded at Pearl Harbour, led by the mighty *Akagi*, his flagship, of 36,500 tons. The others were *Hiryu, Soryu, Zuikaku* and *Shokaku*. In support were four battleships, three cruisers and eleven destroyers. A host of small auxiliary vessels swelled this armada. Nor was there a shortage of aircraft. The carriers in all had 377 modern aircraft, faster than the Allies suspected. Ozawa's fleet included one aircraft carrier.

In the face of an expected Japanese expansion into the Indian Ocean Churchill and the Cabinet were hard-pressed to find adequate answers. They sought to spare what they could from other theatres of war and began a build-up of naval units and maritime air squadrons. By March 1942 there had assembled around Ceylon the largest naval fleet of any during the whole war. The trouble was that some of the ships were obsolete, others untried or unfit, and there had been no chance to weld this assemblage into an effective fighting unit by means of fleet exercises and co-ordination.

To command the new Eastern Fleet the Admiralty sent one of its finest and most experienced leaders, Admiral Sir James Somerville, recently Commander of the formidable Force H in the Atlantic and Mediterranean.

Though known as the Fighting Admiral, Sir James was also wise and adaptable and in the face of severe frustration he made no rash moves. With characteristic drive and humour he set about training his diverse command. He split it into Force A and a slower Force B that included the 'Four R's,' HM Battleships *Resolution, Royal Sovereign, Revenge* and *Ramillies*, which had not been modernised since the First World War. The faster Force A was for more rapid manoeuvring, and included his own flagship, the battleship HMS *Warspite*. Somerville's biographer quotes his typically pithy comments:

'I also hear a lot of blah about how everything depends on our maintaining control of the Indian Ocean,' he complained. 'That's poor bloody me and I wonder how the devil it's to be accomplished. My old battle-boats are in various states of disrepair and there's not a ship at present that approaches what I should call a proper standard of fighting efficiency.'[2]

In Ceylon Admiral Sir Geoffrey Layton was effectively galvanising the island's defences. As for available aircraft to defend Colombo, Air Vice Marshal J.H. d'Albiac, AOC 222 Group, could only acquire a limited selection of 50 Hurricanes, 14 Blenheims (with no experience of attacking ships) and Martlets. The latter, also known as Grumman Wildcats, were tough radial engined fighters with a top speed of 310 to 320 mph. The Fleet Air Arm provided Fulmar fighters, together with Swordfish and Albacore biplanes, but mainly to the north at Ratmalana and Trincomalee. What Somerville urgently needed were long-range reconnaissance aircraft despite which only eight Catalinas were available.

They comprised three from 240 Squadron, and one each from 202 and 205 Squadrons; another, with Lieut Hamers as Captain, came from 321, a Royal Netherlands Naval Squadron, and it had only just managed to escape, following the squadron's battering in Java. The final two arrived from 413 Royal Canadian Air Force Squadron, newly posted from the icy seas of Sullom Voe in the Shetlands.

Some remarkable work was being carried out by American cryptographers in MAGIC, the equivalent of the British ULTRA decoding organisation. This predicted a Japanese fleet moving across towards Ceylon at the beginning of April, 1942. What Somerville had to know at the earliest moment was when and where the invaders would approach. Lieutenant Commander 'Hank' Rotherham of the Fleet Air Arm, in his autobiography, *It's Really Quite Safe*,[3] recalls the occasion in Colombo.

'I was sent ashore by Somerville to make arrangements with the RAF to set up a reconnaissance patrol that would intercept the Japanese the day before their attack so we could attack them that night. Such a patrol line was laid on, using Catalina flying boats operating from their base at Koggala at the south end of the island.'

One of the two 413 Squadron pilots who had arrived from Scotland was Flight Lieutenant Rae 'Tommy' Thomas DFC, a South African from Kenilworth who landed on 28 March 1942. Rae's brother Mr E.M. Thomas of Rondebosch tells me that his brother went to the Diocesan College there and did not work too hard until he found he might be able to get into the RAF. He then slogged at exams till he was able to do so, and joined up in 1937. Thomas had been decorated during his time as captain of Catalina Y/413 on patrols over the North Sea.

The other pilot was Squadron Leader Leonard J. Birchall of St Catherine's, Ontario. He had started his war by forcing an Italian vessel to run aground when it was escaping from the St Lawrence waterway, and he touched down in Ceylon on 2 April. Flight Lieutenant O.G.E. 'Bobby' Roberts, with G.H.U. Bayly in his crew, was delayed in Karachi with autopilot trouble and the fourth Catalina, that of the new Commanding Officer, Wing Commander J.C. 'Johnny' Plant, was followed by the remaining Catalinas.

The squadron's ground crew of 331 comprising other ranks and nine officers, who took passage in HMT *Nieuw Holland*, did not arrive till 1 May 29. Rae Thomas was first to reach Koggala where the base had been established among coconut plantations. The lake was full of obstructions and was surrounded by marshes and tall palms. Only a short clear stretch existed for landings and take-offs.

Birchall's Second Pilot was Pilot Officer P.O. Kenny, whose father was a sea captain – he was born on the shores of the Indian Ocean. Kenny also qualified as a Merchant Navy Second Mate. "Bart" or Warrant Officer G.C. Onyette, the Navigator, was the only other Canadian in the crew. The rest were all sergeants. Brian Catlin, Flight Engineer, hailed from Chinley in Derbyshire, and had enrolled in the RAF at 16 as an apprentice, with a solid grounding.

Another sergeant, W. (Ginger) Cook, Flight Mechanic, stood in for Catlin when required. F.C. (Fred) Phillips hailed from Stoke-on-Trent where he had been a Local Government Officer and was now Wireless Operator-Air Gunner. Another gunner, J. Henzell, was also Flight Rigger. The remaining two were also WOP/AGs. Iain Davidson came from the Isle of Skye, his father being Sheriff there; while L.A. Colarossi had been a dance band leader who played at the Palm Court and Trocadero in happier days.

Rae Thomas and his crew were tasked with a patrol on the night of 2/3 April. They flew for seven hours but saw no ships, hostile or otherwise. His crew members were Flying Officer R.K. Bourne (Second Pilot), Flying Officer R.G. Hervey (Navigator Canadian), Flight Sergeant C.C. Gurney and Sergeants D.L. Housely, J.D. Moxham (Flight Engineer) P. Bourke and J.K. Hooper, a second Canadian.

To avoid another Pearl Harbour Admiral Somerville had dispersed 42 merchant ships from Colombo to other ports and now sent his slower Force B to Addu Atoll (see map). This was a new and secret naval base 600 miles south of Ceylon in the Maldive Islands. There the Four R battleships, which had a rather limited range, could take on water and fuel. Somerville joined them with Force A carrying out a sweep to eastward to try to contact the enemy. He could not afford, with such an unprepared fleet, to engage the enemy by day but hoped to attack them with torpedo bombers during night hours. It became, therefore, hour by hour more urgent to have information on the exact whereabouts and likely course of the Japanese Fleet.

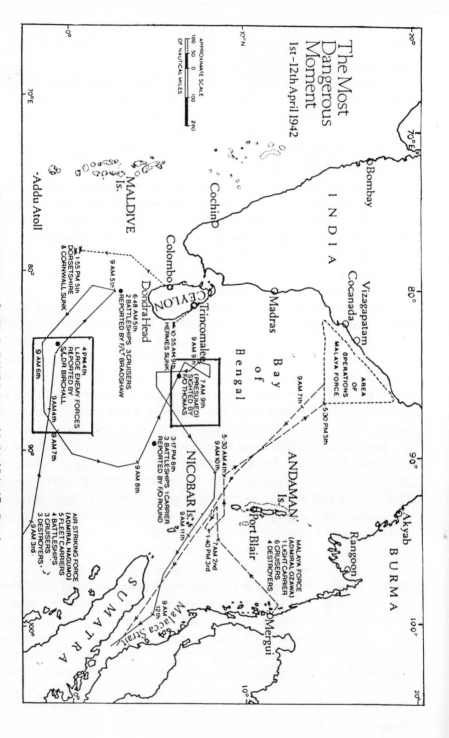

The Japanese attacks on Ceylon, April 1942 (courtesy of the late Michael Tomlinson)

The Most
Dangerous
Moment
1st–12th April 1942

APPROXIMATE SCALE
100   50   0   100   200
OF NAUTICAL MILES

Bombay

Vizagapatam
Cocanada

AREA
OF
OPERATIONS
MALAYA FORCE

I N D I A

Madras

B a y
o f
B e n g a l

9 AM 7th

5.30 PM 5th

ANDAMAN
Is.

MALAYA FORCE
(ADMIRAL OZAWA)
1 LIGHT CARRIER
6 CRUISERS
4 DESTROYERS

Port Blair

Akyab

Rangoon

B U R M A

Cochin

MALDIVE
Is.

·Addu Atoll

Colombo

Dondra Head

CEYLON

Trincomalee
9 AM 9th

10.55 AM 9th
HERMES SUNK

6.48 AM 5th
2 BATTLESHIPS 3 CRUISERS
● REPORTED BY F/LT BRADSHAW

1.55 PM 5th
DORSETSHIRE
& CORNWALL SUNK

9 AM 5th

9 AM 6th

9 AM 4th

9 AM 7th

9 AM 8th

7 AM 9th
(PRESUMED)
SIGHTED BY
F/O THOMAS

4 PM 4th
LARGE ENEMY FORCES
REPORTED BY
S/LDR BIRCHALL

3.17 PM 8th
3 BATTLESHIPS 1 CARRIER
REPORTED BY F/O ROUND

5.30 AM 4th
9 AM 10th

NICOBAR Is.
9 AM 11th

7 AM 2nd
1.40 PM 3rd

AIR STRIKING FORCE
(ADMIRAL NAGUMO)
5 FLEET CARRIERS
4 BATTLESHIPS
3 CRUISERS
3 DESTROYERS
·9 AM 3rd·

S U M A T R A

Malacca Strait

9 AM
12th

Mergui

70°E

70° E

80°

90°

100°

20°

10° N

0°

80°

90°

100°

Len Birchall's crew spent 3 April unloading the aircraft, Q/LA-413 (AJ-155), while the Captain carried out a familiarisation tour of the RAF station and checked accommodation for the officers at a hotel in Galle and for the crew in a commandeered mission girls' school called appropriately enough Richmond Hill.

The Fleet Air Arm officer, Lieutenant Commander Rotherham, back on board his ship in the evening, went below decks.

> 'That night I lay in my bunk thinking about the situation and trying to put myself in the shoes of the Japanese Commander who was planning the attack on Colombo. I decided that I would have flown off from a position to the south-west of Ceylon to make landfall some 20 miles south of the city so that there would be no doubt which way to head along the coast for the attack. To my horror I realised that the patrol line we had set up would not intercept such an approach. I hastened ashore the next morning to reposition one of the Catalina flights to cover this gap, and I slept much better that evening feeling that all contingencies were covered.'

At the same time Admiral Somerville's fleet was carrying out another fruitless sweep to the north-east. The Admiral then detached the cruisers *Dorsetshire* and *Cornwall* and sent them back to Colombo, at the same time ordering the light aircraft carrier *Hermes* and her Australian destroyer escort, *Vampire*, to Trincomalee. Somerville and the rest of Force A and Force B then headed for Addu Atoll for refuelling. Thus, when the attack on Colombo came on Easter Sunday, they were too far off to influence the outcome. At least the destruction of the Eastern Fleet, Nagumo's second aim, was frustrated.

On the evening of 3 April, Birchall was approached and asked unexpectedly to undertake a long-range patrol next day because the Dutch Catalina was unable to go. Sergeant Brian Catlin, later Squadron Leader, the Flight Engineer of QL-A, begins his narrative:[4]

> 'After our first night in the girls school, we were taken back to Koggala and I went straight on to the boat. We had come from Pembroke Dock with a lot of ground equipment and I spent all day getting this ashore because we had no indication of doing a patrol the following day.
>
> 'That night we were all, except for Birchall, Kenny and Onyette, back in the schoolroom. I was the only one awake when someone came in. "Where's the crew of A?" he said. I said "Here we are," and he said,"You're on strike at first light in the morning." So I said, "But we're not refuelled or rearmed or anything." He said, "That's all right, everything will be taken care of."'

51

In the dark the crew and Birchall, with no breakfast, were taken down to the jetty on the lake to prepare for a 24-hour flight. Because there had been no time to practise night landings on this hazardous take-off area, the Catalina would have to stay aloft all night to land by daylight. No rations were provided and it was fortunate that they had some food left from Karachi, with 15 gallons of water. The Captain's briefing as to what to expect was also inadequate. He was given no clear idea which Allied ships might be encountered nor an adequate warning about the known presence of the Japanese fleet. Charts were a makeshift.

This was bad enough but as they set out on and continued their flight the crew discovered that at some point since leaving Pembroke Dock all their pans of special ammunition had been replaced with ordinary rounds, omitting the vital tracer bullets (which in fiery streaks would show where hits were striking). The guns also tended to jam when needed later. The two inflatable dinghies had been inadequately secured, which in different circumstances might have cost their lives. These, along with other difficulties, made their subsequent enemy engagement even more courageous and triumphant than generally realised, even in the Readers Digest account of 1983, which made the exploit well known. And their capacity to 'make do' with inadequate materials was stretched to the limit.

Birchall, in his diaries,[5] writes:

'We were to do a cross-over patrol about 250 miles south-south-east of Ceylon. The general theory of this is that you search the area during daylight far enough out from land so that the enemy cannot sail in during the night and launch an attack at dawn. We were to be at about 2,000 feet so that we could spot anything on the water including periscopes.'

Catlin continues the story.

'When dawn broke, as soon as we could see, we cast off and taxied to the end of the (water) runway. Then we took off and got over the trees with about a hundred feet to spare. Birchall remarked on the intercom, "High Street Tokyo here we come!" I was on watch then and I thought, "That's a queer thing to say," because I didn't know where we were going.'
Birchall's diary moves on:

'The weather was perfect and by noon the sun had cleared up any trace of cloud, leaving a brilliant clear blue sky. Around this time we received orders to alter patrol. [This was the new area planned by Rotherham.] 'There we stayed all day at about 3,000 feet and our one navigational aid was taking sunshots. This only gave us longitude and no latitude but we had no worries as we had all night to get back to Ceylon and there would be bags of stars. Just as it got time to start home, the navigator, [Bart Onyette], asked to do one more patrol of the area as the moon was coming up and he could get a good cross fix for an accurate position. We did another patrol and he got a good fix indicating we were about 500 nautical miles south of Ceylon as against 300, but this error was to the good and so no problem. We continued on and just at our most southerly point as we started to turn we saw some specks on the south horizon. [It was Sgt Colarossi watching in one of the blisters who spotted them first.] As we got closer there were more specks and then they started to take form. Obviously they were warships and so there was nothing to do but to go in and identify them. We had just obtained a good position fix and so it was easy to tell their position, course and speed. As we got into range where we could identify by binoculars we ran into the outer air screen of fighters [the scouting aircraft from the carriers].

'What we saw were 4 battleships, 5 aircraft carriers, with cruisers and destroyers. We still could not see enough of the fleet to justify an assumption of nationality as the number we saw still was less than the number of ships given to us in the Allied naval section. Just as we started our transmission five flights of 3 Zeros each peeled off over the top of us and we were into it.'

Previous accounts have described six Zeros only, taking off from the deck of the *Hiryu*, but Birchall's two diaries written during the war specify flights coming in from above. This is confirmed by the Japanese War Diary of the Third (Fast Battleship) Squadron as seen in the letter from Tokyo to Air Commodore Birchall. It describes no less than 18 Zero fighters coming in to attack the Catalina. (See appendix)

'Once we were close enough to identify them as Japanese, it was too late. We did a hurried count and set up a first sighting message.'

Catlin, in his engineer's tower, the tiny compartment inside the wing root that supported the mainplane, must have been busy with his dials.

'[But] about ten past four [he says] I looked out of the window and saw this great fleet beside us. [Dropping down from the seat] I told Cook to get up there. Then I got out the big RAF camera. I had heard nothing over the intercom but I must have assumed it was the Japanese fleet. After I'd done the fleet, aircraft started coming close to us and I began to take photos of them so that people back home would know what aircraft they were using. I'd never seen a Zero fighter or even a picture, and I thought, "When we get back to Koggala this will be just the stuff for the Daily Mirror." But this is the peculiar thing – there was no shooting!

'I was taking photographs of each aircraft coming past, 30 yards away, and there were the pilots with their hoods back smiling at me while I snapped them. Then the next one would come past, actually waving to us! I thought, "This is madness! Something's going to happen soon!"'

Sergeant Fred Phillips who sent off the vital message about the Japanese fleet on 4 April 1942 from A/413. *(courtesy Fred Phillips)*

It did! Later, in prison camp, Kenny told Catlin that the crew on the Japanese ship where they finished up informed him that the Japs had been expecting a captured Catalina coming from Java to meet with them. 'It was going to do a recce (reconnaissance) and lead them in,' says Catlin, 'and at first they thought that we were the one that had come from Java, according to Kenny. Anyway, I went to put the camera away and suddenly the bulkhead door disappeared!' The bulkheads, as in ships, were the heavy metal panels dividing the Catalina into watertight and fireproof compartments. 'This was the first burst of cannon fire which the lined-up Zeros now began to deliver as Birchall looked for cloud cover of which there was almost nil.'

The crew of A-413.

LEFT: Sgt Brian Catlin in uniform with his brother Jack while passing through Alexandria en route for Ceylon (and unwittingly, Japan). *(courtesy B. Catlin)*

CENTRE: S/Ldr Len Birchall OBE DFC CD at Pembroke Dock. *(courtesy L. Buchall DFC OBE)*

RIGHT: Sgt W. 'Ginger' Cook with his wife Eileen, whom he married after she had nursed him through his leg amputation in Australia. *(courtesy Mrs E. Cook)*

When Catlin got back to the blisters Colarossi was lying there with his leg shattered at the knee. He went for the First Aid kit but even that had been rifled so there was nothing he could do for poor Colarossi. He took over the twin machine guns in the starboard blister while Davidson manned the port guns. All the guns kept jamming however due to the changed ammunition. Cannon shells were now beginning to slam through the aircraft in all directions and one of the first casualties was the radio.

Fred Phillips[6] recalled:

'I had been on radio watch doing my four hours when the action began. When the first cannon shells blasted in they knocked out my receivers but left the transmitters luckily. I'd got two transmitters but I had to use the generator of one to support the other. And I'd got a smashed Morse key so I had to bang the parts together hopefully. People say I got two messages out and had stopped during the third.

'How many went out I don't know, I just kept on. There was no time for encoding but I used the priority code known as O-Break-O which

55

implied an enemy air attack. I had a vague hope that if anyone heard it they'd realise there was an aircraft out there in trouble. I was also sending the ordinary observation reports like 4 BS meaning four battleships or 2 AC for two aircraft carriers and so on.

Some of the explosive cannon shells smashed into the fuel tanks above the tower and burning gasoline ran down the engineer's compartment to set the hull alight. Catlin left the guns to tackle it. He writes:

'When we went on fire I grabbed the fire extinguisher and went up to the bulkhead door. I pulled the extinguisher lever and pointed the cone at the fire but no foam came out. I thought "Here's something else that doesn't work" but the fire started to disappear [with the carbon dioxide in the cylinder]. Cook who was by the Navigator's table came aft with his fire extinguisher – the fire was just pouring down into the radio operator's cabin but between us we got it out.'

Fred now continues: 'the lads were keeping the fire off me with a Lux extinguisher.' The author asked Phillips if he sustained any wounds in all this. 'Yes,' he said.

'The shrapnel from the shells had hit me too – one at the base of the right lung, a lot of shrapnel on my back and leg, machine-gun bullets also and explosive bullets in my hips and about 4 down my leg – Oh, yes, and burns too.

'Now, it isn't often you hear the reverse side of the story. I knew one of the blokes in the Navy at Colombo and when I got in touch after the war he turned out to be one of the lads that received our message. He told me, "We picked the message up, which did sound garbled but we got it down. When we saw what it was the place went deathly quiet and for a heck of a long time."'

As is usual when O-Break-O is heard over the airwaves the transmissions all over the region fall silent. Phillips says the message was also picked up in Addu Atoll. So, the vital warning got through. It was garbled but clear enough to warn the Navy where the Japanese fleet was. Colombo needed a repeat of the sighting report, however. This was a normal requirement for authenticity.

In the aircraft the cannon shells tended to come in from the tail, thundering and howling through the aircraft, causing explosions everywhere. As Catlin was struggling to open a bulkhead door one Jap pilot did him a favour and blasted off the hinges. Shrapnel was hitting the crew as they continued at their jobs. Davidson and Catlin were back at the blister guns and Henzell in the front turret. 'The front gunner,' writes Birchall, 'collected a burst and I saw him slump down out of action.' Then again the blister guns jammed. Brian crawled back into the tunnel compartment below the tail and got hold of the tunnel gun there. It was off its mounting and the sights had been removed (another mystery) but he carried it back to the blister and fired it from the hip, like a tommy gun, as the Jap Zeros swept in one after another, guns and cannon blazing. He had trouble though because along with other shrapnel in his body he had collected some in his left arm and his left hand couldn't grip. So he put the gun up on the blister mounting. Later he found it had fallen into the sea because of the way Birchall was throwing the huge unwieldy Catalina all over the sky.

The Skipper explains in his diary:

'I might mention a few of the manoeuvres I carried out. Whenever a Nip[7] came in from the side I would lift and roll slightly toward him. I noticed that this caused him to dive a bit. Consequently his tracer would miss below us and it also gave the front gunner a chance at him. Whenever I felt a burst coming in from the tail it was only necessary to do a flat turn one way or the other and it stopped at once. I can see the large blobs of red when they floated by as near misses and how they resembled fireworks.

'You could feel the old bus shake and quiver as she took a full burst and the noise of the bullets and shells going through was terrific. It was at one of these times I felt a jolt in my right leg and knew that there was one of them there. During the fight a side burst knocked most of our instrument panel into pieces and it took Kenny and me all our time to hold the nose up despite full elevator control.'

At this stage the fuel tanks in the wings went on fire and the Catalina began to resemble a huge fiery cross in the dusk flaming towards the sea. Birchall comments: 'The fire started up again and this time we couldn't get it out.' Catlin adds:

'It got to the state where the aircraft was taking a lot of punishment. We got into a little bit of cloud and I thought "Oh, we've made it! "Then we came out of it. Kenny told me later the only cloud he saw was the hot air coming off the decks of the carriers which had risen and condensed into a cloud, when we were right over the carriers. I took over Colarossi's guns again and aimed [at the Japanese]. I had a go at each as it dived but there was always another behind it.

'I changed the pans of [inferior] ammunition and so it went on. I got hit once or twice myself and then the guns finally jammed so that I couldn't clear them. So I went up to Onyette and said, "You'd better tell the boss the aircraft has taken as much as it will take. Tell him to get out of it and go home."

'Shortly after that [Catlin continues] the Zeros burst the tanks externally and the whole wing span was a mass of flame from end to end. Clearly the end was near and burning petrol started to come down the tower again. I thought: "This is it!" So I left the guns, went and got the Mae Wests, tossed a couple out and put one on myself.

'I could only do the bottom tie up because my left arm had gone. I wasn't conscious of being hit [Catlin was found later to have 74 separate wounds, as well as burns], only that I couldn't use my hand except the little and fourth fingers. I knew I'd been hit in the chest because I felt that one. Then I passed out the parachutes but Davidson waved then off and pointed downwards. I had a look and we were only about 50 feet up. Colarossi had his harness on and I'm almost sure he had a Mae West but apart from his eyes being open there was no other sign of life.'

Birchall was now heading for the sea to try to get the Catalina down before it fell apart or exploded.

'Someone (I am told it was Cook) got up in the engineer's seat and [winding the handles] lowered the wingtip floats for us to land. He did so with flaming gasoline coming down through the tunnel all over him! We managed to level out over the water and she skipped a couple of times before she stopped. The Nips kept strafing us as we abandoned aircraft which made it rather difficult.'

As they were helping each other down into the water Ginger Cook was assisting. At this point another burst of fire caught Henzell but also broke Cook's left leg in several places (making amputation necessary after the war.) 'I jumped into the water,' Birchall says, 'and held on to the mooring cables for a bit.' He continues:

'The aircraft sank very quickly and the spread of burning gasoline made it necessary to leave the area. I saw Kenny and another lad, off to one side, so I joined them. The strafing continued and we had to duck under the water all the time to get out of the way. I can remember going under and seeing the bullets hitting the water over me and spinning along through the water.'
How did Catlin and the others fare in the rear of the aircraft?

'We hit the water and we stuck. Petrol poured out of the main plane and certainly on the port side there was a pool of flame on the water. I told

Davidson to get out. By sign language he pointed at the dinghies – I had forgotten them – so we went for the starboard dinghy and that blew up, inflating itself as soon as we touched it.' [The inflating mechanism was not restrained because someone had cut off the long braided ropes which should have been wound round their canvas holdalls.]

'Then we tried the port dinghy and that did the same. We needed to get out but the dinghies were blowing up all the time and they were swinging the guns across our exits. I had to push Davidson out.'

There was no way Colarossi, even were he conscious, could have been got out of the blister by that time. He drowned inside the aircraft, but at least protected from shark attack. The failure of the dinghies proved a blessing in disguise because if the whole crew had taken to them the strafing of the Japanese might have wiped them all out. Catlin again:

'Then it was my turn but there was nobody to push me. This was on the port side. I tried to move Colarossi but I couldn't so I jumped out. Now, I hadn't blown my Mae West up and I'd only got the bottom tied, and that helped. I stayed under water as long as possible – I was past swimming. When I came up I was clear of the fire. Davidson was floating about 20 yards away. His Mae West was blown up but I did not use my gas bottle. When the bullets started splashing I sank myself doing a reverse dog-paddle. There was one very big burst round Davidson and I never saw him after that. I kept going unconscious and I guess I prayed plenty.

'I had little regret of dying – there never was much future to wartime flying – but I did regret I had lived 22 years and done nothing to be proud of. I regretted I had struggled, worked hard, got over serious illness, and recovered from motorcycle accidents just to go and die in the middle of the Indian Ocean on the 4th of 1942. Each time I came round I spat to see if there was any blood in my spit because in cowboy films before the cowboy dies he always spits blood. There was this round hole in my chest bullet-sized and I think the bullet's still there actually. When I eventually got back to England they said it was too near my heart – so leave it there.

'I saw nothing of the others at this time. [Colarossi had died in the aircraft and Henzell and Davidson in the water, leaving six of them]. The next thing I remember was this massive ship. Then about three waves away from me, there was a whaler-type boat being rowed, with a soldier in the front with a rifle.

'They pulled me over the gunwale of the boat and put me in the bottom and the first words they said were "Your frequency? Your frequency?" So I said, "Engineer" and they said "Ah so! Engineer." I passed out again and the next thing I remember was other people being dragged in over my feet.'

IJN *Isokaze* which picked up Birchall's crew after the Zeros had shot them down on 4 April 1942. *(Courtesy Air Cdre Birchall)*

The reason the Japanese stopped strafing and decided to take the survivors aboard was to discover if they had sent out a message and whether it was received. 'Next,' says Catlin, 'we were lying on the deck of this picket boat – it may have been a destroyer, but the Captain said it was the smallest in the Japanese Navy.' Commander Shunichi Toshima was the Captain of the *Isokaze*, meaning Surf Wind, at the Battle of Midway and the ship survived till near the end of the war, but was sunk near Manila. Toshima's treatment of the six prisoners, however, was harsh in the extreme. Realising the Japs would be looking for the Radio Operator, Catlin continues:

'Kenny used his loaf and he took all our clothes off, the three lying on the deck, and dropped them over the side. What I remember there was about 300 men on every quarter, looking down on us with field glasses. And then Birchall said to Phillips, "You're an Air Gunner and nothing else." He told the Japanese, "If you hadn't shot us while we were in the water you'd have had the radio operators." Of course they denied shooting us, but they'd lost face.'

Birchall's account goes on:

'They asked for the Senior Officer. Once I identified myself, I had to stand up and was beaten. The big problem seemed to be the fear that we had gotten away a message. I denied we had ever opened up our radios. The same question was asked several times between beatings and we stuck to our story. Just as we started to get them convinced, Colombo came up on the air and asked for a repeat of our message. It was game over. Beatings all round and they then put us all into a paint locker up in the bow. Colombo asking us for a repeat seemed to indicate they had not gotten our message which was sad news indeed.[8]

'In the paint locker we had room for three badly wounded to lie down, two to sit and the sixth to stand. There were some straw mats and blankets to lie on, practically no ventilation, water and rice about three times a day. No medicine or medical treatment and lavatory facilities on demand or whenever they wished to grant them. The wounded had to be carried back and forth.'

As one of the wounded developed diarrhoea this proved distressing and the atmosphere was described as 'rather high'.

Catlin does recall on the second day that 'they gave me a glass of passion fruit juice, bright green and ice-cold, and then I decided I was going to live, because it was delicious.' The six were kept in these blistering, inhuman conditions for three full days. Then they were rowed across in a whaler to Nagumo's flagship, the *Akagi*. The three wounded were then given the best medical treatment the ship could offer, equivalent to that for any Japanese casualty.

All of them were kept together under bright lights in the fore part of the ship but the three least wounded were taken out repeatedly for interrogation with beatings in the officers' quarters. Birchall adds:

'Phillips kept a diary of our trip out to Ceylon and had it with him. We had not wanted to disclose the route we took so made up a story that we came out to India by boat. When we found Phillips' diary, while we were on the *Akagi*, we had to eat it page by page. I can still taste that paper and ink!'

They remained on Nagumo's ship till they reached Japan on 22 April 1942 and began three years of barbarous captivity. Birchall writes:

'Back in Ceylon the message was received, a bit garbled but essentially correct, and passed to all services. Admiral Somerville was informed immediately. A listening watch was kept all night and when we failed to show in the morning we were presumed to have been shot down.'

Since Japan did not adhere to the Geneva Convention, for the next year no one was informed that they were prisoners and they were assumed to be dead. Mercifully all six survived the war.

Sir James Somerville's staff calculated that the attack would come the next morning, Easter Sunday. Colombo Harbour was cleared of as much shipping as possible, the cruisers *Dorsetshire* and *Cornwall* being ordered to rendezvous with Somerville near Addu Atoll. On the morning of 5 April they were spotted by Japanese reconnaissance aircraft. Captain Augustus Agar VC, Captain of the *Dorsetshire*, then had to decide whether to head south west for the main fleet and thus risk giving away their position or stick to his original course south east which could mean the sacrifice of the two cruisers.

He chose the latter. A force of 50 bombers arrived, came in with low, fast and accurate bombing and sank both cruisers. 424 men were lost and after 28 hours in the water, at risk from sharks and the cold night, 1,122 men were saved by the cruiser *Enterprise* and two destroyers, HMS *Pamther* and HMS *Paladin*, summoned by a Fleet Air Arm aircraft on reconnaissance.

205 Squadron's solitary Catalina had been the only 205 flying boat to escape to Ceylon from the Japanese invasion of Singapore. Flight Lieutenant Jock Graham and his crew were now tasked with a similar mission of equal danger, to go and find how far the Japanese fleet had come. We know nothing more of Graham's crew than their toughness in surviving Singapore. At 22.37 that night Colombo received from them the following message: 'One enemy destroyer in 01˚ 59' North, 82˚20' East, course 315˚, speed 20 knots.' A second message came at 0045F on 5 April. '6 destroyers in 02˚54' North, 82˚10' East, course 325˚, speed 20 knots.' After that, silence. Like Birchall's crew they had been shot down but this time, none survived. Their warning, nevertheless, gave the vital confirmation that the attack on Ceylon was about to begin.

The next Catalina to take over reporting was 240 Squadron's 'L' for Leonard which, as Tomlinson informs us, 'had a patch on her hull where the *Bismarck* guns had holed her. Her Captain was Flight Lieutenant W. "Bill" Bradshaw DFC with Pilot Officer Charles Gardner, at one time taken to be a BBC broadcaster, as her second pilot.' Gardner had reported some of the Battle of Britain with all the excitement of a racing commentator from a vantage point on the top of the cliffs of Dover.[9]

At 06.48 Bradshaw was reported as having sighted some of Vice-Admiral Mikawa's escorting warships acting as an advance guard to Nagumo's carriers. He described one battleship and two cruisers in a position 110 miles, 195˚, from Dondra Head, Ceylon, and at 07.21 he sighted four other ships. 240's L for Leonard continued to shadow the enemy fleet for the rest of the day, using cloud to hide from the fighters, and was able to return safely to base.

The Easter Sunday raids have been described in several histories and nowhere better than in Michael Tomlinson's book, so suffice it to say this. Nagumo's hitherto all-conquering divebombers and fighters met with unexpected and fierce resistance as the attackers, *Akagi's* Commander Mitsuo Fuchida and his Pearl Harbour veterans bombed Colombo Harbour. (The city itself was left almost untouched.) The new radar, RDF – radio direction finding – failed to give warning, being still under installation.

So the first inkling of the attack was seeing the Japanese bombers overhead, through heavy cloud and rain. The RAF, the Fleet Air Arm and the guns were ready however, and the aircraft quickly got into the air.

30 Squadron RAF had 22 Hurricane II fighters; FAA Squadrons 803 and 806 from Ratmalana came in with 6 Fulmars and 258 Squadron RAF added 9 Hurricane IIs and 5 Hurricane Is, a total of 42 against the hordes of Japanese bombers, dive-bombers and fast fighters. For the first time however, the dive-bombers found powerful modern Hurricanes on their tails in their defenceless moments and suffered unexpected heavy losses. 30 and 258 RAF Squadrons claimed 22 shot down and others probable for the loss of 15 of their aircraft. The six Fulmars, being slower aircraft, lost four of their number for one enemy shot down, while, sad to say, six slow torpedo-carrying Swordfish of 788 FAA Squadron en route for Ratmalana from China Bay came all unawares through cloud into the huge dogfight and were gunned down to a man by Zero fighters.

Fourteen Blenheim bombers of 11 Squadron RAF from Ratmalana aerodrome set out to find the enemy force but were unable to do so. One naval report blames this on an erroneous Catalina report earlier that day. Damage at Ratmalana and Colombo Harbour was extensive but less than feared. The aged destroyer *Tenedos* was sunk; the Armed Merchant Cruiser HMS *Hector* was set on fire and sank later and other vessels were sunk or damaged.

A signalman/gunner of the Ceylon Royal Naval Reserve, Mr 'Rock' Jayasiri Gunesekare,[10] was the only sailor in the Ceylon Navy to have been commended by the General Naval Signal. He says that his ship, the minesweeper HMS *Sambhar*, had just tied up when the attack began. 'We were about to go on shore leave when suddenly we saw the aircraft flying over us very high.' The bombs rained down on ships and harbour alike, while dogfights broke out all over the sky and the anti-aircraft gunners claimed three aircraft shot down and others damaged. Rock, now a Justice of the Peace at Katunayake, continues:

'After the Japanese aircraft left, we went out and saw lots of bodies all over. That was our first experience of blood and people dead. And some of the Ceylon harbour workers who were helping on the ship, where it was tied up, were also dead around there. So it was a very sad experience for us. After the raid we went around the dockyard area transporting the wounded to hospital.'

Then the bombers were gone and Nagumo's forces departed with unexpected losses and without repeating their Pearl Harbour coup.

Meanwhile on 5 and 6 April Vice-Admiral Ozawa conducted a blitzkrieg against shipping on the eastern coast of India. Using his cruisers and attack planes he sank 18 merchantmen with a total tonnage of 93,000. At the small port of Vizagapatam, halfway up the east coast of

India, some warning was given by a gallant old Westland Wapiti biplane of the Sixth Indian Coastal Defence Flight.

This 'flight' of two Wapitis had just arrived on 5 April in a field behind the town, with no hangars, no phone and as yet no airmen. A CDF pilot, David Small, acting as Navigator and Gunner in the open rear cockpit, took with him a young Indian pilot named Barker, who hailed from Agra. The two set out on 6 April for the same sort of dangerous patrol as the Catalinas further south but with only a single engine to get them home and no way of landing on water. Wing Commander W.W. Russell in his lively book, *Forgotten Skies*, tells the story.[11]

> 'They were not more than thirty miles off the port, barely clear of the swept channel, when David saw flashes to the north-east. He looked closer and witnessed the unbelievable sight of an aircraft carrier, several cruisers and destroyers belching fire at a merchant vessel, like hounds round a fox at bay.'

Drawing closer he realised that this was the Japanese fleet. As Barker climbed to 8,000 feet, the sturdy old biplane trundling along at 100 miles an hour narrowly missed being seen by three fast, yellow, radial-engined Japanese aircraft which passed below and which would have made mincemeat of it.

David, having sketched the fleet, then turned to head for home. There, taking an eight-mile taxi ride, the two pilots passed on their message for Ceylon and Calcutta. Ozawa's Kate bombers, without doing significant damage, nevertheless terrorised the ports of Coconada and Vizagapatam and the whole exercise served to paralyse shipping in the Bay of Bengal for some time to come. Vice-Admiral Nagumo hadn't finished with Ceylon, however. He prepared a further strike, this time against the naval base of Trincomalee in the north of the island.

At 15.17 on 8 April 1942 the sole serviceable Catalina from 240 Squadron, L for Leonard with Flying Officer Round as pilot, reported sighting an enemy force of three battleships and one aircraft carrier 540 miles from Colombo, course 330°. They shadowed for about an hour but were attacked by fighters and took avoiding action in the clouds, returning safely to base. The next flight however, paid the supreme penalty when 413's Catalina Y for Yorker, again piloted by Flight Lieutenant Rae Thomas DFC, took off to find Nagumo's fleet. At 07.00 a message was received reporting the position, course and speed of a large Japanese convoy. The signals were interrupted before the message was completed and Thomas's crew was presumed shot down by the Zeros. Enough warning had now been received at Trincomalee to minimise the damage, however.

Fuchida's 91 Kate bombers escorted by 38 Zero fighters easily outnumbered the gallant force of 16 Hurricanes and 6 Fulmars, who came up to meet them. In the battle ten Hurricanes and a Fulmar were lost, shooting down a Zero and two Kates and damaging ten more. Heavy damage was inflicted on the port facilities. There were only three ships now in the harbour, the Dutch cruiser *Heemskerck* having no ammunition, but a witness thinks she was not hit.

HMS *Erebus* was not a destroyer but a naval monitor, built pre-World War One for work in shallow waters. Here, in Trinco Harbour, she had been sent to supplement the Royal Artillery anti-aircraft guns on shore in defence. For this she had, as well as her two 15" guns, two 4" guns and four four-barrelled pom-poms on either side, plus an Oerlikon forward. These guns were controlled by two Transmitting Stations, small box-like rooms on port and starboard sides of the ship. In the port one, as *Erebus* joined the barrage against high-flying Jap bombers, was Able Seaman Ron Wheeler of Eastbourne. At 18 he had just arrived in Ceylon with other young seamen, he tells us.

He had just bent down towards the floor when a stick of bombs landed right alongside the port side of the ship and blasted all the men and structures there. Ron's room was riddled with shrapnel and as he straightened up he saw a large hole in the wall just where his head would have been. Had he been sitting upright Eastbourne would not have had him in later years as Coxswain of their lifeboat, in which he became a well-known figure on the south coast of England.

Thirteen young sailors died instantly. Cecil Philcox, who was with the Royal Artillery in Ceylon, tells me six were aged 18, six 19 and one a veteran of 23. Thirty-three men were wounded, but like Wheeler, not all badly enough to go ashore. The *Erebus* survived but not so the *Saigang*, the third ship, a merchantman close by which caught a full load of bombs and became a blazing hulk, to drift ashore. When Cecil Philcox revisited Ceylon in 1992 for the 50-year commemoration of the Easter Raids, *Saigang* was still lying there. On behalf of Ron and the Eastbourne Navy Club, Cecil laid two wreaths for the 13 graves in the beautifully-kept war cemetery at Trincomalee.

More satisfying to the invaders was the discovery of the aircraft carrier *Hermes* moving down the coast with its Australian destroyer *Vampire* and other ships, all of which were bombed and sunk, except for the hospital ship *Vita* which was spared. In return nine of the Blenheim bombers found the Nippon fleet and attacked the *Akagi*. Little damage was inflicted, though they shot down two Zeros and lost four bombers in return. Catlin, a reluctant witness on the *Akagi's* mess-deck, recalls feeling the near-misses on both sides.

Thereafter peace descended on Ceylon while the two Japanese fleets headed back towards Japan. On balance neither side had achieved its aims. Admiral Somerville on Admiralty insistence sent back his slow Force B with the Four Rs to East Africa leaving Force A at Bombay, and later followed with more of his fleet to the Kilindini base at Mombasa. This left the eastern Indian Ocean practically undefended.

Based on author's watercolour painted in a 209 Sq Cat blister, A Convoy, 1943. Similar view to that in Birchall's Cat. *(RAF Museum, Hendon)*

Sir James, however, had preserved the Eastern Fleet to fight again and, by reducing the impact on Ceylon, had foiled Nagumo's other aim of destroying the island's harbours. The Japanese Admiral was satisfied that he had inflicted serious losses on the British fleet and the bases at the cost of only 19 of his aircraft. In truth his force had been weakened by the battle. Air Commodore Birchall has recently written:

'Those first serious losses of highly trained (Japanese) aircrew led to further heavy losses at the Coral Sea. The culmination of this was that the carrier forces which the Japanese employed at Midway were greatly reduced in number and heavily diluted with inexperienced or unskilled air crew. The ripple which started at Ceylon ended in a disastrous tidal wave at Midway which was, without doubt, the decisive battle of the Pacific, sounding the death knell of Japanese naval power.'

For the next three years, apart from using some submarines against shipping, the Japanese left the Indian Ocean largely to others. Credit must be given to the American code-breakers who gave the original warning, to the Royal Navy, with its Fleet Air Arm, the RAF and the spirited defenders of Ceylon. The sacrificial patrols of the Catalinas helped to achieve this result.

Shortly after, Flight Lieutenant Rae Thomas received a Mention in Despatches of 222 Group. The squadron diary noted that 'F/Lt R. Thomas DFC was one of our best pilots and his loss will be keenly felt by the squadron.'[12] When one looks at Birchall's flight and battle with the swarm of powerful Zeros one can only marvel at the resilient strength of an American aircraft, the trusty Catalina; the skill of its pilots and the unwavering courage of its crew.

Leonard Birchall was, *in absentia*, awarded the DFC and after the war the OBE for his role as Commanding Officer in various POW units in Japan. There, at the frequent risk of his life, he repeatedly stood up for the men and protected the sick. Winston Churchill, speaking to Lester Pearson, later Prime Minister of Canada, said he considered this attack on Ceylon as the most dangerous moment of the war, when 'we were saved from this disaster by an airman on reconnaissance who spotted the Japanese Fleet.' Other aircraft crews, whether lost in action or experiencing uneventful patrols, shared equally, with other services, in the honour of defending the Indian Ocean.

N O T E S

[1] *The Most Dangerous Moment,* M. Tomlinson (William Kimber), Wellingborough 1976.

[2] *Fighting Admiral,* Capt. Donald Macintyre (Evans Brothers), London.

[3] *It's Really Quite Safe,* Lt/Cdr G.A. Rotherham (Hangar Books), Ontario 1985.

[4] Unpublished diaries and interviews, Squadron Leader Brian Catlin (RAF Retired).

[5] Unpublished diaries and other writings, Air Commodore L.J. Birchall OBE DFC CD (RCAF Retired).

[6] Interview with Warrant Officer Fred Phillips (RAF Retired).

[7] 'Nip'- abbreviation for Nipponese or Japanese.

[8] Birchall never heard that their message got through until he was at Manila on his way home from Japan at the end of the war. He then telegraphed the rest of the crew.

[9] The rest of Bradshaw's crew comprised: Sgt Bert Walmsley, Nav. Sgt Harry Westby 1st F/Eng. Sgt Ron Osborne 2nd F/Eng. Three WOP/AGs – Sgt 'Ginger'

Smith; Sgt Cliff Misset; Sgt 'Sticks' Harris RCAF. Also Sgt Ken Pountain FMA/AG. Their Catalina had on 26 May 1941 taken over from Dennis Briggs' 209 Sq. Cat the shadowing of the *Bismarck*.

[10] Rock's interview - Courtesy Henry Tomlinson, from his film video *The Most Dangerous Moment*, 1994, in which his father, the actor, David Tomlinson, speaks the epilogue.

[11] *Forgotten Skies*, Wing Commander W.W. Russell (Hutchinson) London 1945.

[12] 413 Squadron records, courtesy: Captain Fleet RCAF, Squadron Historian, 413 Transport and Rescue Squadron, RCAF Greenwood, Canada.

CHAPTER 3

MADAGASCAR ONWARDS

A fter Japan's assault on Ceylon, her capital ships in general were withdrawn from the Indian Ocean. Only her submarines were employed to wreak damage on military and other shipping from time to time. In *The Penang Submarines*[1] Dennis Gunton thus comments on Japan's attitude:

'Before 1941, submarines were given a strategic importance by the Japanese their later performance was never to justify. They were equipped to carry midget submarines or (light) aircraft and intended for important operations that would sink capital ships or aircraft carriers. Superior US equipment and anti-submarine technique kept Japanese submarines at a disadvantage and, as a result, they fulfilled neither Japan's highest hopes nor the Allies' worst fears.'

This was the problem in 1942. The Admiralty had no clear idea whether or not Japan would go on expanding into the Indian Ocean and so had to be prepared for the 'worst fears'. In fact Japan was returning her fleets to the Pacific, even towards Australia. The First Sea Lord, Admiral Sir Dudley Pound, not only had to try to bolster up defences in the Indian Ocean, but was fighting a bitter struggle to convince the Government that maritime squadrons in general should be built up,[2] just as much as those in Bomber Command. There were two urgent needs, first to improve long range reconnaissance in the Bay of Bengal, the second to increase patrolling in the Bay of Biscay and catch the outgoing U-boats. Both of Sir Dudley's hopes were met and ultimately proved of great value. As a start 413 Canadian Catalina Squadron had been posted to Ceylon and in June 1942 209 Cat Squadron, after a three-month work-up in Pembroke Dock, South Wales, arrived in East Africa. An immediate answer had also to be provided for limiting future Japanese expansion. The most likely place Japan might want to use as a base, with the co-operation of the Vichy

69

French there, was the island of Madagascar. Its finest harbour was Diego Suarez at the northern tip of that 900-mile-long country, which it was decided to capture in May 1942.

209 Squadron was involved at a later stage, having only just arrived in June, but the Flight Commander, Squadron Leader Barraclough, now Air Chief Marshal Sir John Barraclough KCB CBE DFC AFC, has kindly summarised for me events as they developed on the strategic side.

'As a pre-emptive strike, planned from London and approved by the Joint Chiefs in Washington, a substantial naval force, plus the 29th Independent Brigade (with others forming FORCE 121) ex-UK en route to India, with No. 5 Commando, attacked Diego Suarez on 5 May and captured it by 8 May. The object was to ensure that the Japanese did not occupy this strategic island controlling the Moçambique Channel or, more probably, be invited in by the bitterly hostile Vichy Government and forces. Air support was from FAA aircraft on *Illustrious* and *Indomitable,* there being no operational RAF aircraft in the theatre.'

The expedition was code-named OPERATION IRONCLAD and confined itself to Diego Suarez, the whole island not being taken over till September. Japan had meanwhile decided to keep the pressure on by sending a flotilla of five large submarines to the seas near Madagascar. They were the First Division of the 8th Submarine Flotilla commanded by Rear Admiral Ishizaki and comprised I/10, I/16, I/18, I/20 and I/30 with two supply ships. At that time they were not after merchant ships but they missed the large British fleet that headed north from Durban under the command of Rear-Admiral Sir Neville Syfret, a South African by birth. However, I/30's spotter plane later told of the Fleet's approach and the Japanese headed towards Diego Suarez through rough seas.

In Syfret's fleet, Force F, the battleship HMS *Malaya* was accompanied by the battleship HMS *Ramillies*, in which young Prince Philip, later The Duke of Edinburgh, had served from January until May 1940. In May 1942 he was serving in HMS *Wallace* based at Rosyth. Two reports had stated he was in Madagascar at that time. The Aircraft Carrier HMS *Illustrious* (Captain A.G. Talbot) carried American Grumman Martlet (Wildcat) fighters flown by 881 and 882 Squadrons to attack the shipping and naval opposition in the harbour of Diego Suarez. She also carried 820 and 829 Squadrons[3], flying 20 Swordfish torpedo bombers.

With thirty thousand troops, including the 3rd battalion of the Royal Welsh Fusiliers, OPERATION IRONCLAD got under way on 5 May 1942. The invasion of Madagascar is one of the few parts of the Indian Ocean saga which is better known. The action was fiercely fought on both sides but was over in three days and HMS *Ramillies* steamed into the wide bay of Diego Suarez harbour on 7 May 1942 to anchor there.

A wing of the South African Air Force, popularly known as the Sugarcane Wing, under Lieutenant Colonel J.T. Durrant DFC, was sent up in support of the Fleet Air Arm forces. Colonel S.A. Melville as OC Air Force Madagascar, was to command also the later air operations in the whole island. The SAAF had already carried out aerial photography of the invasion area, but for the invasion of Diego Suarez the Wing, with its 37 aircraft, was not required. They came into their own when the whole island was taken over in September 1942, using Beauforts, Marylands, Lodestars and a SAAF Junkers 52.[4]

The Fleet Air Arm had the task of covering the Diego attack and fought vigorously in various actions. For instance on HMS *Indomitable* (Captain T.H. Troubridge) the squadrons 800 and 806 flew Fairey Fulmars. 880 Squadron had Sea Hurricanes and 827 with 831 flew 24 Fairey Albacores, according to John Winton. *Indomitable's* aircraft attacked the airfields. The nine Sea Hurricanes of 880 Squadron also dealt with the Vichy French sloop, *D'Entrecasteaux,* whose guns were causing trouble. After a frustrating month the Hurricane pilots were glad to be in action. Winton quotes one of these Fleet Air Arm pilots, Hugh Popham:

'We flew in low all the way over the sea, over the low bare hills of the northern part of the island, until the great harbour opened up in front of us, with the sloop in the shallows to the north of the town. She had steam up, and as we raced across the water, she let loose volumes of oily smoke that blew in a dense cloud towards us. One after another we tore into her, guns blazing. The tracer showed up briefly as it went sparkling into the smoke; our tracer going in and theirs coming out. I held it, thumb hard down and that intoxicating drumming of eight machine-guns shaking the whole aircraft; into the smoke until, a yard or two in front of me, the mast and aerials suddenly loomed up. I hauled back on the stick, and we went wheeling round for another run.'

Two weeks after the capture of Diego harbour on 7 May, the battleship HMS *Ramillies* and other naval and merchant ships lay peacefully at anchor in the north-east corner. A spotter plane from the Japanese submarine I-10 came back from Diego Suarez to report this fact. The decision was made by the Japanese to attack, forthwith. Two submarines were ready and able to go in, I/16 and I/20, each with one midget submarine. These would be released 10 miles out to sea and then they would enter the harbour and try to torpedo the battleship.

Adapted from *Submarines* by
Richard Humble, 1981, and
Submarines with Wings by Terry
Treadwell, 1985.

IMPERIAL JAPANESE NAVY SUBMARINES

I-8 (Lt/Cdr T. Ariizumi) made remarkable voyages but also sank the *Tjisalak*, the *Nellore* and the *Jean Nicolet*.

SUBMARINES WITH MIDGET SUBMARINES OR AIRCRAFT

I-20 along with I-16 and their midget subs attacked HMS *Ramillies* in Madagascar, 1942 after I-10 had sent over a spotter plane.

I-37 (Lt/Cdr Nakagawa) sent its aircraft over Mombasa on the night of 16/17 November 1943, but also sank the *Ascot* (see *Blood and Bushido*, Bernard Edwards).

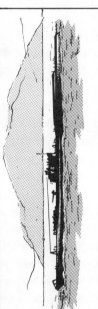

(below) I-16 which sent her midget submarines into Diego Suarez.

AIRCRAFT-CARRYING SUBMARINES

The huge I-400 class (401 feet long) was developed too late in the war for actions with the enemy. Lt/Cdr Ariizumi took two of them in a flotilla across to the Hawaiian Islands in 1945.

AITCHI SIERAN

Scouting float plane. The wings are folded and the floats removed when stowing in a submarine.

MIDGET SUBMARINE

On its cradle with two torpedoes at the bow end

Both mother subs had had a rough time with heavy seas and swell. Captain Imaizumi, of I/20, pointing to some hills, arranged a pick-up point for the brave submariners. On I/16 the midget submariners were by no means 'midgets' – Petty Officer Second Class Takato Takata being so tall he could scarcely squeeze into the cramped quarters of the submarine. Ensign Katsusuke Iwase was short, but both men had nerves of steel. Their story with the full Diego invasion account is dramatically told in *The Coffin Boats*.[5]

At 5 p.m. on the evening of 30 May 1942 the midget sub from I/20 was the first to head for the harbour. On board were the only two married men out of the 24 special crewmen. Lieutenant Saburo Akieda had not wanted to get married yet but his future 'father-in-law' had told him it was a warrior's duty to leave children to his name, and fiancée Fumiko had agreed. Saburo now had a daughter. His Navigator, Masami Takemoto, who hailed from a railway family in Takehara, wrote to his wife Hifumi asking her to care for his small daughter, Yoshiko. Under a bright, full moon the two midget subs slipped out of their storage tubes into the still heaving waters to face the unknown.

The men of the *Ramillies* had sighted the Japanese spotter plane and assumed it to be French, not knowing that Japanese submarines were close by, nor that they were able to carry an aircraft. After this, however, the battleship had steamed around warily, and was at anchor when at 8.20 p.m. an enormous explosion reverberated from the bowels of the ship and she took a list to port. As she settled the ship became flooded up to and above the main deck. 'Half drowned by the cascades of water thrown up by the explosion and blinded by the smoke, men worked feverishly to pump out the water and to jettison ammunition and fuel,' states *The Coffin Boats*.

For twenty minutes or so pandemonium reigned in the harbour, with sightings of small conning towers and periscopes, and guns firing. The 10,000-ton tanker *British Loyalty* carrying furnace-oil and other cargo was anchored near the entrance to the harbour, next to a fully loaded ammunition ship. *British Loyalty* struggled to weigh anchor and move away past the battleship, but she moved into the path of a second torpedo which had been destined for the *Ramillies*. *British Loyalty* settled in a short time on the bottom of the harbour. The battleship eventually proceeded to Durban and then Plymouth for repairs, while the tanker was salvaged only to be torpedoed later by U/183 (Commander Schneewind).

No further sign was seen of the midget boats within the harbour. Next day, however, came a report that two Japanese had been seen at a village 12 miles north. and a British 15-man patrol pursued them for two days. Finally they were seen on a hill above the beach where they should have been met by the I/20. They refused to surrender but used their pistols and a sword, killing one soldier and wounding four others. Years after the war, their identities were discovered to be Lt Saburo Akieda and P/O Masami Takemoto, the two fathers. It was their torpedo which had nearly sunk the *Ramillies*.

By mid-June of 1942 S/Ldr John Barraclough and his colleagues in 209 Squadron were taking their Catalinas out from Mombasa in anti-submarine sweeps. The next requirement was for a stepping-stone between East Africa and Madagascar, one of the islands in the Comoro group – Pamanzi. S/Ldr David Fitzpatrick, now Air Commodore D.B. Fitzpatrick CB OBE AFC, was Deputy Flight Commander and recalls that:

'Mine was the first Catalina into Diego Suarez and I flew in Brigadier Lush, the Chief Political Officer and Air Commodore Taylor of AHQ East Africa, with Group Captain Cahill (my old 1939 Calshot friend – splendid officer). One purpose was to set up the flying boat base there.'

Sir John now continues:

'In Diego Suarez when I first arrived, Colonel Dick Crewe Reid, the Garrison Commander, generously allotted me an ox cart for our squadron transport. Pamanzi had to be taken from the Vichy French. In early July '42 David Fitzpatrick went ashore in an R boat (landing crafts) with twelve strapping black soldiers of the Kings African Rifles. They were led by a gallant Scots Guards officer who had left his right arm in the desert, Colonel David Kemble. In the middle of the night they captured the Governor in his bed. The latter pleaded for "un quart d'heure" in which to replace the other youthful occupant of the great double bed with his elderly wife. He then surrendered with full dignity, nightcaps, Napoleonic bedheads, mosquitoes and all.'

209 Squadron was already a famous outfit. Its history dates back to the First World War as a fighter unit, when Captain Roy Brown shot down the universally known[6] Red Baron, Manfred von Richthofen, who flew the red Fokker Triplane beloved by model-makers today. In the Second World War 209 took to Catalina flying boats. Another exploit came when the great German battleship, *Bismarck*, had temporarily disappeared in the chase by the Royal Navy during the final stages. It was rediscovered by Flight Lieutenant Dennis Briggs DFC of 209. Also aboard was one of the American Catalina pilots who had come over to Britain to advise on the Catalina – Ensign Leonard B. Smith USN – and it was he who spotted the battleship. Briggs' Catalina stayed with the ship four and a half hours. He

then handed over to Lt Johnson USN and F/O Goolden pilots in Catalina M/240 which later took part in the battle for Ceylon. Despite flak damage they completed the watch on the *Bismarck*, enabling her later to be sunk, after a torpedo from one of *Ark Royal's* Swordfish had jammed her steering gear.

Barraclough and Fitzpatrick now set up the base in Pamanzi. The former explained to me this August (1995):

'At last week's international Flying Boat Reunion [at Pembroke Dock] I was very strongly reminded of the extraordinary efforts and achievements of our air and ground crews. I think today's Air Force would find it difficult to believe, for instance, that we had no motor boats at Pamanzi and access to our aircraft was entirely by rowing boats manned by aircrew or ground crew according to whether it was a flying or maintenance task. This included loading depth charges!

'Mostly we had no flare paths and took off in the dark without visual aid and remained in the air until dawn as might be needed. It was this that led to the loss of Flight Lieutenant John Wylie's aircraft and crew on the first sortie for the Majunga landing: he either hit something hard in the dark or porpoised and went under with all 8 depth charges exploding. When flying, although we had good W/T (Morse) and radar, we had (at first) no homing or landing aids at our bases, including Mombasa, so getting home by day or night was very much a matter of bush-flying, sometimes in cyclonic weather.

'At Pamanzi we had, until a ship left us a 3-ton truck, only a 1903 steam roller left after the construction of the causeway between Pamanzi and Dzaoudzi before the first war. Our fitters set about getting it going and we drew lots or played cards to see who should drive it. Flight Lieutenant[7] Ken Murray (later to sink the last U-boat in the war off the Shetlands) was the lucky driver. But with too much steam up he lost control and knocked down the prison wall. The liberated prisoners attached themselves to us and became an invaluable addition to our working parties.'

With the strong urging of Field Marshal Smuts, South Africa's Premier, the final invasion of Madagascar began on 3 September. Of particular importance was the capture of the two ports, Tamatave on the East Coast and Majunga on the West Coast.

'The operation was code-named STREAMLINE JANE and was under the control of the C. in C. Eastern Fleet and the GOC East Africa', says Sir John. 'The South African Air Force maintained bomber support and 209 Squadron 'provided maritime reconnaissance and close anti-submarine support to the assault forces on both coasts, operating from Pamanzi and Diego Suarez.'

The conquest of the island was completed without too much bloodshed on 5 November. South and East African forces provided the ground troops and two FAA squadrons and RAF Lysander spotter planes were added to the Sugarcane Wing with its South African aircraft.[8] Madagascar's capture enabled 209 Squadron to set up a flying boat base at Tulear, on the south-west coast of the island.

Meanwhile, the Japanese craft turned their attention to merchant shipping. In all they sank 20 ships, of 120,000 tons. Later their suppliers, the *Aikoku Maru* and the *Hokoku Maru* were taken on by a gallant little Royal Indian Navy vessel, HMIS *Bengal,* with one 12-pounder gun, escorting a Dutch tanker, the *Ondina.* In a brave action Lt/Cdr W.J. Wilson sank the *Hokoku Maru* and drove off the *Aikoku Maru* on 11 November 1942, 500 miles south of the Cocos Islands.

Thereafter Japan sent only submarines to the Indian Ocean, except on occasions like that in March 1944, when three heavy cruisers were told to disrupt shipping. By then the Japanese Navy had started to 'dispose of' survivors and the captain of the HIJNS *Tone,* Captain Mayuzumi, was ordered by Vice-Admiral Sakonju, despite his pleas, to decapitate 65 survivors of the SS *Behar.* After the war the Admiral was executed but not the Captain.

The next major task after 209 Squadron settled in at Kipevu, Mombasa, was to open up bases on the islands from which the flying boats of 209 and other squadrons could operate.

So Squadron Leader Barraclough was asked to undertake an island tour, taking with him G/C Cahill and Brigadier Hancock with his staff. Squadron Leader Fitzpatrick recalls how on 5 October he lost his 'old boat', VA 727, when it blew up at moorings and Barraclough suggested that he should join his crew as Second Captain. With several VIPs aboard, they set off to survey new bases for Cats. They went to Pamanzi, Diego Suarez, Mauritius and were to look at the Vichy French Reunion Island. Later were added Durban, St Lucia Lake and Langebaan. Sir John concludes:

'These pioneer efforts were led principally by myself and Fitzpatrick with strong support from our CO Dicky Drew (Wing Commander P.R. Drew), at the main base back at Mombasa with the unenviable task, among other things, of keeping C. in C. Eastern Fleet and 246 Wing placated!'

At Mauritius Barraclough was asked by the Navy to go to Reunion with his Catalina to see if there were any guns hidden at the harbour entrance, as at Diego Suarez. Sir John says that the crew saw none as they swept over the trees, and reported so. When the cruiser HMS *Ceres* approached the harbour, however, she got a hot French reception from cunningly camouflaged cannons and promptly withdrew, no doubt muttering rich nautical phrases about RAF myopia.

Fitzpatrick's pride and joy was his 'old boat', the lost aircraft referred to above, VA 727 or 'P' for Peter. What happened was this. She was due for a 'Daily Inspection' (a D.I.) by the various 'tradesmen', electricians, armourers, radio mechanics or riggers to make sure she was prepared for the next day's flying. On 2 September 1942 'P' was lying out in Mombasa Harbour and Leading Aircraftman Cyril Johnson from Merthyr Vale was one of those carrying out a D.I. on her. He writes:

Some maintenance staff of 209 Sq. Inset LAC Dai Thomas, Ground W/Op, 259 (209) Sq. *(courtesy H. Hughes)*

Back row left to right: Cpl Meecher, Fitter; LAC Cyril Johnson, Instrument Repairer; LAC Don Haines, RCAF, Radar Mechanic; Cpl Pete Mole, Fitter.

Front row left to right: LAC Erin Costello, RNZAF, Radio Mechanic; LAC 'Pamanzi' Jones, Rigger; CPL Elwyn Jones, Fitter; LAC Harry Hughes, electrician.

'D.Is. normally, except during "flaps", were carried out at no great speed. When the call came for one on P-Peter, I called in next door for my fellow-Welshman, LAC Harry Hughes of Neath, an electrician, so we could go together and save motor boat fuel.

'Soon out on the "kite" we split up to carry out our D.Is. and in some short while along came the dinghy with the customary call, "Anyone for the slipway?" Harry and I went ashore.'

The two airmen then climbed the hill behind the slipway back to the sections. They knew that two technicians were still working on the aircraft. These were Corporal Hughes of Wrexham, a rigger, and Sergeant Dawson, an armourer.

'We returned to our sections and I walked to the window and looked out at the Cat we had just left, and saw it lift out of the water: the next instant there came an almighty series of explosions as the wings appeared to fold up from their extremes and the hull began to sink. With others I ran to the slipway, fearing the worst. [The Catalina then caught fire.] When I saw the brave Marine Craft Cox'n try to get near to it, I realised THEY hadn't got off in time.'

The 'Coxswain' in question was Aircraftman One Jim Ginn of Northampton assisted by Aircraftman One Ralph Coombs – they took turns to be cox'n. Jim knew Corporal Hughes and Sergeant Dawson well and remembers them as Big Taff and Little Taff. Jim Ginn gives his account of the event, seen from the 'dinghy':

'Big Taff said they were to do a check on 'P'. Coombs and I were just off to the *Manela*[9] for our 3 o'clock tea break. I said "We'll drop you off on 'P' and get our tea later." Well, we got alongside the kite [aircraft]. I lifted the blister cover and Little Taff got in and Big Taff turned to me and said "You get your tea and then come back for us." As we went off I stood with my back to the towbar, looking at the blisters.

'At that moment a depth charge (DC) on the port wing dropped into the drink.[10] I yelled to Coombs, "THROTTLE UP, THE BLOODY DCs HAVE GONE!" He did not mess about. The marine tender's bows rose up and we were off like the clappers.

'She caught fire on the mainplane only. The Fire Tender, a little way off, was trying to start the Coventry Fire Pump but failed to do so. This was strange because only seconds before it was shooting out loads of water. Fitz stood on the jetty almost in tears. We could not get near to her, the heat was so intense. On the carrier [HMS *Illustrious*] the pipes sounded off for Action Stations and the guns all tilted up, as they thought the Japanese were bombing the harbour, but nothing could be done. All craft had to be kept away in case the remaining DCs went up.'

Early next morning as one or two airmen combed the shore, the two bodies were found, strangely peaceful and looking unhurt by the explosion. They were given a military funeral with full honours. 'Later,' says Jim Ginn, 'the salvage team from the "Illy" [aircraft carrier, HMS *Illustrious*] came with a cutter and gear to haul "P" out.'

LAC Harry Hughes (209 Sq) inspects the engine of 9/209, VA 727 (S/Ldr D.B. Fitzpatrick, Captain) which blew up in Mombasa Harbour, killing two, on 2 September 1942. S.S. *Manela* is in the distance.

The Court of Enquiry convened by Group Captain C.H. Cahill DFC AFC concluded that the trouble lay in using American bomb racks with British depth charges. 'No blame can be attached to any individual,' the court said. The adaptations for British racks went ahead.[11]

We return to John Barraclough, who had been appointed CO of 209 Squadron in November 1942, a young Acting Wing Commander at twenty-four and a half years old. While at Mauritius, he says, a signal came through via the Governor that he should 'report back [to Mombasa] at full speed for an urgent mission.' Sir John continues:

'I discovered that the mission was to go down to Saldanha Bay, 100 miles north-west of Cape Town, and open up a base there. On the route round the Cape, ships had been getting sunk in alarming numbers through a German submarine offensive. Eleven had gone down in a week including the liner *Orcades*. South African coastal aircraft, such as Venturas, were too limited in their range to cope with this.'

The offensive was by the *Eisbär* (Polar Bear) group, consisting of four IXC boats – U/68 (Merten); U/504 (Poske) and U/172 (Emmermann, who features in Chapter One); U/156, the fourth, was under Hartenstein who sank the Cunarder SS *Laconia* full of Italian prisoners on 12 September 1942. Hartenstein organised a three-U-boat rescue.

While his U-boat had aboard 200 refugees,[12] including an English nurse, was towing four lifeboats and showing a large red cross, U/156 was bombed by a mystery bomber thought to be a Liberator.[13] Many survivors were killed or forced back[14] into the sea and the rescue was left to the Vichy French cruiser *Gloire* from Dakar.[15] The episode led to the Laconia Order by Dönitz,[16] at U-boat Command (BdU) which was originally at Kerneval, near Lorient, but had moved to Paris in March 1942. In all, the *Eisbär* group sank 24 ships.

A later batch of IXD2s was called the *Paukenschlag* or 'Drum-roll' group and reached the Moçambique Channel. They were U/159, U/177, U/178, U/181 (Lüth), and U/195. We shall meet some of them anon. There another 24 vessels plunged to a watery tomb, amounting to 127,000 tons of vital shipping. No wonder, with 48 ships sunk in two or three months, the British Government became worried. Sir John explains further:

'Saldanha Bay proved to be a wide and windswept stretch of water. At Langebaan, on the bay, there had been an old whaling station with a large hotel beside the beach there. This was one possible source of accommodation and other buildings had to be sought out. The large Panoramic Hotel was owned by two Scandinavian brothers, Ossie and Ziggy, who seemed to be pro-German and not unsympathetic to the Ossewa Brandwag, a banned, subversive Boer organisation, a brotherhood who approved of and co-operated with the Nazis. I set up a wireless station and improvised on other facilities. Depth charges, for instance were stored on barges.'

At this point Squadron Leader Barraclough developed a poisoned foot which had to be lanced. It was then strapped to half of a smoke float, which had a padded centre, to walk on. Some days later on the beach, when he was hobbling along, he was told that an Admiral's pinnace was heading for the jetty, some way off. In a limping trot he managed to reach the jetty, to welcome not one, but two Admirals.

'These proved [he says] to be Admiral Jimmy Somerville, Commander-in-Chief Eastern Fleet, and Admiral Danckwertz, C-in-C South Atlantic. The former was witty, sharp and "a lot of fun"; the latter more severe and not a little stuffy. They came up to the Panoramic and sat down in the rush chairs. Then, while being plied with drinks brought by Ossie and Ziggy, they proceeded to get down to developing their naval strategy for the Atlantic and Indian Oceans in this hotbed of Nazi sympathisers. So with many improvisations the base at Langebaan became established, while the Catalinas, of which there were never more than a half dozen, continued to do sorties far out to sea.'

Congella, in Durban, was then established as a flying boat base but night take-offs in the crowded harbour were a problem so W/Cdr Barraclough made the first reconnaissance into St Lucia lake, 150 miles north of Durban, to set up a base more easy to use there.

In 1942 the British Government did try to reinforce the Indian Ocean with ships and aircraft, but the urgent needs of Arctic convoys to Russia demanded major fleet reinforcements. The Far East needs had to be put aside for a while.

Some maritime squadrons were already in operation by 1942, such as 8 and 203 (flying Blenheim bombers from Arabian airfields) and 36 Squadron (risen from the ashes after the fall of Singapore, and receiving new Wellington bombers in India).

Others arrived after 209 squadron, in 1942. The landplane squadrons were Nos 22 (with Beaufort bombers flying from Ceylon); 244 (with Blenheims based at Sharjah near the Persian Gulf); and 353 (flying Lockheed Hudson IIIs from DumDum, Calcutta's airport). The latter had an 'Indian Air Force component', according to Rawlings,[17] 'and these flew this Air Force's first operations in World War II.'

The flying boat squadrons were 212, at Karachi; 240, at Madras; 262, at Durban; 321 (Dutch) at China Bay, Ceylon: and 413 (Canadian) at Koggala. All were flying Catalinas, except the Dutch who, like the US Navy, flew amphibian Cats, with wheels that stayed retracted when landing on water. The rest of the reinforcements, including 230 (the only Sunderland squadron), arrived in 1943.

In October 1942 the Drumroll Group of U-boats overtook the Polar Bears operating off Cape Town and began sinking ships off Port Elizabeth and Durban. The South African Air Force torpedo-reconnaissance squadron No. 22, with its Avro Ansons and Lockheed Venturas, was sent out on constant patrols and on 24 October a Ventura depth-charged an oil-slick, but nothing showed up. Later another dropped bombs round a suspected periscope, which was Ibbeken's, but without damage. A Kittyhawk unit, No. 10 Fighter Squadron, formed in April 1942 at Reunion, near Durban, also carried out many coastal patrols.

In the 'Drum-roll Group', the U-boat U/177, with 14 ships sunk, was one of the successful operators, under Lieutenant Commander Robert Gysae (Knights Cross). The captain was known for his humane attitude to survivors. Christopher Lowe records[18] that 'there are numerous instances where Gysae helped the crews of the ships he sank, with provisions and medical aid.'

One of his sinkings was of the 10,799-ton *Llandaff Castle* on 30 November 1942 off Oro Point (between Durban and Lourenço Marques). My father, Canon Ralph Banks, with my mother Dora and two younger sisters, Mary and Muriel, had travelled out from England on her to East Africa in 1940. Muriel recalls the ship losing her anti-mine equipment off Cape Town, which meant they travelled up the mine-strewn eastern side of Africa unprotected. My father, a shortish, cheerful cleric, had been Father Neptune at the Crossing of the Line Ceremony, to immerse in a tub those who had not crossed the Equator before. Since 1937 the ship's carpenter had been Stanley James Reynolds, of Hundleton, father-in-law of Mr John Worley of Pembroke Dock. John and Margaret well recall his story of her sinking which I give in brief. He told them:

'At 5.29 p.m. the ship was hit by two torpedoes, which made the ship list and then she stayed capsized. Before this, all had taken to the lifeboats and remained a mile from the upturned ship. Later U/177 surfaced and its crew manned the guns on deck. It approached and the U-boat commander spoke in good English to the boats. After asking in vain for the ship's Captain, he apologised for sinking us, explaining it was his duty. He asked if anyone required medical attention and if there were sufficient provisions in the lifeboats. He gave the survivors a course to steer for the nearest land and wished us all a safe return to our families. U/177 then proceeded to sink the *Llandaff* with her deck gun and finally submerged.'

In after years Stanley Reynolds always spoke with respect of the U-boat's Commander.

The U/177 was another IXD2, a U-cruiser which carried 442 tons of diesel; range 23,700 miles average, enough to sail the world's equator circumference without refuelling. She was 289 feet long, with a displacement of 1,616 tons surfaced. Her speed was 18/19 knots surfaced using her two diesels but 7/8 knots submerged relying on the two electric motors run from banks of suitcase-sized batteries. These needed nightly recharging on the surface, which could leave the boat open to attack. In case of damage the battery acid might also produce a fatal chlorine gas. This added to the numerous risks faced by submariners on both sides of the conflict.

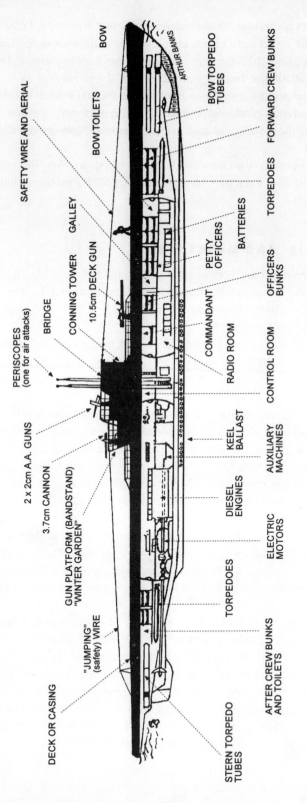

IX D2 U-BOAT

BOW

ARTHUR BANKS

BOW TORPEDO TUBES

FORWARD CREW BUNKS

BOW TOILETS

SAFETY WIRE AND AERIAL

GALLEY

TORPEDOES

BATTERIES

PETTY OFFICERS

COMMANDANT

CONNING TOWER

BRIDGE

10.5cm DECK GUN

RADIO ROOM

OFFICERS BUNKS

CONTROL ROOM

PERISCOPES
(one for air attacks)

KEEL BALLAST

AUXILIARY MACHINES

2 x 2cm A.A. GUNS

3.7cm CANNON

DIESEL ENGINES

GUN PLATFORM (BANDSTAND) "WINTER GARDEN"

ELECTRIC MOTORS

TORPEDOES

"JUMPING" (safety) WIRE

DECK OR CASING

AFTER CREW BUNKS AND TOILETS

STERN TORPEDO TUBES

Besides 24 torpedoes, in accordance with *BdU's* policy a IXD2 was so well armed she could fight off an attack on the surface or sink small ships and dhows with her 10.5 cm gun forward of the conning tower. The anti-aircraft guns aft of the bridge were 2 or 4 x 2 cm cannon on top, and one 3.7 cm cannon below, equivalent to the Oerlikon and Bofors guns. They stood on gun-platforms called the Winter-garden, known by the Royal Navy as the Bandstand and in the American Navy as the Cigarette-deck.

Now turning to the general hazards faced in this unpredictable ocean, we find two examples of a struggle by 209 Squadron against the forces of nature.

JOHN INGLIS' TWO MARATHONS

Quite apart from enemy contacts the problems and possible disasters to be faced in the air could be formidable. This is shown by two of the flights made by Flight Lieutenant John M Inglis of 209 Squadron during the early days, 1942 and 1943.

The first of John's two remarkable flights began on 12 October 1942 when he left Mombasa for Durban as captain of 'S' for Sugar, or WQ-S/209, registered AH 543, a Catalina Ib carrying six ground staff as passengers.

The weather report for the area was good and there was nothing to cause misgivings about tropical storms. The following account of the trip is an amalgam of the memories of Flight Lieutenant John Whitaker, WOM/AG, and Sergeant Derek Nobes, one of the two Flight Engineer/Air Gunners, who came from Berkshire and was a good pianist. The story is told in an article by Derek and the late Brian Philpott.[19] With Inglis piloting was Sergeant Gordon Millom, Second Pilot; Sergeant Geoff Mobley of Wolverhampton, Observer; and Sergeant Bernard Shaw, the other Flight Engineer/Air Gunner. One of the Wireless operators was Sergeant Parker, a WOM/AG and one of the WOP/AGs was Sergeant Staniforth. 'Titch' Bowers was the Rigger but other names are unknown.

After a stop at Pamanzi they took off at dusk, passing down the eastern seaboard of Africa which lay on their starboard beam. The weather was clear but after a while the horizon ahead seemed to become blacker with tiny flashes of light in it and the boat began to rock and shudder a little as the first tatters of cloud drifted past them. Millom was piloting first; then Inglis tried climbing over the thundery barrier but ran into incessant lightning and St Elmo's fire[20] which danced off the wing edges and propellers. They tried the other alternative of flying below the clouds but this too, proved impossible. It was now too late to turn back so they flew on through the storm and for the next seven hours were tossed up and down like 'corks on the ocean'.

In the compartment behind the pilot's cockpit sat John Whitaker at the wireless desk on the starboard side (right, looking forward) and opposite was Geoff Mobley at his navigating table by the port window. Between them at times on the metal grid catwalk were standing or clinging several of the ground staff passengers.

> 'All of them had been sick [says John] into a bloody great saucepan provided by the rigger, who did the cooking – not a very pleasant thought – and it was standing on the navigating table where Geoff had also been sick into it.
>
> 'I, being a good traveller, was about the only one who wasn't sick but just then we hit a terrific bump and the aeroplane went down – the pot went up – it carefully crossed the catwalk where all these passengers were standing just getting in the way and then emptied itself all over me. We hadn't had tinned meat but I finished up looking like a tin of Maconochie's stew![21] Of course old Geoff Mobley laughed his head off.'

With Inglis and Millom fighting the controls, Brian Philpott writes, 'the Catalina flew into several towering cumulo-nimbus clouds in which the violent currents carried it aloft one moment, even up to 13,000 feet where ice formed', and then forced it crashing down almost to sea-level, which could not be gauged, with the altimeter unreliable. He continues:

> 'John Inglis struggled to control the aircraft and on one occasion a down current gripped the flying boat and despite the fact that Inglis had the engines at full power climbing upwards, it hurled the aircraft towards the sea at almost 2,000 feet a minute. Baggage and passengers were thrown about the fuselage.'

The skipper, now wedged into his seat by many cushions, even on his head, despite his discomfort 'called on all his piloting skills to find a way through the unrelenting storm but there was no escape.' After six hours the storm made a final attempt to down the flying boat, flinging it up the centre of a thundercloud again then forcing it down so hard that the pilots thought the wings would come off, which in any aircraft less flexible than a Catalina could have happened. However, they broke out of cloud just above the angry sea.

At dawn the storm abated. Geoff Mobley as Observer tried to find out what part of the sea they were over with his damaged sextant. 'The compasses,' says Whitaker, 'were spinning like inebriated Catherine wheels.' Geoff indicated a rough course to get to land. The Wireless Operator Mechanic/Air gunner, Sergeant Parker, managed to get the radio going and obtained a bearing. Two hours later with 15 minutes of fuel left they spotted the coast and just inland, providentially, a small lake where John Inglis made a perfect landing. They were, in fact, on Lake Kosi, in Portuguese East Africa, about 70 miles south of Lowrenço Marques, now Maputo. Even more 'providential' than the lake was the appearance of an Imperial Airways civilian Empire flying boat overhead. Against regulations Captain J. Algar of *Caledonian* courageously decided, not having passengers aboard, to land beside the Catalina and take off the crew.

Unfortunately the wind blew the Cat on to a sandbank where the Germans were able to repair it and take it back to Portugal, but its fate thereafter is not known. By this time a truck was arriving by road at the lake and spotted four of the crew but all got away safely down to Durban where, it is said, the Captain of *Caledonian* was grounded for three months as punishment. In Derek's later career as band leader and a Resident Pianist, whenever he was asked 'Can you play Stormy Weather?' he would smile to himself. In the *Natal Daily News* John Inglis was praised by Gordon Millom when he said: 'In my opinion he undoubtedly saved the lives of all of us and deserves a medal for his airmanship.' No medal, however, was normally given for single examples of good flying.

The second 'marathon' was more of a struggle against the sea. In the roving U-boat U/177, Lieutenant Robert Gysae was still present the following July when he involved John Inglis by sinking an American Liberty ship. These 7000-ton prefabricated wonders, constructed sometimes in ten days at shipyards like that of the amazing Henry J Kaiser, were welded together and not often riveted. They were surprisingly resilient, though not without exception.

At Mombasa one evening I well remember clambering, in swimming trunks (with Ron Avery, my sergeant in the Met Office), up the gangway of a Liberty ship, from the waters of Port Reitz Creek. The two of us were taking a swim, after a sweaty day's work on Met charts, across the mile-wide creek, hopefully beyond the area of crocs, sharks and barracudas who mainly kept to the harbour further down. Swimming to the centre of the creek we were faced with a broad river of black oil, and decided to climb over this American Liberty ship to avoid it. On deck we were chatting to some of the bronzed sailors when a bell rang and the crew gave us a warm invitation to their evening meal, and showed their appreciation of the Navy and Air Force patrols. After the drab RAF food at Port Reitz the meal tasted like a banquet.

UPPER LEFT: Liberty ship being checked by Leigh-Light Catalina VA 732 of 240 Sq. *(Author's painting courtesy of Harry Collier)*

UPPER RIGHT: U/177 from the bows. (Captain Robert Gysae) which sank the *Alice F. Palmer.*

(Courtesy of Horst Bredow)

LOWER LEFT: The US Liberty ship *Alice F. Palmer* sinks. Photo taken from the U/177.

(Courtesy of Horst Bredow)

LOWER RIGHT: F/Lt John Inglis, whose Catalina rescued 20 of the Alice F. Palmer crew. *(Courtesy of J. Whitaker)*

It was another Liberty boat, the 7,176-ton American *Alice F. Palmer*, which was ploughing northwards, unescorted, up the Moçambique Channel at dawn on 10 July 1943. Robert Gysae spotted her and gave chase. It took U/177 a long struggle. Two torpedoes slowed the ship down but it needed 99 shells from her 10.5 cm gun to stop her and set her afire, after which she gradually sank. A number of survivors got away and were spotted from the air by Wing Commander Wallace on 11 July 1943, according to Canadian Flying Officer Bob Bower, his navigator. We are here concerned with the Captain and 19 survivors who were in one lifeboat on 13 July, about 50 miles off the south west coast of Madagascar. I found this report by Flight Lieutenant John Inglis tucked away at the end of 209 Sq microfilm records in the Public Record Office at Kew. He said:

'On 13 July 1943 I took off[22] as captain of Catalina M-209 (VA 703), at 04.30 from Tulear, ordered to search for a lifeboat previously contacted and drop supplies on same when found.'

John found it at 11.30 and dropped supplies which were picked up. Generator trouble then put their radio out of action so John had to decide on his own what to do next. They could not radio Tulear's tug, nor could they allow the lifeboat to drift or be rowed towards a rocky coastline. Westerly currents could sweep it out to sea and the boat might not be found again. John was (incorrectly) informed that the survivors had been at sea 17 days. Looking down on the frail boat and tired men, he considered the option of picking them all up.

The wind was light and the sea calm, with the dreaded mid-ocean swell (which could bounce an aircraft landing or taking off into uncontrollable danger) scarcely in evidence. John knew that such rescues had been carried out before in worse conditions than this so he decided to risk it. The business of getting the survivors all transferred, after a short landing, took time. John could not now jettison his depth charges without blowing everybody sky high so he shed petrol instead, for the heavily laden take-off.

Meanwhile a strong wind blew up and the swell rose so that when he tried to take off,

'. . . we bounced badly twice and on the third bounce took the air at 35-40 knots to a height of about 35 feet, hitting the side of a wave and landing at right angles to our run into wind and in doing so springing some rivets in the pilot's compartment. The wind was now too strong and the waves on the beam too high so I decided to taxi to the shore and steer for the beach, past the reefs.

'By dark I had made good about 40 miles and was within approximately 7 miles from the coast and within sight of it. It was necessary to continue baling, as much water was made through the bow turret hatch. Instead of going ashore in the dark I decided to lay off into wind overnight with the engines ticking over. Meanwhile we had managed to get the Auxiliary Power Unit (APU) going intermittently and signal our intentions etc before it broke down again. At dawn after weathering some very high seas and wind we had drifted 15 miles out to sea and turning round we made the shore about 10.00 hours.'

With both blisters now broken it would be unwise to delay, so John prepared for landing. The Catalina then headed for the high breakers at the only sandy spot between the murderous rocky reefs. In the breakers the aircraft became uncontrollable and at times felt almost submerged! It slewed side on and was smashed down on the sand, the starboard wing then breaking off. The survivors and most of the crew had jumped out and swum for the shore. John's report continues:

'Flight Sergeant Parker stayed at the wireless set (which he had just got going) till the last minute very bravely and got ashore with all his log books. Flight Sergeant Wiles, a gunner whose conduct throughout was exemplary, was also there with the water almost to the roof and the aircraft being badly pounded, throwing ashore through a small hatch what he could salve. With the water near the roof of the Pilot's compartment and the aircraft breaking up quickly, I left with the captain of the American ship.'

They not only watched from the shore the break-up of the tough US-built Catalina, as the flame floats caught fire and set alight the wings and the engines fell off in the huge pounding breakers, but John Inglis and his crew made fanatical efforts to salvage everything that might be possibly be used in the equipment-starved RAF bases. Mercifully the depth charges had disappeared into the welter of foam.

In the meantime an RAF truck was on its way from Tulear to pick up the survivors and crew. Squadron Leader Fitzpatrick, who had flown over John Inglis' Cat on the shore, was asked, because of his knowledge of French, to go with another vehicle up the coast on the search. The crew and their human cargo safely reached base.

In all Flight Lieutenant Inglis in his Cat must have taxied 62 miles in stormy seas with an aircraft overloaded with 20 passengers and brought every one safe home. However, once again there was no medal in this for him, although he did make sure that Flight Sergeant Wiles received one, the Distinguished Flying Medal. Whereas the DFC is given to RAF officers, the DFM is awarded to Non-commissioned Officers or other ranks, and is less often seen. Wiles was also later promoted to Warrant Officer and posted back to the UK.

Flight Lieutenant R.A.P.H. 'Bob' Dutton DFC CPM, who in 1944 received his award for tracking *Charlotte Schliemann*, adds this comment:

> 'I reckon there should have been two or three "gongs"[23] for Jack and his crew, but I expect he got a rocket for losing the aircraft. In these calamitous circumstances he did a tremendous job in getting the battered Cat ashore. In fact I think all his crew did a splendid job, each according to his individual ability. There was nothing else they could do but it was their dedication to duty that at least saved all their lives.'

No one could say the American people back home were not grateful when their shipwrecked loved ones reached home safely. Where goodies were not as restricted as for rationed English families, they would send parcels which reached appreciative squadrons who were doing Air Sea Rescues. Some intended for the Arctic were diverted and reached the Equator.

One hot day Bob Thomas of Cardiff, a Flight Mechanic (Engines) with 265 Squadron, was working at Kisumu on Lake Victoria. He writes:

> 'I received a parcel from the good ladies of a US town. On opening it I found it contained (among other things) a dozen Air Force Blue woollen Balaclava helmets. The next day saw a gang of African "boys" [workmen] chipping away barnacles on a Cat's hull, complete with the helmets' [and mighty proud of them].'

Africans, Asians and Islanders performed many necessary tasks for the RAF in the Indian Ocean and deserve much credit for their contribution.

MORE SQUADRONS ARRIVE

On 30 April 1943 in Stranraer, on the south Scottish coast, the 265 Squadron Flight Commander, Squadron Leader T.P. 'Pete' Seymour, from Penn, in Buckinghamshire, set out with one of the Catalinas to join the migration to East Africa. He was a popular but very efficient leader and kept notebooks which Mrs Liz Seymour has kindly allowed me to use. His almost lyrical diary of the trip out from England ends unfortunately after a few days, due to his duties. This is a brief glimpse.

'Today I have said goodbye to England; not to my own England, the southland, but to the coasts and the craggy islands that make the British Isles. Spring has come to England as it has for the past thousand years: even my own home village, sleepytime Penn, wakes from its winter lethargy and shakes itself into green glory for the coming summer. But today I have said goodbye to all this . . . for a while.

'Our months of ferry training at Stranraer are now over. I have retaken embarkation leave till I fear to face the patrons of the "Horse and Groom" again; have been inoculated, vaccinated and injected against the promise of dread tropical diseases. Now, floats up! Tucker will already be erasing our name from the training board and the last of 265 is on its way. One last beat-up of the ops room!'

The next stop was Pembroke Dock at the southern tip of Wales, among warm-hearted Welsh people. This was the great flying boat base, familiar to thousands who set out for tropical climes, or used it as the base for long Atlantic patrols. At P.D. the Captain, Flying Officer Temple-Murray 'executed a tasty if rather terrifying landing. It seemed a toss-up between the trees and the sandbank,' writes Pete. Later colleagues will recognise TM's dashing style. After Gibraltar the route south took them down West Africa to Freetown in Sierra Leone and Jui, its sweltering nearby RAF base. Thence they would cross Belgian Congo (now Zaire) to East Africa.

For Flying Officer Joe Pack, also a pilot of 265 Squadron, the route was the same; first Gibraltar, where 'our white knees and tropical clothes seemed a little out of place among the old diehards there.' Then down the West African coast to Port Etienne, where 'another Cat captain, Pilot Officer Moore, and myself were briefed.' He continues:

'There seemed to be a large landing area at Bathurst with no swell and no problems. We took off (about 15 November 1943) for the 4-5 hour trip to Bathurst. The landing was difficult, I could not see the surface of the water, there was no wind, not a ripple. I did a careful landing, lots of engine, the aircraft nose well up until we hit the water safely.'

After tying up at the moorings and de-briefing ashore they heard an uproar.

'We followed the general rush to the water's edge and half a mile across the water was a great column of black smoke – which had been the other Cat with its crew of our chums. Some of the missing bodies were retrieved during the next 24 hours, savaged by barracudas, we were told.'

Sgt. (WOP/AG), later WO John Elms, of Storrington, recalls three bodies which had been recovered being 'buried in a clearing on the edge of the jungle. Our crew laid them in their last resting place and I can still vividly remember standing to attention at the foot of that continuous grave with an oversized lump in my throat as a native soldier played the "Last Post".' A glassy surface for landing meant extreme danger and even in 1945 accounted for two Catalinas on Lake Victoria, carrying double crews.

Most of the East African Cat Squadrons used this Congo (Zaire) route to reach Kenya. Pilot Officer G.O.P. 'Ox' Watson (now Bob Watson DFC) also took his 230 Squadron Sunderland, EJ 141 'R', from Pembroke Dock on 23 February 1943 on the Congo trail. Stops at Gibraltar, Bathurst, Freetown, Lagos, Leopoldville (now Kinshasa), Stanleyville (now Kisangani) and Kisumu on Lake Victoria led them to Dar-es-Salaam.

Nearly all the flying boats arrived safely, despite having to cross hundreds of miles of virgin forest in which they could have vanished without trace. Bob recalls one disappearing between Gibraltar and Bathurst. One can imagine the privations of anyone who survived the crash through the jungle canopy. No one was ever heard of again. 'It must be remembered,' Bob writes, 'that we were very inexperienced pilots with no previous operational experience as Captains and only about 400 hours total flying. Such were the demands of war at the time.'

Another route, while the Mediterranean was still open, went via Cairo, as Warrant Officer Geoff Guy, a WOP/AG of 259 Squadron and Co-founder with the author of the 350-strong Indian Ocean Flying Boat Association, recalls in a lecture to the Catalina Society. 'At Cairo,' he says, 'mysterious minor repairs were required which took two or three days while the crews enjoyed the city'. He continues:

'Then we followed the Nile with landings at Wadi Halfa and Khartoum until reaching the East African coast – all the way taking advantage of the BOAC bases for refuelling and rest. Flying the last leg across Kenya, the crews had a glimpse of Mount Kilimanjaro and the plains with vast herds of game which flourished in those days. Flying at 3,000 feet, it was like looking down on a 1930's African film set.'

Before the furious Mediterranean campaigns closed that route, 212 Squadron's Catalinas could journey to Karachi 'down the Med'. The first was E/212 (FP 175) piloted by Sergeant John Gallagher, adopted son of Willie Gallagher, the Communist MP. With them, as they took off on 22 October 1942, was Wing Commander Dickie Gething AFC who was to be the new CO when 212 was reformed at Korangi Creek, Karachi, after being an RNAS squadron in WWI. Arthur Davies, of Willowdale, Ontario, being an RNAS squadron in WWI. Arthur Davies, of Willowdale, Ontario, Secretary of the 212 Squadron Association, sent me his own long history about 212 and 191 Squadrons and takes up the tale.

'As crew came Pilot Officer Slade, Flying Officer Cooper, Sergeants Bundy, Spry, McKay, Lowe and Reese [with Arthur himself as Flight Engineer]. The Catalina left the icy waters of Lough Erne, Northern Ireland, on a cold night, 23 November 1942, with tropical and other gear carefully stowed. Heavily laden, it lumbered down the flarepath and headed for the Bay of Biscay, landing after 14 hours, in bright sunshine at Gibraltar.

'The war was not going too well at Gib so Wing Commander Gething allowed the 212 Cat to be pressed into service for a couple of ops. 2 December saw them heading once more down the Med but overland as far as Sfax to avoid the possible shooting around Malta. However, as they approached Sfax Harbour all hell broke loose as aircraft attacked shipping in the harbour. Gallagher did one of his famous split-arsed turns and climbed to 10,000 feet where they felt a lack of oxygen [none was carried].'

They then passed over hostile seas to Abu Qir (RAF Aboukir) near Alexandria; and from there they followed a route via Iraq to Karachi, RAF Korangi Creek.

Arriving at the Creek, known to airmen as El Gapio after a gap in the distant line of hills, they surveyed the tented camp. Beyond it the Sind desert stretched away into a grey haze. There was no pier so the MC bods beached them on the shore and bearers carried their bags to the camp. Alex Lowe of 240 Squadron, on his way to RAF Redhills Lake, near Madras, also found Korangi a 'miserable place where we were rationed to a *chatti* (2-foot high jar) of water a day.'

Alex, in his long and fascinating account of the journey out, says that Flight Lieutenant John Baldry was skipper in Catalina Ib, K/240 (VA 718). He had eight crew (Campbell, Shaw, Coker, Lindley, Lovick, King, Rushmore and himself), and flew via Aboukir with a landing on the River Euphrates at Basra where the heat was intense. It was no less at the Redhills base at Madras. One day while Alex was refuelling on the aluminium-topped wing, through a large chamois leather filter, a friend fried an egg on the burning wing-surface beside him, to win a bet.

Some aircrew and all the ground staff for maritime squadrons were transported to the Indian Ocean by sea, on routes no less risky than the Congo trail. To avoid Atlantic U-boats and Condor planes, south-bound convoys might first head towards USA or Brazil. Others snaked down Africa's western seaboard to Freetown and thence to Cape Town.

Airmen often suffered overcrowded troopships and poor food, the most scandalous being the refrigerator ship SS *Rangitata,* during return trips, minus its meat, to New Zealand. The British commandeered it, welded meat hooks all the way up the 70-foot steel sides of the empty holds and slung aircrew cadets in hammocks, one above another to the 'roof' – the future desert Hurricane pilots! Imagine being sick near the top!

Johnny Hackett, whom we meet later, wrote his diary as a 17-year-old in this hell-ship, where there was only a small exit in the massive hatch cover 70 feet above them. Any torpedo would have entombed the lads, while the officers in the spacious saloons above them would have had a better chance near the lifeboats.

Tom Weaving, now in Canada, had been Head Wine Waiter at the Hyde Park Hotel during the blitz and came out on the New Zealand ship *Rangitiki* as a Fitter 2E (Engines) in the Marine Craft Section, to operate with 209 Squadron. He sailed on 22 December 1942 from the Clyde and apart from storms remembers more the journey on from Freetown, playing continuous bridge and suffering foul purple diesel fumes below decks from a blown 6-foot gasket. Bob Thomas of 265 Squadron also came via *Rangitiki* to Durban where he missed the boat to India, so travelled, as did many airmen, overland to Mombasa, 3,500 miles in four weeks. The day after arriving he was flown back to Durban in a few hours, to pick up a Catalina. He never reached India.

It was not only flying boats that reached the tropics. 36 Squadron was re-formed at Tanjore after being wiped out in Malaya, and it used Wellington Mark Ics and VIIIs. John Cox would have been an Air Gunner but for his eyesight, and became instead a Flight Mechanic (Airframes), posted to 36 Squadron at Tanjore, south of Madras. The Wellington bombers were for maritime work. John also sailed on the *Rangitiki* but left Liverpool earlier on 28 July 1942.

The convoy made a bad start when one ship's guns were being tested and they shot down a Sunderland. However, the rest of the trip was unexciting, performing lifeboat drills and playing cards until, ashore at Durban, they were overwhelmed by South African hospitality.

In 1945 I returned to UK as a corporal, with an idyllic two-week trip from Nairobi by air up the Nile and in a troopship across the Med. I spent the idle hours painting a 24-page diary now in the RAF Museum, of which the wry sketch, 'Shipping Space', is one extract.

We were somewhat cramped, in our hammocks on the waterline, but the bath depicted for washing utensils after meals reminds me of Dai Thomas from Anglesey, a ground wireless operator with 259 Squadron, who had been a Cranwell apprentice. His scores of pages of description include the *Nia Hellas,* one of the seven troopships he sailed in, and the atrocious food on the trip to Durban. He writes:

Two of the author's sketches in an RAF travel diary, 1945, showing two scenes on troopship S.S. Batory. *(courtesy RAF Museum, Hendon)*

'I always looked after my own knife, fork and spoon (RAF Cranwell training), but it was the practice for the table orderlies [seen in the author's sketch] to wash the cutlery after a meal. We had a bit of a thick Brummie lad who one day emptied the lot with the slops overboard. You can imagine what nearly happened to him!'

While in Durban, Dai was one of the thousands who experienced the hospitality shown by all communities there. Dai's wife Maggie has heard

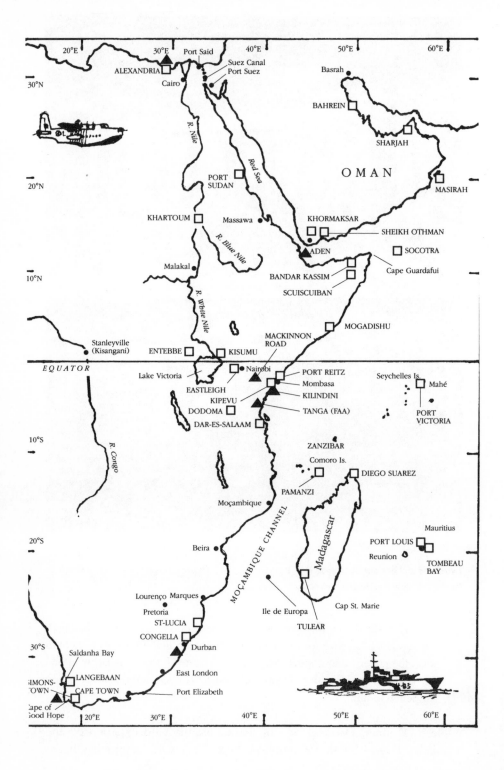

20°E 30°E Port Said 40°E 50°E 60°E
ALEXANDRIA Suez Canal Basrah
30°N Cairo Port Suez
BAHREIN
SHARJAH
R. Nile Red Sea O M A N
20°N PORT SUDAN MASIRAH
KHARTOUM Massawa KHORMAKSAR
R. Blue Nile SHEIKH OTHMAN
Malakal ADEN SOCOTRA
10°N BANDAR KASSIM Cape Guardafui
R. White Nile SCUISCUIBAN
MOGADISHU
Stanleyville ENTEBBE KISUMU MACKINNON ROAD
(Kisangani)
EQUATOR Nairobi PORT REITZ Seychelles Is. Mahé
Lake Victoria EASTLEIGH Mombasa
KIPEVU KILINDINI PORT VICTORIA
R. Congo DODOMA TANGA (FAA)
DAR-ES-SALAAM
10°S ZANZIBAR
Comoro Is. DIEGO SUAREZ
PAMANZI
Moçambique Mauritius
20°S Beira PORT LOUIS
Reunion TOMBEAU BAY
Lourenço Marques Ile de Europa Cap St. Marie
Pretoria TULEAR
ST-LUCIA
CONGELLA
30°S Saldanha Bay Durban
LANGEBAAN East London
SIMONS-TOWN CAPE TOWN Port Elizabeth
Cape of Good Hope 20°E 30°E 40°E 50°E 60°E

MOÇAMBIQUE CHANNEL
Madagascar

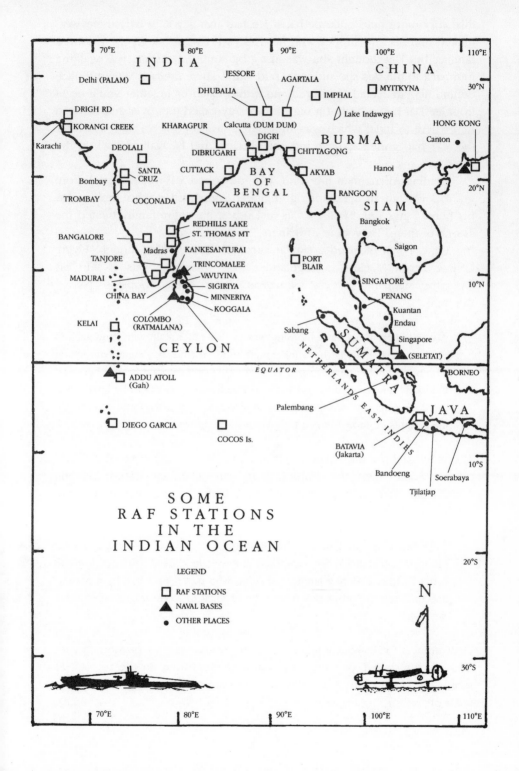

SOME
RAF STATIONS
IN THE
INDIAN OCEAN

LEGEND

☐ RAF STATIONS
▲ NAVAL BASES
• OTHER PLACES

N

this story more than once perhaps. He had met a young lady there who invited him back to supper with her folks who were one of the coloured families but Dai thought she was just a bit sunburnt. As she was walking him back to the bus she suddenly said: 'Run! There are two Military Police behind us. I'm actually coloured and if they catch us together you'll be in trouble.' Dai hared off but a big African lady called him over and showed him where to hide, which was 'in a public lavatory for blacks only'. After the MPs had gone she gave him the all clear and he walked back to the camp.

Leading Aircraftman Jim Ginn, who described P for Peter's explosion, got to know an air conditioning engineer from Durban who 'took me to his home,' says Jim. 'Whilst I was in Durban his entire family treated me as one of them. They were Afrikaners.'

Cape Town received a similar accolade from visiting airmen. Flying Officer Lewis MacRae, a highlander from Glasgow, was a Wireless Operator Mechanic in 262 Squadron, when their troopship passed through:

> 'My first view in the early morning was of Table Mountain with its tablecloth of cloud, resting along the whole length of the mountain, a sight that anyone who has seen will never forget, I'm sure. Two or three days ashore here and the local white population made us very welcome, cars would be lined up at the dock gates and anyone who wished would be whisked away to sample the delights of Cape Town, a truly heart-warming welcome.'

The story of how the squadrons settled in, with many make-shifts, will follow. Some met 'the tropics' early on, like my friend Leading Aircraftman Ron Smith, a shoemaker of Oxford, who was in the MT (Motor Transport) Section:

> 'I do remember my first arrival in East Africa, they were killing a green (or black) mamba outside the cookhouse at Port Reitz. Later I had to pick up an Army Officer on duty guarding the camp who had been bitten by a mamba and took him from our sick bay to the hospital in Mombasa. He died three days later.'

Most airmen fresh from England, despite the damp heat of Mombasa or Bombay which left you dripping, enjoyed the variety in the tropics, as tourists do today, but after two or three years the novelty did tend to wear off.

NOTES

1 *The Penang Submarines*, Dennis Gunton (Georgetown City Council), Penang 1970.

2 *The War at Sea* (4 vols), Capt S.W. Roskill DSC RN, HMSO London 1954-61.

3 *Fix, Find and Strike*, John Winton (Batsford), London 1980.

4 *Eagles Srike*, James Ambrose Brown (Purnell), Cape Town 1974.

5 *The Coffin Boats*, Warner and Senoo (Leo Cooper), London 1988.

6 Von Richthofen is personally credited with 80 Allied aircraft shot down.

7 Ken Murray in Catalina X-210 on 4 May 1945 won the DFC for sinking U/320 (VIIC) off Norway, 20 hours before the end of the War. Fortunately all the U-boat crew survived and invited him and his wife Harriet in 1986 to a reunion weekend, in Germany, where they were presented with two albums. *See RAF Coastal Command 1936-1969*, Chris Ashworth (Patrick Stephens Ltd.) 1992.

8 *War in the Southern Oceans*, Turner, Gordon-Cumming, Bezler (Oxford University Press), Cape Town 1961.

9 The *Manela* – a small RAF ex-British India liner used for transport and accommodation in ports, right up to the end of the war in Burma.

10 The Drink – RAF slang for the sea.

11 RAF Squadron Records, Public Records Office, Kew.

12 *Atlantic Torpedo*, Doris Hawkins (Gollancz), London 1943 – worth searching for archives.

13 'Liberator'- see Chapter 9, page 316 footnotes CHECK GALLEY PROOFS LATER.

14 Able Seaman Tony Large BEM (SANF) of Durban was one of four survivors out of 51 in a boat not picked up for 39 days. Dr Large describes the sinking in *Beyond the Laager*, Louis Duffus, Hurst and Blackett, London.

15 *Der Laconia Fall* – German, source unknown.

16 The Laconia Order 17.09.1942 contained this first clause; 'All attempts to rescue members of ships which have been sunk, including attempts to pick up swimmers, or to place them in lifeboats, or attempts to right capsized boats, or to supply food and water, will cease. The rescue of survivors contradicts the elementary necessity of war for the destruction of enemy ships and crews.' (In the Indian Ocean this was rarely adhered to by U-boat Captains.).

17 Coastal, Support and Special Squadrons, Rawlings (Janes), Coulsden 1982.

18 Christopher Lowe, Nottingham, adviser on U-boats.

19 *Can you play Stormy Weather?* article, based on Derek Nobes account, by Brian Philpott (*Aviation News*, London), 8/21.1.88.

20 St Elmo's fire. A spectacular display of static electricity along the surfaces of the

aircraft, or ships' rigging in thunderstorms.

21 Maconochie's stew. Army tinned stew dating back to World War One, at least in origin.

22 209 Squadron Records, Kew.

23 Gongs – RAF slang for medals.

CHAPTER 4

SQUADRONS IN THE TROPICS

230 Sunderland Squadron, which had been in Singapore at the start of the war, moved to the Mediterranean in 1940 where it saw much action, as discussed in Chapter One. It was then transferred in January 1943 to the palm-fringed harbour of Dar-es-Salaam in Tanganyika, the country of my birth. The aircrews prepared themselves for long-range patrolling over the Indian Ocean; the ground staff adapted their work to humid conditions in Tabora Creek, off the beautiful harbour.

For Leading Aircraftman John Foxon of Northamptonshire, the change was unwelcome. He was an administrative clerk in 230 Squadron Orderly Room, remembered by his CO, Wing Commander Dundas Bednall, as being hard-working and reliable, necessary qualities to keep the squadron affairs running smoothly. Not long after this he was commissioned as a Pilot Officer. Having spent some time in the dry clean air of the Western Desert alongside the Eighth Army, he found the dripping humidity, the palm trees that hemmed one in everywhere, and the dreaded mosquitoes, which began to spread malaria through the squadron, an unpleasant contrast.

John died in 1989 only the day after he had contacted me in the village where we both lived, Great Baddow in Essex. Mrs Mary Foxon generously passed on to me the large collection of John's overseas letters to her, with her own replies as well as many photographs. They show the importance of home links to the airman overseas, while some servicemen, partly through mail getting held up with detachments, experienced misunderstandings that could lead to a divorce.

His colleague Norman Worth, then Corporal in the administration at Dar, describes the tasks behind squadron organisation. Orderly room work consisted of maintaining all records relating to men and the squadron, arranging sick leave, promotions, postings and various travel, and all correspondence between other units or between UK and the unit. At times there were two or three detachments of aircraft, crews and ground staff away from the home base which stretched capacities to the limit. Hard work was in fact welcomed as it helped to pass the time.

John Foxon felt no praise was too high for the members of the British Legion who 'opened a large building,' he writes, 'with Reading Rooms, Lounge, Billiard Room and a canteen upstairs. The European ladies do all the catering and you can get an awfully decent hot meal there for about 1/9d.' I was able to enjoy these meals a year later. Warrant Officer Mike Taylor, at that time a Fitter IIA/Air Gunner, tells me that this scheme was the work of Dr C.H.R. 'Roly' Formby of the Government Medical Department encouraged by 230 Squadron's Commanding Officer, then Wing Commander Rupert Taylor, of Durban. Roly's family adopted Mike as one of the family in his off-duty times. In the New Year Honours list for January 1943 Rupert Taylor was awarded a Mention in Despatches, according to the records and later an OBE.

From the author's watercolour of Pegasus engines on a 230 Sq Sunderland Mk III, Dar-es-Salaam, 1944. *(courtesy RAF Musem, Hendon)*

Further contrasts were seen in the functioning of the Bristol Pegasus XVIII engines on the Sunderland Mark III aircraft when they reached East Africa. Wing Commander Bednall was now the commanding Officer and he recalls 230's Sunderlands in the Middle East having a high reputation for reliability. Here, in Dar-es-Salaam, despite the struggles of the maintenance crews, the exhaust valves of the cylinders had a tendency to stick and then break off when the engines were running. The engines might keep going with the valve head and stem floating about inside the cylinder. This meant that at some awkward moment the cylinder could have a hole blown in it, or explode entirely.

There were nine cylinders (known as 'pots') in each radial Pegasus engine (known as a Peggy). If a pot blew up, the engine could stop but in Sunderland IIIs there was no way of 'feathering'[1] the three-bladed propeller ('prop') to prevent the wind turning it in flight ('windmilling'). The prop could fly off into the cockpit killing the pilots, or it could further damage the engine. In this way Sunderlands were put at risk. In Dar-es-Salaam there was trouble enough but when the squadron moved to Koggala in Ceylon, W/Cdr Bednall recalls at one period ten successive missions having engine trouble. F/Lt Alan Pedley DFC also experienced, in one trip up the Nile from Kisumu to Khartoum at Christmas, 1943, cylinder trouble in three of his four engines! His amusing account ends with exchanging one of his crates of bully beef, a rarity in Khartoum, for a brand-new engine installed by the grateful BOAC engineers.

At this stage, in June 1943, 230 Squadron had to provide a detachment of several Sunderlands for two months to go to Bizerta, opposite Sicily, to cover Air Sea Rescue in Operation Husky, the invasion of Sicily and Italy. F/O G.O.P. 'Ox' Watson and F/O D.W. McNichol, both Australians, won their DFCs there rescuing the downed American crew of a Marauder aircraft. McNichol, in Q/230(JM 659), had spotted the dinghy, through its torch flashing, the night before, and wanted to land but was approached by a Ju88 German night fighter. Landing on the water, with his upper gun-turret not in action, would have lost the aircraft so, noting the position carefully, he returned to base.

Next morning, in 'R' (EJ 141), Bob Watson, to quote from his full and thrilling account, 'came directly upon the six men floating in the sea (thanks to the skill of McNichol's navigator and mine, George Schroeder).' After bouncing down on a 4-ft swell, they could no longer see the men as 'their one and a half dinghies were floating below the surface. In the half dinghy the Americans had put the one injured man; the other five were treading water and taking turns to rest in the remaining dinghy.' After a search and a struggle Bob's crew[2] got the men aboard and back to Bizerta, where later a warm letter of appreciation was received from Colonel Karl E. Baumeister in charge of the US 320th Bombardment Group. The Pegasus engines on their journey up the Nile had given little trouble, nor did they in the Mediterranean.

UPPER LEFT: Crew of R/230 (EJ141) after Bizerta rescue (see Chapter 4) Left to right: Wadsworth, Hitchcock, Peattie, Thomson, Watson DFC. (Capt) Schroeder, Preston, Murray, Davies, Wood.

(Courtesy of Jack Davies)

UPPER RIGHT: Japanese 'sugar dog' being attacked (see Chapter 12) by Sunderland Q209 (F/Lt E. Yeomans DFC).

(Courtesy of Norman Wilson)

LOWER LEFT: 240 Sq Sunderland 'up the slip for a major' at Koggala, early 1946.

(Courtesy of A. Moorwood)

LOWER RIGHT: H.M. Aircraft Carrier *Indomitable* supplies fuel to Cat S/240 in Hong Kong (see Chapter 10). *(G/Capt Abel via A. Moorwood.)*

Radar and Radio.

UPPER LEFT: Cpl Giff Blarney and LAC Erin Costello ground radar mechanics 209 Sq Mombasa.
(Courtesy of G. Blarney)

LOWER LEFT: Sgt A. Moorwood – WOP/AG/ASV operator – Despatcher of FP152 in 240 Squadron.
(Courtesy of A. Moorwood)

UPPER RIGHT: Jim Drew WOP/AG 240 Sq at the .5-inch Browning guns, Catalina Starboard blister.
(Courtesy of J. Drew)

LOWER RIGHT: Jim Drew at his wireless desk.
(Courtesy of J. Drew)

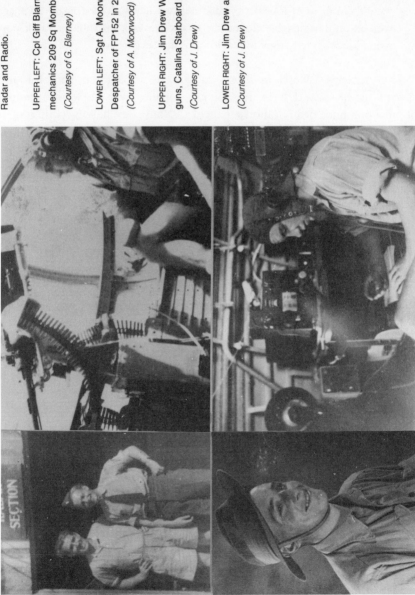

An example of a Sunderland nearly lost at sea with sticking valves is part of an absorbing account by Giff Blamey of Auckland, New Zealand, on a tape. He was then a Corporal Radar Mechanic with 209 Catalina Squadron, based on Mombassa. On 1 October 1943 he was a passenger on 230 Squadron's Sunderland 'N' leaving Mauritius for Diego Suarez. After a faulty start, the engines gave no trouble.

'But when we approached Diego harbour and the pilot eased the engines back, they start to spit like hell – backfire – so anyway we got down all right, no problem – then they had to tow us to the blooming mooring buoy! We were there three or four days, while our two fitters and the Flight Engineer worked on those engines round the clock. We took off with the outer port motor looking pretty ropy to me, towards the Seychelles.'

(The Seychelles Islands in those days were a paradisal spot for any airman to be stranded in for aircraft repairs, with a warm friendly population, and Beau Vallon's beaches. Many Seychellois young men were away on war service, as in the UK, and a surplus of unattached daughters was a notable feature. As an RAF base and a naval port of call, the island played a vital strategic role in the anti-submarine war.)

'[When Giff Blamey landed again] we had to be towed to the mooring buoy! We were at Seychelles four days and they still couldn't get any joy out of those bally engines. Then 230's Sunderland "V" came in, so they said to us: "Everybody out of here, into the other Sunderland." This one was brand spanking new. Only 200 hours flying – all nice and clean, new paint, new motors.

'We took off in a tropical rainstorm but we got clear of it and the pilot climbed to about 8,000 feet, which proved to be very, very fortunate. She was fine. The crew fetched round mugs of tea and bully beef sandwiches. I stretched out there in the bomb-bay (which is like a room) on the cargo and went to sleep. About ten in the morning, I got a knock on the shoulder. It was one of the crew. "Here you are, Kiwi, have a cup of tea." I said: "Thanks. Hey, Sarge, I can smell petrol," because this is what you have to do when you're flying. If you smell burning or any petrol, you have to report that whether you make a fool of yourself or not. He says: "I should bloody think so! We've just jettisoned 400 gallons."

'"Oh, my God, what's the problem?" I said. "You just look at that outer port motor." he replied. There the prop was, just going round in the wind like a windmill and pouring out oil. Apparently it had backfired and smoke came out of it and they had shut it down.

'Later on the skipper kept coming round and talking to us. He was an

Australian, F/Lt McCallum RAAF, and he was reassuring us. "We've kept our height," he says, "but we've lost a few miles per hour on our speed. We'll be all right." We were beyond the point of no return, and we cruised on. Then all of a sudden the inner starboard, she started to cough. You can see all these flames and smoke coming out of it – God, what a horrible frightening sight. Anyway, the skipper came around and he said: "Prepare to jettison everything. Open up the bomb-bays." [These, unlike bomb-bays in bombers, were one on each side of the aircraft. The bomb racks are slid out under each wing to drop depth charges].

'We opened up the bomb-bays and he says: "Right. Throw out all the freight. Just keep your personal kits, your tool-kits and all the mail – keep that, but everything else – over the side!" So over went the guns and over went the ammunition, everything we could find, including a ship's anchor. It was a darned shame but it was either that or curtains for us. We were gradually losing height and Flight Lieutenant McCallum kept coming round to see. Somebody grabbed a gramophone belonging to Squadron Leader Chaffey Moore, who was the Padre for East Africa Command, to throw it overboard but the Chaplain appealed to the Skipper and he said: "No, we might need that." Then someone grabbed a pile of 50 prayer books, but the Skipper said: "No, we might need them." By golly we did, too!

'We soldiered on, still losing height. Then Flight Lieutenant McCallum said: "Right, I want two pairs of eyes to every porthole. We're lost. I don't care what you see whether it's a ship or an aeroplane or a dinghy, for goodness sake report it." I was at one porthole with John Jones, the Instrument Repairer and we were on the starboard side, up near the nose. There were 42 of us on board.

'We took turns of ten minutes, because it was so hard, peering into the haze. All of a sudden Jonah gives me a nudge and says "Here, Giff, what's that?" And I could see this white smudge. "God, I don't know, I think it's a bit of cloud or a bit of smoke or something." Anyway we shouted to Mr McCallum to come down and have a look at it. And being a true Aussie, he says "You bloody beauties! That's Nyali Beach, Mombasa! we're home." Gosh, were we happy about that. We went across Mombasa harbour with one hundred feet to spare, so it was a pretty close run thing.

'We glided over Mombasa and we just stalled right on the water, made a beautiful landing and what motors were still there they just stopped and that was the finish! [The fuel had gone]. A couple of the crew had to get up on to the mainplane and shout to get a tow to the mooring buoy. By God, Sunderlands! Marvellous aircraft but those engines were just terrible! No good at all in the tropics.

'I can remember the 29th of January 1943, Auckland Anniversary Day, we had four of them at Mombasa for a special op, and about twenty Cats up there from all over the area and they couldn't put a Sunderland in the air! Anyway they towed us to the buoy and Squadron Leader Moore, he suggested we have a little service in the "Wardroom" (in the central part of the Sunderland). He crammed the whole 42 of us in there and he gave a little sermon. I was never a great one for that sort of thing and I used to dodge church parades as much as I possibly could, but by Jove, it was very, very impressive. And we all sang the hymn "For those in peril on the sea". We got ashore and we were very glad to get our feet on *terra firma*.'

Warrant Officer (Group 1) Frederick 'Gus' Platts was a very experienced Flight Mechanic Airframe/Air Gunner and for a year he was with 230 Squadron. Now resident in California where, at the time of writing, he had just lost his home in the Los Angeles earthquake, Gus sent me this comment.

'It seemed to me that our efforts were wasted. Our unserviceability (U/S) rate was bad and sickness during my year was chronic. Hence this little song, dedicated to one, Sergeant Dean.

"There's a blackboard by the mess,
        Nelly Dean
where our kites are all U/S
        Nelly Dean
When they're not U/S in red
They're U/S in green instead
Don't show surprise.
230 . . . Never . . . Flies."'

'We used two colours to show the reasons for our not being serviceable,' Gus adds. His Sunderland had actually come out from Invergordon bearing the logo, on its port bow, ALL FLAP – NO FLY. It showed a penguin tethered to a mooring buoy and was F/O Lumsden's V/230 (EJ 140). V had got over her teething troubles but the motto was a reminder. Sadly, on 29 December 1943 she flew into the 3,500-foot Sangalla Hill in thick cloud during a calibration flight, near Voi, Kenya with the loss of the crew. Gus was away at the time.

Yet thanks to unceasing efforts by the maintenance crews, 230's flyers *did* carry on with the convoy escorts and anti-submarine patrols, and they were usually 'uneventful'. The whole Squadron *did* manage the move, round the Indian Ocean to Ceylon in January 1944, with F/Lt Alan Pedley bringing up the rear and carrying a spare engine in case anyone had trouble.

But, what was wrong with the Pots of Pegasus? At Koggala in Ceylon Wing Commander Bednall struggled, through 222 Group headquarters, for the squadron to be supplied with the new Sunderland Mark V which had Pratt and Whitney engines, like the Cats. In his very readable autobiography, *Sun on My Wings*[3], he writes:

'Our problems became an obsession with me and I must have irritated many sympathetic officers at Group HQ as I felt I must never let this rest. After all, a whole squadron had virtually been rendered unoperational by an engine fault and not by enemy action.'

When the author consulted him, Dundas Bednall said:

'The original Pegasus XXIIs on the Sunderland Mark I were superb. The Mark IIIs were equipped with Peggy XVIIIs with two-speed superchargers. Although the engines were basically the same, the XVIIIs were thus stretched to allow an increase of all-up weight of nearly 5,000 lb.'

BOAC also used Pegasus XVIII engines, and I asked Captain Johnny Hackett, whom we will see flying Empire boats down via East Africa to Durban, what *they* did to keep their Peggys going. He told me

'We had an infallible remedy. We filled the grease guns with graphite grease and if there was any trouble on a particular engine in flight we would get in the engineer at base. He would track down that cylinder and valve and pump it full of graphite grease. It might be needed every two or three days, but it did the trick.'

John learned that, in the Atlantic, Sunderlands did not have this trouble so he felt that it must be due to the extreme heat. W/Cdr Bednall doubted if the graphite would have solved all the problems.

In search of further light on this mystery, I sought a 'second opinion' from a distinguished engineer, the retired Air Officer for Air Training Command, UK, Air Commodore Eric S. Baddely C. Eng., FRAeS, FIMgt. He just happens to be my son David's father-in-law and in WW2 he was Engineer Officer to No 40 (Liberator) Squadron in Italy. He writes as follows:

'The engine problems of the Sunderland flying boats and the usage of huge aircraft in the Indian Ocean region may seem strange to some readers. A warplane loaded with a gang of mechanics is unusual, but the legendary flying boat squadrons were accustomed to independent operations, demanding that support crews and their gear were carried to any base where they were deployed. This freedom of operation made the 'boats' a very popular posting for groundcrew.

'The strangely localised problem of exhaust valve failures in the engines needs study in the light of wartime conditions. The "Peggy" was a very well proven engine, built in thousands by the Bristol Aero Engine Company and used in many military and civil aircraft, including of course the Sunderland's progenitors, the magnificent Empire boats that were the luxury liners of air travel in the late '30s.

'Why then should these trusty workhorses fail again and again for the same reason, in one limited part of the world? Climatic conditions were suspected, but once up in the air, the ambient temperatures in the Indian Ocean were not greatly different from the Med. Basic manufacturing faults, or operating practices, can also be ruled out since they would give trouble anywhere. So what remains? Consider the engine's lifeblood – OIL!

'Piston engines depend on valves to fill and empty every cylinder thousands of times a minute and the Peggy's normal, mushroom-shaped valves had a narrow stem sliding in a close-fitting metal guide, dependent on adequate lubrication. Exhaust valves, which release extremely hot gases after combustion, work at very high temperature – so what happens if the oil film on their stems breaks down?

'Engine oil specifications exist to prevent such breakdowns – in particular to ensure that hard waxy deposits do not build up on the hot valve stems. But in wartime, provision of "the right stuff" in adequate quantities, to remote areas of operation, cannot always be guaranteed. The possibility that local oil supplies in East Africa, perfectly adequate for automobile engines, might fail to meet the *extreme* needs of aero-engines, becomes a likely cause. All the reported symptoms could support a diagnosis of failed valve stems, preventing the valve springs from closing the valves before the rising pistons could strike the valve head and break it off inside the cylinders. One such broken valve could destroy an engine in a short period of operation.

'Seen in retrospect such a problem ought to be quickly identified and overcome by replacing the oil supply – but the supply route at that time could imply a long delay in correcting the difficulty, even if it were identified. Truly a case of "for want of a nail".'

Only when Alan Pedley was sent back to UK to bring out the first Sunderland Mark V, with its American engines, did 230 Squadron's 'pot' troubles finally clear up. These had the Pratt and Whitney 'Twin Wasp' engines that had proved so reliable on the Catalina flying boat.

We saw the squadron in action when Ceylon was attacked but after Easter 1942 convoy escorts and anti-submarine patrols continued uneventfully. In July 1943 a detachment from Coconada flew 'Operation Breach', bombing attacks on Tavoya airfield. Otherwise there was no action till 22 January 1944.

On that night F/Lt Jack Groves of Weymouth was flying F for Freddie, Catalina VA 723, on guard for Convoy CJ 13 with 16 merchantmen and two escorts along India's eastern coast. The Senior Naval Officer in the leading escort had delayed Jack's departure at dusk, by transmitting up to him, on Aldis lamp, a lengthy Morse message which included a number of ships' names. Leaving the convoy in the darkness, about 16 miles behind them, the radar operator switched his aerial from the beam (where there was not a trace) to the Yagi aerials pointing to the bow. On the small vertical screen a blip appeared dead ahead, and they went down to investigate.

So near the coast, Jack was concerned that this might be one of the RN Motor Torpedo Boats and didn't want to upset them with a shower of 'friendly' depth charges. By waiting till he was sure, however, he nearly missed a diving U-boat. All the crew could see was a swirl of phosphorescence, with a black space in the middle that grew smaller as the U-boat dived. Jack released flares and dropped four 250-pound DCs over the spot. Back in the blisters F/Sgt 'Hopalong' Cassidy and Sgt Bill Gleaves prepared their Twin Browning guns. Says Bill:

'The Klaxon had already been giving us warning of the attack and Frank commenced firing using the red control lights as a point of aim – he was sure he could see the red dimmed control lighting in the conning tower. The explosions created a background of white light momentarily, with black and green round its edges.'

The Captain also ordered flame floats to be thrown out to mark the spot where the sub had dived.

'We again flew over the location and saw the results, oily patches on the sea surrounded by a brownish foam. We knew the WOPs had been busy sending details and were pleased to see they were effective.'

In other words a 'Hunt to Destruction' was mounted, over the next two or three days, involving A/240, M/205, H/321, C/413, J and R/205 with V/191. Six squadrons! No luck, but the Dutch Cat H for Harry did drop DCs on a 'possible', which they swore was not a whale. 'Numerous whales were sighted before and after the attack,' states the record[4], 'and H/321 had herself taken an excellent photograph of a whale some five days previously.' Obviously my Dar-es-Salaam training cartoon on the cover of this book, was a libel. Anyway the U-boat escaped with damages.

SHIPPING SUNK

The newly-arrived squadrons now settled down to their various maritime duties between Africa and Burma. Axis submarines, with surface raiders, had their heyday in 1942, sinking 205 ships of 724,485 tons, whereas 1943's tonnage was 486,324 and the number of merchant ships sunk was only 72.

413 SQUADRON

Harking back to 1942, this Canadian squadron had preceded 230 at Koggala and one of the routine incidents had also involved 205 Squadron. It was not only engines that could go wrong. This time it had been the depth charge release mechanism. The 205/413 combined effort was thus described in the 413 Squadron records[5].

'On August 26 1942 S/Ldr Stacey of 205 Sq [of whom more later] in Catalina H/413 (Z2135), set off to search for survivors of a ship sunk by an enemy submarine – possibly Japanese. Three lifeboats with approximately 60 passengers were sighted. Supplies were dropped to them and S/Ldr Stacey circled overhead for 10 hours till relieved by F/Lt Roberts in B or P/413 (W8412). While shepherding the lifeboats till the arrival of HMS *Shoreham*, Roberts spotted an enemy submarine and twice dived on it but the depth charges failed to be released. The submarine dived and thus escaped any further attack.'

The passengers were picked up but the crew went home naturally disappointed.

THE HUNTING U-BOATS

Admiral Dönitz, after commanding the U-boat arm, was promoted to Grand Admiral (*Grossadmiral*) and became Commander-in-Chief of the German Navy at the beginning of 1943. He retained personal control of his beloved U-boats and would do his best to meet each crew when they

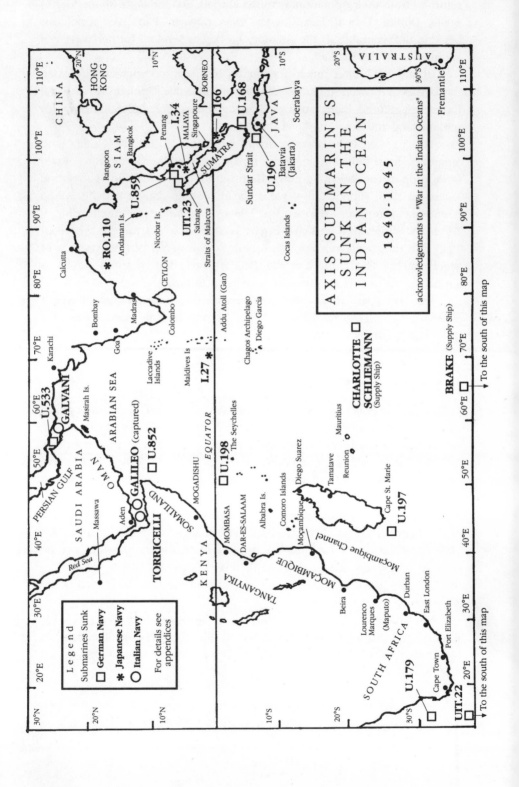

AXIS SUBMARINES
SUNK IN THE
INDIAN OCEAN
1940-1945

acknowledgements to "War in the Indian Oceans"

Legend
Submarines Sunk
□ German Navy
* Japanese Navy
○ Italian Navy

For details see appendices

To the south of this map

BRAKE (Supply Ship)

CHARLOTTE
SCHLIEMANN
(Supply Ship)

CHINA
HONG KONG
SIAM
Rangoon
Bangkok
Penang
MALAYA
Singapore
SUMATRA
Sabang
Straits of Malacca
Nicobar Is.
Andaman Is.
BORNEO
JAVA
Soerabaya
Batavia
(Jakarta)
Sundar Strait
Cocas Islands

I.34
U.859
UIT.23
RO.110
I.166
U.168
U.196

Calcutta
Bombay
Goa
Madras
CEYLON
Colombo
Laccadive Islands
Maldives Is
Addu Atoll (Gan)
Chagos Archipelago
Diego Garcia
I.27

ARABIAN SEA
Masirah Is.
PERSIAN GULF
OMAN
SAUDI ARABIA
Aden
Massawa
Red Sea
SOMALILAND
MOGADISHU
KENYA
MOMBASA
DAR-ES-SALAAM
TANGANYIKA
Beira
MOCAMBIQUE
Mozambique
Mozambique Channel
Lourenco Marques
(Maputo)
Durban
East London
Port Elizabeth
Cape Town
SOUTH AFRICA

The Seychelles
Aldabra Is.
Comoro Islands
Diego Suarez
Tamatave
Reunion
Mauritius
Cape St. Marie

EQUATOR

U.533
GALVANI
GALILEO (captured)
U.852
TORRICELLI
U.198
U.197
U.179
UIT.22

Karachi

Fremantle
AUSTRALIA

110°E 100°E 90°E 80°E 70°E 60°E 50°E 40°E 30°E 20°E
20°N 10°N EQUATOR 10°S 20°S 30°S

To the south of this map

returned from their operational cruises abroad. *BdU* or *Befehlshaber der U-boote,* Dönitz' U-boat Headquarters was now in Paris. As conditions became unfavourable in the Atlantic, he began sending further waves of submarines to the Far East.

In late 1942, after much negotiation in Japan, co-operation between the two Axis powers included the arrangement for Germany to use the Japanese-captured bases such as Penang, Singapore and Sourabaya for replenishing and repairing her U-boats.

The use of Penang as a main base for 33 U-boat Flotilla and Singapore for dry-docking or major repairs enabled the Germans to obtain fresh support for their long-range U-cruisers. Their oil-carrying submarine U-tankers and supply ships were in increasing danger as the Allied countermeasures were stepped up. The two *Mutterschiffe* (mother-ships), *Charlotte Schliemann* and the *Brake,* escaped the net for the whole of 1943, but they were not enough to supply the needs of fresh groups of 'steel sharks'. The *Quito* and the *Bogota* also acted to some extent as suppliers, but mainly as transports, going up to Japan.

The Japanese had already used Penang as a base for their Eleventh Submarine Flotilla. Now, in April 1943, the port became headquarters for their Eighth Submarine Squadron.

THE NEXT WAVE

Following the Polar Bear and Drumroll waves, the Seal *(Seehund)* group of U-boats consisted of U/160 (captained by Lassen), U/182 (Clausen, whose widow my friend Chief Engineer Karl-Heinz Wiebe later married), U/195 (Buchholz), U/506 (Würdemann), U/509 (W. Witte), and U/516 (Wiebe – no relation). All were Type IXC except Buchholz's boat which was a IXD1. The only real success story for the Seals was U/160 with Lassen who demolished a badly-organised Convoy, DN 21, between 1 and 5 March 1943 south of Durban. Out of eight freighters escorted by HMS *Nigella* and three RN trawlers he sank three and the trawlers lost the convoy. Elsewhere Lassen later sank three more. An Italian submarine, the *Leonardo da Vinci* also sank six ships about the same time, two in the Atlantic.

Nevertheless, both German and Allied historians find Germany's Far Eastern ventures as a whole unsuccessful. Günther Schomaekers finishes his erudite article, *Far East U-boats*[6], with a quotation from the American A.M. Saville[7].

'So ended the U-boat Operations in the Indian Ocean and Far East: "Misconceived, misdirected and tragically wasteful in spite of devotion to

114

duty, the valiant efforts, sacrifices, and success of the Far East cadre.'"

Dennis Gunton[8] points out that

> 'Of the forty-five German submarines that set out for the Far East from Europe, only three returned to German or German-occupied ports . . . this makes the success of the remainder all the more remarkable. Twenty U-boats actually took part in operations in the Indian Ocean and between them sank 150 ships of nearly 1,000,000 tons. In addition four Italian-built, German-manned submarines sailed for the Far East.'

Another German authority[9], recounting the work in the Far East, seems to indicate that there were many more than 45 U-boats originally intended for the Far East. The author's table in the appendix which includes five ex-Italian boats lists 66 in all.

LAND-BASED RAF MARITIME SQUADRONS

Those land-planes which used wheels and landed on runways, such as Blenheim and Wellington bombers, made excellent maritime reconnaissance aircraft, but experienced different problems from those which flying boats had to cope with. (I am not referring to the amphibian Catalinas used by 321 Dutch, Squadron). Until the four-engined Consolidated Liberators joined them, their range was far less than a Catalina's and if they had to make a forced landing on water, they were in great trouble. My contacts with these squadrons, for personal operational material, have unfortunately been only too few, in the time available.

160 SQUADRON

This was set up afresh at Ratmalana, Ceylon, with Liberator IIIs performing maritime reconnaissance, and Meteorological Flights. Rawlings states:

> 'In September [1943] a detachment went to Cuttack for photographic reconnaissance of Car Nicobar Islands and here Wing Commander Cohen's crew, flying FL 939 "M", was attacked by Japanese Zeros. They shot one down but were then shot down by another. Further fights with Zeros ensued and another Liberator was lost in October. On 8 November the Squadron found its first enemy submarine which was attacked by Pilot Officers Hill and Hall unsuccessfully.'[10]

More will be heard of 160 in 1944 when the Libs started minelaying, as will 36 Squadron.

OTHER LAND SQUADRONS

Joe Edis flew with 353 Sq Hudsons in 'uneventful flights' on the Madras coast but also in support of the Burma campaign. When Joe arrived on 28 August 1942 some Indian Air Force squadron members were still part of the squadron, and for the first month his log-book was signed by Squadron Leader Chaudhuri as 'CO of "A" Flight, 353 Sq, I.A.F.'

Keith Scott, of Robertson, Queensland, and Don James of Formby both flew with 244 'Arabian' Squadron on Blenheims and Wellingtons and have sent me much detail. 217 Squadron, between 1942 and 1944, used first Lockheed Hudsons and then Bristol Beauforts in anti-submarine work but without enemy contact.

In 1943 the squadrons were all under separate commands. The northern section was under Aden Command; the east coast of Africa was shared by the East Africa Command with an AOC at Nairobi and the Southern Africa Command based on Durban. The widest Asian command was 222 Group at Colombo which extended as far as the tropical islands in the south and had overall direction over the other groups. Co-ordination was difficult at times, as Air Vice Marshal John Stacey recalls in the hunt for the supply ship *Charlotte Schliemann* in 1944. On the whole, however, inter-command cooperation worked fairly well, along with the Royal Navy. The Germans and Japanese also worked out separate areas for operations but the former decided not to adhere to these. Convoys were organised whenever there was a bare minimum of ships and aircraft to escort them.

413 SQUADRON

This squadron had more excitements than, say, 36 or 191 Squadrons but not always due to the enemy, as we see in the following incident.

RANDY AND THE FULMARS

The best description of this episode, in which Catalina F/413 was mistakenly shot at by the Fleet Air Arm, comes in the 413 Squadron records kindly provided by Captain Fleet, recently Squadron Historian in Canada.

'On 3 August 1942 Squadron Leader Lawson Randall ('Randy' for short) in Catalina AH 549 took off to engage in an exercise with the Navy. At 18.47 hours local time the naval force was sighted and the aircraft turned away to send a sighting report. Almost immediately thereafter two Fairey Fulmar fighters of the Fleet Air Arm were sighted by the blister watch and Lawson Randall turned the aircraft toward the sun to make any dummy attack more difficult.

'The Fulmars [from HMS *Illustrious*] each armed with eight 0.303 machine guns, opened fire in a quarter position [i.e. partly from behind the Cat] and shot away its rudder aileron controls. After the first attack Randall's co-pilot, Flying Officer Larry Gardiner, fired the red-red recognition signals of the day.

'The fighters once again attacked from above and behind, killing Flight Engineer Sergeant I.R.E. Meiklejohn, wounding the Wireless Operator, Sergeant G.K. Palmer in the legs[11], and grazing the Navigator, Pilot Officer S.S. Williams.'

The Electrician, Leading Aircraftman Leslie Craggs of Bridlington, says he was standing next to Meiklejohn in the port blister and sustained bullet wounds in his hands, while Sergeant Ireland in the starboard blister was hit in the leg, he thinks. The gas tanks were leaking dangerously but, says S/Ldr. Bill Bayly in his memoir *Cats*, 'they were holed sufficiently high for fuel to remain in the tanks.' The squadron report continues:

'S/Ldr. Randall with tremendous flying skill managed to control his flying boat by manipulating engine and elevator controls. The Fulmars, perhaps finally realising the error of their ways, quickly left the scene.

'On approach to landing it was discovered that the wing floats would not lower; however, amazingly, a successful landing was completed. S/Ldr. Randall's skill in handling his crippled aircraft undoubtedly saved the lives of his crew. The only Japanese flying boat even remotely resembling a Catalina was the twin-engined Yokosuka H541 (Cherry) only seen in Japanese home waters.'

Air Vice Marshal Stacey adds the sequel.

'A word to illustrate the stature of Johnny Plant (then CO of 413 Sq), who later became Air Member for Personnel on the Royal Canadian Air Force Board. He was then a Wing Commander and one of his aircraft, taking part in a naval exercise, was mistaken for a Japanese by a naval fighter. Our Headquarters in Colombo instructed that another 413 aircraft should be sent to continue the naval exercise and Johnny Plant refused. The Air Officer Commanding in Colombo, an Air Vice Marshal, spoke personally to Johnny who responded by saying he would comply with the order to have the aircraft ready but it would not take off until the AOC arrived to fly it. The order was rescinded.'

However, the Fleet Air Arm fighters at that time *were* conducting some very vigorous operations against the Japanese and had recently, in attacking two Japanese cruisers, shot down a four-engined Japanese Navy aircraft.

A ROUTINE PATROL

Very few anti-submarine patrols held the excitement we have seen in some of these encounters. Aircrews themselves speak of routine flights as being 'nothing to write about', yet they were the mainstay of the whole RAF campaign and actually concealed a frightening array of hidden dangers which crews took for granted. If they worried about the risks, to others they shrugged it off.

Roy Sheppee, Flight Engineer with 265 Squadron, who has written me sheaves of description about everything to do with Cats, has also produced a long and careful description of a convoy escort. He mentions the setting out on patrols at Diego Suarez:

'It was the custom after take-off to shoot up the camp i.e. low-fly over it. However 265 OC, Wing Commander Louw (see Chapter One) gave an order for this to stop, no doubt sensibly on the grounds of safety. After this order was given it was surprising how many Cats had rough take-offs and requested permission to low-fly over the Control Hut so that the Controller could inspect the hull and count the number of rivets sprung on take-off!'

Raymond Cox, an FMA/AG (Rigger) of 259 Sq also wrote a letter summarising his time overseas. Among many aspects of routine flights he describes the difficulties of mooring up a Cat to the buoy.

'On Cats I would describe my job as general dogsbody. If you hadn't exchanged the long wooden boat-hook for a short aluminium variety, you were likely to hit the port prop and end up in the drink. You also needed to be as agile as a cat for mooring up or slipping mooring, another diabolical way of having an enforced swim not to mention the risk of a crushed leg.'

Sheppee adds a note about mooring:

'After a night landing in Dar-es-Salaam we were taxiing to the mooring (usually a flattish red dome) to moor up, when the "buoy" disappeared. Any other Cats tried to moor up to a hippo!'

Sgt 'Nobby' Hudson (now Norman Hudson OBE DSC CEng, Emeritus Professor of Engineering) was Second Pilot in W/O Carr's Cat JX593 and has summarised 'The Routine Patrol' for us in a 1945 flight which ought to come into a later chapter[12]. 191 Squadron was based then at Koggala and this was a flight to the Cocos Islands about 1,700 miles to the south over a trackless sea. The islands were halfway to Australia, which also *could* be reached in one 3,000-mile hop by a Catalina[13]. On 6 June 1945 the whole flight to Cocos took 16 hours 25 minutes, five and a half by day and eleven hours in the night.

'Took off late afternoon, tanks full to the last pint, once more just crawled over the palm trees at the end of the flight path (on full tanks we could have done with another quarter of a mile to get off comfortably). Light a fag for the skipper as soon as we are safely above the trees, up to 100 feet at the coast and head out to sea. It's going to be a very long boring flight. We struggle up to 1000 feet, do a couple of those triangular jinks for the navigator to get a wind, then it's fiddle about the boost and revs for the minimum fuel consumption that will keep the lumbering old cow in the air. As I recall, we took off at something like 75 knots, cruised at 80k and landed at 65k.

'Two hours after take-off, same height, same airspeed, Joe brings coffee, nothing in sight as far as the eye can see.

'I leave the flight deck (cockpit) and take up my unofficial role as DJ. I have a wind-up gramophone and a box of "78" records and sit in the port blister with an intercom mike hung over the gramophone. Eric (navigator) likes Marlene Dietrich singing *Falling in Love Again,* flip side *Lilli Marlene*. Taff the flight engineer likes Victor Sylvester; they thought I was funny to want Haifetz playing Brahms' Violin Concerto especially as it was on a 12-inch, so needed a special box. I can't remember the other favourites but with a crew of nine it was a wide-ranging collection.'

'Four hours after take-off, dusk approaching, Joe starts cooking supper. The most important member of a Cat crew is the rigger/front gunner. He does not do much rigging or gunning but he hooks up the mooring cable when mooring to a buoy, which is quite important, and he is the cook, which is very important. Vaguely I think alternately sausage and beans or Spam and beans.

'Six hours after T/O, chugging along at 100 feet, no moon, no stars, no lights, no anything. The WOPs and WOMs in the crew take turns at watching the ASV (a sort of primitive radar) and listening to unidentifiable squeaks on the radio, and we take it in turns to try and get some rest on the bunks. Joe makes coffee every hour on the hour, the pilots change over every two hours.

'Ten hours after take-off – as before!

The Routine Flight Crew as far as is known.

Back row left to right: no name (WOM/AG); 'Taff', (F/Eng); no name (2nd Eng); 'Len' (WOM).

Front Row: no name (WOP/AG); Sgt 'Nobby' Hudson, 2nd Pilot; F/Sgt Harry Carr (Captain); Sgt Eric Knight (Nav); 'Joe' (FMA/AG). *(Courtesy of Norman Hudson)*

LOWER PICTURE: L/209 (K. Murray) being beached after crash-landing, Tombeau Bay while on 'routine flight'. Note beam aerial. *(Courtesy of Harry Hughes)*

'Twelve hours after T/O, big excitement – cloud clears and stars appear. Eric and second pilot (self) try to figure out which star is which [remembering that the stars of the Southern Hemisphere are coming up. The Plough rolls on its back before sinking below the horizon and the Southern Cross appears with myriads of unfamiliar stars]. Eric takes sextant shots and starts ploughing through calculations to get a fix. He says the wind has changed and we are 100 miles south of where we were supposed to be. Well, after 12 hours in an ocean bigger than the Atlantic that is practically spot on. He gives us a course correction.

'Fourteen hours after take-off same boredom but a vague lightening of the sky and soon after, a much more substantial lifting of the spirit as there comes drifting up to the flight deck the most wonderful smells of coffee, then of toast, then of frying bacon. I can't remember what Joe cooked on, but there isn't much space in a Cat and I don't suppose we had bottled gas or paraffin, so it was probably a two-ring hotplate. Anyway it took a lot of time to cook nine meals and since the principle was food in the reverse order of seniority it seemed ages (about four coffees plus ten fags) before it got to the pilots' turn, but there can be few meals more appreciated and enjoyed.

'Sixteen hours after take-off. I can't remember how we found that microscopic dot in the middle of the Indian Ocean. The pseudo-radar was primitive, Eric's navigation was pretty good but I doubt if this dead reckoning and our combined astro-nav could have hit it so I suppose there was some sort of radio beacon to home in on.

'Radio contact ineffective as usual, but we approached, shot off the Very pistol colours for the day – always nervous about that; there were several possibilities of self-inflicted injury in Cats. Apart from the second pilot's Very pistol, the blister O.5 Browning machine-guns had no control stops on the mounting to stop you shooting off your own tailplane or wing tip; the front gun was a relic from the last war and fortunately always jammed before it could do any damage. The latrine in this case was a small hatch in the floor – fortunately too small to fall through, but also a small target in a 60-knot wind.

'With no radio contact and no answer to Aldis lamp (well, after all it was at least 100 miles from anywhere; they were not expecting us, and it was 4 o'clock in the morning) we landed, taxied to a mooring buoy and waited for a [marine] tender. After a sticky and boring sixteen-hour flight the clear blue water was inviting so we stripped off and bathed. The cowards like me, jumped from the blisters, the dare-devils jumped from the wings and one show-off did swallow dives from the wing tips. Eventually the tender arrived and took us ashore.

'Later in the day when we went back on board to sort out and prepare for the return flight, we were startled to see that the lagoon was seething with three and four foot sharks. We will never know what they were doing during our early swim, maybe they were not expecting the possibility of food so early in the day.

'A routine patrol – very long stretches of mind-numbing boredom with some minor flickers of interest. The real crunch is that I cannot remember a single thing about why we had to fly sixteen hours to Cocos and back again two days later, but at least that was quicker, only 15 hours 30.'

THE SABANG RAID

Squadron leader John Stacey (later Air Vice Marshal J.N. Stacey CBE DSO DFC) at the end of 1942 was a very youthful-looking Flight Commander of the re-formed 205 Catalina Squadron. In fact he was universally known as Swee'pea after the infant in the Popeye cartoons. This disguised the fact that he was already, at the age of 22, a highly experienced pilot with a background in the Shetlands (240 Sq) and in Gibraltar (202 Sq) on Mediterranean convoy battles. He brought out to Ceylon four Catalinas from 202 as a gift for 205 Squadron to help build up the strength after the Easter Raids on Ceylon. He was now one of those chosen for an unusual bombing raid on Sumatra.

Looking back, Air Marshal Stacey writes:

'Our controlling body No 222 Group in Colombo came up with the idea in December 1942 that three Catalinas should look to see what was destroyed on two airfields, one at the north end of Sumatra and the other on the island of Sabang, just north of Sumatra and to drop a few bombs at the same time.

'It was decided that one aircraft from 413 Squadron, flown by Scotty (W/Cdr J.C. Scott, the new CO) would carry out the reconnaissance of Sumatra and two from 205 would deal with Sabang. I no longer had my own aircraft. However I felt that Flight Commander should be involved and therefore joined Flight Lieutenant 'Dirty' Lowe and his crew in W8406. [Scott's Catalina was 413-K for King].'

The other 205 Catalina was flown by Flight Lieutenant Tom Maxwell-Hudson with Gordon Bracken RCAF as second pilot. This bombing raid was reckoned to be the longest ever made anywhere in the world up to that time, 1,000 miles each way.

Stacey continues:

'Our briefing was to take off on 20 December at a time to reach our destination at about midnight, to make a first run over the airfield to note

122

any aircraft seen and then to bomb, from low level, harbour installations about two miles from the airfield. Since Sabang was about 10 hours flying from Ceylon I had plenty of time to ponder this plan and my conclusions were not comforting.

'Although it was night, the moon was full with a clear sky. Our planned approach to the airfield was over the harbour installations at 110 knots, delightful for the likely defence of Bofors-type anti-aircraft guns. I decided a dive bombing attack offered not only greater chances of survival but also greater chances of success, since the high level approach would offer better selection of the most juicy target.

'We carried out the airfield reconnaissance without incident and then climbed to 4000 feet for the harbour attack. I well remember it took so long to get there that I imagined half the Jap fighters in SE Asia would have time to intercept us. We then approached the island again and I selected a line of wharf buildings as the target and started the dive bomb attack. We were soon subject to light flak. The multi-coloured tracer was very pretty with the usual impression that it is all coming at you until the last moment; in fact it was well behind. I had closed the throttles for the dive but as the flak began to catch up I opened them somewhat to keep ahead of it. I continued this pattern until, at the bottom of the dive, about 500 feet, I had full throttle including the emergency gate.

'I have no idea what speed we were doing (I'd guess we reached some 180 knots). Anyway after dropping our four 250-pound bombs the crew reported seeing them hit. The flak was uncomfortably close and we kept full power on and withdrew at low level. Tom Maxwell-Hudson, being a better disciplined officer than me, carried out his task as briefed.'

In point of fact Tom's aircraft, O for Orifice as she was known, sailed in to the hornets' nest already stirred up. Squadron G.H.U. (Terk or Bill) Bayly in *Cats* explains what happened next to Tom. He dropped his bombs and shot out of the harbour so low that the aircraft bounced on the sea and put one engine out of action. Then, the Jap gunners having woken up, it collected 143 holes in its frame. Tom now flew home 1,000 miles on one engine and was met and escorted to base, only to find that there the other engine started up perfectly. W/Cdr Scott met with no enemy fire over Sumatra and returned safely home. Stacey and Maxwell-Hudson both received a DFC and Scott the DSO.

THE SS CITY OF CANTON

The Portuguese East African harbour of Beira lay drowsing in the sun on the sultry afternoon of 17 July 1943. The author was there the previous year and found that everything in the town appeared to stop between 10 a.m. and 4 p.m. for the usual siesta. Only at the docks on this day was life stirring as the 6,692-ton freighter, the *City of Canton*, cast off at 2 p.m. and nosed out of the harbour. In her holds were 2,000 tons of general cargo and some 4,500 tons of coal.

The following account is combined from the reports of the *City of Canton's* Captain[14]; of Captain John Hackett, Second Pilot aboard the BOAC 'C Class' Empire Flying Boat, *Cameronian*, G-AEUE[15]; and of Herr Walter Schöppe, a German War Correspondent aboard the U-boat, U/178[16]. A translation from the German account has been kindly made for me by Miss Eleonore Taux, of North London.

U/178 (Captain Lt Cdr Wilhelm Spahr) returns to Bordeaux after a rigorous voyage from Penang. Photograph taken by Walter Schöppe who was a War Correspondent aboard U/178, till its return. *(Courtesy of Walter Schöppe)*

By midnight on 16 July, after a few rain squalls, the weather was again clear but a strong wind had got up and under the full moon the sea was rough. Scrymgeour, on the bridge, could have wished for worse visibility. Unknown to him the U-boat U/178, a IXD2 under Captain Dommes, had been stalking him since 7 o'clock that morning. At 15.26 the submarine closed range and fired a stern salvo of two G7e electric torpedoes. Down in the U-boat's Control Room, after a tense silence, a muffled detonation was heard, says Walter Schöppe. It came after 58 seconds or 820 metres travel but the freighter blithely continued to steam ahead at full speed. The tall Dommes and his Torpedo Officer Petran were horrified after all

124

the careful calculations they had made. Either the battery had exploded inside the torpedo or there had been a defect in the guidance system, due to its long stay in the tropics. For the next nine hours the steamer unwittingly played hide-and-seek with the U-boat.

U/178 was a formidable opponent. I have a mass of details about her kindly supplied by Christopher Lowe of Nottingham[17]. His knowledge of U-boats is encyclopaedic and he has generously provided much of the submarine background in this book. U/178 was launched on 28 October 1941. She did three long-distance Indian Ocean patrols under three fine Captains, *Kapitän zur See* (Captain) Hans Ibbeken; *Korvettenkapitän* (Commander) Wilhelm Dommes who suffered from asthma, I believe, and moved ashore to command the Penang German base; and *Kapitänleutnant* (Lieutenant Commander) Wilhelm Spahr.

Spahr was a very experienced sailor, having been the Navigator who guided Günther Prien's famous U/47, when it slipped into the Navy's great naval base of Scapa Flow, in the Orkney Islands, north of Scotland one night in October 1939. She sank HMS *Royal Oak* with the loss of 800 lives. U/178, in her patrols, sank 13 ships of 87,024 tons and damaged one, being attacked herself at least once by aircraft and once by a Royal Navy submarine.

U/178 continued to stalk the *City of Canton* through rain squalls and at midnight fired two more torpedoes, this time the G7a type. Over the intercom the crew listened to the orders and tension mounted as the moments ticked away. At 132 seconds (or 2700 metres) a detonation could be clearly heard. Walter Schöppe's account continues:

'A huge cry of relief comes from the crew [writes Walter Schöppe] they congratulate each other; "We got him! We got him!" The Captain (through the periscope) sees the stern of the ship engulfed in smoke. The sonar operator reports that the steamer has stopped.'

'Captain Dommes fires another 4-cylinder gas-steam torpedo (G7a) but this misfires. The Captain turns the U-boat quickly, the steamer must not escape! At 00.31 a final shot is fired from the bow torpedo tube. It hits the steamer amidships. Shortly after the detonation Captain Dommes sees, in the periscope, the steamer break in half and sink.

'Dommes surfaces and goes to the scene of the sinking.

'He finds two large lifeboats full of men, one small lifeboat and countless rafts drifting in the water. Almost all the survivors are coloured people. Only in one boat does Captain Dommes find a Ship's Officer in white duty clothing. He is ordered on board and made a prisoner of war. His name is Reginald Harry Broadbent, the Second Officer, born 27/2/08 in Port Said. He comes from 262, Kingsway, Liverpool.'

UPPER: 209 Sq Catalinas 'on the trots', Kipevu, Mombasa, with two of their freighter charges. *(Courtesy Norman Wilson)*

LOWER: Some of the survivors of the Norwegian SS *Breiviken,* sunk 4 July 1943. Photo taken from U/178 which sank her. Amazingly most of this crew reached shore. *(Courtesy Walter Schöppe)*

Broadbent was taken, in lieu of the Captain, as part of the German High Command policy to remove experienced Allied merchant ships' officers and thus weaken the war effort. Meanwhile what was happening to the other boats?

According to Captain Scrymgeour's report, No 4 lifeboat was smashed by the first torpedo. The other three lifeboats were lowered and 'all the crew, including the natives, behaved very well,' writes the Captain. No 1 lifeboat had a raft fall on it from the ship which damaged it. All escaped, jumping overboard from it, except the engine-room storekeeper who was hit and partly paralysed.

The Captain, who had jumped off the sinking ship, rescued him and the two finished up, with Herculean efforts by Scrymgeour, on a raft for six days. The men in No 2, a motor lifeboat, reached shore at the Pinta lighthouse the same night. No 3, with the Chief Engineer, was at first towing two rafts, but as they were 20 miles from shore the lifeboat went ahead, to a strange encounter.

Captain E. Scrymgeour was obviously a man of great determination and courage. While he was transferring the injured storekeeper from the damaged No 1 lifeboat to a seaworthy-looking raft he saw the buff-coloured U/178, about 350 feet long, 'flying the Nazi Ensign' and heard voices which sounded German. His crew later told him the U-boat's captain was a very big man, which Dommes was. However, Scrymgeour was not approached, perhaps because a rain squall suddenly blotted everything out. The crew also later said that when No 3 lifeboat was getting near the submarine the men told Reg Broadbent to take off his white uniform jacket, but he refused and eventually ended up as a prisoner of the Japanese till the end of the war.

The next six days for Scrymgeour and the storekeeper were a saga of hopes raised and dashed. The food lockers and water-tank under the raft had been torn open on falling off the ship so they were without food or water – also without the flares, smoke floats and other necessities, except for two paddles. They found a large box floating, the ship's icebox. In it were three oranges, one rotten apple and a half-gallon bottle of water. This kept them going six days.

They saw two prisoner-of-war ships passing far off, all lit up, and by day lifeboat sails which were nearer; they were not seen by either despite Scrymgeour waving a yellow and blue lifejacket on an oar. On three occasions Catalinas passed right overhead, without finding them, five to fifteen hundred feet below. This does not mean that the aircrews were all asleep – it shows how difficult it is to spot a tiny raft in a choppy sea. On the sixth day two Vichy French cruisers saw their small raft and the *Sufferin* picked them up in a very weak state.

Days earlier, on 19 July 1943, No 3 lifeboat was observed by Hackett's civilian flying boat flying southwards via Moçambique to Durban. The airliner was the *Cameronian,* G-AEUE, commanded by Captain Dick Reid with Bob Hitchens as his Radio Officer. Alan Macgilivray was the Purser who looked after the 25 passengers on board. They flew as usual without any engineer on board.

To summarise Johnny Hackett's account, Captain Reid had been asked at Dar-es-Salaam, a stop on the way south, to keep an eye open for any lifeboats. 230's Sunderlands were all fully engaged elsewhere.

'We didn't climb above 3,000 feet, in order to scan the surface of the water more easily and we diverted our track some 20 miles further out to sea.'

After seeing one empty lifeboat, possibly the damaged No 1, the two pilots spotted another with 20 men in it, six of them standing, with arms linked, across the centre of the boat as if to give shade to the others. They were mostly sunburnt, just in shorts – it was not realised these were the brown-skinned Indian (lascar) crew – and all were apathetic with only feeble waves from those in Merchant Navy uniform. The BOAC pilots thought the survivors must be suffering badly from exposure to the elements.

Cameronian radioed back the information to Dar-es-Salaam but were told that no Sunderland or ship would be able to reach them that day. This persuaded the Captain to take the very courageous step, against regulations, of landing on the sea with a mild swell to try and pick up survivors. Johnny Hackett recalls:

'We taxied over to the boat and stopped, bobbing up and down on the swell, engines idling once more. The skipper went up on the top of the wings and hailed them through a megaphone. No matter how loudly he called them they could not hear us for the noise of our four engines. If we had stopped the engines on the open ocean what would happen if we couldn't start them again? We and our 25 passengers would merely join the others in the lifeboat, doubling the number of lives at risk. It was a hell of a decision to make! I'm glad it wasn't me. "OK", shouted the skipper, "Stop the engines!" I hit the magneto switches and all four clanked and chuffed to a stop.'

The BOAC crew decided it wasn't safe to bring the lifeboat over to the aircraft because of danger to the big hull or floats. To pull the survivors over to the plane by rope seemed the only way. The *Canton's* Chief Engineer, Mr Potter, in charge of the lifeboat, discovered the lascars had not the strength for the trip across, so the three Europeans were pulled over and all the food, water, blankets and Very pistol were passed back to the lascars. This would last until they were picked up by a boat that would be sent out to bring them in next day.

'Then we settled down to start the engines,' continues Hackett. 'Thank God they all started first go, all four of them. God bless Bristols and the designer of the Pegasus engine!' *Cameronian* then continued on down to Moçambique and the rest of the survivors were all picked up.

And how, one may ask, was Reg Broadbent getting on, under the waves in U/178? After arriving on the U-boat's decking, says Walter Schöppe, Reg climbed the iron-runged ladder to the 'wintergarden' gun-platform 'like a cat'. Inside the conning tower everything was dark, except for the very faint light from the slave compass. He climbed down into the control room, where quietly spoken German commands could be heard around the central space for the periscope.

Then Reg was conducted through the bulkhead door past the Captain's cabin, past the Radio Officer's post into the Officer's Mess. Over the step into the Galley, he then reached the Petty Officers' Mess where he was given a bunk on the starboard side. 'I can still picture him today all wet and dirty from the sinking of his ship,' writes Walter. He continues:

> 'The Chief Engineer, Lieutenant Wiebe [whom the author met in Bremen], is one of the first to lean down from his bunk and open his locker. He takes from his personal store linen and underwear to hand to the prisoner.
>
> 'To be fair to Broadbent I can't say he was frightened,' the account goes on, 'only everything in the underwater world was strange to him. There he could not experience night or day. Had he thought his rescue from a sinking ship to be good, he would soon realise he had jumped out of the frying pan into the fire. He had a warm clean bunk, regular food and even proper coffee, but he was not allowed to smoke because of the danger of a gas explosion. He had been used to 50 cigarettes a day and here he was only allowed 10 a day, the same as the crew, when up on deck.'

Schöppe continues to describe the next weeks on board in detail, including the sighting of an aircraft which alarmed Reg, and the re-fuelling of an Italian submarine. Italy was about to capitulate and this boat could defect to the Allies so it was escorted as far as Sabang on Sumatra and then U/178 headed for Penang.

By this time Broadbent could not stand the fug and atmosphere down below so he was allowed to go on *Kapitänleutnant* Spahr's watch and even allowed to be a lookout. When given a look through the Zeiss binoculars he was astonished at their quality.

Second Officer Reg Broadbent sits beside the conning tower of U/178 which took him prisoner. He survived as a POW in Japan.

(Courtesy of Walter Schöppe)

Approaching Penang, Reg confessed he was very frightened of being handed over to the Japs. Walter thought Reg might not get much chance to write home after this, so arranged for him to write a letter to his wife, a copy of which is in our possession, which the war correspondent would smuggle illegally back to Germany and hand over to the Red Cross in Berlin. This did reach his wife and family.

Before landing, Reg was handed back his white uniform all washed and pressed. At Penang he said good bye to the crew and began, on 27 August 1943, two years as a prisoner of war under the Japanese. He survived this and the crew of U/178, who also came through the war, were delighted to hear in post-war Germany that Reg had got back to Liverpool. When he became a Captain of a ship in the Mall Line of Water Street, Liverpool, they still kept in touch till Reg's death in the fifties. At Penang Lieutenant Commander Dommes, because of his chest trouble, was appointed to command the German U-boat base there. Lieutenant Wilhelm Spahr took over as Captain of U/178.

A further incident did occur in 1943. It is described by Karl-Heinz Wiebe, a holder of the Knight's Cross, under the title 'WARLUCK'[18]:

'In the early hours of 2.11.43 the submarine HMS *Tally-Ho* had approached Penang, North Entrance, after a week's passage from Colombo. Its captain, Lt/Cdr Ben Bennington RN was one of the famous submarine captains in the Far East. He sank the Japanese cruiser *Kuma* and the ex-Italian U-boat UIT/23. On 6.11.43 the Chief Petty Officer for the engine room of U/178 was still repairing the port diesel engine. CPO Eutebach was very angry that he has only the one engine OK but that was luck for us, as we should experience some hours later. At 5.00 p.m. we leave the pier with only the starboard diesel working.'

Wiebe then mentions the account in *The Hunting Submarine*[19] where Bennington fired a spread of five torpedoes broadside at the U-boat and was amazed when none of them struck. One even turned round, came back and was only just avoided by skilful steering. Wiebe continues:

'That happened on *Tally-Ho*. What happened on U/178? CPO Eutebach and his men were working in the engine-room, naked except for shorts. Even with one diesel running there was a lot of heat. About five minutes to 8.00 p.m. the diesel engine was ready. That was nearly at the same time *Tally-Ho* sighted U/178. I, as Engineering Officer of U/178, scrambled up the tower and announced to the Captain the port diesel was OK. The engine was just running up to half speed when the sailor on aft starboard lookout announced: "Torpedo trace behind!" The diesel was fixed just at the right moment, not too early, not too late.'

The arrival of a Japanese submarine-chaser prevented Bennington following up the U-boat.

Tally-Ho did not make a habit of missing, and had a most distinguished record. *Tally-Ho's* Lieutenant-Commander Bennington eventually retired as a Captain with a DSO and two bars, and a DSC with three bars.

Captain Hackett added a postscript to the U/178 story. At the time when Reg Broadbent was living out his uncomfortable but relatively safe existence on the U-boat, the crew of *Cameronian* and the officers of the *City of Canton* got together in Durban for a celebration supper. There they all drank a toast to Second Officer Broadbent whom they firmly believed to be lying dead at the bottom of the deep blue sea. They were only half wrong.

N O T E S

[1]   "feathering". Rotating the propeller blades so as to reduce wind resistance or drag. (i.e. sharp edge to the front.)

2   Watson's crew. G.O.P. 'Ox' Watson DFC, Captain; F/O A.J. Thornson, Second Pilot; F/O G. Schroeder, Navigator; Sgt F. Wadsworth, Flight Engineer; Sgt A. Peattie Rear-Gunner; Sgt S. Hitchcock, Rigger; Sgt A.A. Preston WOP/AG; Sgt N. Murray WOP/AG; Sgt J.C. Davies, FME; Sgt Wood, WOP/AG.

3   *Sun on My Wings* W/Cdr Dundas Bednall (Paterchurch Publications), Pembroke Dock 1989.

4   240 Sq Records, PRO Kew.

5   413 Sq Records via Capt. Fleet, 413 Squadron Historian, RCAF Greenwood.

6   *Far East U -boats*, Gunter Schomaekers, Article, Source not found.

7   *German Submarines in the Far East*, A.M. Saville, US Naval Proceedings, August 1961.

8   The *Penang Submarines*, Dennis Gunton.

9   *German U-boat Operations in Eastern Waters 1943-1945*, Extracted from C.B. 4523, *The War in the Atlantic, Vol III* (translated from the German).

10 *Coastal, Support and Special Squadrons*, Rawlings.

11 *Cats*, G.H.U. Bayly (Graphic Images), Ontario 1993.

12 Crew of JX593. W/O Harry Carr (Captain) from Sunderland; Sgt Norman Hudson (2nd Pilot), from Yorkshire; Sgt Eric Knight (Navigator); Other full names not known. – "Taff" (F/Engineer), "Joe" (Rigger Airframes/AG) also one WOM/AG one 2nd Engineer, two WOP/AGs.

13 When the Australian airline QUANTAS started weekly civil flights between Australia and Ceylon across dangerous Jap-held waters, the first non-stop survey flight was carried out by W/Cdr J.C. Scott DSO RCAF of 413 Sq and the second by W/Cdr M.D. Thunder RAF on 3 and 12 May 1943, respectively. 205 Squadron also carried out weekly flights from Koggala.

14 Report via Harry Hutson, Marine Author, Cleethorpes.

15 From a talk for radio, Capt. J. Hackett BOAC.

16 Herr Walter Schöppe, Author, Wilhelmshaven.

17 U-boat Summaries, Christopher Lowe, Nottingham.

18 *Leitender Ingenieur*, Herr Karl-Heinz Wiebe KC, of Bremen.

19 *The Hunting Submarine*, Ian Trenowden (Kimber) London 1974.

CHAPTER 5
FAR-FLUNG DETACHMENTS

If I take the wings of the morning
and dwell in the uttermost parts of the sea,
even there shall Thy hand lead me,
and Thy right hand shall hold me.

Psalm 139.9.A.V.

As operations multiplied in 1943, without a matching increase in naval vessels and maritime air squadrons, the Admiralty and Air Ministry had to pursue a policy of responding to urgent situations. This meant that wherever a need arose, the Air Ministry authorised the regions to send one or more 'detachments', three or six aircraft, away from the squadron bases for several months or longer 'in the uttermost parts of the sea'. As we have seen, officers like Squadron Leader Barraclough had, in 1942, surveyed and opened up bases as far apart as Langebaan near Cape Town, Masirah Island near the Persian Gulf and Diego Garcia, a remote island over 1,000 miles south of Ceylon.

So when, for instance, two passenger ships, the *Jean Nicolet* and the *Nellore,* were sunk by the Japanese submarine I/8 in the same area and about the same time, July 1944, the RN and the RAF acted together. A detachment of 413 RCAF Squadron with elements of 230 and 205 at Diego Garcia joined naval vessels, particularly HMS *Lossie*, in rescuing survivors.

According to Pilot Officer John Foxon of 230 Sq who was posted to the temporary Operations Room there, Diego Garcia was an unusual detachment. It was quite unlike, say, Diego Suarez which, though dusty and windy, was a busy harbour in Madagascar. Diego Garcia was a coral atoll, part of the Chagos Archipelago, south of the Maldives. John wrote to Mary, his wife thus:

'The atoll is a horseshoe-shaped reef with a lagoon in the centre, with one outlet to the sea. The water in the lagoon was moderately calm, but on the outside shores terrific breakers beat up over the coral reef. All night when everything is quiet you can hear the breakers crashing on the shore. By day you would find the most wonderful colourings in the sea.'

Colin Stones of 205 Sq recalls the simple French Creole islanders who were employed in the one copra factory, where a noisy variety of braying donkeys provided the motive power of the grinding mill. In one of his fascinating stories Colin describes being on boatguard duty one night in a moored Catalina, when he was handed up through the blister, by one of the crews, a heavy four-gallon fuel tin in sacking, to be secretly stowed in the 'tunnel' behind the blister compartment. It contained the body of a piglet which had been extracted at dead of night from the French factory manager's private piggery, not without squeals, to bring some relief from the restricted diet the crews had at Diego Garcia.

Colin got to know the Creoles a little and was sad to hear, after the war, that the island had been handed over to the Americans for a huge tracking station and the peaceful inhabitants dumped by the British in the 'foreign' island of Mauritius where they languish today. I am told that other inhabitants of Chagos islands were deported too. John Foxon tells his wife of Diego Garcia:

'I've had a most exciting time and worked damned hard. During the whole fortnight I had only one complete night's sleep. And I did nearly thirty hours flying too.'

For an 'admin' type like John, this was a treat. They were co-ordinating, with the Navy, the rescue of survivors from SS *Nellore*. Later he mentions that some ratings had been told the island belonged to no one and that everything was theirs for the taking. 'They came ashore with kitbags,' he says, 'and stripped the orange trees (which had very bitter fruit), hacked all the bananas off the trees and carted them off to their ship. When the factory manager saw them it was too late and all his 'Mon Dieuing' was wasted. 'Whacko!' adds John's letter to Mary Foxon, 'Following the inherent British policy of appeasement, our CO gave the Froggie a bottle of whisky – the sailors, on the other hand, gave him a "soldier's farewell".'

SS *NELLORE*

The story of SS *Nellore* is another where the details are shrouded in confusion. One aviation author calls her a P & O liner, but marine sources[1] say she belonged to the Eastern and Australian SS Co of Greenock. Then some of the passengers and rescuers were convinced the

AIR SEA RESCUE

B-212, (FP175) prepares at Korangi Creek, for ASR. *(courtesy Arthur Davies)*

B for Bertie sinks and the crew join 16 survivors of S.S. *Montana* with their dinghies. *(courtesy Arthur Davies)*

Survivors of S.S. *Nellore*, two naked, await rescue. *(courtesy Mrs Mary Foxon)*

A 413 Squadron Catalina guides H.M.S. *Lossie* to the boat. *(courtesy Mrs Mary Foxon)* ship had been sunk by a German U-boat, because of the instructions in a German accent from a courteous white submariner, who 'did his best to spare them as much danger as he could'. This is what was gathered from survivors at Diego Garcia by F/Sgt A.W. 'Bill' Badlan, a WOP/AG in one of the 413 Sq Catalinas, who spoke to them on the island. *Nellore* was torpedoed on 29 June 1944.

The main authorities, both German and British, say she was sunk by the notorious Japanese submarine I/8, under Lieutenant Commander Tatsunoseke Ariizumi and the report by a *Nellore* ship's officer speaks of 'guttural Japanese orders' being heard.[2] No 3 lifeboat occupants were forced to give up their lifebelts, a command typical of Japanese, not Germans.

I/8 was notorious because Ariizumi had carried out, with the most unbelievable cruelty, a massacre of 98 unarmed survivors of the Dutch ship *Tjisalak* on 26 March 1944 and was about to do so again on the next ship he torpedoed after the *Nellore* – the American *Jean Nicolet.*

Both the massacres are faithfully portrayed in *Blood and Bushido* by Captain Bernard Edwards[3], so suffice it to say that Ariizumi did not merely carry out the Truk orders[4] for 'the complete destruction of the crews of the enemy's ships' by machine-gunning or ramming lifeboats as other Japanese captains did in 1943 and 1944. He forced the *Tjisalak* passengers, including an American Red Cross nurse, Mrs Verna Gorden-Britten, to come on the deck of his submarine where one by one they were bludgeoned, slashed, decapitated or shot to be pushed overboard for the sharks to finish off, with a cine-camera to record it. By superhuman courage and luck five men out of the 103 survivors, escaped to tell the story.

The surprising thing is that the *Nellore* passengers were spared this. Japanese submarines sometimes carried German liaison officers and Captain Edwards tells me he thinks some of the lifeboats may have been instructed by such a German. Be that as it may, seven lifeboats got away and out of a possible total of 240 souls[2], 150 to 160 survived. Three German U-boats are supposed to have been in the vicinity, but no German logbook records this sinking and they were both comprehensive and meticulous.

The first Catalina from 413 Squadron to spot the lifeboats was that of Flight Lieutenant J.F. Irvine RAF at dusk on 1 or 2 July (log-books missing). Bill Badlan, one of his wireless operators, now takes up the story:

'We started our detachment at Addu Atoll in the Maldives and were diverted to Diego Garcia to search for survivors of the *Nellore* and *Jean Nicolet* and were away from Koggala several months. On the first of two flights a lifeboat was seen. At 50 feet up we could see the joy on their faces and [it thrilled us] to see them all jumping up and down and waving to us.

'The skipper then organised that we collect our own Mae Wests, semaphore flags, all the food we had on board and drop it to them. They retrieved it straight away. The seamen on board then started signalling with semaphore flags. I told the skipper I couldn't read the semaphore. He found that Jack Scannell, who was on the radio set at the time, could. So we changed over. Jack identified "-ELLORE" which of course was enough for the skipper.

'We then told SEAC HQ that we had located the lifeboat, which had at least two women aboard, in the after part of the boat. We were instructed to home in some naval units to the lifeboat. We started transmitting just before dusk to HMS *Lossie* and HMS *Foxdale*. Just at that time there were sharks following the boat which were longer than the boat [could they be 30 feet? The aggressive varieties such as Tiger and Great White are more like 20 feet in length]. The skipper told the blister gunner: "Open up on the ones furthest away from the boat," and we managed to wound or kill one of them. The rest turned on that one and left the boat alone.'

Talking to survivors later, Bill found them very aware of the sharks. Apparently one of the women had bathed over the end of the boat and they thought some of the blood must have been spilled and attracted the sharks. He continues:

'We transmitted through the night and shortly after dawn I spotted the wake of two fast-moving ships coming over the horizon and they came alongside. They picked up the survivors and we returned to Diego Garcia, having been airborne 24 hours, using extra load tanks. We were on the ground for refuelling and airborne again for the next 20 hours. [Catalinas did have bunks but with changing round duties, radio to guns to radar, no one had a long stretch on them. The Navigator couldn't swop with anyone.] During the 48 hours we located six other lifeboats. One of the boats following the course given them by the German for Madagascar 2,000 miles away, was contacted on two successive days and given a course for Diego Garcia only 56 miles away. Unfortunately they missed the atoll and actually reached Madagascar 28 days later. *En route* a Eurasian girl gave birth to a baby which died after they arrived and only 11 of the 47 survivors in the boat lived through the ordeal.'

S/Ldr G.H.U. Bill 'Terk' Bayly DFC in his memoir, *Cats*[4], recalls sighting, along with Jack Glasier and George Bennett, three lifeboats on two or three days, between 6 and 8 July, and sending messages to HMS *Lossie*. It seems that *Lossie* picked up seven or eight boats full of survivors and the other one got away to Madagascar (where 'all were in good health' – this varies from marine reports). Several Catalinas were based at Diego Garcia, from 413 and 205 Sqs and Badlan saw one Sunderland there, probably from 230 Squadron (hence John Foxon's presence in the Ops Room). Bayly quotes a comment by Jack Glazier:

'If you recall one of the women in this (different) lifeboat had a pair of bright orange slacks which they raised as a flag. Roy Grimley spotted the lady coming ashore at Diego Garcia and told her how it had made it much easier to spot their lifeboat, whereupon she took off her slacks and gave them to Roy as a souvenir.'

For a survivor landing with next to no belongings, this was something!

Postscript: The *Nellore* was 'nicknamed the Rolling *Nellore* as she rolled to port', according to the 205 Sq Flight Engineer Jim Bowden of Norwich who sailed in her after recovering from injuries at Broome, in Australia's 'Pearl Harbour'. His Cat later took part in the *Nellore* rescue.

SS *JEAN NICOLET*

The story of the *Tjisalak* was now to be repeated in the dark hours of 2 July 1944 with the American Liberty ship *Jean Nicolet*. Neville Mudd was a Wireless Operator/Air Gunner in 413 Squadron's Catalina Z for Zebra, captained by Canadian Warrant Officer Don Wells and navigated by Jack Campbell during the survivor search. As well as Captain Edwards' story, Andrew Hendrie's *Flying Cats* has an RAF description[5]. They had left Addu Atoll at 18.15, says Neville.

'Two hours later in the pitch darkness over the Indian Ocean I suddenly spotted a flicker of light many miles away. We altered course and approached a blazing ship. My main memory is of the shock of seeing this huge funeral pyre, in the glare of which survivors could be seen in the water. Our first task was to radio back the position and the state of the ship then to find the submarine responsible. During the long Square Search that followed I recall the sudden indication of a submarine, and flare dropping but nothing came of that.

'At first light we were back approaching the ship and it was a sad and chilling sight to see it sink below the waves. It was obvious that in spite of sharks there were still some survivors and I helped to throw out dinghies, Mae Wests and rations, even a large thermos of coffee, though I doubt it would survive the impact.'

The aircrew could never have guessed what a scene of carnage had been enacted below them, meanwhile. The *Jean Nicolet* was an American Liberty ship of 7,176 tons, heading from Fremantle to Calcutta, via Colombo. She had about 100 people aboard, including the crew of 69. At 1905, in the dusk, three torpedoes suddenly slammed into the ship's starboard side and exploded. Captain Nilsson ordered 'ABANDON SHIP' and all the passengers got away in boats or rafts. This did not last for long.

The submarine surfaced and all those in the boats were ordered to come on to the deck. As the first men clambered up the watery sides of the sub, they were surrounded by chattering sailors in khaki uniforms[6]. The Japanese opened the proceedings by shooting the young deck boy, William Musser, in the head and booting his body overboard. Later they sank the lifeboats by machine-gun fire. As the stunned Americans came aboard with the prodding of bayonets and a rain of blows, each man was roughly stripped of his lifejacket, and black boots, watches and rings. (Able Seaman Robert McDougall was about to have his finger cut off when his ring finally budged.) Then, with hands tied securely behind their backs, they were forced to sit on the foredeck, facing away from the conning tower. They could not see behind, but each man in turn was called back. First Assistant Engineer Charles Pyle recalls:

'Somewhere around midnight I was picked out and led aft. I then found out that the Japanese crew were employing a tactic somewhat similar to the old Indian practice of running the gauntlet and were forcing the survivors to pass between two lines of Japanese sailors, armed with clubs, iron bars [swords] and other instruments, and when the victims reached the end, pushing or knocking them into the sea . . . I was pushed between two lines of sailors who rained blows on my head and body with various objects. When I reached the end of the gauntlet I fell into what appeared to be a white foamy sea.'

Amazingly three men survived this ordeal, Able Seaman First Class Robert Applegate, Charles Pyle and McDougall. They were able later to give a report. When there were about 30 men left on the foredeck, Don Wells' Catalina finally returned from her hunting. Alarm bells sounded on the submarine and she began to dive. Able Seaman George Hess had managed to use his fingernails in two hours to saw through his bonds.

With Hess's hands free, and with one or two concealed penknives, about six men were set loose before the waves closed over the deck and its doomed prisoners. Against enormous odds some of the bound men managed to swim to the nearest wreckage while Neville Mudd and his crewmates above dropped dinghies near the site of the sinking, still unaware of the drama below. Shortage of fuel forced them to head for base but they were replaced by 413's Catalina Y (FP 282) piloted by F/Lt Johnny Gowans DFC.

Out of the 100 people who had been on board the *Jean Nicolet* the Indian Navy's rescue vessel HIMS *Hoxa* could only find 23 still alive. Submarine I/8 was sunk off Okinawa the following year, with only one survivor, on 31 March. Lieutenant Commander Ariizumi had moved elsewhere, but, while taking a squadron back to surrender in Japan, he shot himself. Up to 23 known Allied ships had suffered, at the hands of Japanese submariners, cruelties which matched the inhuman treatment of Far East POWs and subjugated Asian peoples. Yet all of the Imperial Navy's submarines in the Indian Ocean had been sunk with their crews eventually and only one man was ever tried for these marine war crimes after the Armistice.

LOCAL FAUNA

For airmen on detachment, close encounters with the fauna of the Indian Ocean region could be amusing or occasionally hazardous. The worst enemy was the malaria-carrying anopheles mosquito. Aircrew sickness hampered operations, especially in 230 Squadron. Some airmen, like Dai Thomas's friend Glyndwr Jones, died of Cerebral Malaria. Dai, from Anglesea, was still with 259 Squadron but at 209 Squadron's Kipevu camp, Mombasa.

Glyn the Post, from Rhos-on-Sea, 'had a lovely Welsh tenor voice. He was booked 'to sing at the Welsh Club in Durban if they ever went back, see?' says Dai. He continues:

'My bed was next to Glyn and one morning he was so ill he could not get up. I went to the sick bay and told the fat corporal and after breakfast took a mug of tea for him and put it on his locker. At lunchtime I ran back across Snake Valley and found the mug of tea untouched with Glyn still in bed. Once again I went to the Sick Bay and told the fat corporal in no uncertain terms what I thought of him.

'That afternoon I worked late at the slipway and walked home across Snake Valley. Then I saw an armed party coming out of the camp. I asked a Cockney named Green what it was and he said: "Taff, your mate is dead and that's the burial party".'

Next day Dai was able to be one of the pall-bearers at Glyn's funeral with full military honours.

Most people recovered from their bouts of malaria though some needed convalescence up-country with the hospitable white settler families of Kenya and Tanganyika, who also provided memorable leave-times on their ranches. John Foxon, sick at Dar-es-Salaam, went to Mrs Howe-Browne's in Morningside, Morogoro. Kenya RAF letters frequently mention names like Tony and Molly Ryan at Molo or Mrs Falconer-Taylor at the Bell, Naivasha, whose daughter Popsy, now Mrs Marsh, was a WAAF in the Met Office at Nairobi, where I worked in 1943 and 1945.

For Ron Carter of 191 Sq, then at Koggala, Ceylon, elephants were the more useful kind of local fauna:

'They were helping the army constructors build a runway and the precision they were using in removing and stacking the large coconut palm trees was truly amazing. The bulldozers were uprooting the trees and two elephants then weighed them up, and got the point of balance worked out before walking off to stack them, with equal precision.'

Not so your African elephant. Group Captain 'Peter' Bryer, while CO of 246 Wing, tells of an experience with one at Port Reitz. After the Ceylon attacks, the Fleet Air Arm regrouped in East Africa for training and the Admiralty asked Admiral Rawlings[7], who was attached to the Eastern Fleet, to visit East Africa and report progress to Admiral Somerville in Ceylon. Assisting him was his Flag Lieutenant, as usual known as 'Flags'. Arriving fresh in Nairobi, Rawlings took a Walrus to the Fleet Air Arm base at Eastleigh, Nairobi, to inspect the flight of Walruses there, but his pilot was told to taxi away from the line of expectant aircraft. Group Captain Bryer continues:

'"Why", said the pilot, "are we to go away from where the Admiral wants to do the inspection?" Back came the answer: "Well, there's a bunch of lions chewing the wings off one of the aircraft at the end of the runway." The Admiral later proceeded to Port Reitz where Bryer set up a conference for him with the Commanding Officers of the other two RNAS training stations. However, because of heavy rains and flooded roads the CO of the Fleet Air Arm at Mackinnon Road, up-country, was unable to come, so the Army fixed up a telephone land line from there to Rawlings at Port Reitz.

'While the Admiral was speaking to him about his efforts to get the squadron ready, there was a crash and the voice stopped. Rawlings handed the receiver over to me and I kept talking to the Army operator.

'Then he said, "The line's working again, Sir," and after a while the CO's voice came on again from Mackinnon Road. He said, "When I was talking to the Admiral just now a ruddy great cobra came out of the thatch

LEFT UPPER: Young shark, Langebaan, with Henry Smith (left) and 'Pop' Enderstein.

(Courtesy of H. Smith)

RIGHT UPPER: RAF Elephants tea-break, Koggala. (Courtesy of R. Carter)

LEFT LOWER: Larry the Lemur on Dick Brown's shoulder at Dar-es-Salaam.

(Courtesy of R. Brown)

RIGHT LOWER: Mamba at Kipevu, Mombasa, plus African Campworkers.

(Courtesy of F. Elliott)

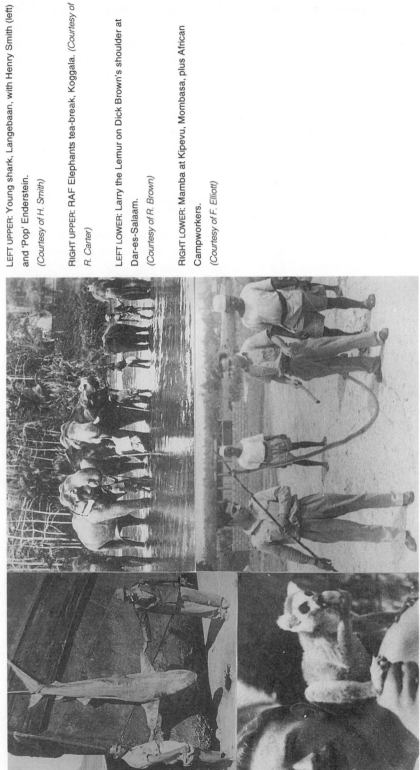

and poked his tongue out at me and I thought it was discreet to go." The crash was the dropping of the telephone.

'So that was two things. Then my adjutant came in and said to me: "Would the Admiral like to see an African elephant? There's one on the aerodrome." So I asked him and he said: "Yes, we'll adjourn. Flags, get your cine-camera out and we'll go over." So I ran them across in the Jeep to the far side of the airfield, where there happened to be some slit trenches for airfield defence.

'This really fine specimen of a bull elephant with enormous ears was standing there, rubbing his backside peacefully against a coconut tree, so we thought. Flags, with his camera, was taking him from port and starboard, moving round [both he and the Admiral in their spotless white uniforms]. Suddenly the elephant charged. Flags jumped into one trench and the Admiral into another. Unfortunately, with the heavy rains, both trenches were full of dirty water. The elephant went off hell for leather somewhere. We had to provide them with khaki drill instead of white. We resumed the meeting and in a day or two sent them off in a Catalina to Ceylon.'

FLEET AIR ARM DETACHMENTS

If RAF flying boat crews felt that some detachments were a trial, the Fleet Air Arm squadrons were even more on the move, partly because their aircraft carriers sailed from port to port. In writing this account the author at first felt that the history, as an attempt to cover at least the highlights of the Anti-submarine Campaign, ought to include something of the sister flying service, the Fleet Air Arm, as space permitted.

That was until he looked into the FAA 'bible' on the subject, *Squadrons of the Fleet Air Arm* by Ray Sturtivant.[8] It shares the same size and tiny print as older versions of Holy Writ. In that tome there appear to be not only many aircraft types of which one has never heard, but scores of squadrons to be found on a host of aircraft carriers or in shore stations with outlandish names, buried deep in the jungle. The author realised the task, for him, was too great. It would have to await a naval historian with a leaning towards air combat.

One example will suffice. China Bay, in Ceylon, played host during the war to the following FAA Squadrons: 733, 788, 800, 802, 803, 804, 806, 807, 808, 809, 810, 812, 814, 817, 818, 822, 824, 828, 830, 831, 832, 834, 837, 845, 847, 851, 854, 879, 880, 888, 896, 898, 1700, 1830 1831, 1833, 1839, 1844, 1851 – a total of 40 squadrons who took part in the ocean war or on the drive to the East, as Japan was forced backward.

Author's painting of two
Fleet Air Arm Walruses at
Port Reitz, Mombasa 1944.
*(courtesy RAF Museum,
Hendon)*

The hunting and sinking of the *Brake* German supply ship in March 1944 and the later destruction of U/198, both in cooperation with the RAF, were notable operations. In the meantime the FAA trained in East and South Africa, and at Mombasa shared the Port Reitz base with the RAF. The author recalls giving Kiswahili lessons on hot nights to a class of Fleet Air Arm ratings, who always signed up for anything cultural. RAF airmen left them to it and got down to the serious business of sinking clusters of beer bottles at the NAAFI canteen tables, to take away the taste of the food and perhaps homesickness. However in the Met Office at Port Reitz we enjoyed much cooperation between FAA and RAF.

Combined RAF/FAA staff of Met Office, Port Reitz, Mombasa (minus forecasters).

Back row left to right: LAC 'Mad' Barnes (RAF); Sgt Ron Avery (RAF); FAA (Scottish) (name forgotten); L/S (Killick) Champion (FAA).

Front row: LAC Warner, of Doncaster (RAF); LAC Banks (author), 1943-44.

THE LOST SWORDFISH

Some dangers were greater for FAA aircraft than for RAF flying boats because most were 'landplanes'. Running out of fuel at sea was a particular risk. The Supermarine Walrus (known to some African workers at Port Reitz as 'Motor-car-belong-Jesus') was safe enough, landing like a boat on the sea, but for Fairey Swordfish biplanes with only undercarriage and a short range the sea had no mercy.

Lieutenant Andrew Stewart RNVR, a friend of mine from Dar-es-Salaam, commanded a pinnace in the Tanganyika Naval Volunteer Force which assisted the RN along the East African coast. He recalls a flight of five FAA Swordfish from the Royal Naval Air Station, Tanga, north of Dar-es-Salaam, which set out to bomb a wreck that was dangerous to shipping, out at sea 10 to 15 miles north of that port.

A sudden rain squall blinded and scattered them and they were forced to head for base, each as best it could. Four eventually straggled back but one remained missing. As on other occasions the RN, RAF and its Marine Craft Service with coastal forces searched the seas and shores and forests several days for the Swordfish but to no avail.

Months later Andrew took his pinnace up to Kilindini naval base and there was given the task of transporting the bodies of the three FAA aircrew of the missing Swordfish back to Tanga. What had happened was this. The Swordfish had struggled along almost to Mombasa but its fuel had run out just 20 miles short of home. The pilot glided down but there were no clearings in the endless miles of forest all round. They crashed through the canopy of very tall trees and probably the pilot and observer were killed outright. The TAG (Telegraphist Air Gunner) in the rear open cockpit was trapped by his broken legs and would have been in great pain. We know this because all his emergency stock of morphine injections was used up. We don't know how long he lived but it was clear he had, with dwindling hope, used up all his stock of ammunition. He had fired it off with the aim of attracting help, perhaps from nearby African villages but no one heard him. Yet, at Jadini, he was not very far from places like Diani Beach, now a very popular tourist resort, south of Mombasa. I vividly recall walking under the forest canopy there and gazing up at the tall treetops, some years ago. Yet the Swordfish was not found for months.

SQUADRONS AT WORK – 262 SQUADRON

Though 262 Squadron had arrived at Congella, Durban, in November 1942, for all the Air Ministry's efforts, it did not receive its first Catalina Ib till February 1943. Sgt 'Willie' Lock, who is featured in Chapter 6, flew the squadron's first operation, a convoy escort, on 26 February 1943. On 19 May F/Lt Grant's crew found and attacked U/198, a IXD2 then commanded by Captain Hartmann, 150 miles NE of Durban. The aircraft's port engine was hit by fierce gunfire during the attack and nearly crashed but Grant dropped his six DCs, without damage to the German. He then nursed his Catalina home and was later awarded a DFC. F/Sgt Street, WOP/AG, was given the DFM. F/Lt Fred Roddick, of Alberta, Canada, and his crew found the second U-boat on 12 July, 100 miles off Inhambane. This was U/197 whose fate was sealed in Chapter 6, but this time Lieutenant Commander Robert Bartels had a narrow escape.

Roddick attacked with guns firing and dropped four depth charges but two hung up. The U-boat was taken by surprise but finally submerged with her cannons blazing away until the last moment.[9]

For 262 Sq tragedy struck on 25 June 1943 when the Australian, Flight Officer Fred White's Catalina H (FP 265) was taking off at St Lucia lake to escort convoy No WF 30. It exploded either in the air or on impact with the water. All were killed except Sergeant Ben Lee, Flight Engineer and 3rd pilot from Highgate, North London, who could never remember the crash. A rescue tender came racing up and found the wreckage of the Cat burning in a fiery lake of petrol from the 1,460 gallons spilled.

The crew of Flight Officer Fred White's H262 Catalina, at Jui, West Africa en route for Durban. They crashed on 23 June 1943.

Back row L to R: Smythe; F/O White RAAF, Sgt Barrington; Sgt. Jock McKay; Sgt Ben Lee; Sgt Dick Cork.

Front row: Sgt Ron Jenkins RAAF. F/O Mitchell (Nav.) F/Sgt Frank Sody RAAF.

(Courtesy Ben Lee)

The marine craft crew could hear shouting but when the coxswain tried to approach, his boat started to catch fire. Then, in an incredible act of bravery, he dived into the sea of flame and swam [presumably under water where he could] over to the wreckage and brought out Ben Lee. Lee was already badly burned, especially on the face, but Roy Sheppee heard that he was said to have been found laying the bodies of his crewmates on the wing of the plane. We do not know who the coxswain was nor whether he was received any commendation for his courage. The waters were also crocodile infested.

Lee was thereafter given plastic surgery for his burns to the face at Brenthurst Hospital, Johannesburg, which had been donated by Sir Ernest Oppenheimer and was run by a dedicated team of doctors and nurses under Major Jack Penn. He had 20 skin grafting operations to his face over 16 months and then in England came under the famous plastic surgeon, Sir Archibald McIndoe, at East Grinstead, who ordered further corrections. His is a long and fascinating story, including the reaction of his mother in Highgate, who cried when she saw him, his family and friends who had to adjust, the girl whom he married later and the neighbourhood folk who treated him as a war hero. His face was wonderfully restored. Now an Estimating Consultant, he attended our Indian Ocean Reunion and one would scarcely know what he had been through.

Catalina H for Harry had a Kookaburra as logo on its nose. The dead were the Australian captain F.N.C. White, with three other Australians, F/Sgt Lane, Sgt Sody, and Sgt Jenkins. The English were Sgt Mills, Sgt Cork, and Sgt Trevor Barrington.

262 Sq operated alongside the squadrons of the South African Air Force. On 14 August 1943 a Lockheed Ventura, No X of 22 Squadron SAAF sighted a submarine on the surface and attacked it, dropping six DCs but unfortunately it escaped.

212 SQUADRON

This Catalina squadron settled down to its anti-submarine work at Korangi Creek RAF base in 1943. We saw one captain, Sergeant Gallagher, bringing 'B' for Bertie (FP 175) down the Med. Now, on 8 June 1943, his crew engaged in the rescue, between Bombay and Oman, of a lifeboat from the torpedoed American freighter SS *Montana*. Arthur Davies, still Flight Engineer, says that Gallagher took the tricky decision to land and pick up the 16 survivors visible in the boat below.

The dangerous mid-ocean swell was not in evidence, but there was indeed a 10 to 12 foot swell. As they landed 'B' for Bertie's nose went in, flooding the aircraft and sinking it. The crew finished up in two inflated dinghies roped together, for safety, with the big American lifeboat. After being missed by several high flying aircraft their very last flare was spotted by a DC3 of the US Army Air Corps. While awaiting rescue they landed first at the Oman coast and then Masirah, from whence they were flown back to Karachi with the survivors. A second lifeboat from the SS *Montana* was never found. Perhaps it ran out of flares.

Throughout 1943 this squadron flew about 30 sorties a month, mainly long and boring escorts and anti-submarine patrols. It had many detachments around the coast of the Indian sub-continent, each with their own story chronicled by Arthur Davies in a personal record.

WAAFS IN AFRICA

Harking back to WAAFS in Nairobi, the Women's Auxiliary Air Force were rarely allowed to work on the Kenya coast or in the Islands but, as in New Delhi, there were scores in the Kenyan capital, as the VE parade photographs showed later. WRNS were freer, but in India the WAAF were also mobile. In East Africa two or three worked in ciphers at Mombasa and there were two cipher officers in the Seychelles, Heather Leake and Doreen Guthrie. Assistant Section Officer Leake came from Bournemouth, says W/Cdr Don Bleach.

'Of course they had a tough time marooned in the Seychelle Islands, away from the happenings in Nairobi, but we did our best to keep them entertained.'

At the Nairobi Met Office, two of the WAAFs with whom I worked, covering the Indian Ocean under Air Headquarters East Africa, were the Foster twins Patricia and Pearl, from Kenya. Pat, now married to another Weymouth College contemporary, Peter Kennedy, recalls 'every day being loaded into the back of a lorry and taken to work where we slogged away plotting reports. There was a time when Italian prisoners of war worked with us.' A note on the WAAFs in Ceylon will come later.

'MAKE DO AND MEND'

The keyword for any airman landing up on a detachment or even joining a tropical RAF base, was improvisation or, as the Navy has it, 'Make do and Mend'. The reason was that the home country could in no way provide all the facilities and stores that one found near to hand in UK. Even when the powers-that-be tried, the war kept interfering. Take Jim

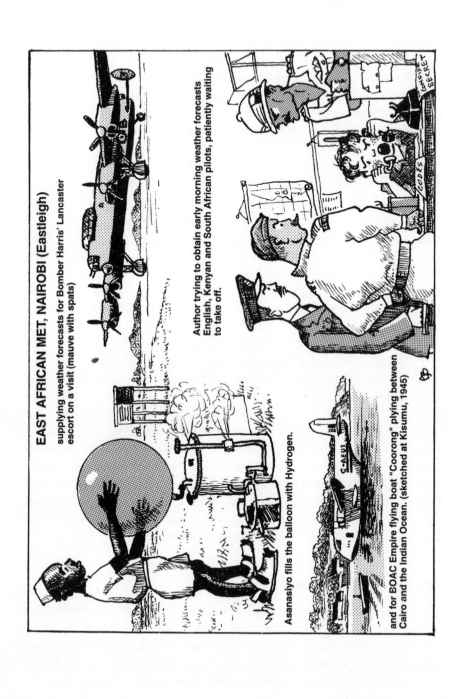

EAST AFRICAN MET, NAIROBI (Eastleigh)

supplying weather forecasts for Bomber Harris' Lancaster escort on a visit (mauve with spats)

Author trying to obtain early morning weather forecasts English, Kenyan and South African pilots, patiently waiting to take off.

Asanasiyo fills the balloon with Hydrogen.

and for BOAC Empire flying boat "Coorong" plying between Cairo and the Indian Ocean. (sketched at Kisumu, 1945)

Ginn of the Marine Craft Section, for instance, who had once been a merchant seaman. The RAF sent him out to Mombasa with 209 Squadron on the *Duchess of Bedford* CPR liner but at Durban transferred them to a very old Yankee ship, the SS *Woodlark*. Says Jim:

'It had – wait for it – BEAM ENGINES! In our small convoy to Mombasa along our port side we had this Clan motor ship. Well, she had all our nice marine craft boats and, it transpired, all our gear. Alas! She was sunk before our very eyes – in the Moçambique Channel.'

'The whole Marine Craft Section [whose ranks can be formed in the index], Taffy, Jones and Reace; Head, McBurney, Lofty Whiteside, Coombs, Pamment, McDougal, and Yank, from Seattle, turned up at Mombasa to look after 20 flying boats with . . . .NOTHING. Not a boat, not a spanner!

'Well, we looked around and began to acquire boats. EA 1 (East Africa No 1), the Dumb Dinghy was a rowing boat. EA 2 was a flat-bottomed Dumb Bomb Scow, but never used, too unstable, the armourers said. EA 3 was a captured Italian launch – Alfa Romeo engine. The hull leaked like a sieve, gear box VERY dicey. She stayed tied up. EA 4 a very nice, fast speedboat, borrowed off an earl who was at one time in clink.'

Gradually the CO and other officers acquired new or second-hand boats for them from the Middle East or UK. Jim continues:

'Meantime what about spares? No wire, or rope or shirts. What did we do? We begged, borrowed or nicked off the Navy, that is when they were not looking. (Fortunately Kilindini was a big naval base.) Our stores was a big crate – late of the Iti Air Force, used to transport bombers in. Yank was our stores basher [like Tony Curtis in the Pacific film] – he could scrounge anything. Taffy Reace appointed himself ships rigger, as he could wire-splice better than all of us. (I could but did not tell him that.) So I helped by holding the wire.

'Marlin spikes were made on the main line to Nairobi after the last train had gone. The line itself was our anvil. Mooring ropes were spliced and then taken down to the apron (slipway) where we made concrete sinkers for the trot (the line of mooring buoys for the Cats). Behind the submarine *Osiris* was her depot ship, *Chambellaine* 2nd – a mobile machine shop, full of grinding, and milling and turning machines – and a very nice line in canteens!'

So, Jim and the others made do and managed.

Returning to Diego Garcia a moment, we find, in *Tropic Tusker Tales*, a lively ex-413 Squadron newsletter, this example. In the Squadron's

Canadian jargon, a Catalina Driver (pilot?) crashed the nose of his Cat into a fuel barge, with no hope of taking off for Ceylon. An Aero Engine Mechanic, H. Glen Baker of Longview, Oregon, with another mechanic named Jupp, was asked to see if they could effect a temporary repair. With palm wood, fuel tins and a tin of aircraft dope they laboured for several days, and the Cat, with a new nose, was able to fly back.

When the Cat was sent up to Bangalore for a nose job, the experts said the work was as sturdy as the original. Both in the Mediterranean and the Far East, Sunderland squadrons in the early days carried crews whose training and skills enabled them to be self-sufficient in repairs and servicing the aircraft on detachments.

Wing Commander Bednall, CO of 230 Squadron, and others in the more peaceful parts of the Indian Ocean had long wished to do away with the Mid-Upper Gun Turret on the back of a Sunderland. It was heavy, an obstruction to the wind and not needed for defence – doing away with it should improve the air-speed and range. When instructions reached 230 Squadron to remove same, FMA/AG Gus Platts was ready again to put his mind to it. From one of his brilliant short stories of those times, I snatch a few details. The Engineering Officer had said; 'Fill it in with timber.' Gus thought this a waste and visualised a removable, perspex escape hatch that would also give light. With his considerable construction skills he devised and built such a hatch, and had it tested in the air, seeing his careful handiwork fall away into the Indian Ocean. This was repeated several times, for the high-ups in Nairobi, and the Exit did become a standard RAF fix, though the Engineering Officer hoped to be given the credit.

Sergeant John Bishop, who after the war was to become one of the most experienced Sunderland pilots, recalls a flying problem that cropped up even in the reliable new Pratt and Whitney Twin Wasp engines. When the new Sunderland Mark Vs were sent out from Britain to East Africa, the technical people in UK had missed out on the M and S gear. The lever to select M or S (Manual or Supercharger?) was not there. Consequently every Sunderland, after 80 to 100 hours flying, began to experience engine failures.

John recalls a hairy take-off run with George McKendrick when first two engines failed, then the other two, fortunately before they got into the air. It needed a technician coming from the factory in San Diego California, to advise on the answer. So the Supercharger, not needed in the tropics, was then blanked off in every aircraft and the Twin Wasp engines did fine.

Among other examples, in the Met Office at Mombasa when the artillery offered us Radar, we were able to track our weather-balloons through thick cloud by hanging a light cross of local elephant grass and copper wire below the balloon. Another Met Office allowed its climbing Hurricane aircraft, which reached 30,000 feet or more, to take up a load of beer bottles to cool them off.

Steve Linsley, over in India with 36 Squadron Wellingtons, heard of a case of sanitary towels being sent in error to an all-male squadron, where the loops were removed and they became excellent oil filters.[10] Even condoms had other uses. As Squadron (Unpaid) Artist the author at Mombasa had to provide huge murals, one week, for the Officers Mess Ball. In the absence of coloured balloons Italian-captured white condoms, in crates, were blown up and provided the right festive touch. Mind you, the RAF was concerned for its airmen's health also.

While Group Captain Rupert Taylor OBE of Durban was CO of 230 Squadron, he spent a while at the neglected detachment of Tulear (it has a different name now). He recalled:

'Tulear was not an exciting place. The Mess and HQ was a double story house which had been taken over by the South Africans when the country was invaded. The young beggars who hung around all day long sang "She'll be coming round the mountain when she comes" in broken English or rather, South African. But it was only after three or four airmen went down with the lesser amorous complaint that I read the Admiralty Pilot and saw that there was about an 80% spread among the locals. I signalled for and got a Dutch Cat to come over with a supply of protectors and amelioratives but I thought the numerous personal messages of sympathy for me were a bit uncalled-for!'

A Flight Lieutenant in a different squadron in a country that shall be nameless, told me of another piece of improvisation in that field.

'I do remember that our flight rations always included tins of pilchards in tomato sauce. Nobody liked them but they had always disappeared by the time we returned to base. It took me a couple of months to find out that two of the crew sergeants used to take them to use in bartering for certain services in the town. Worth their weight in gold apparently.'

It was about Tulear that UK newspapers recorded the bravery of two marine craft airmen who saved a Catalina and its refueller from becoming a mass of enormous explosions.[11] Tom Weaving of the Marine Craft Service, now in Canada, and Tom Ladd recall a similar occasion where one of the two airmen died but both, again, received medals.

One last story of 'initiative-testing', as our New Zealand Corporal

Radar Mechanic calls it, in his tapes to us. Before the Madagascar invasion he, Giff Blamey, and certain riggers, fitters and instrument makers were all sent down to Dar-es-Salaam in 1942 to service the daily Catalina patrols down the coast. What with?

'All we had was what we stood up in, and not even any tools. All I had was a set of screwdrivers which I bought in Blackpool for 1/3d. I didn't even have a spare bit of wire. The others were all in the same boat. And we didn't even have a boat to go ashore in. The local boat-building people and marine services were very good to us. [It doesn't say much for the authorities who posted them down there to make bricks without straw.]

'I had a bit of trouble with a piece of gear one day. After going down the coast at 3 p.m., a kite came in at 7 a.m. as usual and the aircrew reported that the A.S.V. (radar set) was U/S and I thought "Gee, what the heck can I do?" I had a look at it and knew straight away what it was. In the indicator circuit there was a resistor of very high value – 7.3 or 7.8 Megohms, I think. Very unusual value. I was scratching my head wondering what to do. So I took the bull by the horns and took it ashore.

'In the main street there was a radio repair shop and the owner came out in his turban [In East Africa then, all the technicians were Sikhs]. He said he had nothing like that. So I said, "Can you make it up by soldering a few resistances together and make up the value that way?" He scratched his turban then got cracking and sorted out the right value and fitted it. He said there was no charge, as it was for the Air Force.

'Then he said "What's it for anyway?" If the Air Force had known I had taken it to a civvy for repair, they would probably have had me shot. It was still classified, this was 1942. So I told him it was just some high-frequency equipment, thanked him very much and got out smartly. I took it back to the kite and it worked perfectly.'

Examples of how aircrew and the administration had to adapt can be seen in the 'Minelaying' Chapter XI or elsewhere in this book. Many flare paths were home-made; refuelling often had to be carried out by hand from four-gallon petrol tins. Some were rusty, and native girls were employed to stitch together pieces of chamois leather to make funnel-filters which slowed it all up, though some native teams could do the 1,450 gallons for a Cat in half an hour, I am told.

Tools and equipment dropped into clear tropical water could be retrieved by diving, on one occasion by a pearl diver in the Gulf who took *five* minutes under water to find a missing plug. Onlookers had given him up.

MACARTHUR SURVIVORS MEET THE WHALES

In an air sea rescue near Madagascar one of the aircraft taking part was on a far detachment from its base at 205 Squadron, Ceylon. A ship was on its way to the tropical paradise which inspired H de Vere Stacpoole to write his novel *The Blue Lagoon* – Mauritius. The SS *Clan Macarthur*, one of the largest steamers in the Clan fleet, would seem to be suffering from a bout of indecision. She had reached a point halfway from Madagascar to Mauritius and at one moment she would be heading north of the island but shortly afterwards she would be veering south of it. One glance at the date, 12 August 1943, and an inspection of her cargo, 5,500 tons of military stores including 1,200 packets of TNT, in No 5 hold, would give you the answer. The Clan ship was zigzagging to reduce the risk from U-boats.

She had sailed from Durban in company but was now alone, her bow cutting through a moderate sea with a heavy swell. The moon had just set and the 10,000-ton steamer was rolling along under an overcast sky. It was not dark enough to prevent a wide-awake young apprentice on watch from seeing the fine, pale track of a torpedo heading straight for them over the indigo sea.

The lad rushed towards the bridge but, before he could reach the Second Officer to tell him, the torpedo struck the ship under the poop on the port quarter. The shock and the dull boom awakened the Captain, J.D. Matthews, down below, as he tells us in his report. The explosion fractured both propeller shafts and the ship began to settle a little by the stern.

The torpedo had damaged the fo'c'sle (forecastle) in which many of the Indian (Lascar) crew were killed or trapped. More were killed when a second torpedo struck, destroying three lifeboats. It also destroyed the wireless set but Radio Officer Cole managed to rig out the emergency set and received a reply back from Lourenço Marques – 'Way the other side of Madagascar!' The Portuguese would arrange rescue, however.

Five men, Chief Engineer Currie, Purser R.Y. Taylor, Refrigerating Engineer Ruthven, Third Officer J.D. Mair and the Czech Ship's Surgeon, Doctor Ungr, had gone to the aid of the men trapped in the fo'c'sle. They could have got away themselves in boats but they continued battling till, all of a sudden, the third torpedo struck. The ship went down, only Mair and Ruthven out of the five surviving. The Captain, by tradition last to leave his ship, and many of the remaining crew got away in the three starboard lifeboats. Those who jumped in the sea with red lights on their life-jackets were making for the six rafts. All at once from the doomed steamer came an enormous explosion which threw up a column of water 30 feet high. It was probably due to the fires reaching the 1,200 packets of TNT in No 5 hold and it killed all the men in the water instantly.

After this the U-boat, which was Lüth's U/181, surfaced near the Captain's lifeboat. Knowing he might be taken prisoner, Matthews quickly hid under the thwarts, telling one of the naval gunners what to say. The rating had to repeat the name of the ship about six times before it was understood by the U-boat man who knew little English. Finally the German untied their boat from the submarine and said: 'Look out propeller. I go,' and the U-boat slid away.

When daylight crept up over the forlorn scene of wreckage and rafts Captain Matthews kept the three lifeboats together near the site of the sinking, since their SOS had got through. The rays of morning then brought them a wonderful sight. On the horizon the slim outline of a flying boat was spotted. It was Catalina P belonging to 205 Squadron, on detachment from its base at Koggala in Ceylon and piloted by F/Lt McCallum, 'wings of the dawning' indeed.

Matthews reported: 'We hoisted our yellow flag and burnt our smoke flares but I think he had already sighted our sails.' The aircraft circled the boats and signalled by Aldis lamp in Morse: 'Cheer up, help is coming' and then flew off. Another Catalina which spotted them was J/265 (FP 263) based on Madagascar and piloted by an Australian, F/O Johnny Pinkard, known to all as Pinky.

Gil Ewers, also from Australia, was one of the Wireless Operator/Air Gunners in Pinky's crew and noted in his diary:

'Thursday, August 12 1943. Having wizard sleep when Pinky woke me to go on a trip. Anti-sub escort for a merchant ship. Picked up message, "SUNK BY SUB". Found survivors, poor devils. We left them and looked for sub. Saw lifeboats again on way home. Flew over them at zero feet, flashed message.'

The aircrew consisted of Pinkard as Captain; Smith, George McKendrick and Meadows, all pilots; Gil Ewers, Stan Bick, Bob Pow and Alan Gee as WOP/AGs; or WOM/AGs; Dicky Wicks, Flight Engineer; Spike Hunt, Flight Mechanic (Electrical) and Jimmy Atkinson, Flight Mechanic (Airframes). The last named sometimes, as cook, offered a choice of sandwiches – Ham, Jam or Spam.

From the lifeboat's level the seamen saw, in the deepening twilight, the Catalina's winking light as the pilot signalled, says Captain Matthews,

'"I am going to drop you a radio set with full instructions how to use." He flew over the boats and dropped the set by parachute. We picked it up, streamed the kite which flew perfectly then transmitted messages simply by winding the handle until the light glowed, sending out SOS automatically.

UPPER LEFT: 413 Sq Catalina.
(Courtesy of G.H.U. Bayly DFC)

UPPER RIGHT: Masirah RAF Camp, 1944 'The one day in the whole year when it rained' – note Desert Lily and "tin-can" buildings (see Chapter 7).
(Courtesy of K. Scott, Mrs Liz Seymour)

LOWER LEFT: The two 265 Sq crews of Smith and Pinkard (Pinkard was also at Masirah).
(Courtesy Air Cdre Seyman)

LOWER RIGHT: Crew of J-265. Back row left to right: Sgt Hunt; Sgt Bick; Sgt Wicks; Sgt Ewers; Sgt Pow; Sgt Gee. Front row: F/Sgt Meadows; F/O Pinkard RAAF (Captain); F/O McKendrick DFC; F/Sgt Dawson.
(Courtesy G. McKendrick DFC, Mrs Liz Seymour)

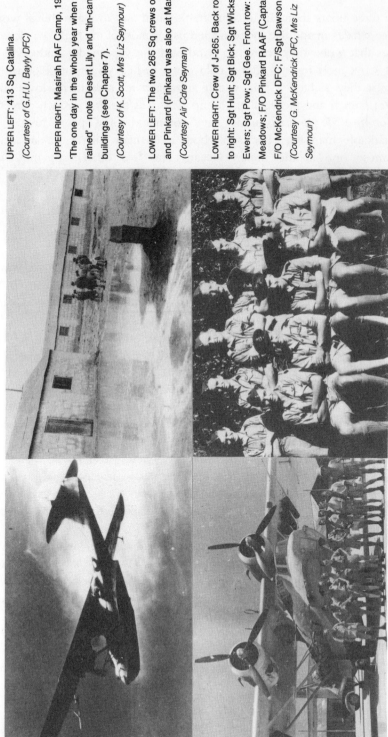

We transmitted these messages every hour for three minutes and I understand a Catalina got bearings from it.'

The three boats spent an uncomfortable night and to make things worse 'three whales in sportive mood circled us for most of the night, so close at times that when they "blew" to windward the vapour descended on us and stank most foully'. After a cold dawn in heavy rain, at 08.00 on 13 August they sighted a ship which zigzagged towards them, lowered a motor launch and picked them all up. This was the Free French corvette, *Savorgnan de Brazza*, under the command of Captain Jubelin, a remarkable man who had sunk both a German sub at Dakar and a Japanese one in the Indian Ocean. The five officers of the *Clan Macarthur* who, at risk of life, tried to rescue the trapped Lascars, all received decorations, three of them posthumously[12].

U-BOATS EASTWARD BOUND

In June and July 1943 Admiral Dönitz decided to send another two waves of submarines, the Monsoon Groups I and II, to the Far East. In Group One there were nine Type IXC boats, as follows (Names of the captains will be found in the appendices): U/168, U/183, U/188, U/200, U/506, U/509, U/514, U/516 and U/532. With them were the larger U/847 and U/533, Type IXD2. To supply them sailed two 'milch cows', U/462 and U/487, both of Type XIV. However, of the 11 boats which set out seven were sunk in the first month or so, mostly in the Atlantic. U/516 was diverted to the Caribbean and reached home but U/533 met disaster in the Persian Gulf, as we shall see later. One seaman survived and caused amazement at the RAF base, being a 'real live Nazi', they said.

In fact, despite the lurid descriptions of some writers who made out the U-boat men to be rabid National Socialists, the vast majority in the Indian Ocean were not Nazis at all. Apart from the national flag, which bore a swastika, that emblem was not displayed inside or outside submarines, with one exception.

In the joint base with the Japanese at Penang the Imperial Navy of Japan insisted on U-boats attaching a large canvas swastika to their conning towers in case they were mistaken for Allied submarines. Away from Penang this was soon stowed elsewhere and Nazi salutes were not to be seen, so I am told by German submariners.

The remaining four from Monsoon Group One, U/168, U/183, U/188 and U/532, along with Japanese submarines, sank 21 ships before reaching Penang. U/168 fought a night battle with a 413 Squadron Catalina. This is the story.

THE RADAR SCREEN BLOB

One of the less boring sorties for maritime aircrews was a night patrol. It was not always easy, and worse in the dark, trying to find the tiny group of ships. 413 Squadron's Catalina Y (FP 282), piloted by two Canadians, F/O Johnny Gowans and Co-pilot P/O Bob Armstrong, was on night patrol over a Bombay-bound convoy on 3 November 1943 off Cochin. The convoy was escorted by two minesweepers of the Royal Indian Navy, the *Rajputana* and the *Agra*. The SNO (Senior Naval Officer) asked Gowans to check on a straggler which had dropped back from the convoy with engine trouble. Just as lions will pick on a wildebeest falling behind the herd, submarines would go for a vessel labouring to keep up.

The lone straggler, seen in my painting, its engines thumping flat out, was actually the second escort, HMIS *Agra*, a converted trawler of 4,569 tons, built in Sweden. W/O Harold (Smudge) Smith, WOM/AG, up in the Cat, was at the ancient vertical radar screen trying to sort out all the ships in the convoy. He writes:

> 'I was only able to see a mass of confused blips on the screen. This was frustrating and I borrowed a piece of paper from the Nav and with a bit of ingenuity found it possible, by turning the paper on the screen and blocking out some of the glare, to discover the relative positions of the ships and the escort vessels.'

Harold then noticed one blip was lagging about eight miles behind the convoy. As he watched the odd-shaped blob, it gradually divided into two, like an amoeba, and Gowans was informed that a possible sub was ahead. The co-pilot Bob Armstrong recalls what happened next:

> 'I could see the sub fully surfaced in the silvery moon path, like a big black cigar. We were close to 2,000 feet so Johnny Gowans turned away into the darkness to lose height for a low-level attack. We carried six 250-pound DCs, four of them set to detonate at a shallow depth and two for a deeper depth. I reached behind my head and set the rotor to release the four shallow DCs in a stick when Johnny pushed the button. We levelled off at 50 feet and approached the sub from the dark side with him silhouetted against the moon.
>
> 'He made a sharp turn [to port] and our DCs straddled his stern – were seen to explode and apparently did some damage. As we came into the moonlight the deck gun got a good shot at us and put a large hole in our tail and severed the cables to the trimming tabs on the elevators – with a loud bang, incidentally – and a lot of noise from our 50-calibre Brownings in the blisters; a lot of shouting from the crew.

'Johnny [Gowans] left his seat to inspect the damage. He went aft and so did several crew members – the aircraft's nose started climbing to the stars with so much weight in the tail. I had an exciting time trying to keep us on an even keel since I had no trim to help the elevators. Thus we lost sight of our adversary and by the time the skipper came back from sending WT and checking out the tail he had disappeared.'

On his 80th birthday, Lt/Cdr Helmuth Pich, of U/168, and his wife Hilde are given Arthur Banks' painting, by W/O Harold Smith. He was a WOM/AG on Y/413 (Captain J. Gowans DFC) which attacked and damaged Pich's boat. *(Courtesy H. Smith)*

Apart from four DCs dropped, a smoke float was also dropped with them, very wisely, to mark the site if the U-boat should disappear. It is seen in my colour plate of the attack which is admittedly not exact in detail, but gives the main impression. The reason the crew of Y were unable to detect the smoke from the float was that it had landed plumb on the deck of the submarine, where a mystified German crew found it later!

So what else happened down on the surface of the sea during that attack? In 1992 Harold Smith got in touch with the Captain of U/168, Lieutenant Commander Helmuth Pich, who was then 78 years old and living in Geesthacht, near Hamburg. The following, with one or two minor adjustments, is part of his reply, which Harold received in return.

'Dear Harold, Thank you for your letter dated 21st August 1992. I'm so glad you didn't leave me out, being on my heels when you "blipped" my boat west of Cochin on the night of 3rd November 1943. At that time I was U-boat Commander of U/168 just trailing a vessel on the port side. The same time a Catalina headed for us and turned off. "Air Alarm!" A lesser risk seemed to be not to dive as the Cat would be back in no time.

'Engines full power ahead – some 16 knots. Then the Cat was up to us dropping four depth charges: two on starboard astern and two on port astern. Our AA opened fire. The Cat was roaring, AA-fire rattled, the boat shaking horribly. The hell!

'Then: nothing! The boat still surfaced, no casualties, the engines on full power, the Catalina off! Except leakings and damages on the torpedo tubes astern, down in the boat all other stations reported no damages. So U/168 turned for Penang . . .

'Harold, you (the Catalina crew) showed an excellent performance of proficiency in anti-submarine actions. You sighted an enemy submarine, attacked it and caused some damage. The boat had to leave the area for repair and last not least the "Lone straggler" could go ahead happily. The dropping of the depth charges very accurate. Congratulations on such outstanding achievement. Helmuth Pich'

Without using Leigh Lights, this night attack by a Catalina using an early form of radar was indeed remarkable. Such was the experience of one Monsoon U-boat and its Captain. More will be heard of Helmuth Pich in 1944, when his boat rescued the crew of the *Brake* and was later sunk by the Dutch submarine *Zwaardvis*. (Most books say *Zwaardfisch*, using the German 'fish', but the Royal Netherlands Navy prefer the Dutch spelling.) This is fully described in Jochen Brennecke's *Haie (Sharks) im Paradies*[13], which is a gripping history of the Indian Ocean U-boats, but unfortunately only obtainable in German.

F/O J.R. Gowans RCAF was awarded a DFC for the exploit. As well as Bob Armstrong the official list gives the crew names as in the chapter notes[14][15].

The second Monsoon Group of four U-boats left Europe in late 1943 but had even less luck. U/848, U/849 and U/850 were all sunk *en route* by American aircraft and only U/510 (Eick) – a IXC – reached Penang and sank five ships in the Indian Ocean on the way. His total number sunk was nine.

N O T E S

[1] via Harry Hutson, marine author, Cleethorpes.

2   Ships reports, Public Record Office, Kew.

3   *Blood and Bushido,* Captain Bernard Edwards (Images) 1991

4   'An order issued by the Commander of the Japanese First Submarine Force at Truk on 20 March 1943 contained the following: "Do not stop at the sinking of enemy ships and cargoes. At the same time carry out the complete destruction of the crews of the enemy's ships."' From *Knights of Bushido,* Lord Russell of Liverpool (Cassell and Co), London 1958

5   *Flying Cats* Andrew Hendrie (Airlife), Shrewsbury 1988

6   *Blood and Bushido* – see above

7   This was not the Admiral Rawlings of the later Pacific Fleet.

8   *Squadrons of the Fleet Air Arm,* Ray Sturtivant (Air Britain), Tonbridge 1984

9   262 *Cape Sub-hunters* Article, Andrew Thomas RAF (Aviation News), 9-22/11/1990

10   A regular free issue of sanitary towels was thoughtfully provided for W.A.A.F personnel in U.K. or overseas through the generosity of Lord Nuffield - one of his many unsung benefactions

11   For this act of bravery and skill in February 1944 LAC R.S. Alexander of Glasgow, and LAC R.W. Chapman of Hollywood, County Down, Northern Ireland were each awarded the British Empire Medal.

12   *The Gathering of the Clans,* N.L. Middlemiss (Shield Publications), Newcastle-on-Tyne, 1988

13   *Haie im Paradies,* Jochen Brennecke (Wilhelm Heyne), Munich 1988

14   The remaining crew are F/O Vernon H.J. Barnes, Navigator; W/O R.E. Limebeer RCAF (known as 'Shandy' – what else!): F/Eng Sgt Ivan Wolloshin, 2nd Engineer; F/Sgt H.J. 'Smudge' Smith, WOM/AG; Sgt W.R. 'Bill' Smith, WOP/AG; Sgt G.R. 'Dickie' Lynam, FMA/AG; Sgt W.E. 'Willie' Winter RCAF; Sgt F.B. Connell.

15   For the radar aspects see diagram in the Appendix. The Yagi aerials, I am told, were invented before WW2 by Professor Yagi of Japan and, ironically, used against Japan by the Allies. They are the basis, I believe of modern T.V. aerials.

CHAPTER 6

A FATEFUL DAY

On 20 August 1943, in the East Africa region, three notable RAF events occurred. The first of these was a mystery; the second was a Catalina tragedy, off Mombasa; and the third was the sinking of a U-boat, U/197, off Madagascar by two Catalinas.

WHEN SUNDERLANDS DISAPPEAR

In the RAF records and in two published lists[1] [2], T/230 (EJ 131) becomes confused with another Sunderland (probably DW 131) which went missing earlier on 27 March 1943. Both aircraft lost their way, presumably ran out of fuel and crash-landed on sea or land with the total loss of their crews.

We will take the March incident first. This was a crash in the morning, recalled by Leading Aircraftman Ron Bradford who was a 'ground' wireless operator in 230 Squadron on detachment at Tulear, South Madagascar. Ron's memoir sets the background for both crashes.

'I was Superintendent of the W/T (Wireless Telegraphy) watch on that day. It was during the morning and after W/T (Morse) contact had closed, that Marine Craft Section were alerted that the Sunderland was due to arrive at any moment. In fact she circled the bay ready, as we believed, to land, but for some unknown reason she continued inland at a height of approximately 1,000 to 1,500 feet. We assumed she intended to come round again, but then the wireless operator on the aircraft frequency suddenly shouted out: "I'm getting what sounds like an SOS and believe it is from the Sunderland."

'Realising the seriousness of the situation I took over from him and did confirm it was definitely an SOS and from "T". I endeavoured to make W/T contact and, in fact, used P/L [plain language] which was normally contrary to RAF signalling procedure during wartime. I came to the conclusion that "T's" wireless operator was either unable to hear or his set was U/S [unserviceable]. The signals became weaker and eventually were lost by us, but other stations on the frequency (either Seychelles or Mauritius) managed to pick it up, though eventually contact was lost.'

Ron ordered a radio silence throughout the area until the last hopes had faded.

In the case of the Sunderland which disappeared on 27 March 1943, the books suggest it crashed in Moçambique and that all nine crew were killed. I have not yet found their names. For 20 August 1943, 'the fateful day', RAF records say this, regarding T/230 (EJ 131?) Captain – F/Lt A.M. Todd which crashed in the evening:

'"T" set out to escort HMS *Albatross* (seaplane carrier) and the destroyer HMS *Nepal* proceeding south through the Moçambique Channel. At 14.50 aircraft message: "Position 19°08' South. 41°23' East. No sign of convoy." At 18.38 "T" sent message to Tulear: "Had they heard engines overhead?" It then asked for bearings for Diego Suarez and Dar-es-Salaam. Tulear told A/C (aircraft) to steer East and pick up the coast. At 19.06 aircraft asked Tulear for D/F (Direction Finding radar) assistance [to home in on]. 20.03, it sent SOS that it was making a forced landing. Nil heard thereafter.'

Three Catalinas, two from Durban and one from Mombasa, searched all next day but found nothing in the Moçambique Channel. 230 Squadron's Sunderland "V" (EJ 140) captained by F/Lt Lumsden also searched along the west coast of Madagascar without result.

209 SQUADRON'S CATALINA LOSS

That same day, 20 August 1943, Catalina R-209 (FP 302), captained by F/Lt Ron (Jim) Roberts, an Australian pilot married to an English WAAF officer, Section Officer Patricia Roberts, had just returned to Mombasa after a 20-hour patrol. A year before, when the aircraft left Pembroke Dock, its last flying boat base, in South Wales on 6 June 1942, Patricia and another WAAF Officer had stood on a vantage point and waved goodbye to their men departing over the horizon. She and Ron had been married just 19 days. R-209 followed the route to East Africa, across the Congo and arrived safely at Mombasa.

UPPER LEFT: F/O Charles Green, Intelligence Officer at RAF Langebaah, at the time of UIT/22 being sunk. *(courtesy F. Roddick DFC)*

UPPER RIGHT: Sgt Derek Nobes, Flight Engineer/Air Gunner on S/209 (AH543) Catalina, captained by F/Lt John Inglis, during the stormy flight to Durban. *(courtesy D. Nobes)*

LOWER LEFT: Mrs Perla Gibson, of Durban, known as the 'Lady in White', who sang on the dockside popular songs to the men in the troopships. *(author's collection)*

LOWER RIGHT: Sergeant Stan Borrill, known as 'Pop', being in his forties, Flight Engineer on Ron Roberts' R-209 which crashed fatally on 20 August 1943. *(courtesy F. Borrill)*

One of the passengers on the night R/209 crashed was F/Lt John Inglis. The Flight Engineer in the aircraft, Sergeant Stan Borrill, was known as Pop because he had joined the RAF in 1918 as a 16-year-old Boy Entrant. This account is mainly based on a booklet written by his son Frank. The full page moonlight painting of R-209 was painted by the author for his son Robert. The personal memories of Lindsay Wilson, a Radar Mechanic from Auckland, come once more via Giff Blamey, another New Zealand Radar 'Mech' with a diary, a phenomenal memory and a tape-recorder heavily used on my behalf.

The story of R's widely mourned crash begins with a little grey tin box. This turned up unannounced from the Middle East in the Radar Section at Kipevu, Mombasa, one day. It turned out to be a modified box for IFF – Identification Friend or Foe, used for signalling to vessels on the sea below the aircraft. This one was to act as a fixed-frequency, long-range homing ASV (Air-to-surface-vessel) radar beacon – a mobile one. It was called a Rooster and was sent from the Middle East to 209 Squadron for the unit to assess. Says Giff, his broad Antipodean drawl emerging from the tape-deck:

'Our blokes would find that if an escort or convoy had it installed, and an aircraft was flying towards the convoy with ASV, they picked the thing up at the absolute maximum range which was 96 miles. Then another time if there was an aircraft over the convoy with the Rooster on board, the relieving aircraft could pick that up at 96 miles too – a big advantage in finding a convoy when there was heavy haze, fog or bad weather. Normally without the Rooster we used to find we could pick up a convoy at 40 or 50 miles at the maximum and that was only if we were flying at about 8,000 feet, so this thing had a tremendous advantage.'

Testing the Rooster was not the main reason for R's flight that night. Flight Lieutenant Roberts was told that he was to 'test the efficiency of low-level bombing with the aid of searchlights.' (These were not the Dambuster type of focusing lights for altitude nor the Leigh Light.) The Rooster was also being tested by the Squadron Signals Officer, Flying Officer Vic Field, WOM/AG, who volunteered to go up and observe results because the Radar Officer was away. The searchlight test interested 209 Squadron's Commanding Officer, Wing Commander G.E. Wallace, who had arrived in May after commanding 262 Squadron for three months. He wished to take part and Air Commodore Fitzpatrick from his own knowledge feels that Wallace was the one flying the aircraft.

Squadron Leader J. Barraclough (CO 209 Sq.) with F/Lt Ron Roberts RAAF before the fatal crash on 20 August 1943 where Roberts' aircraft R-209 was lost with all on board, off Mombasa in moonlight. *(courtesy F. Borrill)*

John Inglis was now a Catalina Captain respected enough to be asked to take temporary command of 209 Squadron when Wing Commander Barraclough had to undergo a throat operation and hand over to the then Squadron Leader D.B. Fitzpatrick. The latter in turn had to take charge at Seychelles and thus Inglis took command for a month.

'R' for Robert also had on board another Flight Engineer, Sergeant E. Mallon; Sergeant E. Hallas was a Flight Mechanic (Airframes)/Air Gunner and there were two WOP/AGs, Sergeants J.M. Snowden and A.W. O'Leary. Finally came a Leading Aircraftman, N. Edwards who may have been a Flight Mechanic (Electrical) doing his training as an Air Gunner. Pilot Officer Alex Larsen RAAF, the Second Pilot in Robert's crew, was not aboard that night, nor W.W.W. Smith, the navigator.

'R' for Robert took off at 19.30 hours and Lin Wilson takes up his story. He had installed the Rooster in the 72-foot pinnace, a torpedo recovery craft with a mast and a winch, which was based at Kipevu for Air Sea Rescue.

R.209 captained by F/Lt Ron Roberts RAAF off Mombasa before crashing in the moonlight on 20.08.1943, losing all on board. Authors painting
(courtesy Robert Borrill)

Snowy Maclean, the Sergeant in charge of Marine Section, took the pinnace out. Everything seemed to be going fine and R was making another run in about 20.30. Said Lin:

'Usually they get down close to the sea, get a bit of height and turn away. This time they did not gain any height at all and for some reason made their turn too early and the wingtip hit the water and she cartwheeled.'

Lin was absolutely horrified to see this thing, in the moonlight, cartwheel into the sea. The sight of it going into the sea lived with him for a long time. Snowy Maclean turned the pinnace straight over to the area and they cruised around for quite a while but all they could find was a bit of debris. No bodies came up. Then they 'high-tailed it back to Kipevu and reported it and 'everything went into a panic.' Next day they searched round and found nothing. All the blisters and escape hatches would have been shut and with the force of the crash everybody would have been killed at once.

A strange fact emerged later and was related to me by Flight Lieutenant Roberts' widow, now Mrs Patricia Thomas of British Columbia. She was then in Blackpool and for some weeks before the accident she began to have a recurrent dream. In it she saw her husband's Catalina flying along close to the sea in the moonlight. The wingtip would then touch the water and the whole aircraft dive into the sea. It was so real that she would wake up crying in her small bedroom and with the paper-thin walls of the billet the other WAAF officers would ask what was the matter.

Section Officer Roberts finally received the news that her husband was 'missing believed killed' and eventually heard the full story all except for one thing. No one could tell her whether there was moonlight that night – not until, through Frank Borrill's research into his father's death, 50 years on, she heard of Lindsay Wilson's eyewitness account on the tape.

The loss of the CO, son of Lady Wallace in Kenya, along with several fine pilot-Captains and the crew, was a severe shock to the Squadron, after the recent changes, but the routine went on. There follows now the third event to take place on 20 August 1943 with a better outcome for the RAF but not for the U-boat.

THE SINKING OF U/197

The crews of the Catalina Squadrons – 259, based on Dar-es-Salaam; 262, whose home was Durban; and 265, operating from Diego Suarez over a large area of ocean around Madagascar were all frustrated with searching a seemingly empty space. It was August 1943. They were hearing of ships being sunk all the time. Now on 17 August, the *Empire Stanley*, a British freighter of nigh on 7,000 tons, had been slammed with torpedoes by an ocean-cruiser U-boat, U/197, under *Kapitänleutnant* (Lieutenant Commander) Robert Bartels.

In reporting to two fellow raiders nearby, the U-boats U/181 and U/196, both also IXD2s, Bartels radioed that the stricken tramp's wireless officer, with the invariable courage these men showed, had succeeded in sending out an SOS which could betray the attacker.

Then the D/F (radar)[3] stations intercepted a message from Captain (*Kapitän zur See*) Wolfgang Lüth in U/181. Lüth, we saw, was the most highly decorated U-boat commander in World War Two. He was reporting to Bartels that they missed a 3,000-tonner with their last torpedo. The despatch was heard by the D/F stations, a number of whose operators were 'very intelligent girls.'

They reported that a U-boat was suspected within a hundred miles of position 28°30' South, 43°00' East, south of Madagascar's southern tip. Combined Headquarters in Durban, to whom the reports came, was the control room that scanned the enormous range of coastal waters round South Africa. It was ready with attack ships and aircraft to send out. This time they despatched a Catalina as a start.

HQ was unaware that in fact there were three U-boats in the area, part of a group which had sunk 22 ships amounting to some 130,163 tons. The third member of the group, U/196, was captained by the tall Commander (*Korvettenkapitän*) Eitel-Friedrich Kentrat. Now German U-boat Headquarters in France (BdU) ordered Lüth to rendezvous with Bartels to receive supplies and take over the keys of the German code ENIGMA and then pass them on to Kentrat. They met on 19 August but it was Kentrat who later offered Lüth five torpedoes and foodstocks on that day. Heavy seas made it impossible to transfer, so U/196 and U/181 resumed their journey southward together.

Back in Durban on 18 August Flight Lieutenant Oscar Barnett and the crew of Catalina Ib, 'C' for Charlie (FP 126) were on detachment from 259 Squadron, Dar-es-Salaam, further up the African coast. They were operating from RAF Congella base in Durban with its crowded harbour and warm hospitable people held in affection by the British troops that passed through. They recall the Lady in White, with her tall ample figure on the dockside, who sang patriotic and popular songs to the convoys entering harbour. (Her name was Mrs Perla Gibson and she worked in a canteen there but she had an operatic voice that would carry to the topmost crowded deck. She received a well-deserved medal in

UPPER PHOTO: Most of the crew of C/259, which helped sink U/197 on 20 August 1943. Tennant was Captain at this time instead of Barnett, and Ernie Brewer had returned after his temporary replacement by F/Sgt Norman Pearce.

Back row left to right: F/Sgt 'Mick' Peters RNZAF; Sgt Rouse; F/Sgt 'Dick' Martin RNZAF; F/Sgt Joe Ball; Sgt N. Collins.

Front row: F/Sgt 'Ernie' Brewer; F/Sgt 'Reg' Anderson; F/O 'Bill' Tennant; F/O 'Len' Eccles; F/Sgt 'Ken' Caligari DFM.

Inset: F/Lt L.O. Barnett DFC. *(courtesy L.O. Barnett DFC)*

LOWER PHOTO: FP126 (Barnett) with squadron letter changed from 'C' to 'L'.
(courtesy K. Caligari DFM)

recognition. After the war the Royal Navy met the expense of a memorial to her, situated on the Bluff). However, Durban, like all ports, had its network of spies who informed the U-boars of their prey.

On that 18th 'C' for Charlie was ordered out on a long-range patrol, partly prepared at Congella and then sent up to the new flying boat haven at St Lucia. This was one of the bases where the Standing Orders for marine craft included the instruction 'Ensure the flight path is cleared of hippos before landings and take-offs.'

Next day saw the crew doing circuits and bumps[4], followed by bombing and gunnery practice. Some airgunners elsewhere were not above putting a crocodile in their log-books as one of their hits. They were now in top form for the patrol and in any case seem to have been a competent crew. The Skipper, Oscar Barnett, was of medium height, cheerful and dapper, with a moustache. As a pilot he was steady and reliable, efficient enough to spend many years after the war as a senior BOAC captain.

According to his colleagues, Flying Officer Len Eccles, the Co-pilot, was also a good pilot. The rest of the crew were all sergeants. The navigator, 'Andy' Anderson, a tallish, quiet Irishman, had never been known to get his calculations wrong. Joe Ball, the stocky, dark-haired engineer from the Winchester area, operated in the tiny compartment in the tower and was very conscientious but a martyr to airsickness. There was no room for a bucket beside his dials so with a sudden loud groan Joe would scramble down and belt along to the Elsan toilet in the blister compartment already stinking from its normal contents and the slops from the meals.

Joe and the remaining crew were all trained air gunners as well. Bobby Peel, the Flight Mechanic, could stand in for Joe as engineer; Norman Pearce, a tall Flight Mechanic (Airframes), detailed to the crew because someone was off sick, was a turret gunner. Ken Caligari, a not so tall Cranwell apprentice from Lincolnshire, as Wireless Operator Mechanic, had the most experience on radio. The two WOP/AGs were collectively known as Martin-and-Peters, since in those days when such friendships had no other connotations they stuck together on or off duty. Dickie Martin, a tall, rangy farmer with a ginger moustache and curly hair, was from Hawkes Bay, New Zealand. He was cheerful, enthusiastic and always very down to earth. Sturdily-built 'Micky', or Warren Manuel Peters, also a New Zealander, had straight dark hair and a narrow Valentino 'tache. He was a great rugby player and with his distant Spanish connection had to keep the ladies in check, as he was engaged to a girl in the WAAF in the UK. He was a keen and skilful gunner as well as being competent on radio and radar. Previously he had worked for 20th

Century Fox. Pilot Officer Woodhouse was third pilot but we have no 'gen' about him. Well before midnight on 19 August Oscar and Andy were briefed at the 'domestic site'.

The U-boat they were to encounter on this patrol had been built quite recently by A.G. Weser, Bremen and launched just over a year before on 21 June 1942. She was one of the IXD2s and after her commissioning *U-Bartels*[5] worked-up in the Baltic with No 4 U-Flotilla at Stettin and then, under No 12 U-Flotilla, she sailed for Penang about November 1942.

The captain, Lt Cdr Robert Bartels, was born at Kiel Priess in 1911. The Chief Engineer of U/178, Herr Karl-Heinz Wiebe of Bremen, remembers him as friendly to his crew but a good disciplinarian. In the Atlantic Bartels commanded U/139 and U/561, when he was awarded the *Deutsche Kreuz in gold* so he was no fledgling. On this trip U/197 had sunk three vessels and damaged another.[6]

We know nothing about the rest of the crew except for young Richard Dietrich who hailed from the little town of Oberrot, nestling in the wooded hills near Backnang, not far from Stuttgart in South Germany. Backnang is twinned with Chelmsford, my home town, so I was able to elicit much information. By 18 Richard would have left the village school to work in the Oberrot chemical factory, but was called up for military labour service.[7] Then, on a cold February day, he volunteered for the Navy. His military passbook or *Wehrpass* came into the hands of Mr Eric Bakker of Rotterdam who kindly presented me with a bound copy. It was then translated from Old German by Mr Karl Wahnig of London who served in U/802, a IXC Atlantic U-boat, and runs a U-boat Museum near Regents Park. As Richard's picture shows, he was a sturdy, handsome young man, just past his 21st birthday. The total number in the crew listed here was 67 and the men were, no doubt, looking forward to going home.

At St Lucia it was round about midnight as 'C' for Charlie's crew prepared to board their aircraft. The lake looked a different place at night with a newly-silvered moon's light shimmering along the black-edged shore and sparkling among the mudbanks. The crocodiles that crowded the sundrenched shores by day were now barely visible. The fish-eagles whose lazy drifting over the lake could be another hazard to planes were long since tucked up on their thorn branches, white head under one wing. The pelican flocks were grey strips of shade along the water's edge, huddled together in sleep.

One by one the aircrew clambered out of the 'dinghy', or marine tender, through the blister and prepared for checks on engines, the guns and the rest. Then, when both engines were running, Norman was ordered to slip the mooring and they taxied to the end of the flarepath.

The moon passed in and out of the clouds, spangling the wake of the broad-winged Cat into a comet's tail with one silver-streaking wing float still dipped. As she rose up on to the 'step'[8] Oscar said to Joe 'Floats up' and the float trail vanished. The comet tail dwindled till suddenly it ended as the Cat left the water and headed out into the blackness of unsuspected destiny.

In the dimly-lit cabin that was the 'flight deck' Oscar, from the pilot's seat on the port side, set a course for the area of operations and the crew settled into their respective positions. The skipper had worked out with Joe how to get the maximum endurance out of the flying boat, Oscar being responsible for leaving as much fuel as possible for the mission.

While Andy was carrying out a variety of checks and calculations one radio operator would be behind the radar curtain in the tiny shoulder-width compartment for an hour's shift on the old-fashioned ASV Mark II radar display. This was not the familiar rotating disc of today but a vertical band fed by the spidery aerials under both wings and on the hull. Shifts continued changing for the gunners during the dark hours but, what with turns on radar wireless and gun-watch, you were lucky if you got two full hours out of the twenty-four on the bunks amidships. Sunrise was preceded by the false dawn when the crew felt they had 'made it' through the night. Then, as always in these zones, suddenly came the real sunrise.

From the pilot's cockpit, from both windows in Joe's eyrie, and in the blisters, patient eyes scanned the rolling swell, first sparkling turquoise then dappled grey, for any speck of ship or submarine, whale or waterspout. Frustration mingled with resignation born of month after month doing the same fruitless search. At midday Oscar went into the rest area for a snack or a breather when, suddenly at 12.10 Len Eccles' excited voice came over the intercom. 'SUBMARINE AHEAD!' He had sighted a U-boat travelling on the surface at about ten knots on an easterly course.

Oscar hurried back to the flight deck, got a sight of the sub and hit the Klaxon horn button. As the deep harsh sound of 'UGA-UGA-UGA' growled through the aircraft for a few heart-stopping seconds, a surge of anticipation rippled around the crew. 'Action at last!' The next few pages are a blend of the different accounts given by six members of the three aircraft crews concerned; Barnett, Caligari and Pearce of C/259; Lock of A/262; Robin and Oxley of N/265.

By this time the Catalina had passed beyond the U-boat so Oscar made a diving turn to port. The German sailors must also have gone to their gun positions. When Norman as front gunner wriggled his shoulders into the bow turret and rose to his feet, he swung down the top door and swivelled up the .303 Browning with its mounting. Removing the hatch enabled him to stand upright in the considerable slipstream to operate the weapon.

Ahead he could see the small stark silhouette of the submarine against a foam-flecked shimmering sea a mile ahead. When they came within 1,000 yards as practised, he tested the powerful gun with a brief burst. The bullets kicked up a line of spray just short of the U-boat so his estimate of range appeared correct. However, the shots also possibly ricocheted off the sea to clang against the sub's casing and put off the enemy crew's aim. At 800 yards, the effective range, Norman opened fire and continued firing until they had passed the U-boat. Below the attacker three German gunners in brown overalls and flat blue caps could be seen returning the fire and their tracer appeared to Oscar, on his left and right, to be drifting up as if it would never reach the aircraft.

Down at the radio deck Ken Caligari watched the bright streaks weaving past his window. Feeling oddly defenceless he pressed his Morse key that much harder. As the Cat approached the sub the port blister gun opened up, a .500 Browning with more menace in its chatter, and the spent hot shells fell clattering on to the platform below. When the aircraft passed over the U-boat two of the Germans had vanished and one was hanging over the rail showing no signs of life. At the same time Oscar was dropping his six depth-charges. Using the 'Mickey Mouse'[9] box at the controls he activated the DC release gear under the wings which controlled the number of DCs dropped. These six Torpex bombs had pistols set to detonate by water pressure at 25 feet depth. Oscar then approached the U-boat in a 'straight-in, low-level attack from 50 feet at about 45° abaft its starboard beam'[10] and released the whole load at what he judged to be the correct moment. As the aircraft swept away from the submarine, thundering explosions rose behind them in a gigantic eruption of white foam, rocking the plane.

Andy, standing poised with the official camera in the port blister beside the hot gunbarrel, caught a dramatic photograph of the scene. The time was 12.13, their position being 28°40' South and 42°15' East. Looking at this photograph later, Oscar surmised what must have happened at that stage. As the Catalina approached to drop its depth charges above him, Robert Bartels had forced his 300-foot U-boat into an amazing swerve and in Oscar's words 'executed a sharp 90° full port rudder turn' by the time the bombs fell. This meant that the DCs, instead of fatally straddling the submarine, would have exploded along the starboard side.

The result was invisible to the aircrew above who saw huge fountains rising to 100 feet or more with the U-boat at their base. Flight Lieutenant Barnett felt quite confident that the enemy had been destroyed. However, to be absolutely sure he commenced a port-hand

LEFT: Leading Seaman (*Matrosen OberGefreiter*) Richard Dietrich, one of the crew of U/197 (Bartels) sunk by N/265 after damage by C/259 off Madagascar. His home was near Backnang. *(Courtesy of Eric Bakker)*

RIGHT: Depth charges from C/259 exploding round U/197, with the submarine seen at the base. It was crippled and had to remain on the surface, firing at the two Catalinas, till sunk by N/265. *(Photo taken by Anderson, Navigator – courtesy of Capt L.O. Barnett DFC)*

climbing turn so that the port blister gun could continue to bear on the spot. Eagerly looking back the crew watched the white sheets of spray subsiding in a welter of turbulent foam but out of this emerged the outlines of U/197. True, it was listing badly to port but it was moving forward. Oscar, sure his charges had fallen on target, felt a reaction of unbelief and chagrin. The crew heard him say in his dry humorous way 'There goes my gong!'

A chorus of gunners over the intercom urged Oscar to 'have another go at the bastards' or words to that effect and make a couple more passes over the U-boat. Ken Caligari felt that the Skipper, now that his DCs had gone, was 'never going to take foolhardy and unnecessary risks because the U-boat was still very capable and ready to shoot at us.' In fact U/197 remained moving on the surface for half an hour with an increasing list to port.

Bartels sent up fresh gunners to man the anti-aircraft guns and the 10.5 cm gun on the casing (foredeck) also opened up with large shells. They exploded as brown puffs near the wary Cat. At 12.23 the submarine dived on a south-westerly course, leaving oil streaks on the surface – to the intense disappointment of the watchers in the Catalina. As far as they

176

knew the U-boat had been insufficiently damaged, thus permitting its escape. Oscar ordered smoke and flare floats to be dropped and started to circle, waiting for another flying boat to arrive.

UPPER PHOTO: Back-up crew A/262 for sinking of U/197 (as far as is known).
Back row left to right: F/S Watson, WOP/AG; F/S Holder FMA/AG; F/S Bill Walton, F/Eng; F/S Bill Little; F/S Bert Peacock; F/S Phil Williams, WOM/AG
Front row: F/S Jack Green RAAF, Observer; P/O Willie Lock, Captain; F/S H.L. Hammond.
(Courtesy F. Roddick DFC)

LOWER PHOTO: Showing well the Radar Antennae on J/265 Pinkard's Catalina.
(Courtesy Mrs Liz Seymour)

The Catalina selected by Durban to join C/259 was from 262 Squadron, 'A' for Apple (FP 251) commanded by Flying Officer 'Willie' Lock, a pilot of much experience. He had been the first and for a short while the only operating pilot on the squadron when it arrived in South Africa. His crew, now coming towards the end of their overseas tour, had been easing up on operational flying so when the order came through they were delighted. A/262 left for St Lucia in the early afternoon.

'C' for Charlie was still circling the oil streak at 13.23 when U/197 reappeared on the surface unable to remain below. Bartels set a course of 200° and once again sent up his gunners to spit defiance at the Catalina with machine-gun and cannon. He also told his *Funkmaat* or Radio Operator to send off signals about his plight to Lüth and Kentrat further south. The first of U/197's distress calls went out with an inaccurate position but the Navigator, *Obersteuermann* Wilhelm Grässle, a 30-year-old Chief Petty Officer, must have risked his neck in the conning tower to get a sextant reading, because subsequent messages were corrected. The two other U-boats were confused and decided to wait for clarification, so Bartels in his crippled boat heard nothing from them.

Meanwhile FP 235 of 259 Squadron, had been out on anti- submarine patrol and by 12.53 was busy on a Creeping Line Ahead operation in position 29°10"S, 40°40"E. It was commanded by Flight Sergeant David Pitkeathly who was later commissioned. As Flight Lieutenant he was to win the DFC not for one exploit but for a high standard of flying in many difficult situations. His aircraft had picked up 'C' for Charlie's signals at 12.02 and by 13.21 they had been permitted to start a Square Search,[11] endeavouring to home in on C-259's morse messages, but in vain.[12][13]

At this juncture down in the radio cabin, says Caligari, calamity struck. The power packs in the big set started to overheat. Ken had no idea why, though he wryly comments: 'I fancied myself as a red-hot operator but I couldn't have been sending that fast, surely!' The radio packing up would have been a major disaster, resulting in the escape of the U-boat and possibly the loss of their own aircraft on the return journey, as with T/230 earlier in this chapter.

265 SQUADRON JOINS THE ACTION

Now a fourth aircraft comes into the picture, 'N' for Nuts of 265 Squadron (FP 313) droning along on an anti-submarine sweep off the African coast. Its captain – Flying Officer C.E. (Ernie) Robin of the Royal Canadian Air Force, who had started adult life as a railwayman in the Canadian Pacific Railway.

Ernie Robin now starts the prelude to his account:

178

'It had been frustrating – a terrific amount of flying time and about the only thing we did was anti-sub escort to naval vessels and convoys – and not a thing to show for it. So I think everyone was a bit jaded, wondering what we were doing in that part of the world.'

Robin's crew on this occasion was the same as when the crew photograph was taken at Killadeas in Ulster before going overseas. With Robin himself as Captain, his Second Pilot was Sergeant George Lynn. Pilot Officer Bill Wilson, another Canadian, was Observer. All the rest were both airgunners and sergeants, Fred Martin and Dave Baty being Flight Engineers. Stan Angelo was an FMA/AG (Airframe Mechanic) while the others, Johnnie Hall and Stan Oxley, were Wireless Operator/ASV Operator/Airgunners; Nick Carter had the job of Wireless Mechanic/Air gunner – a crew of nine with considerable experience.

We must now look at what was happening with 'C' for Charlie. The other Catalina despatched by Durban, C/262, like Willie Lock's A/262, was unable to pick up Ken Caligari's attack message and admittedly weak homing signals, possibly due to the Dead Space. Instead, 265 Squadron's 'N' for Nuts heard the faint bleeping and contacted Durban. Caligari was then advised that N-265 wanted to home in on them. 'C' for Charlie climbed to a higher altitude to give a better homing signal while remaining just out of range of the U-boat's anti-aircraft fire most of the time.

At 14.46 Bartels sent off the same message to his colleagues with the corrected position 28°40'S and 42°40E adding, '600 miles East of Cape St Lucia. Southerly course KQ8252' (The German grid reference). Lüth picked up the message and commented in his *KriegsTageBuch* or Daily Log: 'This position lies 120 miles to our north. In one and a half hours it will be dark but we shall not reach U/197 by then.'

Sergeant Caligari with his overheating batteries and power packs now managed to make contact with N/265 and from then on sent frequent homing signals. The power packs were giving off strong smells of burning but he succeeded in swapping them over to give them a chance to cool off. The irony is that in the hundreds of flying hours previously and subsequently the Twin Bendix radio installation operated faultlessly. At 16.10 Durban Control requested Ken to transmit on 333 kilocycles, which he did until 16.50. At that moment a speck in the shape of 'N' for Nuts appeared on the horizon and a great cheer went up from Oscar Barnett's crew.

Getting there had not been so simple, as Stan Oxley recalls. Stan had left his South Yorkshire school at 14 to 'go down the pit' in the coalmines near Barnsley. After six years, when the Germans bombed Sheffield, he

Author's painting of Catalina C-259 (Captain F/Lt. L.O. Barnett DFC) which helped sink U-197 on 20.08.43 *(courtesy RAF Museum, Hendon)*

threw this up to volunteer for aircrew. His training included an ASV (Air-to-surface-vessel) radar course so secret that the students were allowed no writing and everything had to be memorised. He joined the crew at Killadeas in Northern Ireland. Now his aircraft was heading towards a submarine but no homing signal could be heard from 'C' and Bill Wilson was navigating by Dead Reckoning alone. The first call had been heard at 12.15 through the alertness of Johnnie Hall who was on the set.

The Captain then requested Durban to be allowed to go to C/259's assistance and was asked to wait. After finally being given permission, Robin's course was set towards the scene of the attack but C/259 could not be found. At 18.02 he came down to the blisters and discussed the problem with Stan Oxley.

'We talked briefly about a previous conversation on homing and I suggested using our D/F loop[14] to get on to our target. Robin agreed and asked me to take over the wireless and, with the help of Bill Wilson, carry out the task of homing in on C-259. I requested C to send his call sign so we could home in. This he did and after considerable time our one fear was of missing the target with darkness getting close. There was much sweat on my whole body.

'Bill kept the two needles in a central position when the call-sign transmissions were being made so that bearings could be read off the scale and passed immediately over the intercom to the Skipper to keep us on course towards C/259. Hurrah! We made contact!'

Robin now continues:

'Bill Wilson was a superb navigator – we knew where we were but had not known where C/259 was. When we arrived C was circling in the area and the sub on the surface making about 10 knots on a southerly course. My first reaction was to set our DCs and head right in, however my crew had a better thought.

'Although the sub was firing at us and had a longer range and better guns our crew thought we should try to silence them first, which we did by circling close and using our 0.5s [in the blister]. The boys were anxious to get their licks [shots] in and they were really accurate. They sprayed the conning towers. It was not long before the crew on the sub decided to clear the bridge. So with that done we were free to make a run in without fear of being shot down. The skipper on the sub was obviously experienced and the first time I made a run over him he did the same thing as he did to Barnett – he turned about 90° just when I was ready to press the button. There was no use dropping my DCs if he was not in range. So another pass and again out-manoeuvred by Bartels. However (and I was getting a lot of

181

U-197's LAST BATTLE

UPPER PHOTO: Members of the crew of N-265 (FP313) which finally sank the U/197, on 20 August 1943, south of Madagascar.
Back row left to right: Sgt F. Martin; Sgt N. Carter; Sgt Stan Oxley (MID); Sgt 'Dave' Baty.
Front row: Sgt 'Stan' Angelo; P/O 'Bill' Wilson; P/O C.E. Robin DFC; Sgt George Lynn; Sgt J. Hall. *(Courtesy of C. Robin DFC.)*

LOWER PICTURE: Author's painting of Robin's gun attack, prior to releasing DCs, with Barnett's Catalina on the horizon. *(Courtesy of Eric Bakker, Rotterdam)* flak from my crew), the third time around Bartels made his mistake and turned straight along our path and I hit the button. I recall we were very low and had to lift up to avoid the conning tower and periscopes.

'Three of the DCs landed right alongside the U-boat and one on the deck. I think the reason there was no debris to speak of was because when he went down, due to the three DCs alongside as he reached 25 feet down the one on his deck would have exploded and smashed everything. We knew we had sunk the U-boat and there was great jubilation on the intercom, everyone yelling. Having seen what happened to C/259 and what happened to me on two runs over the U-boat I decided to keep some in reserve. It only takes one DC to sink a sub so I only dropped four of them. For this action I was criticised when de-briefing at Mombasa but when you are on the scene "the Skipper" always takes responsibility. This is the way I elected to handle it. After circling for a while and checking for debris, as it was getting dark we headed for Tulear where we landed about 21.00 hours.'

Surprisingly in the long engagement neither aircraft had sustained any damage, except for a single dent in one wing. Robin and Barnett left the site of the sinking together leaving a large patch of oil and bubbles on the surface. No survivors were seen. All 67 of the crew had perished.

Oddly enough nine of the dramatic photographs taken of the attacks and of the oil slick were shortly afterwards passed to me. In my role as unofficial Squadron Artist, I was asked to mount them with coloured decorations and notes. It was for a display in the Operations Room to encourage other aircrew to emulate this successful attack. Through the courtesy of Group Captain G.M. (Peter) Bryer, OC 246 Wing, the panel is now preserved in the RAF Museum, Hendon, along with the rest of my wartime sketches.

THE GERMAN SIDE

During my enquiries in Germany about Robert Bartels and other U-boat matters I visited, at Osterholz-Scharmbeck, Bremen, Dr Robert Schridde, Medical Officer of the submarine supply ship *Charlotte Schliemann*, who had known Bartels and admired him. He told me that it had been rumoured in the German Navy that during the action Bartels had run up a flag of surrender (which was always black) but that the RAF had ignored it and sunk him anyway. As this implied a lack of fair play I asked the doctor how the Germans could know, when no one had survived to give an account and he thought it must have been in the radio messages. I therefore made investigations, during which two sources were of great assistance: (1) the Logbooks of both U/181 and U/196. I am indebted to

Colonel J.A. Combrinck of the Documentation Service of the Chief of the South African Defence Force not only for extracts from those two U-boat logs but translations thereof; and (2) the official South African history *War in the Southern Oceans* published in 1961[15] and based on what was by then available from *Kriegsmarine* documents. The book features German interviews including one with *Grossadmiral* Karl Dönitz, Head of the U-boat Service. These histories do not hesitate to criticise Allied actions when necessary but at no point is a surrender message mentioned. Bartels' signals in fact caused a difference of opinion between Lüth and Kentrat, meticulously recorded in their logs. It hinged on whether it would be possible to reach U/197 in time to save her but also on how to find her, what with the confusing positions given, plus the uncertainty of ocean currents and doubt as to what Bartels might do. Lüth was short on fuel and torpedoes and felt that if he hung about he might not have enough to reach France. U/181 and U/196 were still sailing within sight of each other so they used semaphore flags to exchange messages. When Bartels' message came through, Kentrat in his log writes:

'At once I signal to Lüth that on no account must we continue to the south; [we] should cruise to and fro in the present area . . . I alter course to East 90°. The attitude adopted by Lüth is incomprehensible to me. First he informs me by visual signals of his approval, turns east and then signals "It is enough if one of us stays here. I am continuing on my way because of fuel position. You have got more, haven't you? You can catch up with me later."'

Having thus signalled, Lüth turns away and follows a course 215°.' Kentrat's flags begin gyrating furiously, saying:

"This is a matter of life and death . . . You will get your fuel all right"'.

Lüth replies:

'Thank you for fuel but hoses are finished'.

[In fact he had only 35 metres of old fire hose instead of the 90 metres of refuelling hose he would have liked.] Kentrat pleads:

'Captain to Captain. Please course East. I really do not understand you.'

Lüth's final reply faded out as his defiant flags disappeared rapidly into the twilight.

Meanwhile, however, over in the Atlantic, Hartmann in U/198 had passed on Bartels' last distress call to BdU in France and on the insistence of Dönitz' Headquarters both boats turned north and spent two or three days looking in vain for the ill-fated U/197. Despite fuel worries the two submarines eventually made it back to Bordeaux.

U/196 and U/181 reached Bordeaux in mid-October 1943, the former after 31½ weeks and the latter 29½ weeks at sea. (Both were record voyages and testified to good crew management, as outlined in an illuminating lecture by Lüth in Germany)[16]

Nowhere among these widely recorded messages was there any hint suggesting that Bartels intended to surrender. To me this proved reasonably that the victory had been gained by fair means.

Not long after the departure of the two Catalinas, Flying Officer Lock's A/262 arrived at the oil-slick in the gathering gloom. They got there first by superb piloting; second by another feat of Dead Reckoning from the Australian observer Flight Sergeant Jack Green; and third by the skills of their well-built Flight Engineer Bill Walton. 'These two,' says Lock, 'were the backbone of the crew.' On the unlabelled crew photograph we have some names. All were Flight Sergeants – H.L. Hammond, Second Pilot, and Phil Williams who had been a Cranwell apprentice in radar. Others were Bill Little, Bert Peacock and two unnamed gunners, one a rigger. They circled all night in case by some ruse or miracle U/197 had survived. Then they set off home with a natural sense of deep disappointment. Nevertheless they had been part of the ultimate victory and, as is clear during the extensive research done for this history, during any war it is partly the 'luck of the draw' who gets the chances and the credit.

Barnett and Robin were both awarded DFCs, Caligari received the DFM[17] and Oxley an MID. Stan Oxley feels that the Mention in Despatches was also for the crew. Ken Caligari recalls the feeling of disbelief, unreality and immense pride when some weeks later 'Oscar came round to my Congella billet in Durban and said, "His Majesty has been pleased to award you the DFM" – just like that! I did not know what to say or do. It was an absolute bolt from the blue and, though I realise and am happy to say the award was as much to my fellow crew members as to me personally, it was the proudest moment of my life.'

Norman Pearce still asks himself why the U-boat's crew did not abandon ship, especially after Norman had learnt that there were other U-boats in the area. It is indeed an Enigma, but from long study on this event the author's personal impression is that Bartels was hoping to hold out long enough for the other U-boats to reach him or to escape when darkness fell and was confident he could outwit his attackers meanwhile.

CREW LIST FOR U/197 (LT/CDR BARTELS)

Rank	Surname	Forename	Birthdate
BtsMt	Alraun	Gottfried	08.08.20
Fähnr	Aurich	Rudolf	26.04.24
MtrOGfr	Baage	Walter	13.03.24
KptLt	Bartels	Robert	28.04.11
BtsMt	Beil	Ewald	26.09.21
MaschGfr	Bicks	Heinrich	23.03.22
MaschGfr	Brandt	Herbert	29.06.23
MechMt	Brauer	Heinz	20.09.19
MtrOGfr	Burghoff	Heinrich	22.11.23
FkMt	Christ	Robert	16.04.19
MaschOGfr	Czipron	Alfred	20.06.20
MaschOGfr	Demnick	Horst	04.04.23
MtrOGfr	Dietrich	Richard	11.06.22
MaschGfr	Driest	Horst	15.07.23
MtrOGfr	v. Ebner-Eschenbach	Horst	09.07.23
MtrOGfr	Eickelkamp	Artur	18.10.20
MaschMt	Eilzer	Willibald	17.11.21
MaschGfr	Eschmann	Gerhard	27.05.24
Lt (Ing) Sub *lieut.* *lnnt.*	Fabricius	Hans	12.11.20
MaschGfr	Fellhauer	Anton	25.10.22
MechMt	Fleischfresser	Siegfried	19.02.21
MtrOGfr	Foitzik	Heinrich	09.07.17
SanOGfr	Freund	Heinz	19.06.22
OStrm/*Oberbootsman*	Gräßle	Wilhelm	08.12.14
MaschMt	Griessinger	Rudolf	04.08.19
MaschMt	Haase	Günter	28.07.23
OMasch	Haller	Hermann	23.11.14
BtsMt	Hannemann	Heinz	31.03.22
OMaschMt	Hansberg	Konrad	12.04.15
Lt	Haß	Rolf	06.12.21
MaschGfr	Heinke	Horst	21.04.23
MtrHGfr	Jäger	Antonius	18.11.19
MtrOGfr	Jakob	Franz	27.04.22
MarSt Arzt	Junghans *Kapitänleutnant*	Eberhard	06.08.16
MaschOGfr	Justus	Fritz	29.12.21
KKpt(n)(Ing)	Kaschner *Lieutnant (Jng)*	Hanns	01.02.15
MtrOGfr	Klein	Walter	09.05.21
MaschMt	Klima	Albert	03.08.22
OMasch	Klinzmann	Otto	11.01.13
MaschGfr	Krahnast	Adolf	27.05.24
MaschOGfr	Kühnbach	Alois	14.01.22
MaschMt	Kurtz	Otto	08.08.18
MaschOGfr	Lafin	Fred	05.12.23
MaschGfr	Lauble	Josef	24.12.22
OFkMt	Liedtke	Hans	27.07.19
MaschMt	Lorenz	Heinrich	05.02.22
MtrOGfr	Lorenz	Gerhard	06.08.24
MtrOGfr	Maraun	Paul	19.11.24
OLt	Marienfeld	Walter	29.04.17
OMasch	Naujokat	Karl	20.08.13
Lt	v. Oesen	Johann	09.07.17
MechOGfr	Orth	Fritz	25.11.22
MtrOGfr	Pampuch	Georg	19.10.22
MaschOGfr	Petry	Erich	11.07.24
BtsMt	Rainer	Viktor	06.01.00
MechOGfr	Reif	Fritz	30.07.23
Fähnr	Reimler	Karl-Hermann	11.08.21
FkOGfr	Reinbacher	Rudolf	29.12.23
FkOGfr	Reisinger	Heinrich	08.08.24
MaschMt	Schmidt	Karl	19.08.22
MaschOGfr	Schwab	Berthold	04.04.23
MaschMt	Schwalbe	Heinz	26.11.21
MaschGfr	Seifert	Ewald	02.06.21
MaschMt	Sommer	Karl	07.11.19
MaschMt	Weber	Herbert	12.10.18
MaschOGfr	Wegner	Gerhard	02.03.22
MtrOGfr	Wöste	Heinz	26.05.23

Crew of U-197 sunk by RAF on 20 August 1943. *(Courtesy of Horst Bredow)*

Ken Caligari concludes;

'I suppose that we [in C/259] probably felt rather cheated that another aircraft had had to administer the *coup de grâce* to our U-boat, but were elated that our 500 hours of patrol had been truly rewarded. With hindsight the whole episode epitomised what we were about – co-operation between crew members, between aircraft and between squadrons [one could add the Naval Forces, Durban HQ and the coastal radar stations] to patrol and escort without gaps in time or space over vast areas of ocean with determination and good humour. I give a regretful thought to the brave men who went down with their ship.'

N O T E S

[1] The Chatham list, issued at the 50th Anniversary of the Sunderland, by Shorts at Chatham 1987, does not mention EJ 131 but dates DW 131's crash as 27th March 1943.

[2] *The Short Sunderland*, Chaz Bowyer (Aston) 1989 says the crash on 27th March 1943 was that of EJ 131

[3] D/F Radar – Direction Finding stations.

[4] circuits and bumps – practice landings and take-offs for any aircraft

[5] material courtesy of Herr Horst Bredow, *Stiftung Traditionsarchiv Unterseeboote*. Museum, Cuxhaven, Germany. In all U-boats the name, such as U-Bartels, was used at times instead of the number, e.g. U/197

[6] courtesy: Chris Lowe, U-boat Adviser, Nottingham

[7] courtesy: Backnang Town Council via Mrs G.B. Nichols, Chelmsford Civic Centre

[8] on the step – where the forward part of the hull became 'stepped' up to the rear section, making take-off easier.

[9] Mickey Mouse – the depth charge selector box also known as intervalometer.

[10] 45° abaft its starboard beam – nautical phrase indicating (supposing the sub were heading North) an approach from 45° south of East

[11] Creeping Line Ahead – back and forth along a line that gradually creeps forward

[12] Square Search – flying round a square that moves steadily forward

[13] The reason why so many U-boat messages and homing signals from C/259 were not picked up may have been the existence of a well-known radio 'Dead Space' round South Madagascar.

[14] D/F Loop – circular rotating aerial on top of a Catalina wing between the

engines for Radio Direction Finding.

[15] *War in the Southern Oceans*, Turner, Gordon-Cumming, Betzler (Oxford University Press), Cape Town 1960

[16] *Problems of Leadership in a Submarine*, a booklet giving the lecture by Commander Wolfgang Lüth, via Karl Wahnig, U-boat Museum, London.

[17] In Andrew Hendrie's *Flying Cats* the Wireless Operator who homed in N/265 is given as Sgt Metcalfe, not a crew member, instead of Sergeant Caligari. As DFMs were rare in the Indian Ocean, I am glad to put the record straight. Correction of any similar errors in this book will be appreciated.

CHAPTER 7

SUPPLY SHIP HUNTING

'From the tanker's mast suddenly we heard the lookout's yell. "Torpedo running on the starboard quarter!" He was just too late. No way could we avoid that steel fish. Yet the dear God held his protecting hands around us. At that moment an unruly sea threw the tanker's bow over to port and the torpedo slid harmlessly past to lose itself in the distance.'[1]

This was no British or neutral tanker which had just escaped being blasted into a raging inferno. It was the German supply ship *Charlotte Schliemann* – a *Mutterschiff* to a family of U-Boats in the Indian Ocean during 1943. She was taking the dangerous passage from Tokyo to Singapore and the torpedo came from an Allied submarine in the South China Sea. The *Schliemann*, sounding the alarm, threw herself into a violent zigzag course and managed to shake off the enemy. She then moved into the Indian Ocean and spent the rest of 1943 making secret rendezvous with various U-boats and refuelling them.

When, in 1942, Germany's tactics changed following losses in the Atlantic, *Admiral* Dönitz decided to supply his submarines from converted tanker-ships.

It was vital to be able to pick up more torpedoes or fuel or food in mid-ocean without having to trail all the weary way back to Penang and perhaps become stranded en route. Of the four tankers chiefly used by the Germans for this service in the Indian Ocean the most notorious was the *Charlotte Schliemann*, the other being the *Brake*. The *Quito* and the *Bogota* supply ships were mainly used as transports. *Charlotte Schliemann* had been cradled in Denmark in 1929 and compared with modern super-tankers she was a shrimp of 7,747 tons, her overall length being only 142 metres.

Now, under a German commander, Captain Rothe, with a crew of 42 sailors and 48 soldiers she carried over 300 tons of diesel and a large supply of torpedoes, ammunition, food, fresh water and other necessities for her U-boat customers. The Ship's Doctor, the late *Marine Assistenzart*

Dr Robert Schridde,[2] assisted me greatly in the writing of this chapter through his own notes and crew lists and by lending me Otto Mielke's booklet quoted at the beginning which was kindly translated for me by Ms Beate Hohlmann through Bob Dutton.

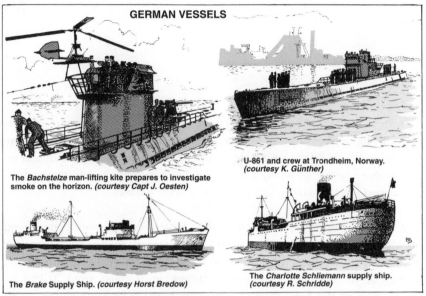

GERMAN VESSELS

The *Bachstelze* man-lifting kite prepares to investigate smoke on the horizon. *(courtesy Capt J. Oesten)*

U-861 and crew at Trondheim, Norway. *(courtesy K. Günther)*

The *Brake* Supply Ship. *(courtesy Horst Bredow)*

The *Charlotte Schliemann* supply ship. *(courtesy R. Schridde)*

The *Charlotte Schliemann's* most daring rendezvous took place from about 21 to 26 June 1943. Considering that the Germans knew half the Royal Air Force and a good part of the Royal Navy would be keeping an eye open for a supply ship, it sounds like madness to assemble six of Germany's crack eastern U-boat captains on the same day for a luncheon party aboard the tanker while their boats were refuelling. Each of the six commanders was a holder of the Knights Cross, one of the highest decorations in the Kriegsmarine. Each had sunk several (in Lüth's case many) Allied and neutral ships.

The list of this elite reads: Lieutenant Commander Gysae of U/177; Commander Lüth of U/181; Lieutenant Commander Bartels of U/197; Captain Hartmann of U/198; Commander Kentrat of U/196; Commander Dommes in U/178. All of these feature in other chapters. They comprised the whole strength of the U-boat force in the Indian Ocean at that time and would have made a prize beyond the wildest dreams of the RAF or RN.

Those submariners who were not on watch on the six U-boats were allowed to row the inflatables across to the tanker and stretch their legs on its deck. They were given a couple of flasks of beer but best of all the chance to stand under a shower. The Captains and their Chief Engineers, who included *Leitender Ingenieur* Karl-Heinz Wiebe, Knights Cross holder of U/178, wined (moderately) and dined (to the full) at a luncheon below decks. Herr Wiebe tells me it was such a heavy lunch he had to find a cabin bunk on which to sleep it off.

UPPER LEFT: Grand Admiral Karl Dönitz, head of the U-boat service, later of the German Navy. *(Courtesy Kevin Matthews)*

UPPER RIGHT: Commander Wolfgang Luth, of U/181 who sank 47 ships, many in the Indian Ocean. *(Courtesy Kevin Matthews)*

LOWER LEFT: Chief Engineer K-H, Wiebe of U/178. *(Courtesy K.H. Wiebe)*

LOWER RIGHT: *Maschinen Maat* (Engineer Petty Officer) Albert Ridder of U/862. *(Courtesy A. Ridder)*

It must have been near dusk when Dr Schridde the ship's MO leaned over the side and saw light streaming from Wiebe's porthole, inviting any passing enemy. Wiebe says that the good doctor came down below, slapped his face to wake him and pointed out the danger. The submarines were meantime under the command of experienced First Officers and Engineers. Lüth's turn came on 23 June but he complained to his crew that the supply of Japanese meat and vegetables was not enough for the increased length of his patrol and he could get no spare parts for his air compressor. After four days of being re-supplied, the U-boats scattered to their grim task.

Through the ULTRA decoding of German messages our Naval Intelligence (Sigint or Y-Service) in the ocean was well aware of the *Charlotte Schliemann's* activities in 1943 but unable to act against her. In one series of sorties Squadron Leader D.B. Fitzpatrick AFC (now Air Commodore), who during 1944 commanded 209 Squadron, was briefed about enemy activity south of Madagascar, involving the use of supply ships.

In April 1943 Fitzpatrick led four Catalinas down to Mauritius where there were frustrating delays and false alarms. On the last occasion he flew in Flight Lieutenant Ken Murray's boat, FP 289.[3] Finally they were recalled without having had the opportunity to have a go at this important target.

From June to August 1943 the six U-boat captains and their colleagues sank 35 ships, July's tonnage alone being 97,214. ULTRA decrypts continued to reveal refuelling taking place with the *Schliemann* and the *Brake*, but it was mid-January 1944 before a convenient opportunity arose. Using the German ENIGMA code which the ULTRA system could decode, BdU sent orders now, which compromised the *Charlotte Schliemann*. . A large operation was mounted by the Eastern Fleet's Commander- in-Chief, Admiral Somerville, called OPERATION THWART, to trap the tanker at last.

From Ceylon came the cruisers HMS *Newcastle, Suffolk* and *Kenya*; from Aden the Aircraft Carrier HMS *Battler* along with HMS *Bann*; the destroyer HMAS *Nepal* with an Armed Merchant Cruiser HMS *Canton* set out from Durban. Finally from East Africa came an eventual total of a dozen Catalinas from three squadrons, 209, 259 and 265. With their enormous range, the latter would provide the eyes of the fleet along with the nine Swordfish of 834 Squadron on the Escort Carrier, HMS *Battler*. 834 also had 6 Seafire fighters, and later Grumman Martlets.

An article about HMS *Battler*[4] mentions that:

'the heat on deck was often fierce and conditions below decks sordid and stifling although the many openings in the hangar made the work there tolerable and the elevator was lowered to catch the breeze.'

In the tropics bugs of many varieties multiplied in the mess decks.

HMS *Canton* also had eyes in the shape of Kingfisher float planes. These Vought OS2U-3 American catapult reconnaissance aircraft had a single radial Pratt and Whitney engine and a single large float beneath them with two small outrigger floats under the wingtips (see plate in appendix "British Aircraft"). Their top speed was 171 mph but they had a range of nearly 1,000 miles and were extremely useful in assessing situations. They were recovered by riding up on to a sled, towed behind the ship.

HMS *Canton* was sent with them to search the southern part of the area in which ULTRA had indicated the rendezvous might take place. This was probably the last occasion in the war when catapult aircraft were used for an enemy operation.

On 23 January 1944 HMS *Canton's* Kingfishers made extensive searches and found – nothing. Two more days in January were equally fruitless. The RAF had no better luck. Flight Lieutenant Harry Laister, a second pilot, recalls that his Catalina N-209 (VA 715), captained by an Australian, Flight Lieutenant 'Alf' Cummings RAAF, flew approximately 20-hour patrols on 23, 26 and 28 January without seeing anything.

HMS *Kenya* sighted possible smoke on one day and later found oil tracks but again drew a blank. It was concluded that the *Charlotte Schliemann* had once again fooled everyone and refuelled a U-boat on 29 January. The operation, designed to 'thwart' the enemy, had been itself thwarted.

ULTRA decrypts from U-boat messages however still indicated that further refuelling would take place. Four U-boats would meet the *Mutterschiff* on 11 and 12 February. OPERATION CANNED was then decided on, to 'can' the wily tanker. One of the four submarines, we know now, was U/532 under Captain (Junior Grade) Otto-Heinrich Junker, born in Freiburg in 1905, a senior Captain who had joined the Navy when he was 19. At the age of 38 he had set out in command of U/532 from Lorient in mid-1943 and had sunk seven ships already. The boat was a IXD40 built in Hamburg.

Junker was now due to meet the *Charlotte Schliemann* and did so on 11 February 1944. One of the crew, Josef Wieser, a former steersman (not navigator) on the boat now lives in Wargrave, near Reading. After being a prisoner-of-war Josef remained on in this country, married an English girl and settled over here. He has kindly told me much of what happened on the U/852 just as Dr Schridde did for events on the tanker.

Because of warnings from BdU that the area was not safe, the U-boat and the tanker delayed refuelling and moved further south.

The Commander-in-Chief Eastern Fleet, Admiral Sir James Somerville, in Ceylon had a choice of three possible rendezvous areas to deal with, deduced from ENIGMA messages. He arranged another operation in which RAF Catalinas from Mauritius would search the three areas with the cruiser HMS *Newcastle* and the destroyer HMS *Relentless* in support at two of the areas. All surface ships were ordered to keep clear. The command of the RAF operation was given to 23-year-old Squadron Leader John Stacey . He writes:[5]

'I returned to Ceylon [from Mombasa as Flight Commander with a 205 Squadron detachment] in February 1944 and was told that I was to go on special, temporary duty to take part with the Royal Navy and, hopefully, sink a submarine "mother" ship, i.e. a refueller and supplier. I took passage to Mauritius in the Flagship, the cruiser HMS *Newcastle*. I was to command the RAF element of the operation, comprising some four flying boats from Mombasa. At this stage the operation was to be predominantly RN with a small element of RAF support.'

Squadron Leader J.N. Stacey at Gibraltar with 202 Squadron, standing between F/O Hamilton, Observer, on left who was 6' 5" tall, and F/Lt Melville-Jackson, Pilot, on right, who was 6'3". *(courtesy AVM Stacey)*

'On arrival in Mauritius I found the Catalinas were under the command of my old friend Squadron Leader Pete Seymour. I cannot recall the details but the first date when the mother ship, later known to be the *Charlotte Schliemann* and which I shall now call the CS was to have been active with a submarine passed with no activity. A second date about 10 days later became a possibility but most of the Navy had other commitments and only the destroyer HMS *Relentless* could remain. The second stage thus became predominantly RAF with only *Relentless* to deal with CS.' [*Newcastle* was searching an adjacent area.]

'The next complication was the threat of a cyclone with winds forecast up to some 80 mph. By this time we had some 12 Catalinas from East Africa and the Air Officer Commanding then in Nairobi instructed me to evacuate them all. I realised that to do this would make it impossible for them to return in time to operate against the CS when it was next expected to succour a submarine. Pete Seymour and I had operated in the Shetlands early in the war, in 1939 and early 1940, and knew that with proper precautions and storm crews aboard, the Catalinas would easily ride out 80 mph winds in the sheltered harbour of Grand Port. I left these arrangements in the capable hands of Pete Seymour and signalled Nairobi of my decision.

'I must now explain a little of the Indian Ocean organisation. Mauritius and the Western Indian Ocean from where all the Catalinas came, were under the command of the Air Officer in Nairobi. To ensure proper co-ordination of all maritime areas in the whole Indian Ocean area, however, overall control of them was vested in the Air Officer Commanding No 222 Group in Ceylon (Air Marshal Sir Albert "Dusty" Durstan). Hence my appointment for this duty was by him. However, responsibility for the safety of his flying boats remained with the AOC in Nairobi.

'When told I was keeping the boats in Mauritius, the AOC in Nairobi sent a long signal to my boss in Ceylon, copy to me, saying I had disobeyed his orders and would therefore be solely responsible for any losses or damage resulting from the cyclone to his boats! Even at the highly confident age of 23 this left me feeling rather uncomfortable but my spirits were restored by my splendid master in Ceylon who responded with a short signal to the effect "I appointed Stacey for this task and have complete confidence in his judgement" – to my mind an epic example of good leadership at long range.

'The boats survived the cyclone but we could only get two ready for the expected first meeting of CS with a submarine and there were two possible venues; one about 1000 miles east of Mauritius and the other the same distance south-east and my decision was whether to send one Catalina to each area or to provide wider cover for one or the other.

UPPER PHOTO: Naval exercises with destroyers HMS *Dido*, HMS *Sirius* and HMS *Orion*. *(Courtesy of J. Foxon)*

LOWER PHOTO: The real thing. Destroyer HMS *Relentless* on her way south to attack the *Charlotte Schliemann*, February 1944. *(Courtesy of R.A.P.H. Dutton DFC)*

'Just before she sailed, the Captain of the *Relentless*, Lieutenant Commander Fell RN, said he would head for a mid-point between the areas and he doubted whether he could intercept before a sighting aircraft had to leave because of fuel shortage. It seemed to me that a Catalina would be fair exchange for the CS and I arranged that a sighting Catalina would remain in contact and ditch in the area if weather conditions were favourable – the decision would be at the aircraft captain's discretion. After my previous exchange over aircraft safety with AOC Nairobi I decided not to tell anyone of this arrangement!

'I well remember examining the sky to decide whether to send the two available Catalinas one to each area or both to one or the other. The cyclone had passed to the south and if affecting either rendezvous area would generate seas making CS/submarine contact impossible. We had no local meteorological service but I felt the sky suggested southward movement of the cyclone and that the east rendezvous was the better bet and accordingly despatched both aircraft there.'

Leaving the commander of the operation pondering his next moves we now turn to what was happening with the Catalina squadrons, on which official records are few. I am grateful, to Mrs Eleanor (Liz) Seymour for letting us use the notebooks and photographs of her husband, the late Air Commodore Seymour which throw much light on the operation.[6] Besides being an efficient Flight Commander of 265 Squadron Pete Seymour was popular with all ranks and characterised by a Canadian Captain as 'the finest Englishman he ever met.'

Well before the final scene two Catalinas of 265 Squadron, M-265 captained by Flying Officer Joe Pack and K-265 under Flying Officer Smith, were sent down from the Squadron's base at Diego Suarez in the north of Madagascar to Mauritius on 16 January 1943. The two aircrews and the maintenance gangs they had brought with them had been told that Grand Port RAF station, down the coast, would not be ready for them till the following day. Their heavy kit and tools were sent on ahead by road in two lorries along with the native servants.

At the RAF station there was no sign of the lorries, apparently they were stuck in the mud. Sheer chaos awaited them at Grand Port Camp. The caretaker who was supposed to be getting the place ready was nowhere to be found and said to be 'hung-over' from his usual Sunday binge. He had all the keys! The 'Officers Mess' was jammed to the ceiling with stores. Beds, pillows and mattresses tottered skywards in drunken heaps; chairs fought with tables for space. On a mountain of tents and mosquito nets giddy piles of basins (large) and basins (small) jostled with utensils (kitchen) and cutlery (airmen, for the use of). In contrast the

265 Squadron officers, Diego Suarez, 1944, with their mixed origins and nicknames.

Front row left to right: (Seymour version) 'Joe' Pack (Eng); 'Doc' Pattinson (Eng); Padre Cross (Eng); 'Pete' Seymour (Eng, Flight Commander); W/Cdr 'Fats' Louw (S. Afr., CO); 'Stan' Jackson (Eng); 'Sandy' Sanders (Eng); 'Paddy' Lawson (Irish); 'Kip' Phillips (Can).
Middle row: 'Mac' Cameron (Aus); 'Cock' Robin DFC (Can); 'Mac' McKendrick (Scots); 'Mrs Smith' (Eng); 'Bob' Bower (Can); 'Tug' Wilson (Eng); 'Jack' Barber (Eng).
Back row: 'Bid' Bidwell (Can); 'Joe' Pinkard (Aus); 'Bob' Pow (Eng); 'Bill' Graham (Aus); 'Dobby' Dobson (Eng); 'Bob' Vercelli (Nat.It.) 'Round-the-bend' Birnie (Can). *(Courtesy Mrs 'Liz' Seymour)*

Sergeants Mess and Airmens Mess were stripped clean as a bosun's whistle.

When it came to rigging beds at night 28 were missing from the list. The telephone exchange, on which everything depended in an operation like this, had no operators. Luckily by evening the two mud-bound lorries arrived laden with Mauritian cooks, houseboys and dhobi 'boys' (all men with families) plus the rations and the equipment so desperately needed to service the aircraft. The Head Boy, Gus, was a good English speaker and organiser and within half an hour,' says Seymour, 'had his mob cracking and cleaning out the mess and brewing cups of tea' (also essential to any RAF operation), making a fire of broken-up petrol boxes for cooking the meals.

The airmen meanwhile having exhausted all the possibilities were optimistically shaking the gaudy tropical moths out of their blue uniforms and polishing monsoon-mouldy brass buttons in anticipation of a night out. It was then decided to 'get the hell out of it' for a while and 'liberty runs'[7] were organised for those wishing to go out to Curepipe, a nearby small town, and explore the amenities, whether feminine, alcoholic or cinematic.

Flying Officer Pack[8] now summarises his experience of that time:

'We were away on the 19 January for an anti-sub/anti-shipping patrol to the east of Mauritius of 18 hours' duration. During the next few days we flew four further patrols from approximately 18 hours to over 20 hours in duration, 1,000 miles into the Indian Ocean and returning. I notice in my logbook I describe them as Blockade-runner Patrols [for secrecy's sake].'

This was about the time, 19 January, that naval units detached from the Eastern Fleet arrived bringing Squadron Leader Stacey and the Flag Lieutenant from HMS *Newcastle*. With them Pete Seymour visited the RN signal station at Floreal. John Stacey decided to direct operations from the RAF Signal Station at Grand Port while Seymour would direct flying from Tombeau Bay. On 21 January while Stacey briefed the aircrews stressing security another Catalina arrived, 'N' of 209 Squadron under the Australian, F/O Cumming.

At this moment came the minor 'Cyclone Flap', previous to the major cyclone described by AVM Stacey in his memorandum for us. On the 22nd M/265 set out on patrol but had to return to base owing to unflyable weather in the patrol area. Joe Pack recalls how disappointing it was 'to turn back 15 minutes or so before reaching our datum point[9]. We had been flying at 500 feet when the complete horizon disappeared in blackness.'

These cyclones not only inconvenienced aircraft, but could cause terrible damage ashore. In the great cyclone of January 1945, the RAF camp at Grand Port with its tin roofs was flattened as depicted by Corporal Ted Foster, of Leamington Spa. He joined the RAF in 1937 as a Boy Entrant and was a 265 Squadron photographer, sent to photograph the damage.

Later on the cyclone flap came through from 246 Wing at Mombasa ordering 'IMMEDIATE EVACUATION OF MAURITIUS BY THE CATALINAS.' In this case the wind for several days held a steady seven knots south-easterly and the real cyclone only came afterwards. Over the next two weeks further Catalinas arrived from 209, 259 and 265 Squadrons until there were twelve available for the next refuelling rendezvous of the *Charlotte Schliemann*. Some moved out again but were reassembled. Squadron Records, for once, wrote a long effort which ended thus.[10]

'Twenty-four hours after the aircraft arrived the missing cyclone turned up and caught them all on the water. The wind sprang up unexpectedly during the evening and by dusk was blowing a steady thirty knots from the South-East. Gale crews, three per aircraft, were put aboard in daylight to fight the storm for fifty-three hours. It was impossible to relieve them, even the replenishment of food and water stocks proved to be a life and death struggle. For half of one night engines were run at moorings in an effort to prevent "snatching" at the buoy.

'The cyclone, although it obeyed all the cyclonic laws (the wind swung round through 210° in four hours), was a comparatively minor one. It was estimated that the centre passed across the north-east corner of the island yet at Grand Port the wind never exceeded 60 knots. All the aircraft came through undamaged though rendered unserviceable temporarily through rain and sea water entering the magnetos.'

During this period, just before the cyclone struck, Flight Lieutenant R.A.P.H. 'Bob' Dutton and his crew took off in 259 Squadron's 'F' for Freddie (FP 133) possibly with a second Catalina, on what proved to be an historic mission. Because of the dearth in official reports it is fortunate that Bob retained the copy given to him of his official report handed in at Nairobi on his return from Mauritius. He comments: 'Going out we flew high to one side of the cyclone which we knew would be in our path on our return.'

In this condensed version of Bob's four-page report, we learn that Catalina 1b FP133 F/259 took off from Grand Port, Mauritius at 05.25 hrs on 11 February 1944. The crew comprised F/Lt Dutton (Captain – South African); F/Sgt Fred Palmer, Pilot (a West-countryman possibly from Somerset); and F/O Davis Pilot; F/O Seddon (Australian), Navigator; W/O Scott RCAF Engineer (a tall, handsome Canadian); Sgt 'Jock' McKenna (also RCAF), FME; F/S Stewart, WOM (a Highlander) Wireless operators F/Sgts 'Charley' Hamill (from Glasgow way), Maclean (West Coast, Scotland) and Royle. (The last five would also be Air Gunners). Bill Kirkup, the Rigger/Air Gunner, who described his crew above, actually was very disappointed to miss this trip. He had completed his tour of 'ops' and was due to return to England. 'At 1137 hrs destroyer HMS *Relentless* was sighted about 12 miles on the port beam.'

Dutton's crew at 2,000 feet then exchanged signals by Aldis lamp in Morse which was difficult when the destroyer was tossing on a heavy sea. It took 40 minutes to establish that the aircraft's latitude had corresponded exactly with that calculated by the ship but that a small ground error had crept into the Catalina's longitude reckoning due to several factors. Dutton accepted the Navy's estimate as correct, which proved vital when homing the destroyer in on the tanker later that evening. 'F' for Freddie moved off and between one and two o'clock went into cloud cover at 1,500 feet. ASV (Air to Surface Vessel) beam was then switched on as they were deliberately blind.

'[In the small radar cubbyhole] a constant watch was kept chiefly on the beam aerials with a change to homing aerials for 10 seconds approximately every five minutes. At 1442 hrs a blip was picked up 14 degrees to port on the beam aerial. Through a break in the clouds a ship was then sighted, identified with binoculars as a tanker, of approximately 9,000 tons. At 1450 a submarine could be seen on the tanker's port quarter, closing it from half a mile at about six knots.'

Neither vessel seemed to be aware of the aircraft. The Catalina switched on IFF (the Identification Friend or Foe transponder) to assist in homing the destroyer later.

Dutton's crew on F/259-FP133 (seen below) which tracked down the *Charlotte Schliemann* on 11 February 1944.
Back row left to right: Maclean Hamill, Royle all WOP/AGS; Stewart WOM/AG
Front row: Scott RCAF, F/Eng; Seddon DFC, RAAF; Dutton DFC, Captain; Davies, 2nd Pilot. *(Both courtesy of Bob Dutton DFC)*

Five minutes after this the Catalina shattered the radio silence to send off a sighting report. '1 TANKER, 1 SUB.' After a more detailed report Dutton broke cloud cover at 1530 five miles away from the tanker. The submarine at that time was one and a half miles away from its supplier. 'Confusion ensued.' This was putting it mildly as we shall see.

Under Captain Rothe the *Charlotte Schliemann* was now sailing southward with its latest companion, U/532, on the surface a mile or so away. Josef Wieser recalls what happened.[11] His captain, Junker, had commanded U/33. Among its other tasks, U/532 was one of the blockade-runners, and Junker had commanded it skilfully since November 1942. Shortly after this he received the *Deutsche Kreuz* in Gold.[12]

In the early afternoon of the 11th, Junker had been paddled across to the tanker in the small rubber dinghy to confer with Rothe. Josef Wieser had been steering the submarine on the morning shift and was now on a standby. However, when the Captain was away from the ship, in case of any trouble the 'Action Stations' klaxon had to be sounded. If the order came to dive Josef would press the button for the forward hydroplanes to tilt down so the submarine would dive at a 25° to 30° angle. Any steeper might cause the acid in the ranks of huge batteries (each the size of two large suitcases) to spill and cause damage to the ship and crew.

However, no order came to dive and in half an hour Junker returned to the ship. At 1611, German local time, the *Charlotte Schliemann* sighted a Catalina and sent off the agreed signal, 'Submarine Fritz, Fritz' expecting to see U/532 open fire on the aircraft as arranged. Instead, as Dutton's report stated, 'the submarine rapidly increased speed and did a running dive, at the same time turning on to an easterly course.' Junker's reasoning may have been that where there is an aircraft the Navy will be hot foot behind and that there was no point in shooting down a single flying boat, an action which could delay or damage the U-boat. As we saw, Dutton was not in a position to depth charge the submarine and he kept a respectful distance from the tanker's battery of guns. Dutton challenged the tanker to identify herself but she gave a deliberately garbled reply. Then, until Dutton set course for base at 1630, hours the tanker shifted direction and finally made off towards the East hoping to lose herself in the oncoming night.

HMS *Relentless*, meanwhile, had not been idle. In an exchange of radio signals with the Catalina, Lieutenant Commander Fell used Squadron Leader Stacey's agreement to request that, if conditions were suitable, the aircraft should use up its petrol circling the spot and then ditch to be picked up (hopefully) later by the destroyer. Bob Dutton took one look at the waves and the 20-foot swell in mid-ocean with a fast strengthening wind of the approaching cyclone and decided that there was a very high risk of the aircraft being broken up on the water even if she could have made a safe landing.

He and one other member of the crew were single but the rest of his crew were married, some with children. 'To hell with that,' said the skipper, 'we will go back.' The *Relentless*, then at high speed hunted down her quarry in the ever-decreasing circles of a St Veno's curve and reached the *Charlotte Schliemann* at midnight.

> Squadron Leader Stacey in the meanwhile was seeing it from another angle. He writes: 'The sighting report stated the sea was unfavourable for a landing and that they would have to return before being relieved. Pete Seymour had worked miracles in bringing the remaining aircraft to readiness and advised that he could despatch some six more aircraft at half-hour intervals starting in about two hours time. He and the Catalinas were at Grand Port while I was on the other side of Mauritius at Port Louis where the communications were located, about two hours by car.
>
> 'I did not have time to work out search patterns and get over and brief crews so I told Pete to get aircraft off as soon as they became available and I would signal search instructions to each aircraft in the air.
>
> 'Disaster then struck! Having worked out search patterns for all aircraft, we were unable to contact the first aircraft which had then been airborne for some two hours. We then tried the others with similar lack of success. We kept at it and finally contacted the first aircraft when it had been airborne for some five hours. We later discovered the Navy were well aware of a signals "flat spot" some 100 to 700 miles east of Mauritius but this was little comfort when I had sent off six aircraft with no operating instructions and was unable to contact any!'

Flight Sergeant 'Dickie' Brown, another WOM, recalls being in the first of four Catalinas that followed Dutton. The aircraft was B-259 (FP 247) skippered by Captain Nick Honey SAAF, another South African, who later lost his life on 30 January 1945 during night flying practice on Lake Umsingazi with 262 Squadron. Unlike Dutton who carried no extra tanks, Honey had overload tanks added. They were told by the Navy that when they reached the tanker, 'Just go on sending call signs till your fuel runs out.' 'What then?' 'Oh just land near the tanker and wait till we come.' 'And be blown out of the water? * * *' One can imagine the RAF comments. Honey's aircraft, like that of 'Alf' Cummings, flew for many hours till they received the signal diverting them to an extended Y patrol after which they turned for base.

Fortunately the first mission that Squadron Leader Stacey had sent off, Dutton's aircraft, proved to be all that was needed. Dr Schridde, at his home near Bremen, recalled for me much of what happened that night. There was little hope on board the tanker that they would be able to escape during the night.

So the ship's engines were running at full power, all weapons stayed fully manned, the Radio Operator scanned the airwaves and those on watch in sou'westers raked the black horizon with their long Zeiss binoculars. Otto Mielke's booklet describes what occurred then. Half an hour after midnight the watch noticed a tiny line of phosphorescence near the horizon.

> "'Enemy cruiser at 220 degrees."
> "'ALARM !"
> "'Steer 40 degrees to starboard.'"

Their only hope was that the destroyer might not have seen them, blacked out as they were, but that was not to be. The Germans did not realise how powerful an advantage radar was proving to have. The enemy ship turned and came haring after them with all the 35 knots it was capable of.

> "'Clear the lifeboats !"
> "'Set the scuttling charges !"
> "'Remove the oil tank covers!'"

It could be seen now that this was not a cruiser but a destroyer and it tried to engage the tanker broadside on, but for a while the old girl managed to show, if not a clean pair of heels, at least a less vulnerable stern. At one a.m. on the 12 February 1944 the last orders were given.

> "'Full astern. Stop engines. Engage the explosives. Fires out. Abandon ship!'"

Suddenly with no warning the destroyer opened fire from two miles away with its six-inch guns at the port side of the tanker. Meanwhile the crew were lowering lifeboats on the starboard side. *Relentless* also fired off her torpedoes. A brilliant detonation rocked the supply ship and she began to go down. The Radio Officer Mosel and *Oberleutnant zur See* Wimmel, the First Officer, were the last two to leave and just escaped being sucked down as the ship foundered. Behind them the whole ship exploded with the scuttling charges and the destroyer's torpedoes. The mother ship that had evaded the Allies for so long came to a brave end.

The well-named *Relentless*, with H-85 painted large on her sides, went round picking up the men who were in the boats or struggling in the black oily shark-infested waters. Dr Schridde, told me how he and the Captain and 39 others had been taken aboard in the darkness. Few casualties had occurred. However, at this moment Lieutenant Commander Fell was informed of a possible U-boat sighting and to avoid the possibility of them all being torpedoed, the destroyer suddenly moved off. The rest of the crew succeeded in getting into four lifeboats.

In the next month two of the lifeboats managed to make it, one with 12 men to land on the shores of Madagascar. Another with ten men had a gruelling 27-day voyage, like those known by many other torpedo survivors, till they were picked up by the *African Prince*, a British freighter, near Mananjori, South Madagascar. Alfred Moser, the Radio Officer and *Oberleutnant* Wimmel, the First Officer, were in this boat and the former has left us a long, gripping account of which this is a brief summary.

The men who had found refuge in the lifeboat were covered in diesel fuel from the centre of the massive oil spill. They found it fried their skin in the burning sun. They managed the superhuman task of turning over the heavy upturned lifeboat which proved to have little food and water. This was doled out in tiny amounts by Wimmel who also navigated. The rest took turns in rowing and in baling out the leaking lifeboat. At night all felt frozen by the waves washing over them.

With water and bread they were given a little corned beef and lemon juice but Moser had swallowed so much diesel that he could barely eat the tiny scraps. Then with raging thirst and crusted mouth it was again hard for the men to eat unless they gargled (and sometimes drank) sea-water first. As the days went by, with swollen joints and pus-covered legs, they fell into sullen silence. A little rain falling was hard to catch and often spoilt with salt water. Death became first thinkable, then desirable as hope dwindled. Misery mounted and food stocks shrank. They made a pact that if no rescue appeared in three days they would spread the sail over the boat and lie under it to sleep for ever.

On the third day a shout of 'Land ahoy!' was greeted with disbelief but the horizon crystallised into blue mountains. Then the appearance of a British-flagged steamer nearby caused some confusion and a desire to escape to the possibly neutral shore. Sanity prevailed, however, and they were helped up on to the deck of the *African Prince,* given sea-rescue parcels of new clothes, and treated with great kindness for some days before being passed on into captivity. Only one of the ten had died but the other two boats bearing 20 men failed to reach any shore. Wimmel's group joined the others in a POW Camp at Londiani, Kenya, where Dr Schridde was allowed to act as Medical Officer for the camp, supplied with his own car and freedom to go into Nairobi to fetch drugs. Now, how did Bob Dutton's Catalina make it back?

We left Flight Lieutenant Dutton and his crew starting on the homeward leg to Mauritius. When they first sighted the tanker the fuel consumption had been cut back to a minimum and to conserve what petrol they had left, the return trip was flown at 1,500 feet, although there was still some headwind at that level. This dropped to eight knots for the last 400 miles. The main trouble was the cyclone they would now have to face. Bob knew there was no way he could get round it or over it so he took the aircraft 'down on the deck' as they approached it. Here the visibility was good and they encountered a 'cushion' of rather compressed air on the sea's surface. Bob writes later: 'The volume of air is diffused but still the densest, heaviest air drops to the bottom giving this cushion effect.'

Flying through the cyclone the pilots were already very tired but could not take a rest and switch over to GEORGE – too bumpy. As they flew towards the cyclone's centre they experienced severe buffeting with winds in one direction; they found dead calm at the eye of this aerial whirlpool and again more tossing as they flew through 120-mph winds coming from the opposite direction. All that could be seen of the sea was a churning mass. Thereafter the force of the cyclone gradually subsided.

'Landfall was made at GRAND PORT at 02.05 hours (D) 12.2.1944 and the aircraft was "waterborne" [in the time-honoured expression used by flying boat pilots everywhere] at 02.20 hours after 20 hours 55 minutes in the air. Fuel remaining was 120 gallons.'

Out of 1,450 gallons this was a very worrying residue. Thus ended Dutton's report.

Several sequels and comments by Bob Dutton after this flight are worth recording. One less happy sequel was mentioned at the end of the Captain's report and pointed up the extreme need for secrecy in such operations. Within three days of their return one of the crew was up on a charge for mentioning, in his cups, the flight to others. A leakage could be catastrophic.

Then Dutton (a South African) and his Navigator Frank Seddon (an Australian) were summoned by the Air Officer Commanding East Africa (a Canadian, Air Vice Marshal Kerby)[13] to Nairobi to give their report directly to him. It was also for them to receive the Distinguished Flying Cross personally (and on behalf of their crew who, incidentally, were Canadian/British.) This sinking, although it could not be splashed over the headlines in Europe, was an enormous triumph for the Royal

Navy and the RAF because for nigh on two years the Admiralty, the Indian Ocean forces and the code-breakers at ULTRA Headquarters in Bletchley Park, Buckinghamshire, had been hunting this particular ship.

The victory (with the sinking of the *Brake* soon after), was one of the principal factors in the winning of the war against Indian Ocean submarines by the end of 1944. Kerby kindly obliged Dutton and Seddon by providing some DFC ribbon for their tunics which was hard to come by in East Africa.

Like Dutton's, Frank Seddon's DFC was well deserved. Bob describes him as a 'craggy Australian cobber – full of dry humour. He was very popular with the crew – they knew he would always get us there and back. Frank was an excellent navigator; he was great on ASTRO (navigation) and astounded the Navy when we went aboard for a three-day exercise. They looked askance at his bubble sextant but were shown it was as useful as theirs.' Throughout the cyclone Frank could not take astro shots and had to get them home by dead reckoning, which amazingly he did.

On the other hand descriptions of Dutton himself are hard to find, fifty years on, but the story he gives speaks for itself. All I have is that he was 'fair and slim and about five foot nine to eleven in height, very approachable and trusted implicitly by the crew; that he was quiet with a wry sense of humour.' Not long after, he married Pamela Higgins in Dar-es-Salaam at the tall spired Roman Catholic Cathedral on the harbour front among the graceful palms, with Squadron Leader 'Pinto' Virr RCAF, the Flight Commander, as his best man. He stayed on in 259 Squadron to become Flight Commander and after the war returned to the Colonial Police, being posted back to Dar-es-Salaam as an Assistant Superintendent in the Tanganyika Police. Later, as Chief of Police in Cyprus, he had the responsibility of arranging Archbishop Makarios' exile in the Seychelles. Oddly enough he became Police Chief in those islands also.

An even lighter sequel illustrates the spirit of cooperation between the RAF and the RN. Harry Laister with Alf Cumming of N-209 shared the general mood. He writes:

'On return to port – in Mauritius – of the *Relentless* the RAF officers were invited to a party on board and we all piled into two cars to travel to where a launch was waiting to take us out to the ship. It turned out to be a terrific party and we all drank more than was good for us. It seemed hilarious at the time for the Naval officers to cut off our ties below the knot.'

UPPER LEFT: F/Lt Bob Dutton DFC, of 259 Sq, marries Miss Pam Higgins at Dar-es-Salaam RC Cathedral with S/Ldr 'Pinto' Virr in rear as Best Man, and Miss Patricia Mackrell as Bridesmaid. *(courtesy R.A.P.H. Dutton DFC)*

UPPER RIGHT: S/Ldr 'Bill' Bayly DFC of 413 Squadron marries Miss Fay Anderson in Bangalore in 1944. *(courtesy G.H.H. Bayly DFC)*

LOWER LEFT: F/O Les George of 209 Sq marries Miss Elizabeth Paddon, a Queen Alexandra nursing sister, at Hong Kong Cathedral in 1946. *(courtesy of L. George)*

LOWER RIGHT: F/Lt Peter Bradford of 230 Sq marries Miss Cornelia van Gennep, in England in 1946. *(courtesy Cory Bradford)*

The RAF departure from the ship was also a bit of a scrimmage, with their trousers thrown down into the boat after them, as the Officer of the Watch saw them off and stood by saluting stiffly. Cooperation on the high seas was not always so easy, especially when communications were lacking but friendly rivalry did not hamper the team spirit that developed in these combined operations. The Naval Report on this one commented:

> 'The performance of the RAF personnel and aircraft was excellent. They were working under the handicaps of weather which also necessitated the use of Grand Port instead of Tombeau Bay where the RAF headquarters are sited. Much of the success of the operation was due to their efforts.'

This was underscored by warm praise from Admiral Jimmy Somerville who visited each of the three squadrons, 209, 259 and 265. Each squadron would be assembled in some long, thatched dining-hall or dark roomy *banda* (hut). Flight Commanders and fitters; Intelligence Officers and instrument-makers; pilots, pigeon-handlers and photographers; WOPs and WOMs; clerks and cooks and cipher-wallahs; MT drivers, MCS dinghy-bashers and SPs[14]; FMEs and FMAs; riggers and radar wizards; engineers and electricians; navigators and mets; adjutants, armourers and all the other trades that make a squadron effective, gathered to hear what the great man said.

With his blunt, down-to-earth humour, says Dai Thomas of Anglesey, Jimmy would tell them that 'the squadron has done itself proud, even if you do nothing else till the end of the war. Thanks to you, a lot of German submarines will never find their way back to base.' The operation was so secret that most of his hearers hadn't a clue what he was talking about.

244 SQUADRON

Like other RAF squadrons in the Arabian region, 244 started with the Vickers Vincent biplanes in 1940, when various wars were going on in Iraq and later Iran. Having played a part in that, the squadron in 1941 received Blenheim bombers and in 1942 went over to anti-submarine patrols. That was when Don James, later W/O, joined them as a WOP/AG. He was on his way to the disaster in Singapore where he might have finished up a POW under the Japanese. Instead, when their Blenheim crash-landed in the desert, he was put under Aden command, in 244 Sq. In between convoy patrols in 1942, Don's pilot in a Vincent took a Russian scientist along to find locust breeding grounds which would then be sprayed by a Russian squadron. However, at one place they mistook soft sand for a landing field and finished up upside down, still strapped in, except for Don who had been thrown out. He later moved to East Africa.

A 244 Sq Bisley (Blenheim Mark V) crash lands off the shore at Masirah in 1943. One sank the U/533 (Hennig) off Oman (Sgt Chapman) in 1943. *(Courtesy Jim Drew)*

244 SINKS U/533

By 1943 the squadron was suffering from engine failures and undercarriages packing up, so that in January and February five aircraft had been written off. F/Lt Andy Thomas, the historian, says this was because they were held in Middle East storage units too long. Nevertheless, on 17 October 1943 (some records say 16th and 1942!) Sergeant L. Chapman (some say Chapple, but that, says Don, was an Australian in the squadron) took off on a routine anti-submarine patrol in his Bisley, C/244 (BA 437), a Mark V Blenheim with the solid nose (some reports say O/244). With Sergeants Bonymgre and Murrell over the Gulf of Oman, he suddenly spotted a submarine four miles away. C/244 slanted down to make a head-on attack with four depth-charges. U/533, whose captain was Lieutenant Commander Helmut Hennig, on his first Far East voyage, sank rapidly and only one survivor was able to escape. He was Seaman Günther Schmidt and was said to be afloat 28 hours. One account says he struggled ashore, another says the Navy picked him up. However, he found himself almost lionised at the squadron base at Sharjah. As the RAF record states:

'The known presence of the enemy – more indeed, the actual presence in the camp of a real German prisoner – has been a spur to the efforts of air and ground crews enabling us to realise that we really are taking part in the same war as others.'

Schmidt's thoughts must have turned to his 52 comrades lying deep in the blue waters of the Gulf. It had taken 1,160 hours of squadron patrolling before this one sighting. Chapman was awarded a well deserved DFM for a 'model attack'.

244 SQUADRON LATER

A tall Australian pilot, F/Lt Keith Scott, now at Robertson, Brisbane, tells me of his time with 244 Sq in 1944. He was posted on detachment with his Wellington XIII to Aden, where we shall hear of him in the U/852 chapter. At that time the squadron operated from the airfield on Masirah Island, which was a jumping-off platform for RAF Jaguars in the recent Gulf War. In those early days, after the tents of 1942, the airmen's quarters were unique – built of petrol tins filled with sand, like breeze blocks. Timber brought in by ship was used for roof trusses under corrugated iron, and the floor was a concrete slab.

Later on, in 1944 or 1945, these buildings were a surprise to the first WAAF to be posted to Masirah, Flight Officer Maureen Guest. Besides living quarters, she said, two churches and a cinema were constructed of these tins. However, 'Earlier on', Keith Scott writes:

'There was no drinking water on the island, and this too was brought in by ship during the non-monsoon season. We were rationed to one bottle of fresh water per day. Alcohol – one bottle of beer per man per week perhaps. There was plenty of cordial in the mess. Food – we lived mostly on M&V (Maconochies tins) supplemented by fish (barracuda caught by the local Arabs), crayfish, seagull eggs, powdered eggs and we even tried turtle meat and eggs. When the AOC passed through one day he was served with the usual M&V whereupon he put on a weekly flight from Karachi to bring us fresh vegetables and some of the more basic delicacies.

'In the evenings we would go to the out-door movies at the American base and occasionally there would be visiting American concert parties. In our camp we had out-in-the-open urinals which we called "desert lilies". They comprised one petrol tin sunk into the ground with a second inserted at an angle to form the top. There was the occasion when a party of American female entertainers drove past in a truck and witnessed one of these 'desert lilies' being used. Shrieks of female laughter caused the urinator to jump in consternation, as he was unaware of the presence on the island of these ladies.'

Among routine patrols Keith describes one where they lost an aircraft due to structural failure during a convoy escort in the Gulf of Aden.

'On this occasion, the mounting holding the starboard motor to the wing snapped and the engine fell forward making the aircraft uncontrollable. It dived straight into the sea ahead of the convoy and four survivors were picked up by one of the ships. One later died in hospital.'

SOMERVILLE AND STRATEGY

In the Indian Ocean between 1941 and late 1944 convoys were a recurring problem for Admiral Somerville and the Admiralty in London. The Eastern Fleet was constantly being depleted to meet emergencies in other war theatres, like North Africa or D-Day. Destroyers were a particularly thorny point. They were needed not only as convoy escorts to round up, with their sheep-dog circling and whooping tactics, bunches of unruly merchant sheep. Their other vital role was escorting Jimmy Somerville's big ships. Without them the battleships and carriers were immobilised like dowager duchesses waiting in vain for their carriages to arrive. So the Admiral was constantly torn between the two, and often the Admiralty could not help with more destroyers. Winston Churchill, our nautical Prime Minister, was also putting in his formidable oar from time to time and disagreeing with both parties. The 'Indian Ocean Narrative' at the Air Historical Branch gives a good example in its bulky unpublished volume, which I was kindly permitted to consult.[15]

'During November 1943 the submarine threat increased in the Bay of Bengal, so early in December Calcutta convoys sailed at 8-day intervals for Trincomalee and Madras. Minimum speeds for these JG convoys was now 8 or 9 knots to speed up shipping while preserving security. Several troop convoys sailed but it was still not possible to escort them all.

'The position in the New Year caused grave apprehensions. In more convoys ships were released, or when submarines suddenly appeared, put back into convoy. Faults were gradually corrected. Fast ships tended to run independently, except when the U-boat threat appeared.[16] Japanese I class and RO boats were still a submarine force to be reckoned with. As time passed they were able to take their pick of a rich variety of targets.

'Convoy routes increased with the mounting material needs of South East Asia. There were movements of the troopships and cargo vessels to and from the Pacific by way of Onslow in Western Australia. There was the build-up of naval bases and the normal needs of air and naval stations. At the end of 1943 the most constructive efforts were being made to rationalise the convoy route system in the interest of more effective air and surface escort.'

Looking at ocean strategy in 1943 and 1944 the aims appeared to be:

1. to use the convoy system whenever there were enough escorts, or when a serious submarine threat arose in one area.

2. To build up Addu Atoll and other bases in readiness for the invasion of South East Asia and for the day when the Eastern Fleet would be prepared for its dual role – serving under Lord Mountbatten in SEAC (South East Asia Command) for the invasion and independently policing the Indian Ocean.

In November 1942, when the cuts were fiercest, Sir James had been called back to London for consultations. The Admiralty, fearing such a doughty admiral would fight his pitch, were much relieved to find the opposite. Sir James well understood that the Indian Ocean's needs would have to await a lessening of the demands in the European theatre, especially in the Mediterranean.

This began to happen in early 1944 when the Eastern Fleet was asked to undertake diversionary operations in the Indian Ocean and a raid on Sabang was decided upon. Somerville had only one carrier at that time, HMS *Illustrious*, so an American aircraft carrier, the USS *Saratoga* was seconded from the US Pacific Fleet. In the aggressive raids that followed, there was excellent cooperation with the Americans. When Jimmy Somerville first visited their carrier, the ship's company expected a 'stuffed-shirt Limey Admiral' and were delighted with the informal figure in white shorts who is seen in our photograph. He made a well-timed impromptu speech and cemented relations, as he was to do later in Washington as Head of the British Naval Mission.

THE KHEDIVE ISMAIL

An example of success was when the Japanese submarine RO 110 attacked a Calcutta-Colombo convoy and was destroyed by the (un-named) RN escorts. Another convoy met instead with disaster when it sailed without an air escort. There were three naval escorts for five troopships (the cruiser HMS *Hawkins* and two destroyers, HMS *Paladin* and HMS *Petard*) in convoy KR 8 heading from Mombasa to Colombo but this did not prevent the Japanese submarine I/27 (Cdr Fukumura) from torpedoing the *Khedive Ismail*. She had 1,527 souls aboard and sank in two minutes. Among the 1,344 troops there were nurses, ATS and 60 Wrens, the latter mainly from the Fleet Air Arm base at Tanga, south of Mombasa in Tanganyika.

That day, 12 February 1944, 1,134 of the passengers and crew went down with the ship, including all but two of the Wrens. After a long battle, in which *Paladin* was put out of action, I/27 was sunk by *Petard*. Next day W/O George Bennett of 413 Catalina Squadron was in a Cat tasked with searching for any further survivors but all they found was the 20-mile oil slick.

N O T E S

1 *Tankmotorschiff Charlotte Schliemann*, Otto Mielke (Moewig), Munich 1955

2 Personal Communications from Dr (Med) Robert Schridde, Ships Surgeon, *Charlotte Schliemann* and from *Leitender Ingenieur*, Herr K-H Wiebe, Chief Engineer U/178.

3 Flight Lieutenant Ken Murray was later Second in Command to W/Cdr Stacey doing the Catalina Conversion Course at Mombasa, and still later in the Atlantic sank the last U-boat of the war. One of the ground crew described him as a 'smashing bloke'.

4 *HMS Battler's War*, Kenneth Poolman – article (*Air Pictorial*, page 262)

5 Personal communication – AVM John Stacey CBE DSO DFC (This is not AVM Sir John Stacey)

6 Notebooks of Air Commodore T.P. Seymour CBE

7 Liberty boat – phrase borrowed from the Navy for a lorry taking airmen for recreation

8 From now on there is a blend of personal communications from the following: Squadron Leader R.A.P.H. Dutton DFC CPM; Flight Lieutenant J. Pack; Warrant Officer R.H. Brown; Warrant Officer W.R. Kirkup and Flight Lieutenant H. Laister

9 'A datum point was a position in the ocean in latitude and longitude where we either turned back to base or flew to another datum point.' (Pack)

10 265 Sq records, P.R.O. Kew

11 Josef Wieser Esquire of U/532, Wargrave, Reading, England

12 Christopher Lowe, Nottingham

13 AVM Kerby, see Caricatures of Air Headquarters East Africa staff on the 3rd endpaper at the back of this book, by one of his Staff, W/Cdr. H. Duke-Woolley DFC.

[14] SP Service Police, like Army Military Police

[15] *Indian Ocean Narrative,* Air Historical Branch, Ministry of Defence, London

[16] OPERATION LONGSHANKS was mounted on 09.03.43 in Goa Harbour to attack secretly four German frieghters, one of which was transmitting messages about shipping to nearby U-boats, it was thought. Members of SOE, Calcutta Light Horse and Calcutta Scottish set fire to the ships, an event immortalised in a book and film – *The Sea Wolves* (see Bibliography). My U-boat informants do not recall any such system of information.

CHAPTER EIGHT

WORLD ULTRA PUT IN DANGER

The *Charlotte Schliemann* had been trapped by the Eastern Fleet's skilful use of decoded German messages from the U-boats themselves using their ENIGMA machine. This was a portable box with an ingenious combination of numbered wheels which determined the coded (or decoded) output of the keyed input. It did this by varying letter by letter (and never repeating) the path of an electrical signal between the keyboard and the output display. ULTRA was not the name of the system used in decoding these messages, but the term for the security classification of the resulting intelligence. However, it has come to be used as an umbrella phrase to cover the whole operation.

The *Kriegsmarine* and other forces relied on ENIGMA to encode their daily messages to base, but it was compromised. Early in the war, with skill and courage, Polish operators had unravelled the code-machine and handed to the Allies a priceless gift. Decoding ENIGMA then became highly developed in a hive of super-intelligence known as Bletchley Park in Berkshire, England. These experts developed in 1943, three years before the Americans, the world's first practical computer. It was large as a single-decker bus, though its complex of 1500 valves and pulleys could now be replaced by a single microchip. The machine was known as Colossus[1] and several like it were built at BP, capable of decoding ENIGMA very rapidly.

Advance information on German plans, quickly sent in secret all over the world to 31 Allied commanders, enabled battles to be won and warships to be sunk to an increasing degree. Till the end of the war Axis authorities refused to believe their machine-ciphers could be broken. However, success for the Allies depended on maintaining the utmost secrecy.

When one or more U-boats were sent orders from BdU in Paris to rendezvous with a fellow-submarine or supply ship, the Admiralty would immediately plan to attend the rendezvous. To protect ULTRA an elaborate plan would be devised to show that our ships or aircraft had arrived through radar D/F fixes on the U-boats' radio signals; or bogus aircraft patrols were set up, 'accidentally' to spot the enemy vessels in the distance and report their position to the Navy.

All went well until the next two successes in the Indian Ocean, one of which was a hunt for Germany's second supply ship in the Indian Ocean, the *Brake;* the other was the sinking of UIT/22. *Schliemann's* loss was a tremendous blow to Grand Admiral Dönitz. Now he must try to refuel many U-boats which would otherwise be lost or stranded. They included U/168, U/183, U/188, U/532 and UIT/24.

Dönitz' HQ signalled that Pich in U/168 should refuel on 10 March 1945 along with Lüdden in U/188 and Junker, whose turn with the *Charlotte Schliemann* was so rudely interrupted by Flight Lieutenant Bob Dutton's Catalina, in U/532. ULTRA had informed Admiral Somerville that the *Brake* would leave Batavia, loaded with fuel and provisions, on 22 February. ULTRA also told him of the rendezvous on 10 March. *Brake* left on 29 February 1944.

The *Brake*, at 14,970 tons, had twice the displacement of the previous supply ship. Built by Bremer Vulcan on the River Weser, she was commissioned in 1937 and her lines were more like those of a modern tanker. She seems to have had only one 10.5 cm gun, beside her anti-aircraft weapons. Captain Kölschenbach was quite unaware of what, apart from the general dangers, was building up around him. His ship may be seen in the plate showing German Vessels in Chapter 7.

THE NAVY SIDE

Admiral Jimmy Somerville, persuaded by the Admiralty for security reasons not to wipe out the tanker en route, called into action five warships. The first was our old friend HMS *Battler,* the *Bogue*-class Escort Carrier with a mixed Martlet/Swordfish squadron aboard, No 834. She may be seen, at Mauritius, in the "Royal Navy" plate in the Appendix. BOAC's Captain Johnny Hackett, whom we last saw rescuing *City of Canton* survivors, recalls *Battler* turning up in Durban.

> 'The arrival of an RN Carrier was quite a rare event as were the uniforms of Fleet Air Arm pilots. We met in the Cosmo Club on 7 February by accident and were very soon drinking together and talking shop. The one taboo subject was where they were bound for and when. It was on a test flight next day that I saw *Battler* in the Naval Berth.'

The next warship was the cruiser HMS *Newcastle*. A friend of mine from Bulawayo Mining School, Allister Stanley of Dar-es-Salaam, had joined the Royal Navy as an Ordinary Seaman in Mombasa and eventually finished up as a gunner on HMS *Newcastle*. He describes her thus:

'. . . a good ship, new and fast and one of the first to have radar which was very useful especially when we were near Japanese warships coming from the Cocos Islands. We were the leading ship of the 6th [and later the 4th] Cruiser Squadron as we had an Admiral aboard. He was a nice guy, Admiral Tennant, who used to put over the ship's intercom some of his exploits.

'For instance, when he was Captain of the *Repulse*, as it was being sunk by the Japanese bombers at the fall of Singapore, Tennant was coming down from the bridge. He was pulled down under water but somehow managed to get out and eventually came to the surface almost unconscious. A couple of matelots were on a raft and they pulled him aboard whilst one of them said ; "We'd better pull this old bastard aboard." Tennant thought it was very good.'

In the RAF we airmen had little idea of the situations that could occur on a ship like the *Newcastle* in a fierce enemy action. Even on 'cruise' watch, as a gunner, Stanley recalls being in the cordite room as:

'Not a very pleasant job. As you went down the ladders to near the bottom of the ship, steel hatches were closed and screwed down . . . then through the Handling Room into the Cordite Room, where cordite was stacked all round. In the wall was a special way of passing the cordite through the Handling Room and up to the three guns in the turret. Ventilation was cut off in both rooms in case of flashback or fire. Also if a shell fired at us landed anywhere near the cordite, the Cordite Room would be flooded and, of course those in it drowned.'

The alternative could be for the whole ship to go up like HMS *Hood* with over a thousand crew. Actually, Stanley was not on the *Newcastle* when she set out after the *Brake*.

We also have a note about the third warship, the destroyer HMS *Roebuck*. She too was a new ship, launched on 10 December 1942, her displacement being 1,705 tons with a very useful top speed of 37 knots. Under the command of a certain Lieutenant R.E. Roe, she served from Trincomalee in convoy work and then in many attacks on the Japanese in the Burma campaign. Her maiden voyage, however, sailing for the Far East on 1 August 1943 with a convoy, was a bit of a disaster, as

Aircraftman (later Sergeant) Dai Thomas of 259 Squadron learned, in Durban, at RAF Congella.

> 'One day in the mess, five sailors walked in and ordered some beer. They sat opposite Norman Owen and me and jabbered away in Welsh. "Ask them where they come from," said Norman. Actually they came from the North Wales coast and were on HMS *Roebuck's* maiden voyage from the UK and she was leaking like a sieve. They had to put her in the floating dock close by.'

Durban Dockyard must have done a good job because by December 1945 she had steamed 153,000 miles, lastly bringing Christmas fare from Cape Town to a ration-bound Britain. Dai Thomas, invited aboard in Durban, certainly appreciated the 1,000 Players cigarettes he bought for 15 shillings at the *Roebuck's* canteen which were 'a great treat after Cape to Cairo fags.' On the other two warships, the cruiser HMS *Suffolk*, and the destroyer HMS *Quadrant*, I have no inside information.

In a plan of action called Operation *Covered*, Sir James Somerville ordered his ships to search the area 300 miles north of the rendezvous on 9, 10 and 11 March.

> 'He also proposed [to the Admiralty] that Catalinas from Mauritius search the more westerly of the two rendezvous alternatives and asked whether, if D/F bearings showed U-boats near either of the two, he could send *Battler* and the two destroyers to search, after a decent interval had elapsed.'[2]

The Admiralty cautiously gave approval, with many provisos over the next few days as the situation changed.

THE AIR FORCE PART

Meanwhile the RAF had prepared seven Catalinas from 259 and 265 Squadrons to take part in Operation *Covered* under the overall command of Group Captain 'Peter' Bryer, who was no longer in charge of 230 Squadron, but now the Officer Commanding 246 Wing in Mombasa. Directing aircraft operations was Wing Commander 'Fats' Louw, DFC and Bar, the South African we last saw in Chapter One. He was now O/C 265 Squadron, one of the three flying boat squadrons in 246 Wing, and his experience was needed in this crucial operation. The late Group Captain Bryer, at 92, provided me in small, beautiful script, with a careful account of his own part in the affair.

'She, the *Brake*, was to rendezvous with a German sub at a position 1,000 miles south of Mauritius. We were asked to make the same rendezvous but some miles to the west. This was done by two Catalinas stripped of guns and with extra fuel tanks. I set up my HQ in the office of the racecourse grandstand in Mauritius, where there were good telephone connections and a high point for our W/T aerials. The two Cats we based in the lagoon at the southern tip of the island (Mahébourg) famed for being de Vere Stacpoole's "Blue Lagoon". To the North is a mountain.

'The flight took practically 24 hours, the latter part with the Captain in his bunk with malaria. To act as a beacon and an obstruction light, I got the small garrison in the island to set up bonfires on the mountain which were lit on an Aldis lamp signal from the lagoon. The Major commanding begged me with tears in his eyes to give his men something war-connected to do. They had the satisfaction of seeing the Cat appear out of the night and flop safely on the lagoon. It made their day – or rather, night.'

We have only one story about Wing Commander Louw's part in the operation. It is typical of him. Flying Officer Ernie Robin DFC says he was standing with Louw on the shore of Tombeau Bay in Mauritius, during Operation *Brake* about 15 March 1944.

'It was dark and raining, windy and a good sea running. One of the aircraft, not 265, was out at the end of the flare path and the skipper using the Aldis lamp signalled back that it was pretty rough and he thought HE SHOULD NOT TAKE THE RISK OF TAKING OFF. Louw signalled back: "TAKE OFF – I'LL TAKE THE RISK!"'

THE COVER FOR ULTRA

The Admiralty said that Somerville should not attack the *Brake* 'until definite D/F bearings had been obtained.' On top of this, says Winton, '*Battler's* Meteorological Officer [known in some ships as 'Seaweed'] had studied the weather conditions in the area for some months and was popularly supposed to have predicted the most likely time and place for a U-boat rendezvous.[3] In the event, Swordfish of 834 Squadron spotted the *Brake* with 2 U-boats refuelling alongside, but were forbidden to attack and recalled. This caused much mystification and anger in the Squadron, especially when HMS *Roebuck* was called in to sink the tanker on 12 March 1944 and missed the U-boats. ULTRA's cautious hand again.'

THE GERMAN VIEWPOINT

After the loss of the *Schliemann*, 'CONSUBS' or BdU Headquarters were determined to take no chances. Intensive preliminary scouting was to be carried out in the area of refuelling, with a wary eye for ships or aircraft. Lieutenant Commander Lüdden's U/188 was filled up; Commander Junker's U/532 received all but its lubricating oil and Lieutenant Commander Helmuth Pich, who appeared in this history before, received only part fuel and no lubricating oil. Bad weather intervened and the group moved south-east.

We saw in an earlier chapter how Harold (Smudge) Smith of 413 Squadron, in connection with his Catalina crew's attack in the moonlight on U/168, recently corresponded with Lieutenant Commander Pich. During an 80th birthday visit to the U-boat Captain at Geesthacht, when Harold presented my painting of their attack, Pich discussed the *Brake* episode with Harold.

It appears that on the Sunday, 12 March 1944, Captain Kölschenbach was holding a memorial service on the deck of the *Brake* for the dead of two world wars, when the look-out shouted a warning of enemy aircraft. At 10.32 in position 31'39" South and 72'32" East, a plane was sighted on the port beam. Shortly after that HMS *Roebuck* appeared and opened fire at 11.26. (The Royal Navy report states she started shelling the tanker at a range of 13 miles, closing till 12.12 and she fired eight torpedoes, which may have missed, along with depth-charges to discourage U-boats.) In the meantime Pich says they dived and carried out underwater repairs for two hours.

Kölschenbach managed to evacuate his crew into lifeboats and of the 139 only four were lost. The scuttling charges were set off and the tanker started to sink at 13.20. The destroyer *Roebuck*, knowing U-boats were in the vicinity, did not hang about to pick up survivors but raced away from the scene. Pich, knowing aircraft were about, also wasted no time in diving and leaving the spot.

Lüdden in U/188 sighted an aircraft and crash-dived at 10.56. His log book records:

'From 12.18 until about 13.30 148 shell bursts and 14 heavy explosions are heard. Boat sometimes shaken as we are in immediate vicinity of *Brake*.

13.20 Loud breaking up noises, followed by about 30 minutes of loud and minor explosions. Tanker *Brake* is sunk.

15.03 Surfaced just after sunset and proceed to scene of sinking.'[4]

Gowans, in Y/413 attacks Pich's U/168 on 3.11.1943. Author's painting presented to Pich by Harold Smith on his 80th birthday. (courtesy Lt Cdr Helmuth Pich)

Slightly earlier, U/168 surfaced, Pich says, to find the tanker ablaze and the *Brake*'s lifeboats all around them. He managed to get all 135 survivors aboard. Night was falling. U/168 moved off to the East. One hour later the British task force returned, complete with aircraft, looking for the missing U-boats. Two rockets were fired at Pich from one Swordfish but missed.[5] He then decided to go down to 250 metres, with 190 men aboard and was forced to stay down for 20 hours. Pich told Harold these 'chronic conditions were very dangerous', implying that, with so many men aboard, oxygen ran very low before they could surface again next evening. The U-boat captain blames this for much ill-health later.

The conversation with Harold finishes: 'U/168 surfaced next day heading for Jakarta (a ten-day trip) via Sunda Straits. They seem to have had some Japanese escort on the way, arriving at Jakarta [Tanjong Priok harbour].' U/168 was sunk on 6 October 1944 by the Dutch submarine *Zwaardvis* (Swordfish), when 22 crewmen were lost but Pich and 22 others were saved.

We have, through Mr Richard Smith, son of Sergeant W.R. Bill Smith, a WOP/AG on Johnny Gowans' Cat Y/413 which had attacked U/168, the Dutch captain's account of the sinking. *Zwaardvis* was actually built in Barrow in 1941, as an RN submarine, HMS *Talent*, and was handed over in 1942 to the Royal Netherlands Navy and HRH Prince Bernhard took the salute in 1943. Her displacement was 1,290 tons (surface). She had a crew of 48, seasoned Dutch submariners, and under her intrepid captain, *Luitenant ter zee der 1e klasse* (Lt/Cdr) H.A.W. Goossens, achieved a distinguished record. In the Java Sea, at 0641 on the 6th an enemy submarine was sighted at 5,900 yards. Goossens fired six torpedoes, two ahead of the U/168 and obtained hits in the forward section and one in the engine room. It sank at once but 27 people were picked up, including Lt/Cdr Pich. Five remained as prisoners, but 22 were transferred to a native fishing vessel. 'The German officers were astonished at the coolness and comfort of our submarine,' comments Goossens.

ULTRA's secret appeared to have been kept, though Commander Junker in U/532, who had been present at both sinkings, reported to BdU thus on the evening of 12 March: 'provisionings have been systematically compromised'. BdU were not convinced. Another success for the Allies, however, brought ULTRA to the very verge of total disclosure to the enemy.

UIT/22 IS SUNK

This third sinking actually took place the day before the *Brake*'s demise and well away from her area. Far to the south of the Cape of Good Hope, in the Roaring Forties, Dönitz had arranged another rendezvous, this time between two U-boats, U/178 and an ex-Italian boat UIT/22. Once again the code-breakers at Bletchley Park were well aware of the meeting place and time.

The Commander-in-Chief South Atlantic set up an elaborate scheme to intercept them and if possible sink both. It was called OPERATION WICKET-KEEPER. The name would have appealed to the cricket-loving South Africans, but what slipped past the wicket eventually was a surprise to the RAF Catalinas who caught it in the slips.

UPPER: 'Gar' Nash's crew (P/262, FP174) which sank UIT/22 on 11.3.1944
Back row left to right: Tromans, Fitter 2E; Bower, WOP/AG; Davey, F/Eng; Hocking RAAF, Obs; Wright, WOP/AG; Walker Rigger 2A.
Front row: Wills, 2nd pilot; Nash DFC AFC, Captain; Hugger, F.Eng; Hanson, WOP/AG.
(Courtesy of Roddick Family)

LOWER: P/262 with Gar Nash on approach to UIT/22 taken by Surridge's crew.
(Courtesy of B. Hanson)

Naval HQ then laid on a reception committee of two SANF minesweepers, and three RN warships, along with SAAF Venturas of four squadrons. Finally seven RAF Catalinas of 262 Squadron (later to become 35 Squadron SAAF) left the bright lights of Durban to head south for the windswept Saldanha Bay at Langebaan, near Cape Town.

Of the two targets in this hunt, UIT 22 had been an Italian submarine with the proud name of *Alpino Bagnolini* when Germany took her over after Italy's surrender to the Allies. The Italian captain Mario Tei handed her over and she was re-commissioned on 10 September 1943 and given the number 'U-IT 22'. *Oberleutnant zur See* (Lieutenant) Karl Wunderlich, her new captain – tall, slim and only 22 years old – was born in Gefell, a little town in Vogtland. He joined the *Kriegsmarine* in February 1941 and in three years had risen to the command of a submarine.

UIT/22 set out as a transport to Penang but she was fully armed and equipped with torpedoes. She sank no ships on the dangerous Atlantic passage south but was attacked herself by an American bomber that damaged her, south of Ascension Island. She lost a good deal of fuel from her outer fuel tanks, which continued to leak. Wunderlich's skill brought her safely to the Cape of Good Hope where BdU arranged for her to be topped up and to exchange other items with U/178. This was THE RENDEZVOUS.

The second target was U/178 which we last saw at the sinking of the *City of Canton*. Her captain, Commander Wilhelm Dommes, troubled with ill-health, had remained in Penang to command the German base there. His place was taken by Lieutenant Commander Wilhelm Spahr. He and his Chief Engineer, Karl-Heinz Wiebe, who spoke to me at his home in Bremen, had been used to the steep crash-dives of the fast-moving Atlantic battles. So they somewhat alarmed the U/178's crew when the Captain made them practice near-35° emergency dives instead of the more leisurely tropical 20° slides. In those one often saw a slow-moving Catalina or Anson far off on a clear horizon, giving one plenty of time to disappear. However, the steep practice dives stood them in good stead later on.

South Africa at War tells us that

'on 8 March the SANF minesweepers, *Southern Barrier* and *Roodepoort*, sailed from Cape Town to patrol an area some 220 km SSW of Cape Agulhas, while the Royal Navy destroyer *Lewes* (one of the old, narrow American four-stackers given early in the war under lease-lend)[6] and anti-submarine trawlers, *Lady Elsa* and *Norwich City*, extended the patrol line another 96 km southward. Five Venturas from 25 Sqn at Port Elizabeth and ten from 23 Sqn at Lombazi moved to reinforce 27 Sqn at Fisantekraal.'

Aircraft of 22 Sqn first sighted the U/178 near 'P.E.' and she crash-dived.

Chief Engineer Wiebe now gives us an account in German about U/178's tribulations, of which I summarised a few paraphrased extracts.[7]

'The sea was rough, the sky overcast and U/178 was again on the surface when a Ventura was spotted through the binoculars. The crew [he learnt later] comprised Lieutenants Evans, C.P. Marais, Fletcher and Langton of 25 Sqn. As we dived, the plane descended from 600 metres and dropped five bombs into our diving swirl. The ship's log stated: "A stick of bombs, well aimed. The boat was at 120 metres, no losses." We had dived so fast at 40° that the depth charges exploded above us and not below.'

Alarm dives became common at that time, Herr Wiebe told me. His diary recorded that on one occasion in the engine room during a dive, two mechanics were changing a large piston which was suspended and swinging. As the boat plunged grimly downwards these two hung on to the piston and despite explosions saved it from damage, getting wounded in the process. After this the weather deteriorated, curtailing the Ventura patrols. U/178 ploughed on towards the rendezvous.

262 SQUADRON CATS ATTACK

OPERATION WICKET-KEEPER was then moved further south. In the early hours of 11 March at RAF Langebaan, three Catalina captains were sent out on patrol together. The future squadron commander Flight Lieutenant E.S.S. 'Gar' Nash DFC AFC, a South African with the RAF, in P/262 (FP 174); a chunky-faced Canadian pilot from Alberta with an engaging grin, F/Lt Fred Roddick, flying D/262 (FP 252); and the tall F/Lt A.H. 'Oscar' Surridge in A-262, were tasked with a vital patrol.

Nash's Second Pilot, F/O Peter Wills, later Group Captain and commander of a Canberra squadron in Cyprus, who has written of this time in his monograph, *Catalina Safari,* allowed me to use extracts from it, along with accounts by three others. Wills opens the batting.[8] Crew names (still incomplete)[9] are listed in the chapter notes.

'In the small hours we were roused and gathered in a small operations hut near the Panoramic Hotel [the Officers Mess], to be briefed by Charles Green, the detachment Intelligence Officer, former curator of Gloucester Museum. He was a slight elfish figure, already in his forties, with large owlish spectacles and over-long khaki shorts. He was always full of irrepressible enthusiasm . . . The search patterns, laid out on a crude table, consisted of

226

three crossover[10] patrols, each orientated North/South and lying side by side along the estimated westerly track of the target U-boats. [P was in the Centre, D the West, and A to the East] . . . The search patterns were only fifty miles deep north and south (seventy was more typical for Catalina speeds) which, allowing for a probable detection range, visually or by radar, of about ten miles, would have meant that the effective area to be searched was 70 miles square.'

Crew of F/O Oscar Surridge's A-262 which helped sink UIT 22.
Back row: L. to R. Chambers, Sweet, F/S Jones, Bather, Rutter
Front row: Ashton, Surridge, F/S Jones, Dicker.
(Courtesy F. Roddick DFC)

Warrant Officer Len Allen, Fred Roddick's second pilot in 'D', takes up the account.

'The flying rations were ready for us by the time we were ready to board the aircraft ("D") and we were on our way about 4 a.m. It was a fine night and it was not long before the rigger, Bill Hill, was getting breakfast ready. Our Australian observer, 'Harp' Davies RAAF, kept himself busy and was constantly checking drift.

[Flight Sergeant Henry Smith, at that time NCO in charge of the Marine Section at Langebaan, recalls how he got the bobbing lights of the flarepath in readiness and how the three great Cats took off one after another across the darkened waters of Saldanha Bay.]

'After about six hours flying, at 4,000 feet, we had just reached our patrol when we saw a boat on the surface about 12 miles away. We were soon close enough to identify it as a U-boat – the skipper sounded the klaxon horn and put the nose down. The gunners went to their places, the wireless operator transmitted S-S-S (am attacking submarine) followed by our call sign, and we were all set.

'In the cockpit I armed the depth-charges and set the *Mickey Mouse* – the device that would release the six DCs at two-second intervals. As we flew in at 50 feet

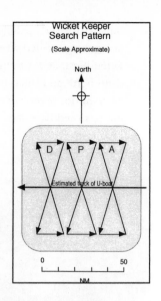

Wicket Keeper Search Pattern
(Scale Approximate)

North

D P A

Estimated track of U-boat

0   50
NM

The hunt for UIT-22 by Catalinas D, P, and A. Diagram of Crossover Patrols. Devised by G/Capt Peter Wills.

above the sea towards the U-boat, the gunners on its conning tower opened fire when we were still four miles from it and we saw the shells falling in the sea ahead of us. As we got closer they were bursting around us – it looked like ping-pong balls going "Pop". The skipper kept on changing altitude to make their gunners' job more difficult and our front gunner (Bill Hill) kept firing away. As the skipper weaved in response to the U-boat's evasive turns, the gunners in the blisters got the opportunity to fire at the submarine with their Brownings. In the last few seconds the captain of UIT/22 made a mistake and turned his boat along our track. Fred Roddick pressed the button releasing the depth charges in a perfect straddle of the U-boat. After passing over the submarine we climbed to 200 feet, turning as we went and saw the sea erupt with the U-boat in the centre. When the sea subsided we saw UIT/22 was listing heavily and the conning tower was un-manned. We flew round the stricken craft firing at the bridge but after a few minutes the boat submerged leaving a large patch of oil.

'Soon after the other two Catalinas came on the scene. We could see quite a number of jagged holes in one of our engine nacelles and the wing and as there was nothing more we could do, we headed for Saldanha Bay, six hours flying away. As we flew towards the coast of South Africa I thought of a quote from Churchill: "There is nothing more exhilarating than being shot at and being missed". How true!'

Upper: Crew of D-262 (FP252) Captain F. Roddick DFC, in which they damaged UIT-22.

Back row: Bill Hill, FMA; D. Barlow, FME; Ted Williams, WOP/AG; D. Wesley, WOM/AG; T. Thomason, RCAF Fitter.

Front row: Vern Snape, WOP/AG; F/Lt Ralph Wharton, Navigator (not on this flight); Fred Roddick DFC, Captain; Len Allen, Second Pilot; (F/Sgt, Harpleigh Davies was Observer, and a F/Sgt Winchester, WOM/AG is mentioned).*(Courtesy of Roddick Family)*

Lower: Catalina F/262 landing in Durban harbour. Note shadow of beam aerial behind cockpit. *(Courtesy of Roddick Family)*

Fred Roddick's crew had thought that this was U/178 they had damaged, but it was UIT/22 doing 10 knots on a course of 270°, 965 kilometres south of Cape Point. (Heading west she was probably tracking back and forward, waiting for U/178.) One of the six DCs hung up and Fred decided to make a further attack using his guns, and dropped the 250-pound bomb just five yards from the bow of the U-boat. By now Catalinas P and A, who heard the S-S-S, had arrived at the scene.

Flying Officer Brian (Syd) Hanson was the Wireless Operator/Air Gunner on P who had picked up the S-S-S. He writes:

'The three WOP/AGs (Sgt C. Bower, Sgt C.N. Wright and myself) alternated between the wireless watch, the ASV (Radar) and the blister gun watch. By mid-morning I was on lookout in the starboard blister, with the headphones plugged into the intercom but able to hear faintly any incoming wireless signals, since there was always a slight leak. I heard in Morse S-S-S followed by D's call sign. I switched on my intercom mike and informed the skipper that D was making an attack and that I would get a loop bearing on it. The loop was operated from the observer's table where Norman Wright was still taking down the message from D giving its position.'

'I quickly got the bearing, checked that it was not the reciprocal and then passed the bearing to the skipper on the intercom so he could head immediately towards D. I then returned to the starboard blister to continue on lookout watch. The Observer, Sgt Doug Hocking, an Australian now in Canterbury, Victoria, was able to work out the relative positions of P and D.'

Arriving at the growing oil patch, Gar Nash's Catalina P communicated by Aldis lamp with D and then A. Peter Wills continues his account here.

'While all this was going on we had been flying a fairly close pattern round the scene of the last attack, which was in clear evidence from the visible oil slick and a certain amount of floating debris.

'Suddenly, while we were actually flying towards the centre of the oil patch, we realised that the U-boat was surfacing again in front of our eyes and that it was practically stationary. We scarcely had to alter heading, and Gar, with a tense expression, reached up to the overhead throttles and drew them back and, as we started to descend, sounded the klaxon horn to call the crew to action stations. I remember watching the U-boat with fascination and wondering what was going to happen. She was wallowing in the slow forties swell and was slightly out of trim, her stern more exposed than her bow. As we came nearer I could see the gun on the conning tower but could not be sure if it was yet manned. Something strange about the flare of the conning tower and railings struck a chord, going back to my ship recognition training in Prince Edward Island, and I was sure that it was an Italian. [This was not confirmed to Wills till after the war].

UPPER: Catalina 1B P/262 (FP174) which finally sank UIT-22, with Panoramic Hotel, Langebaam, in background. *(Courtesy B. Hanson)*

LOWER: P's depth charges explode round UIT-22. *(Courtesy B. Hanson)*

'Tommy Tromans, in the bow turret, began to fire his twin 0.3 Vickers guns . . . With Tommy's first burst I saw that the locking device that should have held the gun mounting in position had failed, so that the recoil drove the butts backwards and upwards into his chest. Nevertheless he continued to do his best . . . In the event, however, there was no need for our gunfire because, in the final seconds before passing over our target at 200 feet, one

231

could see there was no one in the conning tower. Gar's manually released aim was as nearly perfect as could have been achieved, as became evident when the photographs taken by Oscar's crew were developed.

'We remained over the position for another two and a half hours but saw no further evidence of the submarine, except that the amount of oil on the surface increased and spread until we estimated it to cover an area 1300 by 400 yards. Towards the end of that time, Gar became silent and sombre, and remarked that the U-boat crew had only been trying to do their job in the same way that we had, and that perhaps they had wanted to surrender. I think I was less affected than he was, although as time has passed I have come to feel a great admiration for the fortitude of that crew and sadness for their misfortune.'

Brian Hanson goes back to the moment of the approach.

'As we went in to the attack I pulled the 0.5 round to fire along the starboard hull under the wing. After our six depth charges had been released the skipper banked sharply away. As we continued to circle the scene, I took over from Norman Wright on wireless watch and then sent out the message giving our position which the observer had worked out.'

An official report reminds us that Fl/Lt Surridge in Catalina A had stood by in support as P faced head-on the emerging submarine; took the photographic record of the attack and followed Gar Nash in raking the site with gunfire in case the destruction of UIT 22 was incomplete.

Meantime Roddick's Catalina was on the way home with its damaged wing and engine. Len Allen concludes with this description.

'As we approached Saldanha Bay the Skipper signalled for the floats to be lowered and we found that we had been hit at the end of one wing and the mechanism to lower the floats would not work. So the two heaviest members of the crew used the handle and were able to force one of the two floats down. As soon as we were on the water and had lost a bit of speed, Ted Williams, one of the WOPs, got out of the blister and climbed on the wing with the float down, to keep the damaged wing out of the water.'

Back at base, in the bay, Flight Sergeant Henry Smith, organising his waiting marine craft, takes up the tale. (Henry's RAF experience goes back to pre-war days when he knew Lawrence of Arabia who was an aircraftman at Felixtowe, helping to develop the first RAF high speed launches and air sea rescue boats.)

UPPER LEFT: Marine craft personnel at Langebaan with 60-foot pinnace No 87 behind. *(Courtesy H. Smith)*

UPPER RIGHT: 37-foot seaplane tender No 1579 standing by at Seychelles to assist a Sunderland which lost one float. *(Courtesy Les George)*

LOWER LEFT: Mrs Molly Ryan, of Molo, Kenya, whose hospitality was legendary; here with some of 259 Sq crew. Back left to right: George Tweddle; 'Cec' Heck (Aus); Front left to right: Norman Leece and Captain, Buzz Hibberd. *(Courtesy Norman Leece)*

LOWER RIGHT: 230 Sq, Administrative Staff at Koggala, with P/O John Foxon 2nd from left seated, and W/Cdr Bednall, CO, 4th from left. *(Courtesy John Foxon)*

'One of the Catalinas had a wing-tip float badly damaged. We had to dash around filling sandbags [to put on the good wing] and have the pinnace ready to support the damaged wing.

'The sandbags were not needed because as the Catalina landed, some of the crew hopped out on to the good wing – it was quite something to do [Henry adds in typical understatement] because the pilot had to maintain enough speed to keep control while the crew did their scramble on to the wing. If they had slipped and fallen in the water, there were plenty of sharks in the bay who would have made things most uncomfortable [Henry's MCS chaps ought to know, facing those risks daily. A photo shows him with Pop Enderstein and one of the smaller sharks they caught in Saldanha Bay.]

'F/Lt Roddick did a very good job. All we marine bods had to do was to have all available boats ready to close in, in case of emergency. Shortly afterwards the pilot got the DFC and we celebrated with a *bryfleis* (Afrikaans for barbecue) on the beach with basketfuls of meat chunks and sausages cooked on sharpened sticks in the bonfire, washed down with unlimited supplies of free South African beer.'

After the attack there were no survivors from the submarine. The Captain and 42 crew lost their lives. Karl Wunderlich was posthumously promoted and the U-boat service lost yet another promising captain. The RAF report stated:

'Two excellent attacks. Both aircraft made good tactical use of their firepower to subdue the U-boat's gunners. It is most probable that D so damaged the U-boat that it had to surface and face the very accurate and excellent attack carried out by aircraft P.'

Gar Nash already had a DFC for work with 612 Squadron Whitleys based on Iceland. Now Fred Roddick was presented the DFC by the Canadian High Commissioner at the Officers' Mess in Congella. His citation mentioned great courage and determination. This applied also to all three aircrews who were ready to face the firepower of a surfaced IXD2 U-boat.

Wilhelm Spahr in U/178 was still heading for the rendezvous, continues Wiebe's German account. On 7 January 1944 Spahr had been presented with the *Deutsche Kreuz* in gold.

'Now he was running a heavy risk and complained of a "round-the-clock patrol service." Arrived at the spot, Spahr noted the huge oil patch and submerged. Then U/178 set course for Bordeaux. Meeting a Catalina 800 sea miles from Cape Town and crash-diving once more, the Captain wrote in his log: *"Wo ist man im freien Seeraum noch sicher?"* (Where is one safe these days on the high seas ?)'

The journey back to France was slow and painful. In the tropics the diesel engine cylinders had developed worn linings. The first was replaced, but after that, Herr Wiebe wrote, 'there were seven more to be done but no replacements.'

He and Commandant Spahr were discussing this in the engine room, he recalls, with the mechanics present, when one of them, a Petty Officer, suggested repairing the broken parts of the cylinders with sheet metal and packing. Wiebe was dubious at first but then the idea struck him as brilliant. Why not try it themselves? The engine room crew set to and eventually managed the job. This *Reparaturidee* (idea for repair) from an *Unteroffizier*, writes Wiebe in his German memoir, helped them to reach *die Heimat* (Homeland) safely after fourteen and a half months away. U/178 had escaped the WICKET-KEEPER nets.

However, three successes, two supply ships and a U-boat, thought the Admiralty and the ULTRA code-breakers, was not bad going. 'Then gradually,' says John Winton in his book *ULTRA at Sea,* 'an awful realisation dawned upon the Navy's OIC (Operations Intelligence Centre) at Bletchley Park[11].' This was that although none of the rendezvous incidents had been dangerous to security in themselves, ULTRA was now 'under its gravest threat of the war so far.'

'It was not the incidents individually,' he comments, 'but their combination that imperilled ULTRA. Surely the coincidences were too great even for German Intelligence to gloss over.' Nevertheless, so fixed was the idea in German Intelligence Services that ENIGMA could not be broken, that ULTRA was able to carry on till the end of the war and help in its successful conclusion.

In the meanwhile, for three months attacks on U-boats anywhere near rendezvous had to be foregone. Strong words passed between Admiral King, the fiery American chief of US naval forces, and Admiral of the Fleet, Sir Dudley Pound, still in firm charge of the British Navy. The crisis passed eventually and U-boats during 1944 were sunk in increasing numbers, many of their best crews being lost.

In a postscript to his time at RAF Langebaan, 'Gar' Nash's Second Pilot, now Group Captain Peter Wills, wrote his thoughts in a poem about Saldanha's windswept bay. The place is now a popular resort and yachting centre with housing and a National Park, in an irrigated green landscape, but in those days it was a dry, deserted whaling centre and anchorage. From England in 1945[12] Peter wrote:

UPPER LEFT: Lt/Cdr Wilhelm Spahr KC U/178. *(Courtesy of Horst Bredow)*

LOWER LEFT: Lt/Cdr Robert Bartels KC U/197. *(Courtesy of Horst Bredow)*

UPPER RIGHT: Cdr Wilhelm Dommes KC U/178. *(Courtesy of Horst Bredow)*

LOWER RIGHT: Senior Lieutenant Karl Wunderlich UIT/22. *(Courtesy of Horst Bredow)*

SALT ON MY LIPS (Saldanha Bay)

I never thought I'd wish again to see
That barren bay, locked in a Western shore,
Nor ever dreamed that I should long once more
In solitude its wilderness to roam,

Where, endlessly, the white waves burst and foam;
And the kelp gulls cry as the cormorant dips,
There by the bleached bones of forgotten ships;
And the all is alone with God and the sea.

Yet, though I yearn for that forsaken waste,
To breathe once more its special flavoured air,
I know that I shall never see so rare
A thing as sunset on the evening calm,
Nor will I ever know again the taste
Of salt, upon my lips in Langebaan.

DUTCH MOTHER SHIP SUNK

With submarine mother ships, however, the Allies had not had it all their own way. A German success came on 27 February 1943 when Commander Wiebe, in U/516, sank a Dutch submarine depôt ship, *en route* from East London to Simonstown. She was the 10,780-ton RNNS *Colombia*, and due for a refit at the great naval base. Once again my friend from Weymouth College days, Lieutenant B.G.M. (Paddy) Cangley RN, later in Natal and Australia, happened to be on the spot. Extracts from his detailed account tell what occurred behind the scenes.

His ship, HMS *Genista*, a 900-ton Flower Class RN corvette, defined as a small naval escort vessel, sailed into East London early in 1943. The ship's company soon discovered that the job was to escort the *Colombia* down to the Cape. The background story was

'. . . that she had been secured to the harbour wall for months on end undergoing a refit, for so long in fact that the war had passed her by. East Londoners looked on those Hollanders as sons, many being married or engaged to local girls.

'The fact that D for Departure Day had almost dawned seemed to be common knowledge throughout the port. So it was that if South Africans knew the score, the enemy must have been equally well informed, bearing in mind the fifth column in which the subversive Ossewa Brandwag played a part. The extent of the leak became evident when a fair-sized section of East

237

London turned out to wave *Colombia* farewell.

'Course was set for the Cape of Good Hope, the weather remained fine and the sea swell moderate. *Genista* took up station, zigzagging ahead of her charge – and yet, a slow escort for such a valuable prize.

'On *Genista* the hands were contemplating dinner – the writer, being off watch and bored, wandered aft towards his action station, the stern depth charges. When it came, the explosion sounded thin, even muted. He watched a plume of smoke arising from *Colombia's* starboard quarter. *Genista* started searching the surrounding seas, groping for the "ping" which never failed to set the pulses racing.

'Those of us on the upper deck silently watched the lowering of *Colombia's* lifeboats crammed with survivors. Slowly, almost gently, the Dutchman settled by the stern, her bows rising ever higher, until at last the python ocean gave a last greedy gulp to swallow its prey without trace. Throughout, the corvette continued vainly saturating the depths with Asdic pulses.

'The seas off the southern African coasts were, and probably still are notorious for deflecting Asdic transmissions, the numerous cold water layers providing an effective shield against hunter-killers. Once it became apparent that the U-boat would live to fight another day, *Genista's* captain broke off probing and turned to rescue operations, at which point the corvette became a second, stationary target. A nasty moment.'

Not so much as a single depth charge had been fired in anger. Nor had one Dutch sailor been killed by blast or gone down with his ship. Having completed the perfect rescue, *Genista* sailed for harbour depositing the survivors back in East London, presumably into the arms of their loved ones. Forty years later, Cangley read the conclusion of the matter in *War in the Southern Oceans*.[13]

The reason why no escorts other than *Genista* were available, was that seven other convoys were at sea at the time. Wiebe (U/516's captain), fired three torpedoes. At one point in the search, says the book, *Genista* passed close astern of U/516 without attacking. Cangley disagreed with this, preferring to believe that the corvette released a charge or two from the stern rails, with the object of persuading the U-boat to stay deep. My friend comments:

'Finally, bearing in mind the existence of that fifth column, the writer considers the presence of U/516 in precisely the correct interception area, at the appropriate hour, a cause for speculation. An afterthought. The sinking seemed an ideal way of waging war at sea, neither side suffering casualties. For that matter, not a soul so much as got a wetting.'

A special note of tribute must be given to the US Navy and their land-plane American bombers operating from the Ascension Island base in 1943 and on to 1945. Hunter-killer groups were sent to the Atlantic forming, with the RAF, an enormous net spread between the Americas and Africa, which caught many of the Far East-bound U-boats. These groups possessed, besides destroyers, a new breed of aircraft carrier. It was the Escort or 'Woolworth' carrier or 'baby flat-top.' They were smaller, more manoeuvrable and easier to produce in the large numbers needed by the RAF and the US Navy. Most carried a swarm of powerful Grumman Avenger torpedo-bombers and Grumman Wildcat fighters favoured by the Fleet Air Arm.

The hunters also had an immense advantage, thanks to ULTRA's decoding by the 'back-room boys and girls' of Bletchley Park. This gave detailed knowledge regarding U-boat movements and rendezvous with supply ships and Germany could not understand why so many sorties ended disastrously. Also in 1943 the USA intensified its activities on Ascension Island with long-range Consolidated Liberator bombers of the US Navy. These began to contribute to the havoc wrought by the hunter-killers.

The full list of U-boats may be seen in the appendix, but these are some examples of U-boats sunk *en route* to or from the Far East: U/200 sunk off Iceland by US group VP84's Catalina on 24.6.43; U/506 sunk by a US Liberator off Finisterre on the 12.7.43; U/487, a *milch kuh,* sunk by Avengers and Wildcats from USS *Core* on 13.7.43; U/160, a U-tanker sunk by VC 29 Squadron from USS *Santee* on 14.7.43 and U/509 sunk on 15.7.43.

The following month three aircraft from USS *Card* in the Sargasso Sea sank U/847, a IXD2 *milch kuh* which had recently refuelled five U-boats. Finally, in November 1943 Ascension-based US Navy Liberators sank U/848 and U/849, while on 20 December Avengers from USS *Bogue* west of Madeira downed U/850. The RAF meantime had sunk two Far East boats in the Atlantic, U/514 and U/462, and two in the Indian Ocean. Other U-boats would meet their fate the same way in 1944 and 1945 so numbers operating in the Indian Ocean were lessened by the US Navy's Atlantic contribution, along with the Royal Navy and the RAF squadrons, especially in the Bay of Biscay.

What the Allies had done is summed up dramatically by a German historian, Günter Böddeker, when he wrote:[14]

'Anfang Juli stellte die "Zehnte Flotte" in Washington im mittleren Atlantik eine gigantische Falle auf, die über den Booten der Grüppe "Monsun"

zuklappen sollte.'

(At the beginning of July the Tenth Fleet in Washington set up, in the middle Atlantic, a gigantic trap, which should clang shut over the boats of the Monsoon Group.)'

It did!

N O T E S

[1] Colossus. After the war the original machines were dismantled and at first were thought not worth preserving, but recently a group have revived interest in the centre near Milton Keynes, which is worth visiting. Three scientists have now reconstructed a working Colossus. See *Ultra Goes to War*, Ronald Lewin (Hutchinson) 1978.

[2] *ULTRA at Sea,* John Winton (Leo Cooper), London 1988

[3] HMS *Battler's War,* Kenneth Poolman (page 256 *Air Pictorial* magazine)

[4] RAF squadron records, PRO, Kew

[5] 834 Sq Swordfish piloted by the squadron CO, Lt Cdr E. Dixon Child

[6] *South Africa at War* – Vol. 7 *South African Forces WW2.* Henry J. Martin (Purnell), Cape Town 1979

[7] *Leitender Ingenieur,* K-H. Wiebe, Knights Cross, personal memoir

[8] *Catalina Safari,* Group Captain Peter Wills (privately printed memoir)

[9] Crew lists, as far as known, are as follows: 'P'- (E.S.S. Nash) with one change from the crew photo – F/O P.B. Wills, 2nd Pilot; F/Sgt Doug Hocking RAAF, Observer; F/Sgt 'Bluey' Davey, Flight Engineer; F/Sgt E. Walker, Rigger 2A; F/Sgt Tommy Tromons, Fitter 2E; Sgt C.N. Wright, WOP/AG; Sgt C. Baker WOP/AG.

'D' (Roddick) F/Sgt Harpleigh Davies, Observer; W/O Len Allen, 2nd Pilot; F/Sgt Bill Hill FMA/AG; F/Sgt Dennis Barlow, FME/AG; F/Sgt D. Wesley; WOM/AG; F/Sgt Tommy Thomason RCAF, Fitter 2E; F/Sgt Ted Williams, WOP/AG; F/Sgt Vern Snape, WOP/AG.

'A' (Surridge-incomplete, possibly wrong – guessed by colleagues, from an unlabelled photograph. (? F/Sgt) Tubby Ashton, 2nd Pilot; F/Sgt Dennis Rutter, Observer; F/Sgt Bather WOP/AG; F/Sgt Alan Chambers, Fitter 2E; F/Sgt Jones; F/Sgt Dicker; another F/Sgt Jones; F/Sgt Sweet.

[10] The cross-over patrol was a blocking search used to intercept the passage of a target whose general direction of approach was known but track uncertain. The pattern was a long thin 'X' placed transversely across the expected track of the target (see diagram). The length of the short legs was equal to twice the estimated detection range, and that of the long diagonal legs such that the time for one complete circuit of the 'X' was not greater than the time required by

the target to cover a distance equal to twice the detection range. (Wills)

[11] *ULTRA at Sea* John Winton – see above

[12] *My Old Tin Trunk* Peter Wills (privately printed booklet of his poems) 1992

[13] *War in the Southern Oceans,* Turner, Gordon-Cumming, Betzler (Oxford University Press), Cape Town 1961

[14] *Die Boote im Netz,* Günter Böddeker (Gustav Lübbe Verlag GmbH),- Bergisch Gladbach 1981

WELLINGTONS HOME IN

In the Western Desert the battles raged back and forth along the Mediterranean seaboard according to the strength of opposing armies. The campaign in the Indian Ocean was influenced more by events along its shores and it was hard to detect the ebb and flow of fortune. In September 1943, thanks to Allied victory in the north of Africa, the Mediterranean became open to Allied shipping. Now shipping was able to pass into the Red Sea and then to India or South Africa rather than face the long dangerous haul round the Cape of Good Hope.

Both the German Navy and the Imperial Japanese Navy started sending more submarines to Aden and the Persian Gulf. From there tankers ventured cautiously southward through the Straits of Hormuz without a protecting convoy, carrying oil from the Anglo-Iranian Oil company, the lifeblood of the Allies' war effort. The steel grey sharks were ready to pounce.

Number 8 RAF Squadron, based on Khormaksar, Aden, had been in that area a long time as we saw earlier in the capture of the Italian submarine *Galileo Galilei*. In 1943 Blenheim and Hudson aircraft were replaced by Wellington XIIIs, but one Hudson did have a partial success.[1]

The Wellington bomber or 'Wimpy' was so nicknamed, to quote Michael Turner, after a 'newspaper Popeye strip cartoon featuring a chubby, hamburger-eating trencherman named J. Wellington Wimpy'.[2] Whereas Lockheed Hudsons were like short stubby cigars, Vickers Wellingtons, with an overall length of 64 feet, were 20 feet longer, looking more like winged cheroots. This is because the scientist Sir Barnes Wallis, famous for his Dambuster bouncing bomb, invented a geodetic or basket-weave design to give extreme strength and flexibility to the somewhat rounded fuselage.

Up to 1943, Wellingtons were the mainstay of RAF bombing, 11,461 being built in all, and when serving in Coastal Command they sank or seriously damaged 91 enemy submarines, as shown here. The Mark XIII had two 1,735 hp Bristol Hercules XVII engines, which gave it a maximum speed of 255 mph, greater than that of a Catalina but with a range much less than the Cat's 3,000 miles. The rotating gun turret in the nose carried twin 0.303 inch machine guns, with quadruple 0.303s in the rear turret. A small bubble astrodome in the roof was big enough for an observer to keep his head and shoulders there to spot enemy activity above.

Extra reinforcements were now needed against the growing menace around Aden and for this purpose a new Wellington squadron, number 621, was created on 12 September 1943 at Port Reitz, Mombasa, equipped with Mark XIIIs for anti-submarine work. The author, at that time an observer in the Meteorological Office, Port Reitz, must have handed out many a weather forecast for the newly-arrived pilots but the white Wellingtons somehow escaped being recorded in his sketch pad. After a few sorties they were soon moved up to Mogadishu and then to Aden to share the Khormaksar base with 8 Squadron. A healthy rivalry developed between the two squadrons to sink the first submarine.

The two squadrons were joined in the hunt by detachments of Catalinas from 209, 259 and 265 Squadrons, and Wellingtons from 244. By January 1944, when five vessels were sunk in a month, the outlook was bad. Sixteen sightings of submarines had been made but none sunk despite 524 sorties. In 1944 over 2,000 hours were flown in April alone.

On the credit side in the first three months something like 300 ships were safely escorted through the area and on 2 April Wellingtons from 621 found 70 survivors from a torpedoed ship SS *Tarifa* and homed in rescue vessels to pick them up from the boats and rafts, as described by Oliver Gomersal who was then in Wellington E/621. At this period the *John Barry* was sunk in the area by U/859, and has now, by modern deep diving apparatus and computers, been found in the Arabian Sea and relieved of some of its gold and silver coins, which had been bound for the Gulf. U/859 met its fate at Penang as we shall see.

Signals picked up by direction finding units along the coastline of South and East Africa showed a submarine, later identified as U/852 by ULTRA's cryptographers, moving up towards Aden between March and April 1944. A ripple of expectation ran through the commands and squadron bases and Catalinas were kept in readiness in Madagascar and the smaller islands.

U/852 was a new long-range IXD2 U-cruiser launched by A.G. Weser in Bremen in 1943. Between May and June the final construction was being overseen by young Commander *Kapitänleutnant* Heinz Eck on his first assignment at the age of 27. He had started in minesweepers from the outbreak of war till June 1942 when he transferred to U-boats.[3] He must have been efficient for he had only one year's training in submarines before being given command of his own U-boat. Events later showed that he had learnt well the lessons of evading aircraft attacks. U/852 sailed on 8 January 1944 from Germany's great naval base at Kiel.

Eck left at a time when the Americans were using the 'Hunter-Killer' packs which we have seen and sending out bombers from Ascension Island with great success. U/852 managed undetected to reach 10° South when she came upon a Greek tramp steamer, the *Peleus* of 4,695 tons. What followed became a subject of post-war heated debate and bitterness between the Allied and Axis authorities. It can therefore be summarised in the words of a German history writer, Janus Piekalkiewicz, in the third volume, *Seekrieg 1939-1945*, of his well known trilogy, in its English translation, *Sea War 1939-1945*.[4] He writes:

'On Monday 13 March 1944, at 7:30 p.m., U/852 (Lt Comdr Eck) sank the Greek merchant ship *Peleus* (4,695 gross tons) between Freetown and Ascension. The old ship went down quickly, and only two or three rafts bearing a few survivors were to be seen among the wreckage. Lt Comdr Eck ordered that a machine gun MG15 be mounted and a case of hand grenades be brought up on deck. The submarine's doctor, Dr Weisspfennig, was given the order to open fire on the survivors. The U-boat commander wanted to destroy all traces of the torpedoing for fear of Allied air reconnaissance. Twenty-five days after the sinking of the *Peleus,* a raft with three survivors was sighted by the Portuguese steamer *Alexandre,* which picked up the men and so heard about the incident. The '*Peleus* affair' is the only recorded incident of survivors being fired upon by a German U-boat.'

One of the three survivors was the Chief Officer of the *Peleus,* Antonios Liossis. An extract[5] from his affidavit given before a magistrate at Cape Town describes the situation from the survivors' viewpoint.

'The submarine left the third officer's raft and made a sweep. I could see most of the rest of the crew in the water clinging to the wreckage and shouting and blowing whistles. We lashed two rafts together and very soon after, the submarine reappeared and hailed us to go nearer. As we approached, the submarine suddenly opened fire with a machine gun. We all ducked and I could hear cries of pain from Konstantinidis who was hit by bullets in several places. The rafts were riddled with bullet holes but did not sink because the tanks were filled with buoyant material. The Germans also threw hand grenades at us, one of which wounded me. My head was under a bench so that I was only hit in the right shoulder and back. They also threw grenades at the other raft.'

What about the U-boat captain's account? In the hope of obtaining a photograph of Heinz Eck, I wrote to his surviving sister, Mrs Talitha Eck-Constatinescu, in Hamburg, sending her also the account of the brave battle and destruction of U/852 which was, of course, new to her. She not only sent the photograph, but kindly added many documents relating to her brother, his trial and subsequent articles about it. One of the statements is in English by Heinz Eck before his execution. It amplifies what he had said at the end of his trial by a British Military Court in Hamburg in 1945.

Eck stated: 'I gave the order to open fire with machine guns and two cm guns at the bits of wreckage and rafts.' When asked: 'What reasons and ideas prompted you to issue such orders?' he gave this reply:

'When I gave these orders I was in an area over which there was continuous enemy air reconnaissance. I had been informed of this before leaving Kiel and I had seen for myself there were constant air patrols. I was convinced that enemy aircraft patrolling the area would find traces of the sinking within a few days. As the enemy was not aware that we were in the neighbourhood, I thought it best to avoid being discovered through bits of floating wreckage as this would have led to my boat being destroyed.'

Other statements give the impression that Eck thought that any survivors would have jumped off the wreckage and that only rafts then had to be sunk, although he regretted that men still alive would therefore not be able to reach shore. Eck was described in some but not all recent articles as bent on murder and destruction. My feeling is that he was bent on saving his crew and vessel, as he was when the submarine was later attacked. Though well trained in tactics he had never faced before a disaster scene with a torpedoed crew determined to survive. Had he been 'bent on destruction' he would have murdered the crew of the next ship he torpedoed, which he did not.

Having sunk the *Peleus*, the U/852 then reached the Cape of Good Hope and south of it torpedoed, on 1 April 1944, the British ship *Dahomian* of 5,277 tons. She sank in a few minutes and 49 survivors were picked up by South African Naval Force minesweepers[6]. On this occasion there was no attempt to attack survivors. Eck continued up the eastern coast of Africa but by now his boat was being tracked by D/F fixes from radio-monitoring staff along the coast. The history *War in the Southern Oceans* notes: 'Air Headquarters at Aden prepared for his reception. On 30 April he was "placed" as approaching Cape Guardafui.' This was the most easterly tip of Africa and U/852 had reached a point just a few miles south, opposite a small bay called Bender Beila. The operation was under the direction of IOGROPS, a new RN/RAF control group at Colombo. The official report now takes up the story[7]:

> 'As U/852 approached the Somali coast on 1 May 1944, Wellingtons of 621 Squadron from Riyan, Socotra, Bender Kassim and Scuiscuiban (pronounced Shoo-shooban) bases, forewarned by East Africa Command of an intruder, had established a day and night pattern of patrol over the waters south of Cape Guardafui. On its patrol in the early hours of 2 May aircraft E/621 descended to 3,000 feet altitude to evade a towering mass of cumulus ahead.'

In the cockpit was the captain, Flying Officer Roy H. 'Mitch' Mitchell with Canadian Warrant Officer Harvey Riddell as Second Pilot. Flight Sergeant O. 'Ollie' Gomersal was navigator. Before joining up Oliver worked in the Treasurer's Department at Buxton Town Hall. At the table behind and beside him was one of the two wireless operator/air gunners. On this occasion it was Flight Sergeant J. 'Ted' Turner of the Royal Australian Air Force. Sergeant W.R. 'Stevie' Stevenson, the front gunner, was in the Second Pilot's seat at the time keeping watch to starboard. Before coming into the RAF he was training to be a colliery blacksmith. 'Tail-end Charlie', the WOP/AG in the rear gun turret was Sergeant A.R. Philip, an ex-railway clerk known as Sandy because of his hair colour. To continue the story in Stevenson's words:

> 'The time was early morning (0421) and immediately ahead was some awful weather. Harvey switched on his intercom to the Skipper and asked permission to fly under it. That was the first bit of good luck or good flying because within seconds of coming into good weather I spotted out of the starboard window what appeared to be a boat on the surface. Harvey turned and confirmed it was worth investigating. He then called Mitch and immediately everyone was on the alert. I was shut into the front turret, locked and bolted.'

The radio operator sent an SS 465 signal on operational day frequency, addressed to Aden from his own call-sign. The Captain took over the controls at six miles range from the submarine and descended with undercarriage down to 800 feet at one mile range. He then turned 80 degrees to port to meet the submarine head on. He had previously checked that all six depth charges had been properly selected and fused by Gomersal. Stevenson continues:

> 'Mitch had started his run in and I could see the U-boat looming closer. After

months at sea it felt unbelievable that we were going to have a crack. The thing that stands out in my memory was the [German] crew as they ran to the conning tower. I was fortunate that my guns were in perfect working order. I strafed the conning tower from top to bottom, which was made easy by the Skipper's wonderful approach.'

The RAF report continues:

'As Mitchell turned the aircraft to port to meet the submarine head on, Eck's U/852 started to dive leaving a heavy swirl and keeping quite straight. Mitchell straightened out at 1,200 yards range [and continued a more steady descent to the standard 50 feet for dropping DCs], coming in at 10° to the submarine's track. Stevenson's tracer could be seen consistently hitting the base of the conning tower. On the run in the Captain reckoned that only the conning tower would be showing when he arrived. Basing his judgement of distance on a target towed for practice at an Operational Training Unit, 150 feet behind a launch, he aimed the first depth charge to strike 250 feet ahead of the still visible conning tower.

'It was still very early in the morning. The sun was low but it was on his port beam and caused no glare. Both pilots saw large bubbles in the foaming swirl of the conning tower, half of which was still visible when they passed over it. The front gunner kept firing bursts until the guns were fully depressed. The navigator standing in the astrodome, noticed the aircraft suddenly rise and then saw all the depth charges apparently hanging in mid-air. [Gomersal recalls saying to himself grimly, "GET DOWN, YOU BLIGHTERS, GET DOWN!" as the bombs tilted forward.] They all fell dead in line with U/852 and the last entered the swirl. The rear gunner saw the tails of the last two depth charges hurled into the air, the others having gone off and left plumes of water. Mitchell said. "Harvey, get the camera and shoot or they'll never believe us." Within three minutes of release [of the DCs] the navigator had gone to his table, worked out a position, noted the submarine's course and speed and got the sighting report sent to Aden HQ. The oil patch was photographed. The Captain saw a white foaming ring beyond the oil patch with what appeared to be the nose of the U-boat rising at 50° to the horizontal. This was five minutes after the release of the DCs. The nose sank: the submarine surfaced and began firing on the aircraft.'

The following RAF description must have been obtained when the submarine crew was interrogated after the operation. The Germans said:

'The Wellington's attack had fractured the main inlet pipe. The vessel was flooding badly and only able to surface by blowing all air containers and driving the boat to the surface. She surfaced at an angle of more than 45°: all water ran aft, flooded the engine room and started a fierce fire.'

The RAF report continued:

'After the U-boat had begun firing, the Wellington turned to port and made off into the sun, taking corkscrew evasive action. The pilot returned over U/852 and fired, raking the deck and firing tracer into the conning tower until return tracer ceased. Then U/852 opened up with 10.5 cm. shells, [from the large gun on the foredeck mainly used for sinking small ships] at three miles and continued it to a range of seven miles, reopening fire each time the Wellington closed to four miles.

'Two hours and ten minutes had passed since E had dropped its depth charges when the captain saw another white Wellington, U, about to attack U/852 closer in. It was too late for E to close and create a diversion so, near the end of its endurance, it returned to land at Scuiscuiban with only 30 gallons of fuel, all in the tank of one engine, at 08.15 hours after a 7 hours and 10 minutes flight.'

For the next two days U/852 faced an amazing number of attacks by different Wellingtons, first from 621 Squadron and then from 8 Squadron. In all of them where depth charges were dropped, Eck, in the words of the RAF report, 'showed himself as a master of tactics'. He turned his boat rapidly at exactly the right moment, either to avoid the falling bombs or to put off the pilot from dropping his DCs.

The first and most effective attacker, E, was followed by Wellington U/621 (JA 564) whose Captain was Flight Lieutenant J.Y. Wade.[8] It set out from Socotra Island and dropped its DCs at 06.42 hours. These landed about 100 feet ahead of the U-boat's bows causing some damage, it is thought. On U's run-in, however, a 20-mm shell had damaged the starboard air cooler. She then continued to circle while two more reliefs arrived.

The first, F/621 (HZ 803, also given as JA 184) captained by Flying Officer E.E. Read,[9] left Bandar Kassim at 06.40 and carried out two attacks, dropping four DCs on the first run and the remaining two on a third run. They burst close to the boat but caused no visible damage.

Flight Sergeant Mick Bond, a WOP/AG/ASV Operator (radar) was in the swivelling front gun-turret that day, facing the submarine's fire, and wrote a full account of it, of which these are a few points:

'I remember having some difficulty in lining up the conning tower in the gun sight. I know now this was not easy because the Pilot was taking evasive action. During this attack we experienced heavy anti-aircraft fire, balls of black smoke appearing on the same level. I recall seeing these flashes of light on the U-boat and just for a few seconds thought it was a signal in

Left: F/O Keith Scott RAAF with K-244 awaiting attack on U/852, from Aden.

(Courtesy of K. Scott)

Upper right: U852 at 8.18 a.m. on 2 May 1944 seen from U/621

(Courtesy of O. Gomersal)

Lower right: U/852 after scuttling in Bender Beila Bay, being checked by naval parties.

(Courtesy of R.N Submarine Museum Gosport)

Aldis. I soon found it wasn't. During these attacks our second pilot gave us gunners lots of encouragement by shouting through the intercom – he must have been very frustrated just sitting alongside the pilot and not being able to contribute.'

The fourth attack was carried out by 621 Squadron's Commanding Officer, Wing Commander P. Green, in his own Wellington 'T' for Tommy (HZ 940). He took off from Bender Kassim at 06.12, after dawn on the first fateful day, 2 May 1944. There are some inconsistencies in the four reports that can be studied about T's attack in the official record. The third of these was a personal account inserted into the Form 540, written at the time by Green's navigator, Flight Lieutenant R. Whitrod, an Australian (not RCAF!). It is a long report full of vivid details and humorous comments that reveal the story behind the official jargon. Whitrod begins:

'Entering the Ops room to pick up the gen for a routine flight that T/621 was making to Socotra that morning in order to provide the Wing Commander of 621 with an opportunity to inspect all his detachments, the navigator was somewhat taken aback by the unusual amount of activity that met his eyes; a harassed pilot acting as controller and a WOP/AG "clerk", struggling to decipher an "Immediate" that had just arrived. Pressing closer the navigator heard the exciting phrases,"465[10] – still on the surface – off Dante – damaged" – and without any further information he rushed for the Wing Commander.

'The smooth organisation for which Bender Kassim is noted went into operation. The remainder of the crew of Tommy were collected and their belongings thrown into the flight truck.[11] The truck would not start. A fresh truck was commandeered and found to contain a varied assortment of beds, mattresses, mosquito nets, frying pans and small huts taken to pieces and so back rushed the crew to the original truck.

'The Wing Commander, with memories of Brooklands[12] still fresh in his mind, threw the native driver out of his seat and succeeded in starting the engine. Amidst shouts of "feisha feisha" [Arabic for quickly] and "pacee pacee" [Swahili ditto] the crew drove out to the aircraft at dispersal. Thoughts of the arrival of aircraft from 8 Squadron at the U-boat first were sufficient to guarantee a hasty take-off and despite a cross wind that drove the aircraft crabwise down the runway, and assisted by the fervent prayers of the crew, Tommy rose into the air and course was set for Dante [a small coastal village].

'Climbing up through the gap in the mountain range at slightly more than recommended cruising, the crew had time to collect their thoughts and they were not altogether pleasing. Outwardly everybody was smiling and saying "Wizzo, let's kill the baskets", but inside there were some rather uneasy thoughts. Only two 303's in the front turret, and it's sure to be a German and bound to fight back to a finish, and only last week in Coastal Command Review there was an article describing how a Sunderland had been shot down by a U-boat in the Bay, three of the crew being killed outright; and this navigator was due to go home after three years abroad!

'Arriving at Dante, course was set due east to the revised position of the U-boat, Estimated Time of Arrival being in nine minutes flying time. Shortly before the time had elapsed, a broad oil streak, approx 400 yards wide, could be seen on the starboard bow, leading south south east. Turning into this, in a few moments the head of the oil streak could be seen. Yes, there, right at the apex of the streak was a black dot moving at quite a speed, and Tommy metaphorically pawed the ground and moved in closer; but not too close, for Al Winslow, the Canadian second pilot, asked "What is that? Recognition signal?" And the Navigator acting as Fire Controller in the astrodome replied, "Flak", and bursting just short of the aircraft were small bursts of black smoke.

'As a precaution the navigator lowered the astrodome and placed the dinghy emergency pack, and four K-type dinghies under the opening ready for immediate use should the necessity arise. First Aid outfits were stuffed into the pockets of his shorts and his Mae West given a last-minute check over. He then braced himself for whatever might happen. He occupied himself by reporting the accuracy of the flak to the Captain – "Flak – 200 yards starboard. Flak – 100 yards starboard. Flak – 60 yards starboard." He was then instructed by the Captain to cease reporting!

'On this occasion Sgt Lucy was acting as First W/Op and was sitting at the set. On all previous flights he had occupied the rear turret, and for many hours had sat there dreaming of the time when something real and living would be the recipient of his bullets, instead of lousy sea markers; but unfortunately the Wingco had discovered that prior to remustering as aircrew he had been a ground W/T operator so he had been promoted to first W/Op. Lucy was therefore manfully struggling to do his duty and concentrate his attention on the many Ps and O-Ps[13] that were filling the ether at that time. The navigator, knowing Lucy's real thoughts, made an arrangement whereby he would notify him when the kite started its run in, so Lucy would have time to leave the set, rush to the side guns, and at least have the satisfaction of firing a few bursts from them as the aircraft flew over the submarine.

Upper: When 621 Sq Wellingtons destroyed U/852 (ECK), Sgt Walter Stevenson was awarded the DFM and F/O Roy Mitchell the DFC. (see chapter 12) *(Courtesy W. Stevenson)*

Lower left: F/Lt Eric Yeomans received a DFC for 209 Sq anti-shipping strikes off Burma Coast in August 1945. *(Courtesy N. Wilson)*

Lower right: F/Lt Rae Thomas of 413 Sq and his crew were shot down and lost reporting the approach of the Jap fleet in April 1942, but Rae already had a DFC from the Atlantic operations. (see chapter 2) *(Courtesy Mrs Sarah Clayton)*

'Several attempts were made to get an attack in down the submarine track, but smart turning on its part always presented the beam to the aircraft. One attempt to attack down the track was pressed fairly close, and while the submarine's attention was concentrated upon Tommy, another Wimpy, flown by F/O Ogle, hitherto unnoticed by Tommy, saw an opening and coming from the opposite direction dropped a stick (of bombs) right down the U-boat's length. Seizing his chance the Pilot of Tommy dived in for his attack.

'The navigator not wishing to use the intercom, which was being used by the Captain and front gunner, yelled and screamed at Lucy and gesticulated wildly with his arms, but Lucy was devoting all his time to the set. Finally in desperation, he picked up his rubber and threw it at Lucy. The rubber landed on his neck. Just at this moment, a heavy burst of flak above the aircraft shook the old crate and Lucy fell to the floor. He remained still for a few moments and then, very slowly and gingerly, placed his hand on his neck and drawing it back looked at it. Then he jumped up sprightly and resumed his seat on the set.

'Nearer and nearer came the submarine, until for one moment the bared torsos and fair hair of the guncrews were clearly seen, and then – Wham! – out spoke the four guns at the rear and great joy came to the rear gunner. The stick of DCs slightly overshot, No 1 [DC] helping to exaggerate the overshoot by hanging up! Disappointment at the miss spread over the crew, and depression could be seen on all their faces. At this moment a signal from base was received ordering Tommy to return to Socotra at the end of her patrol, but the Captain, taking the initiative into his own hands, decided to land at Scuiscuiban and re-arm, Socotra being 100 minutes flying time away and Scuiscuiban only 30. [There] the Wingco planned a co-ordinated attack by Tommy and F/O James' and W/O Ryall's aircraft, but unfortunately F/O James' kite Q/621 overheated whilst he was on the deck and he had to be left behind. '

Warrant Officer J.P. Ryall[14] of Canada in his report on D/621 (JA 389) later stated:

'At 10.40 aircraft took off from Scuiscuiban on U-boat strike in conjunction with T/621. Saw aircraft T circling what appeared to be a U-boat and only after an attack had been made with depth charges was this found to be a smoke float.'

Whitrod continues:

'The U-boat was sighted ahead. Several Wimpys could be seen circling round, waiting for an opportunity to pounce, and, not knowing whether these were all 621 or of some other squadron, Tommy immediately attacked. On this occasion the flak did not seem so thick but F/Lt Wade in aircraft U/621 later reported that 14 bursts were seen just aft of the aircraft's tail as T went in. By skilful evasive action, the U-boat commander again swung his boat round at the last possible moment, and rather than drop another stick across the beam, the pilot decided to forego this opportunity. Around went Tommy again and this time of the two front guns, one was out of ammunition and the other had a recurring stoppage. W/O Ryall was nowhere to be seen on the first attack and apparently plans for a co-ordinated attack had given way under the strain.

'In went Tommy and just when the flak became uncomfortably accurate, another Wimpy [which later proved to be Ryall's D who had used up her DCs on a smoke float] was seen to float over the top of the U-boat from stem to stern and literally shower bullets down upon it, to the extent that for the last 400 yards of Tommy's run, there was little if any flak. A beautiful stick was dropped right across from the starboard beam, just forward of the conning tower and DCs Numbers 2 and 3 straddled. A huge column of spray flew up and hid the submarine from view. For about two minutes the intercom became incoherent with the cries from the Navigator and the Rear Gunner – "Okay, Boss, a beauty!"

'But when the plumes had subsided the U-boat was observed moving along its old course, apparently undamaged. It did not seem possible! All the experts must be wrong. Anyway there it was, still moving, and apparently untouched by our straddle. A very disappointed crew watched that submarine for a few minutes and then, remembering that it was a strike aircraft and not detailed to shadow, course was set for base.'

All was by no means lost, however. There was hope of bringing in the cavalry in the form of the Royal Navy and efforts were made to home a naval vessel in the vicinity on to the U-boat but had to be broken off when T reached the end of its endurance and flew back to Socotra. HMS *Falmouth* had been ordered at 1206 hours to proceed to assist in the hunt, but through faults in communications and the tortuous course of U/852 she did not sight her until dawn on the 3rd.

Almost a new chapter now begins in the hunt for this apparently unsinkable U-boat and its crew. When T/621 left the U/852, the situation of the submarine was grave but not hopeless. There was still a chance of getting away by night either outward into mid-ocean or (more improbably) by hiding up by day under the land and proceeding south by stages towards the Cape. If any such plan was considered then on 3 May the arrival of most of 8 Squadron's remaining Wellingtons ruled it out.

No 8's aircrews must have been gnashing their teeth by now to think that the long-awaited submarine had surfaced in 621's patch on the 2 May. Their first aircraft,[15] G/8,(JA 413) captained by F/O J.R. Forrester RCAF, had been out on the 2nd, according to one report, attacking the sub at 1355 hours and scoring probable hits. Another 8 Sq aircraft failed to locate the U-boat and had to land at Scuiscuiban with engine trouble, the crew no doubt being forced to listen to the stories of the 621 crowd.

On the afternoon of the 3rd, Forrester flying G/8 returned, passed over U/852 from starboard quarter to port bow and straddled her with a stick of DCs, to no avail. He then shadowed Eck's boat and, having been hit by a 20 mm cannon shell, kept out of range of the formidable 10.5 cm deck gun. Losing radar contact at 1638, Forrester returned home as night came on. Another aircraft, J/8, was ordered to attack but made no contact.

From then onwards a visual search was carried out up and down the coast in the hope that later the U-boat's wake would be visible by moonlight. Nothing was seen until later that evening when the submarine was found by G, lying stationary off the shore with a large oil patch round her. Forrester, anxious to do nothing to encourage Eck to move from his position, did not circle but stayed at long range. He lost contact again and, at the Prudent Limit of Endurance, returned to Scuiscuiban.

Wellington X/8 then found the submarine at 0200 hours lying in shallow water 40 yards from the shore at Bender Beila. At 0220 hours aircraft D/8 also sighted her. Her captain received permission from HMS *Falmouth*, then in the vicinity, to attack but his depth charges failed to explode probably owing to the shallowness of the water.

Air Headquarters, Aden, had also up their sleeve other measures in case depth charges were insufficient. Some 244 Squadron aircraft were on detachment to RAF Khormaksar before returning to base on Masirah Island near the Gulf Of Oman. One was armed up with three anti-submarine bombs possibly 500-pounders and Wellington K (JA199), piloted by Australian Keith Scott, was chosen for this. His crew consisted of Bert Carroll, Second Pilot; Grev Davis, Navigator; Ray Ellick, Jim Bailey and Stan Aldred, all Wireless Operator/Air gunners. Keith wrote:

'I guess that we would have taken off from Aden about 0230 to 0300. We had three hours of night flying and 1 hour 55 minutes in daylight. When we got to Scuiscuiban we were told that our bombs were not required as the submarine had beached itself and that the crew had taken to the land.'

Thus, they 'missed the show'.

We return to the U/852 lying motionless in Bender Beila Bay. Hans Herlin[16] describes the events from the submariners' angle, of which I summarise a few points. The crew by now had all taken to the water and those fit enough had clambered on to the rocky shore. The weakest lay still in the water in their lifejackets near the beach. Suddenly there was a loud explosion and Captain Eck, lying behind the boulders on the shore, looking at his stranded boat saw that the bows and the stern had been blown off but the conning tower and centre section were still standing proudly up in the water. (This had nothing to do with a rather surprised crew of Wellington X of 8 Squadron, which happened to be passing overhead at the time at an altitude of 900 feet.) Eck had himself set scuttling charges, due to go off in nine minutes, according to Herlin.

Reports from the Navy, the RAF and the German sources become somewhat confused at this stage. Herlin describes 12 of the crew climbing desperately up the thorny and rocky cliff and contemplating escape across the blazing desert, but remaining there. Exploring a dried river bed with dwindling food and water they then decided against escape and gave themselves up after three days. Other accounts indicate a shorter period for rounding up the prisoners and speak of a Camel Corps doing the job.

Lt Paddy Cangley RN, who had by now changed his corvette *Genista* for another, the *Tulip*, which visited the wreck at Bender Beila some time later, knew Malcolm Logan who was a Captain in the Kings African Rifles unit covering that mission. Paddy concludes that it was the KAR patrol which would have done the rounding up of the crew and then handed them over to the naval parties which took over the scene. Apart from the *Falmouth* at least two other small ships are reported to have gathered. One of those mentioned in T/621's report was HMS *Parrott*. We know also of the cutter HMS *Fishguard*.

Another friend, Lieutenant Andrew Stewart RNVR, later a mining engineer consultant but then in the Tanganyika Naval Volunteer Force, knew one of the officers on *Fishguard* which had sent a boat on shore to help round up the tired German crew. He described how polite the German officers were, standing up to click their heels and salute any British officer who entered the Mess. Then naval parties explored the U-boat's shell including the helicopter kite or *Bachstelze* (water wagtail) seen in the illustration of the supply ships, chapter 7.

This was said to have been the first time that the British became aware that the Germans were using these man-lifting kites to achieve the spotting of merchant ships over the horizon. The two drums containing the kite, which was a Focke Achgelis, were handed over by the Navy to a party from RAF Mombasa sent up by Group Captain G. M. 'Peter' Bryer, Officer Commanding 246 Wing, Mombasa. He then had the kite tested off some cliffs near Mombasa and a useful, if not powerful, new weapon of the *Kriegsmarine*, was revealed to the Allies. The Captain and crew were taken by various means to Aden. There had been five dead during the action and now on HMS *Falmouth* down in the sick bay the Ship's Surgeon and Dr Weisspfennig from U/852 operated on a sixth crew member but despite their joint efforts he died.

By now the British had become aware of the *Peleus* history and Eck was kept in close custody. To quote the German history again. 'Lt Comdr Eck, Dr Weisspfennig and Lt Hoffmann were taken prisoner. They subsequently appeared before a British military court – the trial began on 17 October 1945 in Hamburg – and were sentenced to be executed by firing squad.'[17] It must be noted that the Chief Engineer, Hans Lenz, when Eck had given the order to fire on the wreckage, had protested against the order but was overruled and then took part in the firing. On this account he received a lesser sentence.

This was, to my knowledge, the only case of a WW2 German U-boat attack upon survivors being tried in a court of law but legal authorities would point to other cases attested before an attorney as being valid also. One of those on the German side was the attack on the *Noreen Mary* by U/247[18] and on the Allied side there was the case of the submarine USS *Wahoo* which torpedoed a crowded Japanese troopship and the US captain reported firing upon the hundreds of survivors in the water some of whom 'used pistols'.[19] In the Indian Ocean German submariners at times helped survivors, even on one occasion actually towing the lifeboat for some distance. Japanese attacks, however, on those they had torpedoed were many and ferocious,[20] acting in accordance with the orders they had received.[21]

Should Heinz Eck have been executed for this order given under extreme pressure and with the motive of preserving his ship? One British admiral thought not. The *Daily Telegraph* of 6 May 1949 records a debate in which Admiral of the Fleet the Earl of Cork and Orrery said of Eck:

'He knew and accepted that there were survivors clinging to the wreckage, but he put the carrying out of his mission and the safety of his ship and crew first. I think myself, though it is a severe view, that is the view every officer ought to take.'

This was borne out in the *Laconia* case itself where Commander Hartenstein in U/156 in the Atlantic was towing four lifeboats full of survivors, had scores of passengers visible on his deck and a large Red Cross draped over his deck gun. The pilot of the American Mitchell bomber[22] nevertheless received orders from Ascension to bomb the submarine which he did unsuccessfully but killed many survivors in the process.

I have before me a copy of the front page of the *Sunday Express* for 4 August 1963 (which cost 5 old pence in those days) revealing a secret that had been kept since the end of the war. In it Brigadier General Robert C. Richardson at Nato Headquarters told the reporter:

Lt/Cdr Heinz Eck.
(Courtesy of Mrs Talitha Eck-Constantinescu)

'I gave the order to bomb the *Laconia* survivors. We did not know there were British among them. But even if we had, it would have made no difference. I would have given the order anyway.'

Lieutenant Commander Eck's sister has a letter which states that her brother tried at one stage to stop the shooting. It was from *Kapitän zur See* (Captain) Hans Meckel, of the Defence team, to Admiral Ruge after the execution. The relevant sentence in German states:

'Eck hatte befohlen, falls Schiffbrüchige in der Schussrichtung erkannt würden, das Feuer einzustellen – Eck had commanded that in the event of ship survivors being perceived in the direction of the shots, firing should be suspended.'

Nevertheless, the legal opinion of the Allies remained that in Eck's case the incidental killing of survivors required the supreme penalty.

Some time after the action two awards were presented by Air Vice Marshal McNamara VC at a ceremony in Aden. Flying Officer Roy Mitchell received the DFC and Sergeant Walter Stevenson the DFM for their fine work at the beginning of the action which crippled the U-boat and enabled it to be driven ashore in later attacks.

How was it this U-boat was able to survive the onslaught of 47 depth charges and 7,000 rounds of ammunition? How could it suffer only a minor fire and the loss of six of its crew until it grounded itself in Bender Beila Bay and was then scuttled by the Captain using his own charges? Looking at the balance sheet, on the German side three factors stand out.

A courageous crew used their anti-aircraft fire to keep the Wellingtons at a distance, between attacks, but hardly damaged the attackers. Secondly, a skilful Commandant correctly judged the moment to swerve as the aircraft zoomed in on him. Thirdly, the U-boats from Type VII onwards, were superbly designed, welded and riveted together, with an inner 1-inch solid steel circular hull that could withstand 14 tons per square inch pressure. It took an explosion of extraordinary accuracy and a measure of luck to rupture the inner hull. A Bisley bomber of 244 Squadron, as we saw in October 1942, managed it with a single drop of four bombs in the Gulf of Oman. Yet in the same region a Navy vessel, circling over a dived U-boat, dropped 55 depth charges without result.

The British, for their part, had done well with ULTRA decoding and D/F radar to track the submarine up the eastern coast of Africa. Then they had enough Wellington bombers ready to give U/852 a hot reception and force it towards destruction on the Horn of Africa. The aircrews were determined, brave and skilful enough in their attacks – so why was the submarine not sunk? Part of the answer must be in the fact that the U-boat was forced to remain on the surface. Depth charges are normally set to explode by water pressure at 25 feet depth. Even if detonated at a shallower level, the effect of the explosions may have been merely to lift the sub upwards without damaging it. Other methods would need to be adopted in this situation. Be that as it may, one can give the last word to the RAF report.

'It was the result that mattered most, whatever the lessons for the future were. Aircraft of British Forces Aden had ensured the safety of all shipping passing through its waters for two more critical months.'

36 (WELLINGTON) SQUADRON

This squadron was re-formed after its being wiped out in Malaya on 22 October 1942 and was supplied with Wellington 1cs in December. Late that month, a Catalina pilot, Flight Lieutenant D.E. 'Ted' Hawkins DFC, was detached to Tanjore from 240 Squadron as a Senior Flight Lieutenant to take command of 36 Squadron. After VE Day he was to command 230 Squadron at Seletar.

36 Squadron – Shades of the TV Serial *It A'int 'Arf 'Ot,
Mum!*, one of many RAF magazines in Asia.
(Drawn by Nick, a squadron artist – courtesy of John Cox)

Ted Hawkins, now Air Vice Marshal D.E. Hawkins CB CBE DFC, had
been with 240 Squadron in the Atlantic. An article in the *Illustrated
Weekly of India* magazine[23] states:

> 'In April 1942, one of the outstanding achievements of the squadron was the
> first aerial reconnaissance of Spitzbergen by F/Lt D.E. Hawkins in a Catalina
> with P/O J.G. Wright as his navigator. This secret and highly dangerous
> mission was altogether successful in weather of arctic severity, on a flight
> lasting twenty-four and three quarter hours across more than 2000 miles of
> sea. F/Lt Hawkins and P/O Wright were both awarded the DFC after
> demonstrating exceptional ability and unusual powers of endurance on this
> occasion.'

During 240's move to India he had also sunk an Italian submarine in the
Mediterranean. The AVM writes:

> 'The squadron [36] having technically re-formed in October 1942 was still
> building up its aircraft strength and its crews had little if any maritime
> reconnaissance experience. My task was to inject that experience.

Upper: 36 Sq Wellington XIII with ground crew at Tanjore. Allan Whiting standing behind 4th from right. *(Courtesy of Allan Whiting)*

Lower: K/244 Wellington XIII (Captain, F/Lt Keith Scott RAAF) patrols Arabian seas. *(Courtesy of K. Scott)*

'If I remember correctly we were under the operational control of AHQ Bangalore and our operational area was the Bay of Bengal. Up to that time 240 Squadron was the only unit covering the Bay and I assume that the intended role of 36 Squadron was to relieve 240 Squadron of its Inshore responsibilities and allow it to give more effort to long range operations in the Indian Ocean. However, the Inshore convoy routes were relatively quiet as far as the U-boat threat was concerned and I have no knowledge of any sightings or attacks by our aircraft at this particular time. Nevertheless, intelligence was scarce and convoy protection was still important, so the task continued.

'Tanjore was an airfield of hard red laterite with the runways marked out in white. There were no buildings and the whole squadron was housed under canvas and I distinctly remember the howling of the jackals circling our tents every night. The whole area was rocky and barren. Apart from training and learning to fly the Wellington, I only carried out two operational sorties, one on the 17 January '43 with Pilot Officer Parker and the other the following day with Pilot Officer Allan. I was then posted back to 240 Squadron having handed over to Wing Commander Mellor. It must have been around this time the Squadron's move to North Africa was being considered.'

AVM Hawkins is quite right. This move did occur in May 1943.

Now, looking at 36 Squadron from the ground staff angle, I was lucky to find, through the 36 Sq Association, three ground crew with an excellent memory for the days at Tanjore. Allan Whiting, an airframe fitter or FME, who died recently at Leighton Buzzard, wrote at length about the trip out from UK in MV *Rangitiki* and later experiences. (In the group photo, in front of a Wellington, Allan is marked with an arrow). On the voyage, near Freetown, came an unsuccessful submarine attack, in which they 'started to get the quivers':

'We were on our mess deck with all the portholes closed and not allowed to smoke for two hours, waiting for the "big bang", while overhead sailors were running about and uncovering guns. Thankfully nothing happened . . . once arrived in Bombay we were put on a troop train for five days journey down the west side of India. I had never seen such poverty. However desolate the countryside, as soon as the train came to a standstill, hordes of near-naked children and adults were running alongside the train begging [possibly a famine situation].

'On arrival at Tanjore we found we had no aircraft and no tools and because of this all the technical trades of the Squadron were sent to a Maintenance Unit at Trinchonopoly leaving behind one engine fitter, myself, and one airframe fitter and a Sergeant. This two months was the laziest time I had during my Air Force career. We had nothing to do after cruising round the aerodrome finding where the petrol stores, oil stores and ammunition dumps were.

'One day our sergeant raked us out in a panic, as there were sixteen Wellingtons landing and they all had to be D.I'd (Daily Inspection done) and refuelled. My friend and I soon realised that our cushy time was over. The first Wellington to land was K for Katie so I duly D.I'd and as required tried to start the engines. The first engine would not start. On removing the starter motor I found the nut and split pin retaining the starter dog was missing – it was obviously inside the engine!

'The only thing to do now was to push the aircraft to one corner and wait for a new engine. As there were no Wellington spares in India at that time, that aircraft became the squadron Christmas tree and it kept the rest of the squadron flying.'

An earlier bomber squadron commander confirmed this to me. They too had cannibalised their Wellingtons. Leading Aircraftman John Cox, a Londoner from Herne Hill, recalls that Wimpy.

'Whatever we took from it had to be replaced with a label giving details of the parts taken. There were so many labels on it that it was called the Christmas tree. The sight of an aircraft in that area of India was unusual and soon bus parties of a middle class type of Indian would come from Tanjore on Sundays to see the aircraft. Some of them expected us to show them over the Wellingtons but they got a firm no from us.'

Allan Whiting also recalls local reaction.

'We had great trouble keeping the local people off the runway when the aircraft were taking off. They would sit all day along the edge. On one occasion a little toddler ran across the runway just as a Wellington was taking off. We just stood there open-mouthed because there was nothing we could do. Then the mother ran after it and luckily she did not stop – she just scooped the baby up and kept running. The wing passed over her head with a big sigh of relief from us.'

Allan also described how, because he was a good violinist (and later a professional), he was asked by an old missionary to play at a service in an empty hut converted into a makeshift church. He was shown an old violin with hairy gut strings and a bow that looked as if it had been used for firing arrows. His playing was a success, however. Cox continues:

'Then we began our duties, the aircrew taking off and doing their patrols while we ground crew serviced the aircraft that remained on the airfield. One day a Wimpy had to have a test flight over the sea and I went with it. The pilot flew so close to the sea that the plane cut a ripple through the water and although we did not know it at the time the squadron leader in charge was on the beach and saw the low flying. The next day the pilot had a good telling off.'

Steve Linsley, a motor mechanic from Malton, North Yorkshire, was a Corporal MT Fitter at Tanjore and later at Koggala in Ceylon. His stories are mainly of people and animals but one illustrates an effect attributed to long years in the Indian sun – Dulally Tap, the tap being Hindi for sun and Deolali a worthy town in Central India but also a very hot military base. In this condition one becomes somewhat mad or eccentric, without being so deranged as to require sending back to UK. He writes:

'Jock was (naturally) Scotch and much older than any of us and talked with a deep Scotch brogue. Unfortunately had got "Sun Tap" severe. Should never have been overseas really. Could only do menial duties with others, so was put on the fire section checking domestic extinguishers. (This was a Koggala story) The Officers Mess on the side of the lake was on a hill and it was steep. It took four or more to pull the cart loaded with extinguishers to the top. Going down Jock was given the handle to hold back, the others all behind. All of them were laughing and joking, telling Jock not to let it get away and gaining speed all the time. Actually they were pushing. Result, it came down the hill like hell and turned over, Jock, cart, extinguishers and all in one big heap. Everybody thought it such a huge joke.'

By April 1943 36 Squadron was carrying out maritime reconnaissance and doing 43 sorties a month, without seeing hide or hair of a U-boat. However, their patrols were part of the combined efforts to keep the submarines away, whether German or Japanese. The previous month, in March, the squadron moved to Dhubalia, north of Calcutta, for three months. This camp was in the jungle, unlike Tanjore's dry flatness. John Cox writes:

'The local natives warned us about a tiger in the vicinity so guard duties were carried out with two men instead of the normal one-man guard. Our huts were made of bamboo material and baboons would roam about outside looking in at us as they sat with their young. We made catapults and sat outside and became wary of snakes after having to chase some out of the hut. Along at the airfield a petrol bowser caught fire when the driver became careless with smoking. The natives worked hard and bravely to roll many drums of petrol away from danger. The tanker burnt for days and the driver was punished with 90 days in the glasshouse [jail].'

The authorities then decided to transfer the whole Squadron to Blida, in the Mediterranean. By mid-1944, when this chapter began, they had led the Navy to three U-boats there which were sunk, and they achieved many other results in the Mediterranean.

Koggala Lake, Ceylon. 240 Squadron Sunderland, with refueller, and Catalina overhead.
(courtesy C. Simmonds, Montreal)

NOTES

1   A Hudson VI (FK628) of 8 Squadron, piloted by F/Sgt N. Miller; with F/Sgt R.W. Sibley navigator; Sgt G.J. James and Sgt R.G. Wood as WOP/AG's attacked a surfaced sub at Cape Guardafui on 14 July 1943. It was the Japanese 1/29 commanded by Lt/Cdr Juichi Izu and was presumed damaged, to be sunk later south of Formosa by an American sub. See Norman Franks' new edition of *Search, Find and Kill*, 1996.

2   *Royal Air Force*, Michael Turner.(Temple Press), 1981

3   Christopher Lowe, Nottingham

4   *Sea War 1939-1945*, Janus Piekalkiewicz, from *Seekrieg 1939-1945* (Sudwest Verlag), Munich 1980

5   *The Peleus Trial*, John Cameron (William Hodge and Co), London 1948

6   *War in the Southern Oceans*, Turner, Gordon-Cumming and Betzler. (Oxford University Press), 1960

7   RAF record via Flight Lieutenant A.L. Thomas RAF, Aviation Historian

8   The following 5 crews' names are by courtesy of Norman Franks, author. U – Crewed by F/O J.H. Wilson RCAF; F/Sgt T.M. Scales RAAF; F/Sgt S. Repchik RCAF; Sgt A.L. Jones; Sgt F. Moxley

9   F – Crewed by P/O R.A. Evans; F/O W. Clements RCAF; Sgt D.Whitehurst; Sgt A.C. (Mick) Bond, Sgt C. Hull

10 465 – (or SSS) 'attack – enemy submarine'

11 T – crewed by F/O A.J. Winslow, 2nd Pilot; Sgt K.P.F. Lucy; Sgt J. Hardiker (Sgt K.G. Free); F/Lt Whitrod's account omits Sgt Free and gives Sgt Palmer.

12 Brooklands in Surrey was the principal motor racing circuit of that period.

13 O-P, known as O-break-P, and P were secret wireless codes.

14 D – Sgt C.L. Buggy, F/Sgt J.C. Miller, Sgt W.S. Lay. Sgt J.,Sinclair, Sgt G. Welsh

15 G/8 crewed by F/Sgt C.H.C. Bellchamber, F/O J.R. Culham RCAF, Sgt J.F. Calnan, Sgt W.G. Lapsley

16 *Verdammter Atlantik*, Hans Herlin, Hamburg, 1959

17 *Sea War* (see above)

18 *The Scourge of the Swastika*, Lord Russell of Liverpool (Cassell and Co), 1954

19 *The Underwater War* 1939-1945, Richard Compton-Hall (Blandford Press) 1982

20 *Blood and Bushido*, Bernard Edwards (Images), Malvern, 1991

21 see *Knights of Bushido* on the TRUK order, in Chapter 5 footnotes.

22 For years this was thought to have been a 4-engined Liberator (B24) but the Sunday Express in 1963 describes it as a twin-engined Mitchell (B25) bomber, in an interview with the man who ordered the attack.

23 *Illustrated Weekly of India,* 27 June 1943.

NAVY-AIR FORCE COOPERATION

ROYAL NAVY HUNTER-KILLERS

Oberleutnant-zur-See (Senior Lieutenant) Burckhardt Heusinger von Waldegg was tall, blond, charming and aristocratic but only 24 years old on his first command of a seasoned U-boat, the U/198.

Now the Middle Atlantic was alive with 'Hunter-killer' groups, some RAF but mainly American. And they were scoring successes. Over in the Indian Ocean Admiral Somerville had long wished to have enough ships spare to form a hunter-killer group. Now, in 1944, this famous Admiral's Eastern Fleet had reached a fair size. Against Admiralty advice[1] he formed FORCE 66, a formidable naval group, to lie in wait for unwary U-boats, being also forewarned by ULTRA as in the Atlantic.

Von Waldegg and his crew of 65 sailed from Bordeaux in early 1944 and managed to avoid the dreaded U-boat traps of that ocean.

Then on 5 July 1944 after unsuccessful RAF Catalina sweeps, the submarine was attacked by a cigar-shaped Lockheed Ventura of the South African Air Force, off Durban. The aircraft's bomb-bay was jammed by an anti-aircraft shell from the U-boat so little harm came to the submarine. Then a second Ventura came in and despite more fire dropped six DCs which did some damage.

By now ULTRA's decoding of the ENIGMA messages led to her being tracked up the eastern Africa seaboard and FORCE 66 prepared a hot reception. There were two escort carriers, the HMS *Begum* and HMS *Shah*, out of Trincomalee, carrying many FAA Avengers; four frigates, HMS *Taff*, HMS *Findhorn*, HMS *Nadder* and HMS *Parrot*; with them two sloops came from the Indian Navy, HMI Ships *Cauvery* and *Godaveri*. A sketch of HMS *Taff* on escort duty may be found in the Royal Navy plate in the Appendix. The latter was captained by Commander A.B. Goord of the Royal Indian Navy.

The whole force was under the leadership of Captain 'Jackie' Broome RN,[2] described by Goord as an 'untiring tough tactician'. Finally came HM Ships *Jasmine*, and our old friends *Genista* and *Falmouth* who were ordered out of Mombasa to meet FORCE 66.

The Force sailed from Colombo on 30 July 1944, headed at 13.5 knots towards the Kilindini Naval Base at Mombasa. At that side of the ocean the RAF's 246 Wing was readying its three Catalina squadrons to play their part in tracking down U/198. They were 209, 259 and 265 Squadrons. In all, on this venture, the three squadrons carried out 58 sorties totalling 871 flying hours between 5 and 14 August. The RN described the hunt as a model textbook one with maximum cooperation from the RAF.

On 5 August 1944, just after midnight, still being tracked by ULTRA and D/F stations, von Waldegg torpedoed Andrew Weir's *Empire City* of 7,295 tons (her third ship) off Cap Delgado in the Moçambique Channel. The wireless operator – a Manchester man named Grant – stuck to his post sending out SOS messages, or SSS (am being attacked by submarine) as the ship was listing and rapidly sinking. The skipper, Captain Basil Jackson of Southampton, was last to leave the ship, diving off the stern, but was badly affected by the fuel oil on the water, according to Donkeyman[3] Smith, who writes:

'Then the U-boat surfaced and came alongside the lifeboats into which we were crowded. The submarine Commander [O/L von Waldegg] told us he had heard our wireless operator sending out his SOS messages and we judge from that they would be picked up by a friendly station. He asked if we had enough provision and we told him we had provisions and water that should last till we reached land. We were 120 miles from the coast of East Africa.

'One of our men asked the German captain, who spoke good English, if he had any cigarettes to spare for us but the commander told us he had not as he was too far from home. He said "goodbye" and wished us "good luck" before he left us.'[4]

William Corkhill, a 'Wearsider' from Seaham, south of Sunderland, was an Ordinary Seaman aboard the ship and now runs a nautical book business in Connecticut. He told us that he and his crew remember the first torpedo hitting the engine room in the 'small hours', killing the two on duty there.[5] William Corkhill continues:

'The 18 minutes which elapsed before the second torpedo struck permitted all the men except the men in the engine room to leave in three undamaged boats. The boat I was in with the Irish 3rd mate, was the first to reach the mainland in about 40 hours. We had been met about two or three miles offshore by some native villagers in outriggers who did not speak English. Nor did they appreciate the chocolates we threw into their boats for they dumped them overboard and retained only the shiny tin boxes. They led the way into a sandy beach behind which was a small village, where women and children were leaving their huts and heading into the trees.

'A fire was lit on the beach and in a very short time a delicious meal of rice and goats' flesh was served on a 30-inch diameter brass tray and we enjoyed sitting cross-legged on the beach. Come to think of it, when that searching seaplane [a 209 Squadron Catalina] on the first day in the boats, dropped tins of corned beef and crackers in a Mae West lifejacket, they tasted pretty good too.'

They were taken in a truck 125 miles down to Porto Amelia, thence found their way via Durban and Cape Town, to Liverpool.

U/198 meanwhile cruised on, unaware of the closing jaws of a trap ahead of her. On 7 August she sank another Empire ship, the *Empire Day*, which failed to get off an SOS or SSS, opposite Dar-es-Salaam. Her captain was taken prisoner[6] and sailed on in U/198. Unaware that ULTRA and the D/F units were listening in, von Waldegg continued to send his radio reports to BdU in Paris and sealed his own doom.

More D/F fixes were obtained and the hunter-killers of FORCE 66 began a hunt to the death. They tracked von Waldegg from the Comoro Islands to the Seychelles. Admiral Somerville asked the Flag Officer East Africa based at Kilindini, Mombasa, to co-ordinate the hunt. The RAF Commanding Officer 246 Wing, also at Mombasa, Group Captain 'Kiwi' Broughton, now Air Marshal Sir Charles Broughton KBE CB, was requested to organise the Catalina air searches by day but also at night because the Avenger pilots had not had much experience of night landings on the heaving decks of their carriers, so the Navy said.

After 209 Squadron's Catalina had sighted the *Empire City* lifeboats on 6 August, and U/198 had reported to *BdU* her sinking of *Empire Day* on 7 August, 246 Wing spread the searches further east. FORCE 66 made all speed westwards to reach the U-boat's area, Captain Broome ordered a large sweep for 10th and at first light Avengers of 851 Squadron on HMS *Shah* and 832 Squadron on HMS *Begum* roared off the aircraft carriers' decks. On that day one of the searching Avenger torpedo-bombers from the *Shah* spotted the sub and screamed down to attack it. However, the bombs apparently did no damage.

Part of FAA-RAF Canteen mural by author, Mombasa, 1944, showing FAA Avenger. The theme was post-war, 'The Jungle takes over'. (Courtesy of William Bryer, grandson of G/Capt Bryer)

Meanwhile the Catalina sorties were building up and 13 separate searches were organised. Although no actual sightings occurred, one 'disappearing contact' was found on radar, in position 03°36' South and 49°45' East. However, changes in the hunt were made at times and the Cats' presence, especially at night, meant that the U-boat was less often able to come up for fresh air and battery-charging. Staying submerged meant a big strain on the huge electric motors banked astern of the now-silent Diesel engines and also on the crew.

Back in Mombasa the ether was humming with incoming and outgoing messages, mostly in code. F.J. 'Jim' Stanyon was one of those in the Cipher Office, including two or three WAAF officers. He recalls :

'The rest of the Cipher Officers and I dealt with messages about this incident as we worked in close cooperation with 222 Group and ACSEA[7] in Ceylon. We also handled all 209's incoming and outgoing signals together with those from all the island and other bases in the area.'

Nothing happened on 11 August but on the 12th an Avenger from *Shah* attacked the U-boat without success. This was not far ahead of the carriers and their escorts *Godaveri* and *Cauvery*. Commander Goord on the Indian sloop *Godavari* now continues the story:[8]

'It was not until 1410 that *Godavari* got off the leash. Three hours and thirteen minutes later, in the seemingly empty expanse of ocean she got a "ping", loud and clear, an unmistakable submarine contact.

'Not being fitted with "Hedgehog" [the large depth charges like oil drums with projections all over them, hurled ahead of the ship), a silent attack was denied her. Thus, she sat patiently on the U-boat's tail, moving at about three knots, for three quarters of an hour until *Findhorn*, captained by Lt/Cdr J.C. Dawson RNVR, closely followed by *Parrot*, came storming up – nothing patient about them.

'With *Godavari* as directing vessel, *Findhorn* sailed straight in and, with a shower of "Hedgehog", scored two hits. Within five minutes, a large explosion was heard on Asdic. It was the end!'

For his part in the action Commander Goord was awarded the Distinguished Service Cross and other personnel received decorations, including the commander of the Fleet Air Arm's 851 Squadron and *Findhorn's* Gunnery Officer (DSCs) and one of the *Godavari's* lieutenants, presumably for holding the Asdic contact.

It was estimated that U/198 was at 300 feet (50 fathoms) so the attack was astonishingly accurate. Light-coloured Diesel oil continued for days to rise to the surface from the entombed submarine on the ocean floor 2,200 fathoms below, where the Chief Officer of the *Empire Day* shared the same grim fate as von Waldegg's crew.

Leading up to the sinking, despite a certain lack of information as to where the naval force might be expected, 246 Wing's RAF aircrews continued to perform search patrols, the night ones being particularly useful. Canadian Fred Joplin, of 209 Sq whom we shall meet shortly, writes:

'I did a parallel track search from Mombasa to Seychelles, with our Squadron Commander W/Cdr Fitzpatrick aboard, on 11 August. Fitz went over to be in command during the hunt. We had good intelligence from the YY boys (Intelligence using the Naval 'Y service') that a sub was in the area. I did a search north and west of Seychelles the night of 14 August. When we landed next morning we were informed that the Navy had destroyed the sub fairly early in the evening of the 14th (!). But the controllers decided to leave us up for the rest of the night rather than recall us to Seychelles.'

The news that the U-boat had been sunk on 12 August does not seem to have reached Group Captain Broughton at 246 Wing till 14 August! RAF records, for instance, describe:

'SEARCH No 13. By 14 August no further news had been received from Force 66 so it was assumed that THE FORCE had moved further east and was still searching. A Parallel Track Sweep of 4 aircraft was ordered to search an area North-East of the Seychelles. While this search was in progress a signal was received from the Force stating that HMS *Findhorn's* last attack had probably been successful. Air Headquarters allowed the RAF search to continue till the 15th, to be sure.'

Flying Officer Norman Leece, now in Huddersfield, an observer with 259 Squadron, Dar-es-Salaam, recalls one sortie, on 12 August 1944. His Catalina was C/259 (FP 256), captained by F/O W. 'Buzz' Hibberd.[9] Leece writes:

'We were taking part with the Navy on a submarine hunt from Diego Suarez, landing at night in the Seychelles. During our patrol, the radar operator reported a contact on his radar screen which might be a submarine and we quickly homed on to it. As we closed, Buzz was cautious as he thought that naval vessels might be in the area. However, the wireless operator reported that if it was a naval vessel it should be transmitting an identification signal[10] and there was no such signal. Buzz decided to make sure and over the target he ordered a parachute flare to be dropped which lit the sky. "It's a frigate!" I heard over the intercom, followed by, "They have switched on their identification signal."'

The Second Pilot on that flight was 'Bill' Martin from Scotland, and from his wide viewpoint in the cockpit he could see more. He recalls:

'We had no identification signal and had not been advised by the Navy that they had ships in the area as we should have been. Buzz decided to set off a flare. Down below were many ships and a carrier. Buzz said, "The whole bloody Navy are down there!" It was a nice sight to see.'

Bill Martin describes the landing:

'We arrived over Seychelles after midnight, circled the flare path and made a night approach which was 70 knots at 200 feet per minute descent. The flare path should be on the skipper's left hand side. As we approached the flare path we drifted right across with the flares on my side, and eventually no flares – total darkness. Buzz opened up and we went round again. This happened again next time – we had a 90° cross wind. After the fifth time I was wondering if this was to be my last flight. The sixth time I said to Buzz, "Let the bloody thing go. We can only run up on to a beach. What the hell!"

We eventually touched down in total darkness. The shouts of delight from the lads behind was something to remember. The motor launch came chasing after us and led us back to the flares, but as we went down the flare path we had to open up some engine to counteract the cross wind. The pilot boat went faster to keep away from the roaring monster behind him and he ran us on to a coral reef.'

Norman Leece adds:

'After being holed we managed to keep the sea water from swamping us by pumping through the night from the aircraft's Auxiliary Power Unit and by much needed assistance from a local man who brought his boat and generator alongside. We were towed to the slipway at Mahé next morning.'

The Admiralty sent a letter to the Under-secretary of State at the Air Ministry, which included the phrases:

'The cooperation of 246 Wing under Group Captain C. Broughton was close and efficient. No less than 871 hours were flown.'

The enormous number of flights and especially the long night patrols by Catalinas had some effect in forcing U/198 to stay down at night until, in desperation, it burst to the surface in daylight and thus encountered the Avengers.

In London the Admiralty remained dubious of FORCE 66. Roskill's official history backed them later.[11] He wrote:

'That solitary success, can hardly be taken to vindicate the departure from the principle which all our recent experience had substantiated – namely that, unless and until a surplus of sea and air escorts was available over and above those needed for convoy duty, hunting for U-boats was unlikely to prove a profitable venture.'

Somerville and the Eastern Fleet were unrepentant. After spending a couple of years trying to run convoys on a shoe-string, they found the present normal complement to be like a surplus. The operation would have been repeated if an influx of U-boats had occurred in the Indian Ocean. As it happened, there was hardly any need. Yet the U-boat whose story follows, escaped the net entirely.

AN ALDABRA STORY – THE FIRST HALF

To the north of the wide Moçambique Channel lies the little atoll of Aldabra, a riot of luxurious vegetation still today. Its three islands form the outer ring of a long lagoon, with a squashed oval shape, where sharks, turtles and other creatures abound.

Catalina S, FP 107 of 209 Squadron, had been down in Mauritius on 'Operation CANNED' from 4 February 1944 and flew back to Diego Suarez on the 20th. Her Canadian Captain, from Vancouver, was F/Lt A. Frederick 'Joppy' Joplin. His crew names will be found in the chapter notes.[12] Joplin's account begins:

'The next day (21st) with our normal crew of ten and six additional airmen we left Diego Suarez in transit to Mombasa. This should have put us into that harbour fairly early in the afternoon without much difficulty; apart from the extra bodies and stores – a routine flight. Our route before reaching the coast of Africa and turning north took us very close to the islands of Astove and Aldabra in the Comoro Group.'

For meals, says Joplin, he and Flash Johnson, added in their Canadian parcels to improve them. The meal was being served by Jack Pheasant, he continues: 'when Reg Greenwood, the Flight Engineer, pointed out that we had an oil leak showing along the cowling of the starboard engine and that we had fluctuating pressure in that engine,' adds Joplin.

'I got down from the Captain's seat on the port side of the cockpit and went through to the blister to see how much oil the engine was leaking. Certainly it was bad enough to consider what action need be taken to get us to base safely. I was at the navigator's table, just behind the cockpit, with Flash looking at how far we were from alternate landing points when there was the most colossal bang and McPherson, the Second Pilot, who was on the bridge at the controls, let out a piercing yell. In less time than it takes to tell I was back in the Captain's seat, had disengaged the automatic pilot, pushed the "feathering" button for the starboard engine, turned the starboard magnetos to off, called for "automatic rich" on the control indicator lights, and put the pitch of the port engine up to 2,300 rpm.

'Reg at the flight engineer's station had us into rich immediately and shut off the fuel on the starboard engine. It was a good thing this was all done almost instantaneously since the reduction gear on the front of the starboard engine had sheared off nearly all the bolts on the gear housing.'

The lightning reaction by Joplin and his engineer saved the wireless operator and his part of the aircraft from being mashed up by the enormous three-bladed propeller and its gear. Another revolution or two might have seen them spinning off straight into the aircraft. Joplin continues:

'With one engine shut down the aircraft took a swerve to starboard which was corrected with full left rudder. The tail trim was set to relieve the pressure on the rudder and the aircraft was manageable again. We were almost half way between Mombasa and Diego Suarez. Continuing north was entirely over open sea. The loss of the starboard engine made up my mind for me. I turned back towards Diego Suarez, which would involve us flying over possible alighting areas at Aldabra or Astove.

'Under normal circumstances the Catalina can maintain itself on one engine. Unfortunately we were too overloaded for that. I dropped the six depth charges, on safe, and all the radar stores but we continued to lose height. With six airmen as well as crew it seemed prudent to land at Aldabra.

'The island is a typical atoll, oval in shape with a lagoon in the centre, a channel opening at the south-west corner and one at the north-west. As the tide changes a strong tidal current of up to ten knots runs in the channels as the atoll empties or fills. We informed Mombasa by radio of our intention to land at Aldabra. We were able to approach straight in. In the Catalina, single engine landings are not difficult of themselves. I had made more than a few while training pilots new to flying boats as they came to the squadron in Mombasa.

'It is different when you are on the water with only one engine. Waterhandling with its need to be always moving and at the same time allowing for winds, tides and the fact that you cannot simply put on the *brakes* when you get into difficulties adds an entirely new dimension to moving about on the surface with a flying boat. With one engine it is that much more difficult.

However, with the strong tidal current and a drogue out on the port side I was able to move along the channel looking for a safe place to anchor. I manoeuvred out of the main channel into a small bay in the coral and anchored. About half an hour later a dugout boat came over from the main south island. We were to meet Clement Hororou and his boat crew. He was operating, at this time, a turtle fishery and a coconut plantation on the island.

'After some discussion with Hororou who came from the Seychelles and spoke English, I started up our engine and taxied, through winding channels where coral could rip a hole in hull or wing-float, to the lee of one of the islands in the atoll. Eventually I was able to get us into a pool with enough room to swing at anchor with a good holding for the anchor.'

A Catalina moored somewhere in the Indian Ocean, author's painting with a marine tender in the foreground, for transporting crew.
(courtesy His Grace the Duke of Devonshire, Chatsworth House)

CATALINA IN THE INDIAN OCEAN.

ARTHUR BANKS

Paddling the dinghy 50 yards to the shore Joplin and the crew were able to set up camp on the island. Now in late afternoon they checked the damaged engine, quite impossible to repair, and radioed Mombasa and Diego for a new one. That night on the beach they celebrated Fred's birthday with a meal and the one bottle of rum which had, 'somehow', escaped being jettisoned with the other stores. Next morning the message came that a small Navy ship the HMS *Sundra*, would bring the engine. 'It arrived on the 23rd of February and,' says Joplin, 'there on her deck was the brand-new engine still in its shipping case. What a beautiful sight! I had thought they might send out some beat-out old wreck that had been recovered from the scrap yard!'

From the ship two rafts were lashed together and the engine lowered on to them with the ship's winches. In the afternoon during high slack water the power boat towed the raft and engine to the aircraft's mooring in the little pool by the island. Before midday a second Catalina bringing an engine fitter, Corporal Moore, arrived and took off the spare passengers, who were reluctant to leave this island paradise. Among them was F/O Jim Lawson, of Belfast, an Observer whom we shall meet further on in the chapter.

The raft was then moored beside 'S' for Sugar and with a tripod erected on it for a hoist, the work began. As the new engine had not been sent with any ancillary equipment, such as generators, starter or hydraulic pump, these had to be painstakingly removed from the damaged engine and fitted to the new. Each nut and bolt had to be secured with locking nuts or wire, while a thick larding of anti-corrosion protection needed to be removed from the new engine.

This took three days of gruelling work under a blazing sun dead overhead at the hottest part of Aldabra's year. Tarpaulins gave some shade for the three corporals, Moore, Stait and Slater, working stripped to the waist along with the Flight Engineer and Fitter of the aircraft. A further irritation was the host of small sharks swimming along the edge of the pool, mainly interested in the nearby shoals of fish. However, Fred Joplin sat up on the blistering mainplane with a Navy rifle taking the odd pot-shot at them to discourage them from entering the pool.

The old and the new engine were laid on the raft back to back while parts were transferred and on the evening of 28 February the new one was hoisted up and the engine bolts set back into the engine mount. The next evening a good meal was laid on, as Joplin writes:

'In addition to sharks and fishes in its lagoon Aldabra is the home of very large sea turtles. They lie in the mud floor of the lagoon and as a result produce a pale coloured shell which is much sought after. It was these

278

turtles Hororou and his men caught and shipped back to the Seychelles. He furnished us one evening with turtle steaks taken from one of his catches. Jack Pheasant grilled these for that evening's meal.

'By 1 March the job was almost completed. After one or two further snags, by the morning of 4 March we had the starboard engine all ready and the dome back on the port by noon. We brought the aircraft up to short anchor and started up the port engine. With that engine going we got the anchor on board after some difficulty. The Island seemed to be reluctant to let us go.

'I was able to swing round in the pool in which we had anchored, keeping a sharp eye for coral all round. Then came the moment of truth. Our new engine caught first time. Still continuing to circle, both engines were brought up to temperature. Both Reg Greenwood and Corporal Moore were at the engine control panel. We were taking Moore with us. After all he was the main functionary at the engine installation and we were not going to let him off the hook.

'All seemed to be well, with the exception that the oil pressure in the new engine was low. It would have to be set up. Back we turned to the pool in which we had lain for eleven days and anchored. Moore was out on top as soon as we stopped. He and Reg with a few minutes of wrenching made the adjustment. Both Corporal Moore and Reg agreed that the oil pressure now showing was still low, but it would not give too much trouble. I headed out into the main channel without delay.

'Now close to the *Sundra*, I waved them a farewell. Then I went off down the channel getting airborne without further delay. I circled back over the *Sundra* while Moore and Reg both pronounced that they were satisfied with the engines. Soon I turned toward Diego Suarez leaving the *Sundra* to clean up the camp and do all the other chores we had left them with, after eleven days. In two hours and forty minutes we were landing at Diego Suarez – a welcome sight. What we needed most was a good bath and a drink at the bar.'

ALDABRA – THE SECOND HALF

This time it was a large grey U-boat, U/861, which put in at the atoll of Aldabra. The *Black Panther,* its symbol painted crouching on the conning tower, was yet another IXD2. She was built at Deschimag, by AG Weser at the port of Bremen, and was commissioned on 2 September 1943 under the command of Lieutenant Commander Jürgen Oesten. Oesten was now 30 and had joined the *Reichsmarine* in 1933. During the voyage, on 1 December 1944, he was promoted to full Commander *(Korvettenkapitän)*. This followed a distinguished career, as Captain of two other U-boats, U/61 and U/106, then Chief of the Ninth U-boat Flotilla, based at Brest. Finally he was Staff Officer to the Admiral Commanding the Arctic. F/Sgt David Pitkeathly, 259 Sq Captain who was later F/Lt Pitkeathly DFC, was also in the Arctic at Murmansk on the convoys that the Admiral was attacking.

U/861's Commander Jürgen Oesten salutes at the commissioning on 2 September 1943. He is standing on the 3.7-cm gun platform, on a misty day in Bremen. This was the birthday of the boat celebrated a year later. *(Courtesy Karl Günther)*

page 190

U-861 is seen in the plate of 'German vessels' found in chapter 7. Exactly a year after her commissioning, she had been five months at sea in a voyage leaving Bordeaux and skirting Iceland and Rio de Janeiro. So they called in at Aldabra Atoll. In a letter to me Captain Oesten wrote:

'Our short visit to Aldabra on 2 September 1944 was just for fun. It was the boat's birthday, therefore I thought we should have some recreation. We did not want to attract the plane's attention and moved nice and slowly on deck. Of course all our guns [one 10.5 cm, one 3.7 cm, and two twin 2 cm], were following the Catalina.'

This needs explaining. Just previously the U-boat, finding no ships in Tamatave harbour on Madagascar, headed north. The Helmsman, or *'Steuermann'* Gustav Götsche, later Captain Götsche, who died in 1989, wrote in the private memoirs his widow allowed me to use, that he was off duty when he heard over the ship's loudspeaker. 'Steuermann auf Brücke', a call to the bridge. 'What crime have I committed now?' he thought because normally the call would be 'Gustav to the bridge'.

He found they were near Aldabra and the Captain was entering the atoll. There was doubt whether the draught of five metres could be accommodated above the coral reefs. Gustav, holding the lead line, sang out, 'eight metres under the keel', then seven and six and so on. 'Your voice sounds shaky, Gustav!' came a shout from the bridge. The depth remained about seven or eight metres, so they anchored in the midst of this profusion of tropical vegetation. The crew pictured themselves with a couple of coconuts and bananas apiece.

Captain Oesten ordered out the inflatable dinghy (rowed, before the days of outboard motors made life easy), plus a party armed with pistols and handgrenades in case of any hostile or consumable life ashore. They set off under the command of *Obersteuermann* Wendelmuth, known to all as Achmed. 'At this moment came an alarm call, "AIRCRAFT!"'

On the bridge the Captain moved his binoculars round. 'It's straight ahead. A Catalina flying boat,' he said. Götsche continues:

'This could be bad. Here are we stuck at anchor with no chance to dive but our 10.5 on the deck and the automatics in the 'wintergarden' were ready to fire. At this moment came the Captain's voice again. "Hold your fire. First we'll see what the fellow will do."'

Oberleutnant zur See Karl Günther was Second Watch Officer at that time and in charge of the deck watch. When my wife and I visited Bremen, a while back, Karl and his wife Lotte kindly entertained us to a sumptuous meal and spoke of that day in Aldabra. He told us:

'As well as having a break from the monotony of five months travel mostly under the sea, the crew were going to do odd jobs and clean the outboard filters. When the aircraft became visible I gave the signal to the rubber boat "Come back!" but the current was so strong the little boat was in some danger. It was lucky for us the Catalina remained at some distance because I was very anxious in case some marksman became "trigger-happy" and betrayed our position by a nervous shot. So I kept shouting "Don't shoot!"'

Eventually the Catalina passed along the horizon without coming over to investigate. It missed not only a sitting duck, if it had depth charges, but the chance of calling in reinforcements to make sure the U-boat did not escape. Joplin comments:

> 'Where he was inside the reef he could not submerge. If he had attempted to run to sea and got out before assistance could arrive he would have had to close down his guns and get his crew in before diving   At this point he would be open to a depth charge attack.'

However, a gunbattle could also have been fatal for the Cat, in view of the fact that H-265 was shot down later by this U-boat's sister ship, U/862.

One of the problems with research is that when you have a story all sewn up and wish to close the book, at the last minute a fact or connection suddenly comes to light. When I had a phone call from Belfast I could hardly believe what I heard. Flying Officer Jim (Paddy) Lawson, a passenger on Joplin's Catalina which forced-landed at Aldabra on 21 February 1944 thinks that he could also have been in the very Catalina which passed along the horizon that morning while U/861 lay helpless in the lagoon on 2 September 1944.

He was the navigator in Flight Lieutenant A.H. Smith's 265 Squadron Catalina on a transit flight that day between Diego Suarez and Mombasa. Aldabra lay some five miles to starboard and had they been armed, they might have gone for a look-see. As it was, a transit flight meant no depth charges and no ammunition in the guns; they were unarmed, either carrying stores or a few VIPs .

Paddy Lawson says he was probably taking a bearing on the island and a fix on the sun to check his course but at that distance the submarine would be invisible within the lagoon. The meeting never took place.

U/861 LOOKS BACK

On 29 April 1943, at the inland port of Bremen, a new U-boat was sliding down the stocks into the broad River Weser from the shipyard of the A.G. Weser Company. She was another long-range IXD2 U-cruiser to be commissioned as U/861 on 2 September 1943 with Oesten as her commander.

One feature of U-boat welfare in Germany was the presence, in a submarine home base, of a *Mutti*, a motherly lady who adopted various U-boat crews, visited their wives and families when they were away and, if a U-boat were sunk, took on the sad task of comforting the loved ones in their grief. For U/861 and 14 other U-boats this lady was Madame

Chief Engineer Herbert Panknin (left) and Commander Jürgen Oesten (right) with Madame Rosiewski, the *Mutti* or 'mother' of 15 U-boat crews (as seen on her necklace) at a pre-voyage party for U/861. *(Courtesy of Karl Günther, Bremen)*

Rosiewski, a well-loved figure at their crew parties, as shown in the photograph, wearing her necklace of the 15 submarines she cared for, taken before the voyage. U-Panther sailed from Kiel on 20 April 1944 with a crew of 64 for the Far East. According to the Ship's Surgeon, *Doktor.med* Hans Possin,

> We passed through the Faroe Strait into the Atlantic Ocean. During that time in the North Atlantic we only surfaced during the night to recharge the batteries and to fill up with oxygen. We had a very healthy crew, all of them volunteers, whom I had given a thorough medical before sailing. Our submarine was fitted with all the necessary instruments for operations and medicine for a long voyage especially for the tropics. We had one case of Middle Ear Inflammation, a young sailor whom I operated on at 40 metres depth below the waves.'

Dr Possin explained to me, that the motion of the waves nearer the surface would disturb such a delicate operation. The youngster was in agony with increasing pain in the head, giddiness and vomiting. Dr Possin realised he would have to operate. He needed to go through the mastoid cavity and evacuate the pus, but he did not have the instruments for this. 'What do you need?' said Herbert Panknin, the Chief Engineer, who kindly wrote me a long letter. 'Our diesel machines are also delicate and I might be able to produce something for you.' 'I need a small chisel and a tiny spoon to scoop out the debris from the mastoid cavity'. The doctor had found swelling there. 'I can do that for you,' said Panknin. 'Give me a little while.' 'Won't this be dangerous?' asked Captain Oesten. Could it wait till we reach a Japanese base?' 'No, he'll be dead by then,' replied the troubled Surgeon,[13] 'but we'll have to take the risk.'

'I will assist you,' said the Captain. So they went ahead with the operation, the instruments functioned perfectly and the sailor, Dr Possin told me, made a good recovery.

On another occasion a crew member was brought to him with acute abdominal pain settling in the right side – a typical appendicitis case. Again the doctor decided to operate to save his life. Once the patient was under the anaesthetic, Possin made the incision at the classical McBurney's point, removed the appendix and again, he told me, the sailor made a good recovery.

Hans Possin said that one troublesome complaint for the Engine Room staff was that of oil-eczema. Chief Engineer Panknin elaborated on this. 'In tropical waters,' he said, 'the temperature normally stood at 35 to 40° inside the submarine, but with an alarm dive, it could rise in the engine-room up to 71°.'

The problem of skin bathed in constant sweat remained, and was not helped by the lack of fresh water. Distilled water had to be saved for the huge accumulators, so washing and laundry had to be done in seawater. One consequence was that the salt crystals drying in the clothes were hygroscopic and later attracted damp from the humid atmosphere inside the boat, which only aggravated the eczema – the itching must have been intense.

One crew member wrote a poem, full of alliteration, in the Ship's Paper, about the tremendous heat 'down below'. It was under the name Dage and kindly translated for me by Mrs Lieselotte Harries of Pembroke.

Die Heisse Hitze

Und wieder sind wir auf der, Linie,
Wo ach so heiss die Sonne sticht.
Damals man von der weiten Weiten,
Heute man von heisse Hitze spricht.

Je heisser du bei heisser Hitze
Das Mittagsmal verzehrts,
Um so heisser Du im heissen Schweisse,
Nach einem kühlen Trunk begehrst.

Doch wird Dir heisser, immer heisser
Das dann nicht mehr heisse Hitze heisst,
Denn das Heisseste alles Heissen,
Tropenkoller heisst !!

WHITE HOT BURNING HEAT

And again we travel along that line (equator?)
Where, oh! so hot, the sun will shine.
Where once all talk was of far horizons,
Today it's of heat like white-hot irons.

As hotter still in the scorching heat
Your midday meal you sit and eat,
And hotter yet, bathed in burning sweat,
You long for that cool, refreshing drink.

Yet as you feel hotter and even hotter,
Its name's no longer just white-hot heat.
It's the hottest heat of all white-hot heat:
It's called Tropical Madness !!

Nevertheless U/861, with all the hardships of five months under water from the Arctic to the Equator, remained a 'happy ship.' Dr Possin says 'the team spirit and the mood on board were excellent all the time.' He saw to it the food was good, the water clean and hygiene observed. He himself ran the weekly typed newspaper on board, of which he donated to the author a bound volume of photocopies, now donated for the Pembroke Dock Museum. The articles were stimulating and humorous. 'Psychological complications were unknown on board, the mental and moral state of mind of the crew was exceptionally good.' What of the job they had to do, grim as it was?

'As you know,' says the doctor, 'we sank several enemy's boats on our passage out, two off the Brazilian coast, auxiliary warship *Vital de Oliveira* and one Liberty ship, *William Gaston*. We sank two (British) ships out of a convoy off Durban (the *Berwickshire* and the *Daronia*) and one boat (the

285

Greek *Ioannis Fafalios*) off the island of Pemba off the East African coast. We saw the enemy's aircraft twice, once off Durban, and once at Aldabra, as described in our ship's newspaper.'

The doctor then describes the four months' stay in Penang and Soerabaya (Java), for the crew an idyllic time with fresh food, tropical scenery and pretty girls. Avoidance of VD was strict, however. One could not afford infections in such a confined space as a submarine, before the days of widespread antibiotics.

In Penang Possin was kept busy elsewhere as a doctor and still had to oversee the provisioning for the long haul home. Hundreds of egg yolks were deep frozen in tins, with all kinds of fruit juice and bread. Potatoes were dried and rolled in talcum powder which stopped them decaying. Everything was stored in the U-boat's deep freeze compartments. Possin had no cases of vitamin deficiency either coming out or going home.

The U-boat took on some stores and ammunition in Penang from the Japanese, but had to go to Soerabaya in the Netherlands East Indies (Indonesia) to load up the ballast in the keel with raw materials vital to Germany's war effort. Chief Engineer Panknin tells me that this consisted of tin, wolfram, manganese, raw iodine and 40,000 kilos of latex rubber. 144 tons of this 'cargo' was later unpacked at Pembroke Dock. Cooperation with the Japanese was good (with the hospital it was excellent), but on the whole relationships were distant.

They sailed from Soerabaya on 14 January 1945 on the long trip to Drontheim (Trondheim) in Norway and reached there on 18 April without incident. They had again taken the wide detour via Brazil and Iceland.

Their precious cargo of raw materials arrived in Norway only a month before the Armistice. Upon surrender U/861 was sent across to the small naval dockyard at Pembroke Dock, the flying boat base in South Wales, along with the Second Engineer and a smaller crew of 19. There the keel was unpacked and the public allowed to visit her for five days.

From the huge heap of latex chunks on the dock many pieces found their way to a new home as souvenirs. The Mayor and Mayoress of Haverfordwest and the Chairman of Milford Haven District Council and councillors paid official visits. The U-boat was then taken to Lisahally, Northern Ireland, to be sunk. The whole crew had to spend two years as Prisoners-of-war, 1945 to 1947, in Britain. Captain Oesten told me he prefers to call himself a Prisoner-of-Peace.

IOGROPS

Navy-Air Force cooperation rose to its heights in the formation of this new organisation with its inelegant initials. I was fortunate in getting to know Air Vice Marshal Avian A. 'Uncle' Case CB CBE shortly before his death and, as one who was involved with the start of it all, he was able to give me a rare insight into IOGROPS. In his own words, then, introduced by a C.V. which is no line-shoot:

'I flew flying boats from November 1935 until July 1946. During that time I flew Southamptons, Scapas, Stranraers, Londons, Sunderlands and Catalinas, among others. He was CO of 202 Squadron at Gibraltar, working the battered Mediterranean convoys throughout 1942.

'In 1944 I volunteered for the job of Staff Officer to Air Marshal Sir Albert Durstan on his appointment as Air Officer Commanding No 222 Group, Ceylon. At that time there were parcels of anti-submarine aircraft spread out all round the Indian Ocean but no central control. For instance the South African Air Force were operating land planes from Walvis Bat, Cape Town etc; RAF flying boats from St Lucia, Madagascar and so on; Pamanzi, Dar-es-Salaam and Mombasa under AHQ East Africa at Nairobi; Wellingtons from Aden, Mogadishu etc under AHQ Aden; Flying boats all round India under AHQ Bangalore; also from Ceylon, with advanced bases as far as Diego Garcia, and landplanes from Kankesanturai etc all under HQ 222 Group.

'U-boat activity was hotting up and the number of sinkings of merchant ships was becoming serious. So, it was decided that some form of centralised operational control should be set up to direct the anti-submarine operations in the 13.5 million square miles of ocean between Cape Town and Penang.

'Air Marshal Durstan and his team decided that as a first step all merchant shipping should be routed in lanes which could be patrolled. This would improve the chances of catching a marauding U-boat and would also mean that any ships sunk would be quickly discovered. The Royal Navy agreed to these measures and appropriate orders were signalled to the Merchant Fleet.

'The Air Marshal and his team also suggested that Naval/Air Operations Rooms (NAORs) should be set up at all the main bases, so that centralised control could be exercised to meet the threat of U-boat activities. It took a little time to get RN agreement to this measure because though the RAF had no qualms about decentralising control of aircraft to the Group Captain at an NAOR, the Senior Naval Officer (NOIC) in a port never had and could not have authority to order ship movements.

'However, agreement was soon reached on a method of overcoming these difficulties and joint Naval/Air operations rooms were set up in

Colombo (C in C Eastern Fleet and AOC 222 Group; Bangalore, Bombay, Karachi, Aden, Mombasa, and Durban, with Colombo exercising overall control. Each NAOR had a Group Captain and a Captain RN in charge. The organisation was known as IOGROPS (Indian Ocean General Reconnaissance Operations).

'There was also the advantage of ULTRA which enabled them to meet specific U-boat threats. I was the lucky chap who got the job of writing the MANUAL OF OPERATIONAL CONTROL – INDIAN OCEAN!'

Air Vice Marshal Case then described at length three examples of operations where IOGROPS directed the response. One was U/852 where Lt/Cdr Heinz Eck, after his defeat, said he was quite sure there were more anti-submarine aircraft in the Indian Ocean than in the Atlantic. In another case there were several night sightings, but the U-boat got through to Penang. The last submarine sounds like U/859. AVM Case writes:

'It was attacked by night off Durban, Tulear and Diego Suarez without success. The U-boat then set course for Penang and once again we set up our parallel track sweep and several night attacks were made as she progressed towards Penang.

'The area round Penang had been mined by both the Allies and the Japanese and the safe entrance to the harbour was long and narrow. By this time cooperation with the Navy was working smoothly and one of our submarines (HMS *Trenchant* – Commander A.R. Hezlett RN DSO DSC) was stationed near the entrance to the channel. When the U-boat surfaced to proceed down the Channel she was torpedoed. Many of the crew were saved and became prisoners. The U-boat captain said that they had been attacked on many, many occasions in spite of the fact that they had never once been on the surface in daylight since leaving the Baltic. [Commander Hezlett went on to sink the Japanese heavy cruiser *Ashigara* off Sumatra on 8 June 1945, a tremendous coup.]

AVM Case concluded:

'These stories show how tremendously difficult it was to find and sink a U-boat. At night one has just one fleeting chance to see the target and hit it – a long shot! By day it was hard work trying to find a U-boat in millions of square miles of ocean.'

One last example of Navy-Air Force cooperation is recalled by F/O Norman Leece, an observer in 259 Sq:

'On 15 April 1945 on our way from Pamanzi to Durban on an exchange visit, we encountered the battleship *Warspite* and two cruisers also heading south. They were in perfect formation, the *Warspite* leading and the two cruisers equidistant on each side. It was most impressive to see from the air. As we circled a signaller started to signal from the deck of the *Warspite* and I felt thrilled that this was happening, only to be disappointed when I learnt the message. "THE CAPTAIN WANTS TO KNOW WHAT NUMBER DRESS TO WEAR ON ARRIVAL AT DURBAN." I expected Buzz [F/O Hibberd] to be flummoxed but he must have called on his reserve of knowledge and promptly replied by Aldis lamp. Goodness knows if he gave them the right information.'

SUBHAS CHANDRA BOSE

Cooperation was also seen on the Axis side between Germany and Japan, when the Indian Nationalist leader Bose was taken out East by U/180 (Musenberg) and transferred south of Madagascar to the Japanese submarine, I/29 (Zyniti-Isu). With him was his aide, Abid Hassan (not an Arab as some books aver.) Vital materials on both sides were handed over from 23 to 27 April 1943 and Bose proceeded eventually to Japan and South East Asia, where he raised the Indian National Army to fight the British.[14]

203 WELLINGTON SQUADRON

We last saw 203 as a Blenheim light bomber squadron in 1940 performing sea patrols and sharing the same hot RAF base at Aden with 8 Squadron – helping to sink Italian submarines.

During 1941 the squadron was rushed to Crete where its assistance was badly needed to escort convoys evacuating the British Army from Greece. In that task they lost all but six of their Blenheims. 203 stayed in the Mediterranean till November 1943 when it moved to India and received Wellington XIII bombers. With these the aircrews carried out sea patrols from the base on Bombay Island, the Santa Cruz airport. While there they worked up to 100 sorties a month on convoy escorts and other maritime duties but saw not a trace of submarines – a familiar story. On 12 March 1944 F/O McKay did see a U-boat; he straddled it with his DCs and saw it no more – a sinking not confirmed after the war.

THE *FORT STIKINE* DISASTER

Shortly after this, on 14 April 1944, occurred one of the greatest sea disasters of this century, right next door to Santa Cruz. In Bombay's

Victoria Dock an ammunition ship blew up and destroyed many ships and supplies.

The cause is still debated but seems to have been a succession of human failures and wrong decisions. The full story is best told in *Unsolved Murders and Mysteries*, a well researched, gripping book with a cover as arresting as its title.[15] In brief, the tragic chain of events began at Karachi where the *Fort Stikine*, of the Port Line, a 7,134-ton freighter built in Canada with Lend-Lease funds, and commanded by Captain Alexander Naismith, arrived from Baltimore, USA. (She was named after Canada's River Stikine). There she unloaded crates of Spitfires, but still had aboard 1,395 tons of assorted shells, mines and explosives and plenty of room in her holds. Under a wartime rule, she had to leave with a full load, and, despite the captain's misgivings, an extraordinary variety of mainly inflammable goods was put aboard. These included 4,100 bales of cotton, badly needed for Bombay's cotton mills, 1,089 drums of oil, and 11,000 pieces of timber. A floating bomb.

Arriving at Bombay she was berthed safely but a catalogue of misunderstandings and uninformed decisions about unloading allowed a fire to start in one hold and go unnoticed to become a raging furnace. It was possibly due to one forbidden cigarette or one saboteur. Eventually there came the first massive explosion – 'like an earthquake and a volcanic eruption combined.' Blazing cotton bales, oil drums and metal fragments killed 336 people, maimed over 1000 more, and destroyed property and sheds full of food and essentials for miles around. A steamer beside the explosion, the *Jalapadma*, had its stern lifted 60 feet into the air and dropped on the roof of a dockside shed!

Half an hour later, as flames reached another 790 tons of explosives, a second, more devastating explosion threw debris 3,000 feet into the air and damaged more residential areas and people. The whole dock became an inferno. In the end 15 merchant ships were sunk or damaged beyond repair, with two ships of the Royal Indian Navy. Three more vessels were repairable. Well over the official death toll of 1,376 people died, and thousands were severely injured. 50,000 people lost their jobs and enough food stocks were destroyed to cause a temporary famine in the neighbourhood.

Firefighting and rescue proved very difficult in an area looking like a bombed section of London or Berlin. Corporal Joe Spencer at Trombay, on the east side of Bombay, was an RAF Nursing Orderly in charge of Station Sick Quarters at the Air-Sea-Rescue Unit. He recalls watching the smoke, flames and explosions going on towards Bombay. Three days later, as he drove a patient to the British Military Hospital, they saw the devastation, and 'natives walking aimlessly amongst the rubble which appeared to consist mainly of flattened huts and houses.'

According to 203 Sq records,[16] 'at 1900 hours that day a telephone message was received ordering the Squadron Fire Section and all available personnel to the scene of the fire and to assist in fire-fighting and salvage work. For his efforts LAC Nelson was awarded the George Medal and Corporal Newstead was mentioned in despatches.' The Army, despite great efficiency, still took seven months to get the docks working again. The loss of Bombay for that time was a huge blow to the war effort.

The maritime author, Captain Bernard Edwards of the Merchant Navy, remembers 'going into Bombay 12 months after the explosion and the port was still suffering from the after effects. We had 4,500 tons of ammunition,' his letter says, 'on board from South Africa, which the Indians were not at all keen to touch. They kept us at anchor in the outer harbour for six weeks, and we were lying there when the Japanese surrendered. What a wasted journey!'. While probably not due to outside enemy action, the Bombay explosion in half an hour caused more damage to shipping and the fragile supply situation than a couple of average U-boats might do in a month.

FOOTBALL AND LIONS

Animals provided some variety of interest in the serious business of war, but the first event was most unhappy. In Mombasa and Dar-es-Salaam there was a great enthusiasm for football, which on the African side was played in bare feet, even against European teams. Mike Taylor in 230 Squadron says:

'We had a very good football team, our goalkeeper Geordie Knox had played for Everton, he enjoyed a tremendous fan club of African boys who, every time he made a fine save, stormed the pitch around the goal area doing cartwheels etc in sheer delight.'

LAC Ron Smith, my friend in the Transport section at Dar, the year after, recalled 'driving one of the football garries after the match, through an avenue of Africans, and the thrill of a hundred war cries as we passed through them.'

On this day in Mombasa, however, it was an all-African match which Roy Instrell of 209 Sq remembers most clearly:

'Mombasa sported a number of teams, while the main Mombasa eleven was a match for any side the services could muster. One Sunday afternoon we

UPPER LEFT: RAF football team plays first-class African side, who are barefoot, Dar-es-Salaam. *(Courtesy of N. Leece)*

UPPER RIGHT: What a drogue is like. This one acts as brake on port side of Cat. *(Courtesy of J. Drew, 240 Sq, Madras)*

LOWER LEFT: The funeral of Glyndwr Jones who died within a few hours of contracting Cerebral Malaria, Mombasa, 1943 conducted by S/Ldr Easton, right. *(Courtesy of Dai Thomas)*

LOWER RIGHT: Refuelling a Cat, using 4-gallon tins *('Debes')*. Some of the crew of FP265 (F/O Fred White RAAF) who later perished (all except Ben Lee) in a crash at St Lucia, 25 June 1943. *(Courtesy Ben Lee)*

were lazing in our huts at Makadini camp, when one of our colleagues came rushing in. "There's been a terrific panic in Mombasa this afternoon," he gasped. "What happened?" we all shouted.

'"There was a football match between two African teams and a large number of native spectators," he went on. "Everyone was intent on the game when suddenly five lions jumped out of the undergrowth at the side of the pitch. They had got on to the island following some cows across the causeway. For a second everyone was frozen and then terrible panic broke out as the lions started chasing people all over the field. At first they seemed to be playing, knocking someone over and then running on to the next. But then blood began to flow and they got really nasty".

Five lions attack football game in Mombasa, killing nine and wounding 40, until three of the lions were courageously shot by this Indian trader (seen with hat) on 18 February 1945. *(Courtesy Geoff Guy)*

'It was reckoned that about nine people were killed and up to 40 mauled. An Indian trader who lived nearby came out with a hunting rifle and finally managed to kill the lioness and two of the young lions. There were some who thought that the lion and cub had got into Snake Valley which was an overgrown valley between our camp and the slipway camp.

'Anyway we were suddenly issued with Sten guns and magazines to carry about the remoter parts of the camp. We fortunately did not see anything of the lions and were in most danger from the guns when the NAAFI turned out at night. Our only temptation was to use the guns on the massive hordes of cockroaches which frequented the latrines.'

293

A happier Mombasa lion story was told by Padre Squadron Leader Chaffey-Moore, the Senior Chaplain in East Africa, in his autobiography,[17] and he has allowed me to use it.

'One of the occupants of the mess was an ancient lion called George. How old he was I have no idea, but he had few teeth and was inclined to be smelly. He belonged to the Duty Officer in the control tower. One day he saw George in the middle of the grass strip, so he called to the Corporal and said, "A plane is coming in and George is in the middle of the runway. Will you go and shift him?"

'The Corporal raced across to shift George, giving him a good kick up the backside. George gave him a weary look and instead of going back to his usual resting place slunk off into the "bush" the other side of [Port Reitz] runway. Feeling a bit mystified, the Corporal returned, only to see George blissfully asleep under the stairs.'

[On Christmas Day (1943) celebrations at Mombasa it was usual for the Officers to serve us Airmen the Christmas lunch. The author missed this, as instead of going to the Mombasa Cathedral service, he joined some friends for a booze-up in the town.] The Padre remembers 'lining up to take my turn behind the cookhouse, when an Australian pilot suddenly spied a black mamba snake. Bending down, he got it by its tail, and whipped it, so breaking its neck. 'Don't ever try to do that,' he said, 'It takes years of practice.'

DAMAGE TO RAF PROPERTY

These animal stories may seem a bit remote from the 'War in the Indian Ocean' but each case could have resulted in injury or death to RAF personnel prosecuting that war. None more so than the Makadini tusker, whom LAC Jim Ginn, of the MCS, recalled vividly.

'One dark night after aircrew had returned to the huts, tired and worn out after a hard night's booze-up in Mombasa, a bleary-eyed WOP/AG got up to go to the nearest palm tree to "water his horse". To his horror, framed in the door was the biggest Tusker he had ever seen. No sooner had he sobered up he yelled out "Wild Elephant!" A chorus from the hut yelled "shut up!" and the end of the wooden hut came in round the tusker's neck. At that moment (so I was told later), a mad charge out of the other end of the hut began! All hell broke loose and we heard the rumpus on our side of the camp, at Kipevu.

'Down in the harbour the "Indom" (HM Aircraft Carrier *Indomitable*) lit up overall and the searchlights lit up the whole camp. This upset the tusker, plus the fact that the bods were spilling out all over the place, they in turn yelling blue murder! They came through the mango and banana plantations over to our camp for safety. Meantime the elephant went from hut to hut, tossing them all over the place. The din was fantastic, it was a mess. By dawn, much of the camp was flat. As the Askari police failed to, or did not want to get too close to shoot it, the Royal Artillery brought up a Bofors gun and that was that. It came to light that the Tusker was a rogue and had been driven out of the herd.'

N O T E S

[1] The Admiralty would have preferred him to use all his ships on convoy escorts. *The War at Sea* Capt, Roskill, see Note 11

[2] *The Royal Indian Navy,* Commander D.J. Hasting RINVR (McFarland and Co Inc) Jefferson, USA 1988

[3] Donkeyman – Senior hand in the engine-room in former days had charge of the donkey-engine on deck, driving the winches.

[4] These accounts are in the *Sunderland Echo and Shipping Gazette,* Tuesday 14 November 1944

[5] The two killed were James Rutter, Third Engineer and a Donkeyman-Greaser, named Critchley of London.

[6] Some reports said this was the captain of *The Empire City* but those are incorrect.

[7] ACSEA – Air Command South East Asia

[8] *The Royal Indian Navy* – as above

[9] The rest of Hibberd's crew on this trip were: 2nd Pilot, P/O W 'Bill' Martin. Observer, F/O Norman Leece. WOP/AGs, Sgt 'Cec' Heck RAAF, and Sgt George Tweddle RAAF. WOM/AG Sgt Pete Mosely. Flight Engineers, F/Sgt 'Taffy' Wilks, Sgt Alan Carlton.

[10] identification signal – see IFF aerial on Radar diagrams in Appendix

[11] *The War at Sea,* Capt S.W. Roskill DSC RN, Volume III Part II page 205, London 1954-1961

[12] The rest of Joplin's crew follow. F/Lt V.C. 'Flash' Johnson RCAF, Navigator; F/O H. Widdefield RCAF, 2nd Navigator; F/O 'Mac' MacPherson (the rest being RAF), 2nd Pilot; W/O Reg Greenwood, Flight Engineer; W/O 'Oggie' Ogston, WEM/AG; W/O Gething, WOP/AG W/O Jack Pheasant, AFM/AG; an FME/AG and an WOP/AG, names not found.

[13] *Coastal, Support and Special Squadrons,* the Rev John D.R. Rawlings (Janes),

London 1982

[14] *The Springing Tiger* Hugh Toye (Cassell and Co, London 1959

[15] *Unsolved Murders and Mysteries,* editor John Canning (Treasure Press) London 1990, essay – *The Great Bombay Explosion* by Michael Hardwick

[16] 203, Squadron Records, Public Record Office, Kew

[17] *Recollections of an RAF Chaplain,* Canon R.G. Chaffey-Moore (the Book Guild)

LIBERATORS COMPLETE THE TASK

As the war rolled on towards 1945, both German and Japanese submarines in the Indian Ocean became scarcer, but three or four U-boats managed to escape the increasingly successful Allied searches. The Liberator long-range bombers were given the task of sealing off the approaches to the Axis submarine bases in the Far East. Meanwhile one U-boat's spectacular tour took her round New Zealand and Australia and she sank the last freighter of the war to go down in the Indian Ocean. She was U/862.

THE SHOT-DOWN CAT MYSTERY SOLVED

On a glorious summer evening, 20 August 1944, over the wide Moçambique Channel, three Catalinas of 265 Squadron were droning away together on a dull anti-submarine patrol. When I say 'together', they were actually 200 miles apart, but moving in the same direction (Bob Thomas of 265 is sure that H-265 was actually en route to Durban with passengers, hence 13 men aboard). This would give them the best chance of finding a needle-like U-boat in the haystack of the vast Channel, anything from 250 to 700 miles wide, and no more aircraft could be spared.

Like all aircrews on long patrols, those of the three flying boats had spent hundreds of hours searching without seeing a thing. Their wireless operators were vainly monitoring the air-waves for clues or directions from base, when – out of the blue – came the call sign of 'H' for Harry, the Catalina at the centre. Then a Morse cry of three triple dots – S-S-S and again S-S-S! Then, silence. When S-S-S is heard radio traffic ceases awhile so that any further message, however faint, may be heard. H-265 (FP 104)[1] with her captain, Flight Lieutenant J.S. Lough of Berwick and his crew must surely have been shot down.

U/862 coming into Penang Harbour, 1944. *(Courtesy of A. Ridder)*

The other two Cats and the base radio station waited anxiously for hours but nothing further emerged from the silence. In one of the accompanying Cats, that of F/Lt E.C. Lawrence from Ontario, was F/Sgt Albert Farmer, a WOM from Ilford. He recalls that the authorities wished them to continue their patrols which they did till evening but the Flight Commander, S/Ldr Pete Seymour, who was in their aircraft, would stand it no longer and told Lawrence to go over to Lough's last position and see.

Also that night Flying Officer 'Ernie' Robin DFC, the Canadian who had finally sunk U/197 exactly a year before, flew across to the area where his friend Jock Lough and 'H' for Harry would have been, but no debris was seen. Back at base, there was indecision about sending further searchers, but fellow aircrews, says Farmer, insisted on it. So flying boats of different squadrons spent the next three or four days searching. All that was seen, however, was the empty yellow dinghy which is automatically ejected and self-inflates in a sea crash.

Almost to this day nothing more was known of the crew's fate, except the fact that they had been shot down by the U-boat U/862. In 265 Squadron records, through some oversight, only eight of the 12 names of this heroic crew were given, as 'missing believed killed'. The stricken relatives could not even be told that they had been shot down, and killed in a brave attack on a submarine, which might have given a crumb of comfort and pride. Such are war regulations. 'Missing' creates inevitably an agony of dwindling hope and postponed grieving, which could have been avoided in this instance, by Air Ministry action, at least at the end of the war.

The squadron records at Kew, due to a regrettable oversight at Mombasa, failed to record the names of the 13 gallant airmen aboard the aircraft. Only eight mis-spelt names were given 'and four others' – this for a crew deserving an honoured page in history. Amazingly, at the last minute, Air Commodore Graham Pitchfork MBE unearthed for me the 13 correct names given in this chapter's footnotes. They include 'Stan' Elliott AFM. This rare Air Force Medal was awarded for gallantry on 24 September 1941 when Stan struggled for 20 minutes out on the wings of a Vincent to remove a burning tyre which would have set light to the aircraft.

It was the paucity of records that made me determined to find what had happened to that crew; a long search ensued, with help from Jim Lawson of Belfast, Bob Thomas of Cardiff and Reg Fletcher now at Nuneaton, all of 265 Squadron. Then Christopher Lowe gave me some names of his submariner friends in Germany and one who had served on U/862.

I wrote to Herr Schirrmann and when he replied, in German, recommending his friend in North Wales – I entered a goldmine. Mr Albert Ridder after his POW days had married a Welsh girl there. He kindly not only replied that he remembered the shooting-down but sent me two full War Diaries to copy, even better than log-books.[2] They were taken from the combined memoirs of several friends, and particularly those of Ist Watch Officer Reiffenstuhl. These both had two-page accounts of the shooting down, which had remained unknown to any save that crew. They were kindly translated for me by Dr Margaret Thiemeier of Soest, Germany. Among many fine photographs was one, perhaps never seen elsewhere, of a shot-down Catalina burning on the water, taken from the opposing U-boat. So what did happen?

We can only extract, from a very full account, some of the features of a record voyage which covered three oceans. U/862 was another 87.5-metre-long IXD2 boat built by Deschimag on the River Weser and commissioned on 7th Oxctober 1943. Her captain, Commander Heinrich Timm, decorated with the *Ritterkreuz* (Knight's Cross) in 1944, was born in Bremen and was now a stocky 34-year-old experienced captain. He was nicknamed Tüte Timm (meaning 'paper bag' – a chimney-sweep with a bag being the emblem on the conning tower). His leisure occupation was playing classical records over the loudspeaker, in between the pop records, which the crew bore with weary resignation.

Unique in military history – the photograph of Catalina H/265 burning on the sea, taken from the U-Boat, U/862 (Captain, Heinrich Timm), which shot it down on 20 August 1944 in the Moçambique Channel. All of Jock Lough's crew died in the crash. *(Courtesy A. Ridder)*

In a map from one of the diaries we see that U/862 with its 66-man crew, took the traditional route of U-boats round Africa and up the Madagascar coast across to Penang. She sank seven ships, four in one week in the Moçambique Channel. For the first of these, we have an amazing story, seen again from both sides.

MAROONED

On a Sunday, 13 August 1944, as the sun went down over that wide waterway, the submarine's 'sonar' detected a vessel some way ahead. A jolt ran through the crew and eyes brightened at the thought of the chase. After a while a plume of smoke appeared on the horizon, and U/862 slowly caught up with the 3,614-ton British tramp, the SS *Radbury*. A spread of two torpedoes was enough to sink her and she went down so quickly that the U-boat detected no SOS and was thankful. In the dark the Germans watched as the survivors swam about or tried to clamber on to five overloaded rafts, made of oil drums. Each raft had a magnesium flare lit, which shed an eerie blue-green light on the scene of the tragedy. But, with the British Navy about, the German crew, having enquired the details of the ship, made haste to get away and took no prisoners.

We next see those struggling survivors ten weeks later, stranded on a desert island called Europa Island where there was no source of fresh water! *Radbury's* captain had gone down with the ship but 55 crew members had reached shore. How then did they stay alive for the rest of the 73 days?

Most of the *Radbury's* crew were Chinese but a few were British DEMS gunners.[3] The island was uninhabited save for goats and chickens existing on the scrub since a previous occupation. There was no spring or stream and for six weeks the party lived on salt water (at first), goat and chicken supplemented by turtles and fish. It was thanks to the Chinese Chief Engineer that all their lives were saved. Sung Tsu Tem, in charge of the party, devised an evaporator out of two buoyancy tanks from a lifeboat and some lengths of piping and from that day on each man had a cupful of distilled water every day. Sung also organised, among other things, a rota of watchmen to scan the horizon for sign of ship or aircraft. Signal fires were lit every day even though nothing was seen. Sung Tsu Tem was a marvellous leader to have on a desert island.

Then, ten weary weeks later, as their food ran out, Catalina A (FP 311) of 265 Squadron, Diego Suarez, was tasked with a photo reconnaissance or 'recce' of a coral reef, the Bassas da India and of the French *Ile Europa*, 205 miles west of Tulear in South Madagascar. 'A' for Apple was[4] captained by F/Lt E.C. Lawrence and navigated by another Canadian, F/Lt D.S. Lyall from Halifax, Nova Scotia.

And it was Albert Farmer who provided me with photographs of the Europa castaways and an Ilford news cutting of the occasion. He told me how 'A' for Apple took off from Tulear at sunrise on 26 November 1944 and carried out the first recce without any incident. They then turned for Europa and as they came near they were surprised to see smoke rising and a number of men round about, on the island. Lawrence's first thought was that these might be a roving band of fishermen from the mainland, but at this point the resourceful Sung Tsu Tem threw some rubber on the fire which produced billowing clouds of black smoke. The Catalina captain said later, 'Probably we should never have seen the fires but for that.'

He then circled low down and messages were written out in the aircraft on the back of some charts. These were rolled up into cylindrical Sea Marker containers and weighted with tins of food. Albert recalls sealing one with a tin of salmon before dropping it from the blister. One message read, 'If in distress lower flag' and this was done. Another said,

View from Catalina A/265 of the men of SS *Radbury*.
The survivors were marooned on the waterless
Europa Island for ten weeks. *(Courtesy of A. Farmer)*

'If medical supplies needed write in the sand'. Replies were marked out with strips of black tarpaulin on the beach. The survivors also said that they had only food supplies for one more day. 'A' for Apple's crew then dropped further supplies of food, water, cigarettes and a First Aid kit before their PLE obliged them to leave, promising a ship would come. The following day they returned with additional supplies for the survivors who were taken off on the morning of the 28 October 1944 by HMS *Linaria* and transported to Mombasa.

THE CATALINA BATTLE

Only a week after the sinking of the SS *Radbury*, the two War Diaries record that on 20 August 1944 as the tropical sun was again nearing the horizon, U/862 was:

'proceeding without problems when – suddenly! – aeroplane – we see him too late – we cannot submerge. This is all we need! It's him or us now!

'Our men work feverishly at top speed. The aircraft is flying towards our beam. It is a twin-engined Catalina flying boat. Only one of our two guns is working. The little Matrose Mumms (sailor Walter Loch) is firing very well and has hit the plane. [This was First Watch Officer Günther Reiffenstuhl writing]. At this time I stay down in the Command Centre of the U-boat. I hear the command suddenly from the Conning Tower: "Hard-a-starboard! Hard-a-starboard!" Now everything depends on the next few seconds. There is a heavy detonation – the boat vibrates – it heels to one side – water comes into the control room!

'On deck there is lots of noise. A hit! A hit! (When the pilot saw he had been hit and realised he wouldn't get out in one piece, we thought he was aiming the aircraft to hit our U-boat.) The Cat came flying just 10 metres above us and it crashes into the sea about 10 metres ahead of us. Because of the explosion there is a fountain of water through which we travel seconds later. Our joy and excitement at being alive is enormous!

'The wreckage of the flying boat is burning for a long time. All the crew are killed, no bodies seen. There is a dinghy and other debris floating around. (Reiffenstühl himself dived in and ignoring the risk of sharks, swam over). The flying boat's logbook is salvaged and also a lot of navigation cards and silk shirts. The logbook gave us useful information -from where the Cat started and where the bases were in Africa.

'During the night another flying boat came towards us [this was Robin's] – now we have been seen, we were able to get away without attack. We had to be on guard as it was a matter of life and death.'

To fill in the story from other bits of the diaries, Lough's Catalina appeared out of the setting sun at 3,000 to 4,000 metres distance. He kept a steady course towards the boat. Friedrich Peitl gave the alarm and went immediately to the 3.7 cm gun on the 'wintergarden' while Walter Loch manned the twin 2.0 cm cannons higher up. In the Cat the bow gunner was firing away. It was too close for the 10.5 cm deck gun to be effective but the other three let fly. Peitl's shooting from the 3.7 cm damaged the right wing and right engine so the plane became unflyable but still hurtling directly towards them. Finally Loch, with his 2.0 cm cannons, scored a hit on the cockpit. The aircraft only just missed them and exploded in the water 30 metres beyond.

Had the RAF heard of Lough's courageous attack at the time, no doubt medals would have been awarded for him and his crew. In the South Atlantic F/Lt Lloyd Trigg, RNZAF from Auckland (described to me by Dudley Dresch, of 200 Sq, later at Madras, as one of nature's gentlemen) was in his Liberator D-200 in the South Atlantic and sank the U-boat U/468. He and his crew crashed fatally as well, on 11 August 1943.

UPPER LEFT: On U/862 which shot down H/265, gunner Friedrich Peitl, on left, damaged the Catlina. *(Courtesy of A. Ridder)*

UPPER RIGHT: Captain Henrich Timm (standing on right in a white shirt) watches the 10.5 cm gun crew at work. *(Courtesy of A. Ridder)*

LOWER LEFT: Bosun of U/178, Max Schley, at Penang, with two Japanese provisioning officers. 10.5-cm gun seat in foreground.
(Courtesy of Watch Officer Karl Günther)

LOWER RIGHT: Heusinger Von Waldegg, Captain of U/198 (holding bottle) with some of his crew.
(Courtesy of Horst Bredow)

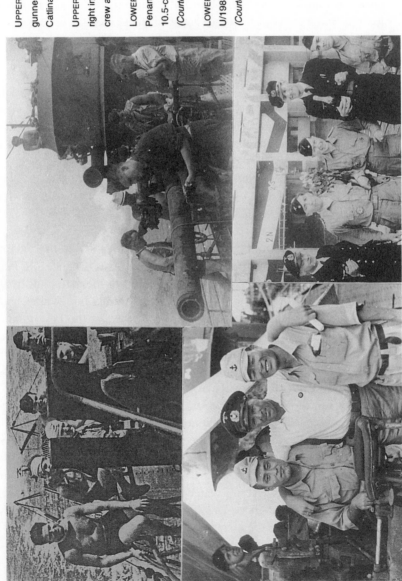

Catalina N/265 captained by F/o Ernie Robin DFC, over Port Victoria, Seychelles. They did a search for Jock Lough and crew, on 20.08.44. Robin also sank u/197 on 20.08.43.
(courtesy C. E. Robin DFC)

He was awarded a posthumous Victoria Cross because the U-boat captain, Senior Lieutenant Clemens Schamong, had survived to become a POW and put together an account of the attack. Now another German crew has witnessed to the brave exploit of a Scottish pilot.

Crew of H/265 shot down by U/862 on 20 August 1944.

BACK ROW LEFT TO RIGHT: F/Sgt Glynn; F/Sgt Baines; Sgt Dow; F/Sgt Elliott AFM; F/Sgt Popple

FRONT ROW LEFT TO RIGHT: F/O Willis; F/O Lough; F/O Watkins; F/Sgt Bickmore; (inset) F/O Dick Chaffée.

(Courtesy Reg Fletcher)

From an address on an old photograph which Ernie Robin gave me, we traced Jock Lough's sister, Mrs Chris Todd, a retired headmistress now in Sunderland. She confirmed that the crew's relatives had been told nothing other than that they were 'missing'. Bill Lough, as he was known to the family, was brought up in Eyemouth and loved the boats there. His father, who died when he was only eight, was a fisherman, and in WW I his drifter was taken over as a minesweeper. Bill went to Berwickshire High School and then into the police, marrying Janet, a Queen Alexandra nurse. He loved his nephew Keith and his nieces, carrying Keith's photo in the cockpit of his Catalina as a mascot. Berwickshire would be proud of him. Jim Lawson remembers Jock as a:

'likeable, tall, rugged Scot, rather unruly and not given to observing the niceties of dress or etiquette but a born leader and someone you would like to have with you if you ever got into a scrap. His co-pilot Johnny Watkins much more an introvert – a quiet shy Englishman. Dich Chaffée was a close friend of mine and was a loquacious Welshman. They were all great guys and I was very saddened when they went missing. Dick's sister Claire, was in Bridgend, Glamorgan I think. It would be a comfort to her and her family to know that his death was instantaneous and that he didn't rot away in a dinghy for weeks.'

In the photograph of Jock's crew, which is not exactly the group who flew on 'H's' last patrol, we at least have names on the back. If any reader knows of relatives who can now be told, this account would be well worth while.

U/862'S RECORD VOYAGE

The submarine, having sunk five ships in the past month, headed east across the Indian Ocean to Penang. There she stopped only three days for supplies and water. After nearly four months at sea with the claustrophobic fug and stenches of U-boat life, Penang was, as ever, a paradise. The war diary extols its virtues:

'10.09.44 Cars are OK here – you never walk – a totally different world. Pineapples, bananas, coconuts. The children of our Malaysian "boy", Oswald, climb into the palms like monkeys. Badminton, tennis and in the afternoon, around the island with Charlie, had a bath in the waterfall. In our villa we had coffee, then went to the "Shanghai" (the local for our sailors – in Penang no duties were given).

'11.09.44 Japanese Admiral on board, also officers of Japanese Marine U-boats. Officers are very mistrusting; they write down everything. They were fascinated with the Snorkel; we didn't like them. Later we were at the Tonga ballet.'

Passing via Singapore and Java southwards, they headed for Australia in November 1944. Rounding Tasmania, up the east coast of Australia on Christmas Eve, U/862 sank, with four 'eels' the 7,000-ton American Liberty ship, the *Robert Walker* off Sydney. Two Americans were lost.

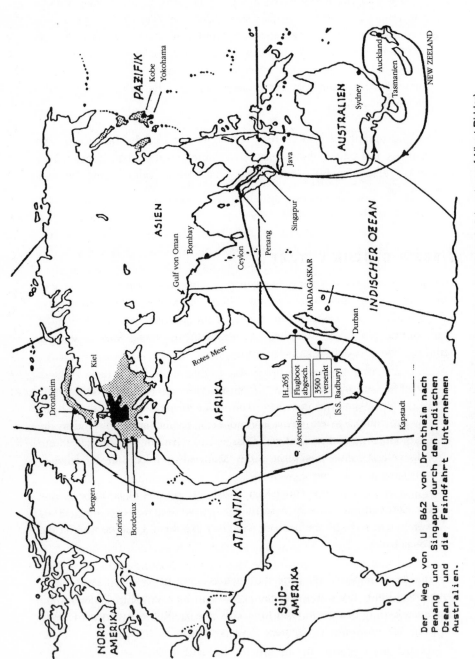

Der Weg von U 862 von Drontheim nach Penang und Singapur durch den Indischen Ozean und die Feindfahrt Unternehmen Australien.

U-862's lengthy voyage. Surrendered by the Japanese at Singapore 10.8.1945 (courtesy of Albert Ridder)

Finally Timm took his boat round the North Cape of New Zealand and began a cruise down its eastern coast, fully described in the New Zealand *Sunday Star*[5] in 1992, with the help of Seaman First Class Albert Schirrmann's diary. The writer of the article, Chris Chapple, comments:

> 'The war was still turning Europe into a boneyard. And on the far side of the earth, the killer submarine U862 made the turn south to hunt on the New Zealand coast. But perhaps it's worth bearing in mind too, as this 12-day voyage begins, that the crew are struck by the beauty of their surroundings at sea, affected also by the imminent ending of the distant war, and perhaps a little in awe of New Zealand's innocence.'

Four times U/862 made for small ships going in or out of harbours, but one was too small to waste a torpedo on and others escaped through rain squalls or other causes, quite unaware of the dangerous enemy below them. One was coming out of Auckland Harbour and another from Gisborne Harbour. This town of 12,000 people was so brightly lit you could see it on the horizon. The U-boat stole into un-blacked-out harbours, watched New Zealand couples dancing on the piers, but found no ships tied up at the quays.

Returning north after rounding Tasmania, U/862 sank another 7,000-ton US Liberty ship, the *Peter Sylvester*, off the south-west corner of Australia, Cape Leeuwin, on 6 February 1945. Commander Timm says he had received the German propaganda saying that these ships 'built by Kaiser were actually *Kaisersörge*' or Kaiser-coffins and easy to sink.' Timm found the opposite, and this ship needed six torpedoes to break it in half – even then the stern section stayed afloat and was last seen by survivors two days later riding low in the water.

The *Sylvester* was heading from Melbourne to Colombo, carrying 2,700 metric tons of US Army cargo, 175 men (including 7 officers and 100 enlisted men of the US Army), and 317 Army mules. Tied in their stalls, and braying on the deck, the latter will all have drowned eventually. A Hellcat pilot, Sub-Lieutenant Eric Spearing from an FAA carrier, HMS *Speaker*, was sent out to look for survivors, but he tells me that all he saw were a dozen of the dead mules floating and some bits of wreckage. Being near Australia, 142 survivors were picked up by various ships, including HMS *Activity*, an escort carrier doing blockade-running and transporting goods and warplanes to the Pacific. Robert Taylor was a FAA Air Mechanic on board and explained how some aircraft were lost overboard in a storm. In an article[6] he had written, he recalled the discovery of one of the lifeboats, summarised herewith:

'The carrier spotted this boat with some figures in it, but the war was still very active and Captain North was rightly cautious. Japanese submarines had been known to fill a lifeboat with dummies and then torpedo an unwary ship investigating. So first the warship circled at high speed using asdic and radar and gradually approached, to find 20 genuine live Yanks, who were hauled aboard and given their favourite hot coffee. The NAAFI even produced a hitherto unseen crate of chewing gum for the guests, who were taken to Fremantle.'

U/862 now headed back to Singapore and at VE day was taken over by the Japanese and renamed I/502. While there, a scratch German crew was still aboard when American bombers came over to bomb the harbour. They were accompanied by Lightning twin-boom fighters, and crew surprised themselves by shooting one down as it swooped on the ships.

Timm and the crew, when VJ day came, finished up as prisoners-of-war, the Captain and officers in a camp near London and some of the crew in a North Wales POW camp. There Albert Ridder and his colleagues worked on a farm in Denbighshire where 'the farmer and his family were very good to them' they wrote, at the end of their War Diary.

MINING OPERATIONS BEGIN

We have seen how a Far East U-boat managed to slip through the clutches of the Eastern Fleet and use Penang Harbour as one of its facilities. The Allies were determined to close this loophole, but how? Laying mines round Penang and other ports seemed a possible answer, and various Royal Navy submarines had tried doing this, but the ports remained open. Submarines also risked being attacked on the sea, whereas the Japanese had no adequate air defence, for their harbours. Their Arado float planes with German pilots were mainly useful as spotters. One acted one day as an air sea rescue boat, the pilot tying many U-boat survivors to the big floats then flying back and forth to Penang.

Could long-range bombers, then, reach Penang from the nearest RAF bases in Calcutta or Ceylon, carrying heavy mines over a thousand miles of chartless sea? One man was determined to prove they could. He was Wing Commander James Blackburn, the Commanding Officer, not of a maritime squadron but of 159 Bomber Squadron based at Digri, near Calcutta. The Allies gave him the task of adapting Consolidated Liberators or B24s, with adjusted power settings, to reach Penang carrying a heavy payload. Air Commodore Henry Probert, till recently head of the Air Historical Branch, Ministry of Defence, has allowed me to use material on this subject from his recent book.[7] He describes Blackburn as 'one of the great unsung bomber COs of the war.' Quoting the Squadron Engineer Officer, the late Air/Cdre Eric Burchmore, Probert writes:

'Blackburn had been working hard to improve his aircraft's performance by removing such things as mid-position gun turrets and armour plating . . . [Though Penang was 1,500 miles away], calculations showed that with a full fuel load, including the bomb-bay overload tanks, four 1,000-pound mines could be carried, provided we had access to a 3000-yard runway and that the aircraft would withstand an all-up weight of 68,000 lbs (the normal maximum was 56,000).'

In October 1944, flying from the US base at Kharagpur, 15 RAF aircraft, led by the intrepid CO, one after another lumbered down to the end of the runway before lifting off and flying down to Penang with their dangerous loads. 60 mines were delivered to the inner approaches of the harbour.

'They had all covered a distance equivalent to London to Moscow and back [says Probert], one of the great bomber missions of the war, and had done exactly what the Navy wanted, placing the mines in "precisely the position ordered", as the AOC, Air Vice Marshal Mellersh, put it. An American expert was sent from Consolidated's factory in San Diego, California, to see how these incredible performances were achieved.'

160 SQUADRON

Speaking of the improvements W/Cdr Blackburn had started, a Flight Engineer of 160, Jack Burgess, writes:

'By January 1945 W/Cdr Stacey, our CO, had taken up and utilised these innovations to enable 160 Sq Liberators to reach Penang Island, lay mines between the island and mainland Malaya, then return to Ceylon.'

160 squadron had really started life in January 1942, with Liberator IIs, carrying out Atlantic patrols. It soon moved abroad, via Palestine, and by May 1943 was doing mainly photo reconnaissance work from Ratmalana in Ceylon with Liberator IIIs, and later from Kankesanturai, known as KKS, at the northern tip of Ceylon.

In contrast to the Catalina, which came from the same stable, Consolidated Aircraft, the Liberator weighed twice as much and could carry heavy payloads as far as the Cat. They shared the same engine, the

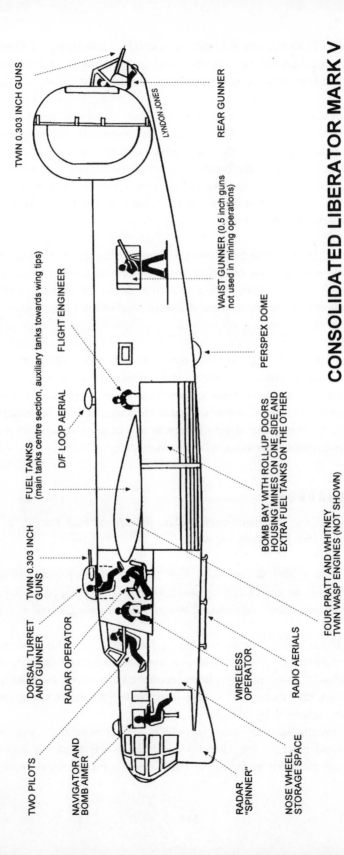

CONSOLIDATED LIBERATOR MARK V

TWIN 0.303 INCH GUNS

LYNDON JONES

REAR GUNNER

WAIST GUNNER (0.5 inch guns
not used in mining operations)

PERSPEX DOME

FUEL TANKS
(main tanks centre section, auxiliary tanks towards wing tips)

FLIGHT ENGINEER

D/F LOOP AERIAL

BOMB BAY WITH ROLL-UP DOORS
HOUSING MINES ON ONE SIDE AND
EXTRA FUEL TANKS ON THE OTHER

FOUR PRATT AND WHITNEY
TWIN WASP ENGINES (NOT SHOWN)

TWIN 0.303 INCH
GUNS

DORSAL TURRET
AND GUNNER

RADAR OPERATOR

WIRELESS
OPERATOR

RADIO AERIALS

TWO PILOTS

NAVIGATOR AND
BOMB AIMER

RADAR
"SPINNER"

NOSE WHEEL
STORAGE SPACE

reliable Pratt and Whitney 1,200 hp Twin Wasp, but the four engines had a sideways oval cowling, like four eggs in a row, and gave twice the power of the flying boat. Libs had sunk 100 U-boats in the Atlantic and the squadron was hoping for one or more here.

When W/Cdr Brady was the CO, the squadron was warned, in October 1944, that the Japanese submarines were bringing over agents to India. Four-aircraft sweeps were therefore started. On one of these, on 27 October, Fl/Lt Lloyd Netherton, a Canadian, with his crew of eight,[8] set off in their white Liberator Five, 'A' for Apple. It had brown and green on top of its fuselage and wings and the large light and dark blue roundel of SEAC on its sides.[9]

Heading north, after some boring hours, they were at 1,500 feet in a sunny sky with light cumulus cloud when Netherton in the port-hand pilot's seat spotted something. It was a fully surfaced submarine four miles off and the captain hit the klaxon button for ACTION STATIONS! As they approached the submarine, there was no indication as to whether she was Japanese or German, but she was taken by surprise. 'A' for Apple descended steadily towards her, but she stayed on the surface and did not fire. One man, in a yellow shirt and white cap, was seen in the conning tower. He was probably shouting down the tube to alert the crew but there was no time for a response.

The sun was behind the Liberator as she dropped her four depth charges from the stern along the track of the vessel. When the huge plumes of spray had subsided there was no sign of any U-boat. Nor was there any sign of debris, but an oil patch gradually spread during the hour following the attack. Netherton and his crew were convinced they had achieved a kill, but it could not be confirmed as their camera film stuck to the glass in the heat and all 12 photographs were taken on the same patch. Apparently as a General Reconnaissance squadron, they were NOT ENTITLED to be issued with the small mirror attachment in their F.24 cameras which would have protected the film from overheating.[10] Bureaucracy is not confined to the late twentieth century!

160 GOES MINING

The squadron now moved from the comfortable brick buildings of KKS to a small RAF airfield at Minneriya. hacked out of the Ceylon jungle which conveniently had a 2,500-yard runway but primitive living conditions. Burgess writes:

> 'Aircrews flying at UK bases had only to complete in some cases 30 operations of two to three hours duration before being grounded for six-

months' rest period. We had to complete 500 operational hours with little or no air-sea-rescue facilities; no home leave; no social life; poor food quality and flying rations. There was the underlying realisation that we could be stuck out here for years, in the Japanese war, and a feeling that if the German Army overran UK – would we ever see Britain again?' The aircrew in 160 consisted partly of members from the Commonwealth with ages ranging from 19-26. The new CO, Wing Commander Stacey, was then 24, and still known as Swee'pea.'

He adds his account to others which he and Jack Burgess and Warrant Officer F.W. (Bill) Cooper,[11] another Flight Engineer, have kindly allowed me to blend into one. Stacey writes:

'Having spent four and a half years on flying boats, I was surprised to learn on my return to Ceylon, early in 1944, of my posting as Flight Commander to 160 Squadron, equipped with Liberators [land planes]. After operating in the bomber role in the Middle East, they needed someone with the sort of maritime background I had. Many of the aircraft captains had been instructors at flying training units and the rest were young pilots direct from training with an abundance of youthful enthusiasm, but little experience.

'Collectively, the senior captains were the most professional and competent bunch of aviators I saw in any one place during the entire war. There was a wonderful mixture of nationalities: Australian, New Zealander, Canadian, South African, even a few Americans and of course from all the home countries. But there was never a suspicion of national jealousy – the only judgement was always how well the chap did his job. Every crew, about eight in each, contained a mix of nations and not once did I ever hear a suggestion that even one crew should be formed on a national basis.

'In November 1944 I was given the command of the squadron and told to prepare the unit exclusively for minelaying: this involved devising a system for dropping mines at low level, 200 feet, at night with a fair degree of precision on targets up to 1,200 miles away in Malaya, Sumatra and the Kra Isthmus. However, it would be wasteful to fly 1,000 miles only to find one's datum point obscured by rain so we also devised a low-level, radar-based approach (our Libs had Mark Five ASV) which would enable us to drop even in non-visual conditions but with less accuracy.'

Burgess here interjects:

'In these long flights, there was no mistaking the four-letter word in everyone's mind – "FUEL"! To carry more fuel, Air Gunners were excluded, the remainder of the crew taking turns at the guns. (I have seen gunners in tears because they desperately wanted to see action).

'Ammunition was reduced to save weight; the rear turret ammo was cut from 6,000 rounds to 600. All equipment not considered absolutely essential was stripped, even oxygen systems.[12] Bomb bay fuel tanks were then fitted in order to stretch the operational range to even greater lengths. [These were flexible bag tanks].'

Bill Cooper adds:

'In order to achieve the range the Mark VI Liberator was exchanged for the Mark V which did not have a nose turret. To further lighten the aircraft the top turret, armour plate and Elsan chemical toilets were removed. *In extremis* crews used nose cones from flame floats *in lieu* of the Elsan. In normal times insects used the outlets from the toilet tubes as a nesting place and woe betide any Flight Engineer who did not shove a long wire through each of the three tubes during his pre-flight checks.'

'Now, engines could only be fed from the main fuel tanks in the mainplane. Therefore it was absolutely crucial timing on the Flight Engineer's part to judge when the main tanks were ready to be topped up. Too soon would cause highly dangerous flooding, too late would cause engine failure.'

Fuel transfer during flight was via an extremely awkward set of rubber tubes in cramped conditions and darkness beside the rigid rubber tanks, with only a small torch and a wrist watch to judge things by. Add to this the pitch and rolling of the aircraft in storms, which on one occasion threw Jack against the ammo rack and covered him with blood, and you have a fairly hazardous process.

'Mutual respect [says Burgess] between aircrew and maintenance staff was very high, However, survival was based on sufficient fuel and flight engineers before take-off would cut the fuel cap locking wire and visually check each tank was full to the brim. [This was a regular practice in 160 Squadron]

John Stacey adds:

'Attention was given to devising easy means of deciding what was feasible and checking in flight actual fuel consumption against planned. Here the professionalism of our ex-Training Instructors was invaluable, especially the three Canadians, Squadron Leader Doug Joy (Flight Commander), and Flight Lieutenants Jack Leeper and Lloyd Netherton. In all this we were given a totally free hand, and it was by this we were able to find solutions so quickly.

'Relevant to this is that, shortly after being given command of 160, my boss, Air Marshal "Dusty" Durstan [Air Marshal Sir Albert Durstan CB AFC], asked me to dinner in his house in Colombo. As we were all leaving, he stopped me and said, "You stay: we'll drink a bottle of whisky, after which we will know each other better." We did finish the bottle. I left at about three in the morning and his valedictory words were: "Remember, you are responsible to me and not to my staff: I don't expect you to bother me with matters they should handle but you must tell me personally if ever you feel I should know of anything prejudicing your squadron's efficiency." I rang him three times during the eight months I had the squadron and something happened within ten minutes every time.'

The preparations started with a tragedy.
Stacey told how

'the squadron was given permission to drop a number of old depth charges to allow the crews to see the effects. Regrettably, on the second lot to be dropped they exploded on impact; as the dropping height was about 50 feet, the aircraft was totally destroyed. The only survivors were the two New Zealanders, Dixie Dean, the captain, and the wireless operator, whose name I forget.

Burgess cannot recall the name either, but he was usually called Kiwi.

'Of Maori extraction, he told me that he held up a crew-mate in the water for five hours when, to his horror, he had to let go through sheer exhaustion. A short time later they were picked up . . .'

Stacey continues:

'Our first attempt at minelaying was on 21 January 1945. The target was Penang harbour. I made the mistake of going in very low to avoid giving radar warning, but it proved impossible to identify landmarks at such a low level and the mission proved abortive.'

Jack Burgess, who was Canadian Les Waterfield's Flight Engineer on that trip, remembers the briefing by W/Cdr Stacey.

'He enthusiastically announced he would be the leading participant along with his crew. He gave us dire warnings about flying too close to Sabang which was swarming with Jap fighter planes. We had been practising low flying for some time, and Stacey now informed us it would pay off as he told us to approach enemy territory at wave-skimming altitude to get under the Japanes radar beams.

'After dropping our mines, Stacey announced that he intended to increase his altitude to reveal his aircraft on Japanese radar and fly on a north-west course. This was to give the impression that we were returning to an Indian base. Holding this course for a short time, he then intended to drop back to sea level and follow our two aircraft back to Ceylon. I can still see the expressions on the faces of W/Cdr Stacey's crew[13] as he announced this. I'm sure they would have much preferred to skip the heroics and get the heck out of it with us.'

A word from Bill Cooper about the details of the operations. Out of 8 targets he mentions, including Singora, which we visit in the next chapter, he did two trips to three of them in the role of Flight Engineer. The range could be up to 1,700 miles each way, and duration up to 22 hours 20 minutes. A Cat might stay aloft over 24 hours but not carrying such a heavy load half-way. Typically three 1000-lb American magnetic mines would be carried, fitted with fins or parachutes. They could be set to allow up to five vessels to pass over them before exploding under the sixth.

Cooper continues:

'In addition to the normal hazards from enemy fighters and ack-ack, the crews on these missions had to contend with an absence of meteorological forecasts, with cumulo-nimbus clouds, electrical storms, unexpected headwinds, shortage of fuel leading to ditching, absence of radio aids – and flak from the always trigger-happy Navy!'

Jack Burgess also told me of more than one Liberator, with its heavy load, failing to get off at the end of the runway, and becoming a firebomb.

Ditching, or a sea landing, due to fuel running out, is illustrated by our Liberator photograph of 'A' for Apple, a B24 Vb (registered BZ 711). She was captained by F/Lt Doug Turner RCAF of Toronto, with four other Canadians, two Scots and a Yorkshireman in the crew.[14] Returning from an operation in a similar B24 on March 1945, the dreaded moment came when it ran out of fuel, says Burgess, and the Liberator crash-landed on the sea. Fortunately there was a Dutch ship on its way to Ceylon nearby but a Lib V goes down in a few minutes, and for this reason: when minelaying, the bomb bay doors roll up either side like a roll-top desk, leaving anyone standing on the nine-inch catwalk exposed to the breeze. Such doors are like matchwood when the sea crushes them and pours in.

UPPER: Crew of Liberator 5b (A/160 BZ 711) who faced the constant dangers of mine laying. Left to right: Dorsey; Yeomans; Hewitt; Turner (Captain); McCreadie; James; Smith; Burgess.

LOWER: Liberator 'A' for Apple showing Bulge or radar spinner under nose. Left to right: Dorsey; Hewitt; Turner (in cockpit); McCreadie; James; Smith; Burgess; (standing – Dorsey).

(Courtesy Jack Burgess)

All the crew escaped except the flight engineer, Sgt Grundy, who when the cables snapped on impact, was enmeshed in their coils, and also by bomb parachute cords. In the air pocket remaining, his cries were heard by F/O Bob McCreadie, 2nd Pilot, who was up on the mainplane as it lay on the waves, trying to launch the yellow dinghy. Bob then dived repeatedly down into the fuselage of the sinking aircraft, came alongside Grundy and with the jungle knife they all carried, hacked and slashed at the steel cables and cords. He still had to tear Grundy out forcibly and get him up to the surface and then to the dinghy. The monster aircraft could have dragged them both down into the depths at any minute.

For this act of determined bravery Bob was awarded the British Empire Medal. Grundy was seriously injured and when the crew went back on ops, Burgess took his place as Flight Engineer and was with them on 29 July 1945. On that day they broke the squadron record for the longest operational flight (supply-dropping in Malaya), 23 hours 25 minutes.

There were other hazards. On one occasion Cooper's crew circled Chumphon Harbour three times in brilliant moonlight before he (Cooper) managed to kick a "hung" mine off its bomb rack.' Burgess mentions another Liberator which was last seen flying along like a ball of flame.

> 'Another unspoken thought [he continues] was the fear of a close-to-shore ditching or crash landing as we knew full well that the Japanese ignored the Geneva Convention regarding prisoners-of-war; and had, in fact, stopped keeping prisoners as such. A 159 Squadron crew had been tortured by the Japs, two officers surviving to tell the tale.'

They were given some basic jungle equipment and training in survival and a ludicrous promise of air-sea-rescue. Our routine Catalina patrols in East Africa sound dull by comparison but a crash by accident there could be no less deadly.

I asked about the loading up of mines. Burgess said he thought they were flown in by the Madras-based 200 Squadron.

> 'The squadron armourers then took charge and undertook the loading from a trolley on to the specified aircraft by means of hoisting gear. The operation was always completed by briefing time. Although we realised each mine was capable of blowing up a ship, such was our confidence in our armourers that we trusted them implicitly to "hang them up" properly.'

Stacey adds a word on the maintenance unit:

> 'The ground crews were superb, which was just as well as they were working under the most appalling conditions. We were at the end of the line on priorities, and it was make-do-and-mend all the time. There were no hangars and all the work was in the open, rain or sun – and it was hot! 120 degrees in the tail turret at midday. The backbone of the ground crews was always the pre-war Halton or equivalent-trained apprentice, with an average age of 21, we were never short of ingenuity or enthusiasm.'

How about dropping the mines? I asked Jack. He answered:

> 'As the mines nestled in the bomb bay our thoughts would focus on this

particular mine destroying an enemy ship, that would reduce the threat to Allied forces in Burma. It was always a relief to make a clean drop and get back on the long 9 to 11 hour flight home.'

Bill Cooper adds:

'It was customary to fly from a landmark at a set speed on a pre-determined bearing and drop the mines on a time interval basis. Accuracy was essential to inhibit Allied naval activity in the target areas.'

This was borne out on the extra-long-distance trip to Singapore, which in the words of Jack Burgess, 'produced an additional surge of adrenalin intensified by the effect of shipping in Singapore harbour extinguishing their lights one by one as presumably air raid warnings blasted out.'

John Stacey led this raid also, the Libs carrying only four mines instead of the usual six. With extra fuel from Catalina tanks, the overall weight was 68,000 lbs which meant that the take-off run would be tight, with 150-foot trees only 300 yards beyond the end of the runway.

He says:

'There was no question in my mind that we should not make it. I must mention our splendid Intelligence Officer, Andrew Boggin, who had been a solicitor and, I think, Town Clerk of Gloucester and who put his heart in to the squadron; I'm sure he wished to be aircrew. He flew whenever possible, and we were together on this Singapore venture, in my favourite Lib, 'N' for Nuts or BZ 752.'

Stacey says that after the lessons of the first Penang trip, the 160 Squadron Liberators would approach at 200 feet but climb to 500 feet about five miles from the target:

'This gave us enough time and vision to identify datum points and remained standard practice. We took off at about noon, eight or ten Libs, on 23 March 1945. The outward trip was uneventful. As usual, we went to sea level at last dusk to check the radar altimeter against actual – any inaccuracy could mean curtains. All our runs started from the southern point of Asia, only a mile or so from the Singapore harbour entrances.

'I nearly wrote us all off here. Having briefed everyone to carry out their runs on "George" (the automatic pilot) because he would be more accurate over this distance, I also told them to disengage him after dropping mines because they would compensate more quickly for the nose-down trend following mine release. After I had released my mines however, I was intrigued to look at Singapore. I left George in, gave the elevator up a good twist, the turn control a similar twist to the right, opened the side window and had a good look through the binoculars.

'Glancing down after a short time I saw the vertical climb indicator showing a loss rate of some 500 feet a minute, the altimeter a height of less than 100 feet (we had started at 200). The Lib's George altitude control worked in the opposite direction to the Catalina's which I had used for several years and under pressure I couldn't remember which way to turn it! So I banged George out of operation and recovered position manually with only a few seconds to spare.

'Coming back direct meant climbing over the Sumatra mountains and we knew we would then have a rough ride because the inter-tropical front was lying from that point to about 200 miles short of Ceylon. But we thought we could avoid the worst storms by radar. At the top of the climb at some 8,000 feet our radar packed up and we had a few very unpleasant and turbulent hours, with lightning striking the aircraft constantly: very frightening at first but you can get used to anything!

'We landed at Minneriya after 21 hours and 15 minutes flying and, if memory serves, about 150 gallons of fuel. All dropped their mines successfully (40 in all) and returned safely. I left the squadron shortly after this by getting an infected throat and went into hospital for a spell. Truth to tell, I was exhausted: for a month or so I had been waking up every three minutes during the night before any operation unless I took a good dose of sedation, mostly Australian brandy, and could get over the after-effects before take-off next day as it was usually about 2 p.m. On leaving hospital I was posted to Headquarters 222 Group in Colombo to look after Special Duty operations.'

Jack Burgess confirms the 'physical and mental exhaustion'. One flight, as with Catalinas, involved many hours preparation for the crew, between 7 a.m. and 2 p.m., the take-off time. The flight of 18 to 23 hours was then followed by debriefing and after up to 36 hours on the go one was too tired to sleep. 'It must have been worse for Stacey, with the responsibility of command,' Burgess thinks.

Anyway, the results were worth it. Apart from isolated U-boats like U/862, activity ceased, and only two merchant ships were sunk in the Indian Ocean in 1945. In the minelaying drive against Japan, 'it was the long-range bombers of the RAF's No 222 and 231 Groups which carried the main burden of the campaign in South-East Asia. These mines sank ten ships totalling 29,294 tons; and in addition they certainly impeded, and finally contributed a great deal to stopping the flow of oil from the ports of Sumatra and Borneo,[15] says the Naval historian.

Admiral Sir James Somerville, C-in-C Eastern Fleet, inspects US Marines on USS *Saratoga*, 1945. *(Courtesy of Imperial War Museum No. A23458)*

The new convoy arrangements and the work of the RAF and Royal and Dutch Navies (especially the submarine arm) had reduced Axis submarines further and the minelaying reinforced this. With the end of the European war, the stage was set for the final defeat of Japan.

TWO MYSTERIES

First

During any war things happen, ships or planes disappear, and even men, in strange circumstances. Occasionally the answer is discovered after the conflict is over, as happened here. This first mystery relates to an American tanker of 10,448 tons called the *River Raisin* from Portland, Oregon, in the closing days of 1943.

Earl Mountbatten, Supreme Commander SEAC, at Sigiriya, Ceylon, thanks 160 Squadron for their work. *(Courtesy AVM J.N. Stacey)*

Of the many detachments experienced by the squadrons of India and Africa, Masirah was regarded as the most God-forsaken, as we have seen. Just before the end of 1943 both 265 and 259 Squadrons had a detachment there, with 212 Sq later.

Masirah is an island off the coast of Oman, used more recently by the BBC as a relay station, by the Americans as a satellite tracking base, and by the present large local population as a base for dhows, probably all motorised. The modern air force base there was used by RAF Jaguars in the Gulf War but is now home to a unit of the Omani Air Force.

In those days Masirah served as well for a staging post for big American transport planes heading from the USA (via West Africa), across to the Burma hills and into Nationalist China. The airfield at Ras Hilf was also host to 321 (Dutch) Squadron's amphibian Cats. The US base offered a cinema show every other night and when the ice-cream-making machine had been left behind, sent an aircraft back to Karachi to collect it. The RAF too, in other lonely outposts, had been known to load up a Catalina with vegetables or beer as in the time of 244 Sq. However, in those days there was hardly a tree on the island and of course no fresh water.

In contrast to the airfield, the RAF aircrews lived on the shore at Um Rasas or Um Rasays, surrounded by a searing hot bare landscape, in tents which were eventually replaced by rough buildings.

The squadron record said that there were 'more flies to the square inch than most places had in a square mile'. This statement puzzled me till I read a letter from Captain John Petschi, of 321 (Dutch) Squadron RAF, quoted in the next chapter. During their detachment on the airfield with their amphibious Cats, he says:

'The Squadron Leader (Admin), S/Ldr Zorab, was a rich London Armenian stockbroker born in the Dutch East Indies where his brother was a judge before the war. One day an American "Sanitary Inspector" arrived and was horrified by all the flies. He discovered that our local coolies did not go to the latrine when they woke up but sat down in the sand outside their tents.

'When Zorab heard this he picked out a hefty airman and armed him with a stick. Any coolie about to hunch down had the stick applied to his buttock and was chased to the latrine. Almost overnight the fly population was reduced to manageable proportions.'

Down at Um Rasas the Catalinas anchored off shore, and maintenance facilities were whatever you brought with you. When the detachment from 265 Madagascar Squadron was stationed there in December 1943, one day the Minor inspection (D.I.) for 265's aircraft 'Q' for Queenie, without which a Catalina could not continue flying, was delayed. The reason was that the only plug spanner on the island, that held by the American Air Transport Command, was dropped overboard from Queenie – thus making the RAF less than popular with their noble Allies. This time there was no pearl diver handy.

On Christmas Eve 1943, preparations for the celebrations were going well. The Officers' and Sergeants' and Airmens' messes were tastefully decorated from petrol tins, scraps of paper and leaves from the only palm tree in sight. However, reports began to come to the control room at Ras Hilf, known as 'top camp', from a ship called the *River Raisin*. She complained that a submarine was chasing her. A Dutch Cat, E/321, with J/265, was sent out in her direction but they saw neither the ship nor the sub – which was, at the end of the war, found to be the Japanese I-26 [Captain Kusaka].'

In the heat, the sweat-stained 265 Squadron Records grumbled ruefully:

'One of two things is certain – the enemy don't intend to give us any rest over Christmas, or the Merchant Navy have started Christmas celebrations rather early.'

Catalina N/265, piloted by Flying Officer C.E. Robin DFC, the Canadian who had sunk U/197, was joined by Q-209, piloted by P/O Bob Birnie, another Canadian, and later by J/265, with F/O Johnny Pinkard RAAF, with E/321, in a 17-hour search on Christmas Day. Flight Lieutenant John Whitaker, this time Birnie's radio officer, writes:

'We did so many bloody searches for that U-boat with no success we think it waited until we were airborne, and then surfaced and used our moorings.'

In the end a message came through to the RAF that the ship had been sunk. After further fruitless search the whole operation was called off. What never reached the RAF was the *River Raisin's* final signal.

'At 0630Z/24 she reported no hit but a near miss and that she had twice sighted the submarine. She was then proceeding on course and using evasive steering.'

However, the *River Raisin* emerged unscathed from the encounter.

The mystery for us in the RAF was that when the list of ships sunk during the war was examined, the *River Raisin* was nowhere to be found. Was there then a *River Raisin?* Could she be a phantom ship, that disturbed the Christmas peace of Masirah? In such cases I invariably turn to my friend, the marine author Harry Hutson, of South Humberside, who can track down a ship like a spaniel sniffing hashish in Felixtowe Dock. The *River Raisin* was indeed a real tanker, and it was *Lloyd's List* for 1947/48 which revealed the fact that she was still afloat – thanks to a stout-hearted American Captain who had given a Jap submarine the slip on Christmas Eve, 1943.

The Second Mystery

Flying Officer Norman Leece, of Huddersfield, was an Observer with 259 Squadron at Dar-es-Salaam. He writes:

'A crash occurred on 5 April 1945, when a Catalina of 259 Squadron plunged into the glassy surface of Lake Victoria with a large loss of life. The Catalina was carrying an experienced crew, some of them possibly Canadian, and a second crew as passengers, who had only joined the squadron in February 1945. Amongst those killed was the captain of the second crew, a young Flight Sergeant Pilot.'

The mystery is that there is no official record of the crash in 259 Squadron records, nor in the monthly records of Air Headquarters, Nairobi, nor even in the list of the fates of UK Catalinas in World War Two, given at the end of Andrew Hendrie's *Flying Cats*. Norman Leece continues:

'I heard about the crash on returning to Dar on 6 April 1945 with my Captain, F/O Wilfred "Buzz" Hibberd, and Flight Engineer P/O Wilks. Unfortunately Buzz died in a civilian air crash in September 1975 and all contact has been lost with "Taffy" Wilks who was in the regular air force and came from Brecon, South Wales, so I am short of corroboration.

'The pilot officer who gave them the news (probably an acting adjutant) told them that he was having difficulty coping with the procedures and was very short-handed. The Intelligence Officer, F/O Goodey, had completed his tour of duty and had left for the UK and the Flight Commander, S/Ldr Dutton DFC, was on leave. Furthermore all the other crews seemed to be on detachment away from Dar.

'What impressed the crash on my mind was the fact that I had been introduced to the young Flight Sergeant Pilot a few weeks before the accident and was impressed by his personality. Then after the crash I was asked by the Station Padre to collect a few of the dead pilot's personal belongings to be returned to his next of kin.'

So Leece was in no doubt. Another confirmation of the accident was the fact that I met one of the Air Gunners of the regular crew in unusual circumstances in the first week of August 1944. While in camp at Dar-es-Salaam I had been invited by my aunt Betty[16], a Church Missionary Society nurse in Tanganyika where my parents were also with the CMS, to dinner in the New Africa Hotel. There, in conversation with an American Mennonite, Bishop Stauffer, I met the Air Gunner, who was thinking of becoming a committed Christian.

Traditionally two subjects not discussed in messes and canteens were religion and politics. Both, however, played a part in men's lives. The Air Gunner had two doubts. If he came out in his crew as a Christian or 'Holy Joe', the others might not want him with them and then his tour overseas might be prolonged. Also how could he as a Christian still be a gunner and kill people in his job – a problem faced by not a few in the past and not to be ducked.

I was thinking of making this move too and the Bishop suggested I keep in touch with the gunner, who had a wife and young child in Devon. The last time I saw him, he was mulling over taking this step, and may indeed have done so. (He was then enjoying *Screwtape Letters* by C.S. Lewis). Through that meeting I did find Christ as my Saviour and later served as a medical missionary in India instead of becoming a mining geologist in Tanganyika, so the occasion was firmly fixed in my mind. I was sorry to hear, in April 1945, the gunner was killed in this particular crash and never returned to his family in Devon. Such sacrifices, as elsewhere in the war, often passed unnoticed except by a few colleagues and grieving relatives.

It is to be hoped that some reader may let us know other details of the accident so the full story may be recorded in the archives. This was not the similar crash of M/259 (FP 115) of the Cat Ferry Flight on a glassy surface at Kisumu on 8 July 1945, also with a double crew, and captained by F/Lt Grainger. Norman Leece and I wish we knew the names of that April crew.

NOTES

[1]   The final crew list of 13 (the number stated in German diaries!)

F/Lt J.S. Lough (Captain); F/O J.H.L. Watkins 2nd Pilot; F/O R.A. Willis, 1st Navigator; F/O G.R. Chaffée, 2nd Navigator; F/Sgt 'Stan' Surtees Elliott AFM F/Eng; four WOP/AGs, F/Sgt R.R. Baines; F/Sgt F.W.A. Bickmore; F/Sgt C. Glynn and F/Sgt F.C.A. Dow; then Sgt. M.S. Popple and 3 passenger Fitters', Cpl. P. Hodoul (?Hodoil); LAC 'Joe' A.W. Statham; LAC Halstead.

[2]   German War Diaries, U/862, via Albert Ridder of Denbigh, formerly *Maschinen Maat* (Engineer Petty Officer) aboard U/862.

[3]   DEMS – Defensively Equipped Merchant Ship. The guns were usually manned by five or ten Royal Navy gunners.

[4]   The rest of the crew comprised:- Sgt A. Gattrell, 2nd Pilot from Greenock; three W/OP Warrant Officers, W. Morgan from Cardiff, R. Williams from Wrexham and another Canadian, B. Foreman; two East Anglians, F/Sgt Albert Farmer, WOM from Ilford and F/Sgt D.R. Cook, FME (Electrical) from Norwich (Squadron Records via F/Sgt A. Farmer RAF.)

[5]   *Unseen Enemy* – article. Chris Chapple (*Sunday Star*), New Zealand, 23.08.1992

[6]   *Our Survivors* – article by R.E. Taylor in the *Sea Cadet*, 1954

[7]   *The Forgotten Air Force*, Air/Cdre H.A. Probert (Brasseys [UK] Ltd) London 1995

[8]   F/O C.D. McPhail, 2nd Pilot; W/O K. Collins, Navigator; F/Sgt G.A. Hopkins,

1st W/OP, W/O E. Lauper; Fl Engineer; F/Sgt F. Duffy, WOM; F/Sgt F. Gurman Ist S/E (radar) operator; W/O H.F. Stratford, Fire Controller; Sgt R.J.F. Eitel, Air Gunner.

[9] The change of colom for SEAC roundels leaving out red, was to avoid confusion with the Japanese red circle on its aircraft in the heat of battle.

[10] 160 Squadron Records, PRO Kew.

[11] Lecture Notes, W/O F.W. Cooper; Personal memoirs W/O Jack Burgess and AVM J.N.Stacey, CBE DSO DFC

[12] 3,339 gallons of fuel was typically contained in Main Tanks (4), Wing Auxiliary Tanks (2) and Bomb Bay Tanks (up to 3). (Cooper)

[13] Stacey's crew on this first mine sortie were: F/O C.W. Gay; F/Lt F.A. Fry; W/O F. Davies, W/O A. Ryan; F/O I.J. Turner; F/Lt S.E. Chandler F/Sgt E.J. Skinner. (Records not too legible).

[14] A/160 crew, minus Sgt Grundy, invalided out. As seen in the photograph, F/O Doug Turner, Captain, Toronto. F/O Bob McCreadie BEM Annan, Scotland. F/O Don Yeomans, Navigator Canada; W/O Jack Burgess; Flight Engineer Kirkcaldy; F/O Jim Dorsey; W/Op Fonthill, Ontario; F/Sgt Ivan Hewitt, WOP/AG Calgary, Alberta; F/Sgt Frank Smith WOM, Chesterfield; F/Sgt Al James, WOP/AG. Calgary.

[15] *The War at Sea* 1939-1945, Roskill Vol 3 Part 2 (HMSO), London 1961

[16] Sister E. Banks MBE of Bukoba Hospital.

SWORDS AND PLOWSHARES

They shall beat their swords into plowshares
And their spears into pruning hooks:
Nation shall not lift up sword against nation,
Neither shall they learn war any more.

Isaiah ch.2 verse 4 (A.V.)

BIRCHALL'S CREW IN JAPAN

When we left Squadron Leader Len Birchall RCAF and his crew at the end of Chapter 2, they were prisoners in Nagumo's aircraft Carrier *Akagi* and going to Japan. So, during all the events we have been looking at, where were they?

We have accounts from three, Birchall, Phillips and Catlin but little about the other three. The Skipper kept two copious diaries and as Senior Officer in the POW camps compiled a dossier of the war crimes which enabled much justice to be done after the war.[1]

The three badly injured men were taken to Yokosuka Naval Hospital near Yokohama and were treated. The other three including Birchall were marched through the streets and subjected to popular abuse en route to prison. Brian Catlin continues:

'The same high standard of medical care was given to us as on the *Akagi*. One time a Japanese nurse sat with us all night and she wrote on a card, "to a brave air warrior". I concealed it in a double wrapper round my tooth powder, but when I was due to be transferred to the Yokosuka Naval Prison, she became frightened and asked for it back.

'After staying there we were transferred to the Interrogation Camp at Ofuna. I was only interrogated once, I don't think they found me very profitable. There was no torture as such. You stood facing the table with a big Japanese corporal behind you and if you refused to reply to a question he just knocked you down. So after being knocked down three times you would say something.

Sgt Brian Catlin (x) with other POWs in Japan, Christmas 1942. The first year they were issued with musical instruments for the group photo, but these were later taken back.
(Courtesy Brian Catlin)

'They would ask me what engines we had on our Catalina. I would say perhaps "Twin Wasps", but they would impatiently say, "Yes but what mark?" So I would think furiously and say, remembering something from chemistry, "They were two KCLO3's". The Japs would thumb through all the books they already had on Catalinas and say, "There is no such mark." So I would say "Those are American books. In England we called them something else." So they decided I was not worth interrogating, and left me alone. We were in solitary confinement but allowed out for half an hour morning and evening. I stayed there several months. We were then transferred to the Baseball Stadium POW Camp in Yokohama, for one and a half years. With us came an influx of about 180 British soldiers from Hong Kong' – these were supposed to be the troublemakers of the camps there, whom the commandants wanted to get rid of. They were mostly First Middlesex Regiment and Royal Scots, the best lot of lads you could hope to be POWs with – they were really tough.'

Fred Phillips suffered the same conditions and saw how Birchall stood up for the men under his care.

'He tended to stick his neck out and more often than not he used to get the chopper. I myself was in control of a section. If anyone of my lads did anything wrong, I used to get the beating as well. The Jap soldiers got the

330

same treatment but I think they were definitely harder on us than they were on themselves.'

And what about Len Birchall himself? He seems to have been a born leader but he had the most horrendous situations to deal with as his diaries show.[1] He recalls the 'real rough bunch' arriving at the stadium. As Squadron Leader, Birchall was the Senior POW and, under the Japs, in charge of the whole camp.[1]

'The first thing I encountered was mass hostility from the troops . . . the feeling that their officers had let them down. In Hong Kong many of the officers had let the troops down, by looking after themselves. They had more food, cigarettes etc. and this caused severe hatred. The troops distrusted these officers and held them in deep disrespect. The officers who had accompanied them to Japan were the exception.'

Birchall and the other officers settled on one objective – 'to do the best we could for the whole camp. Somehow we had to convince the troops that our greatest chance of survival lay in working together.' They started with a fair and open distribution of food, where anyone who wished to change his plate with an officer's could do so.

Then if a man got into trouble with the Japs, an officer would jump in front of him, and give him a chance to get away in the crowd, while the officer usually got a less severe beating. Daily clinics for the sick meant trying to persuade everyone to give up their fiercely hoarded bits of medicine for the common good. In this way the atmosphere changed gradually.

The trouble came when the Japanese insisted on forcing the sick to go out on working parties with the healthy because there were not enough workers. Birchall's part in defending the sick was repeated when he was moved elsewhere and culminated in his beating up a Japanese sergeant who was thrashing a POW too sick to go on duty. Sgt Ushiada (Ushida) finished up on the ground with a broken jaw.

Birchall could have lost his life on the spot but after being in solitary and beaten and hung up by his thumbs, a Tokyo court martial ordered him to be shot. At the firing squad it was decided that was too good for him and that he should be executed. After the sword had flashed past his head, they changed their minds – back in solitary for a long period and that was that.

So for three and a half grim years the POWs of Japan, like others, longed for freedom. After the war Birchall was awarded an OBE in addition to his DFC. Many of the POWs' Japanese captors were executed for war crimes. Meanwhile how were the squadrons faring?

Air Commodore Birchall RCAF says: 'This photo was taken on 6.9.45 outside Yokohama station where we first met up with US troops after beating our way out of Camp Suwa.' *(Courtesy of Len Birchall OBE. DFC. CD.)*

321 SQUADRON

This RAF unit, built up in 1942 from the Royal Netherlands Naval Air Service, flew mainly amphibian Catalinas. Through the kindness of Nico Geldhof, Historian, of Voorschoten in the Netherlands, I have an 11-page history of the squadron in WW2, and Captain John Petschi RNNAS, whom we have met, added his experiences.

What the squadron illustrates more than any other in the Indian Ocean is the theme of 'making do' and adaptation. After the 321 Sq had been reduced in struggles during the Japanese onslaught against the Dutch East Indies, three Dutch Catalinas from a lake hidden in the mountains of Java made it to Ceylon (Y55, Y56 and Y57) and a fourth to Pondicherry. Others followed from Australia. On 1 July 1942 a new RNNAF was born in 321 Squadron, with 9 Cats and just 100 ground staff, based at China Bay, inland from Trincomalee.

Eventually the Squadron built up to 500 in strength (220 being aircrew) from a heterogeneous group of nationalities, many men with no training and their families in Japanese internment camps. They had hardly any equipment and the RAF could spare little. They made tools and bought in equipment and impressed the RAF so much that after one workshop lorry had been granted to 321, the AOC-in-C, Air Chief Marshal Sir Richard Pierse, seeing their work, personally ordered another for them.

From 1943 with eight Catalinas and 11 new amphibian Cats the Squadron started to be called upon for detachments and a large group of 11 flying boats went to South Africa, based on Durban and Port Elizabeth. The report states:

'From the day the Dutch started their activities until the end of the German campaign in those waters not a ship was sunk or even attacked when under the protection of one of their Catalinas.

'Amphibian Catalina Y85 had been escorting a convoy in the night of 23/24 May 1943. A periscope was observed in the morning, moving with great speed approaching the convoy and dangerously near to it. Y85 did not hesitate a second, dived and let go her depth- charges. Some oil and a little bit of wreckage came on the surface and that was all that was left of the submarine. A very important troop-carrying convoy was saved. The Captain, Lt Fl 2nd Cl RNNVR J. Vonk was awarded the DFC.'

The submarine was damaged but it does not appear among those sunk, in post-war and German reports. At the end of 1943 the detachments were moved from the delights of South Africa to the barren rocks of Socotra and Masirah, 'They left Heaven and landed in Hell.'

In 1943 the number of 321 Sq convoy-flights made was 333 with 5,110 flying hours. In 1944 the picture was much the same, 233 convoy flights, 194 anti-submarine patrols and 32 submarine chases. Total flying hours were 8,836. Serviceability was a creditable 70 per cent; and out of 22 aircraft, 15 on average were available for operations.

In 1945 their capacity to adapt and improve was tested again when a batch of Liberator VIs in poor condition was sent to the squadron in December 1944 and intensive training given to ground-staff and aircrews. The Air Ministry sent someone out to investigate and a newer batch was substituted, and in June 1945 six were stationed in the Cocos Islands, carrying out anti-shipping strikes, ASR and other work. In the three and a half years operating in Asia, Africa and Australia, 321 Squadron with an average of 22 aircraft, flew over 30,000 hours, escorting 500 ships with none lost and only one fatal aircraft accident.

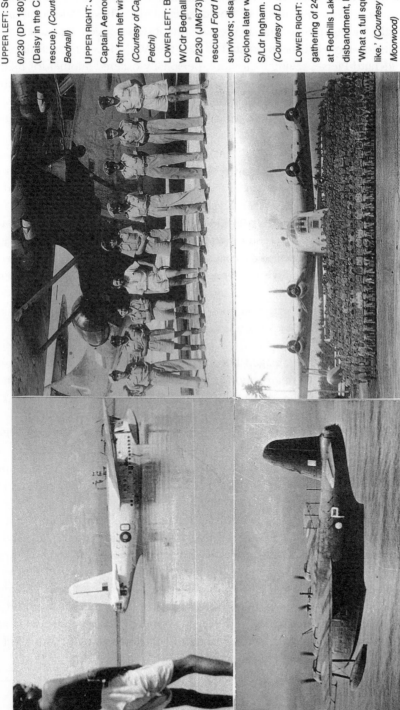

UPPER LEFT: Sunderland 0/230 (DP 180) at Koggala (Daisy in the Chindit rescue). *(Courtesy of D. Bednall)*

UPPER RIGHT: J/321, Captain Aernout RNNAS 6th from left with his crew. *(Courtesy of Captain John Petch)*

LOWER LEFT: Black Peter W/Cdr Bednall's Sunderland P/230 (JM673) which rescued *Ford McLeod* survivors; disappeared in a cyclone later with Captain S/Ldr Ingham. *(Courtesy of D. Bednall)*

LOWER RIGHT: Last gathering of 240 Squadron at Redhills Lake before disbandment, March 1946. 'What a full squadron looks like.' *(Courtesy of A. Moorwood)*

Captain John Petschi realls the early days in South Africa when he was in charge of the St Albans detachment at Port Elizabeth.

'We lived in tents, with candlelight. Outside was a little tripod with a wash 'basin'; a shaving mirror was nailed to the nearest tree. Every 24 hours there were three crews on duty flying, or on stand-by, or off in town (P.E.) enjoying a hotel room with hot bath (and the company of lovely girls!).

'After the months on searches and doing squares round the convoys, we moved to the Arab coast where we did anti-submarine patrols ahead of the convoy. On 28 December I had to give ASR cover for a torpedoed US ship I found the ship listing a bit and the crew in lifeboats. The lifeboats then went back to the ship and the men collected their belongings! They realised the ship could not sink quickly because the holds were full of empty drums.'

The Cocos Islands where 321 Sq moved to were well south west of Java. In March 1944 S/Ldr G.H.U.(Bill) Bayly of 413 Squadron, with F/Lt Fink as his 2nd Pilot and F/O Johnnie Rankin, Navigator, had undertaken a photo reconnaissance of the islands to see whether they were held by the Japanese. With a round trip of 3,000 miles and a duration of 28 hours it established another record for the Indian Ocean, being the longest reconnaissance flight ever made. The photographic results were good and showed no serious occupation by the Japs. In December '44 S/Ldr Bill Bayly and S/Ldr Johnny Gowans received DFCs and G/Capt Randall, who had become 413's CO, also had a DFC in 1944. Bayly's Navigator on the Cocos trip was awarded an Mention in Dispatches. Later a huge base was built in Cocos, Wing Commander Derek Martin OBE[2] being Chief of Staff responsible. This was to make Cocos a staging post between Ceylon and Australia, and an airfield capable of handling 500 aircraft a month. Even when war ended, some uses were planned for it, as W/Cdr. Martin kindly explained to me.

JARDINE AND SCALES IN JAVA

As with Birchall we last saw these 205 Sq pilots, the Canadian F/Lt Alex Jardine and the New Zealander P/O Sid Scales, in Chapter 1 back in 1942 starting life in the prison camps, only this was Java. Alex Jardine writes:[3]

Sid Scales adapts Cyril Fletcher's Ode.

'Bandoeng was a large military camp with full facilities, barracks and gymnasium area, cookhouse, proper sanitation. It was a regular camp, just more crowded. The first year we had a certain amount of freedom within the camp and we had money to buy food from the Chinese and the local natives.

'We had organised classes in all sorts of subjects, that idea was introduced by Laurens van der Post. People who had skills taught them to others. Van der Post was very keen to start a news magazine. I suggested the title Mark Time. Sid Scales did all the illustrations for it.'

Sid explains further about the covers which, each week, featured a caricature of a different POW personality, as with the one of the famous Australian Medical Officer, Colonel E.E. 'Weary' Dunlop CMG OBE KSJ MS FRACS FACS DSc who did so much for the men in different camps. We now have through Sid a collection of his cartoons, both of prisoners and later, secretly, of his Japanese captors, copies of which may be seen in the Imperial War Museum and RAF Museum, Hendon, if one enquires (and Far East POWs do).

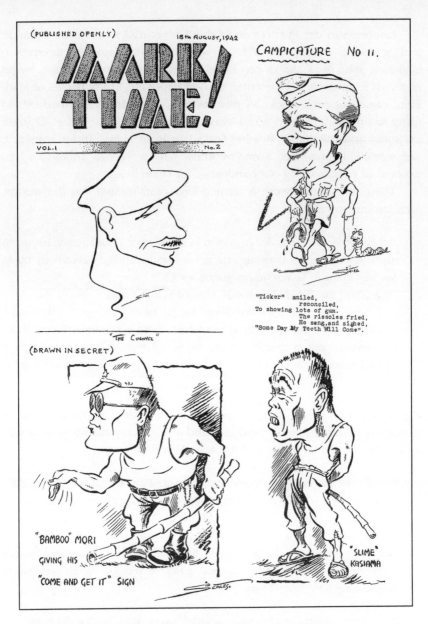

Caricatures by F/O Sid Scales at Bandoeng POW Camp, Java 1942.

UPPER LEFT: Lt Col E.E. 'Weary' Dunlop the CO.

UPPER RIGHT: Sergeant Hayes 'Ticker' Harding RAF, in charge of POW Cookhouse

LOWER LEFT: W/O Gunzo Mori.

LOWER RIGHT: his Korean assistant Private Kasiama, both described in *Night of the New Moon* by Sir Laurens van der Post.

(Courtesy Sid Scales OBE)

Laurens van der Post (Dean of the 'University') who spoke Japanese and of course Dutch, was able to work with the Japanese interpreter, Ishikawa, who 'was almost pro-British,' and the Dutch interpreter, to get materials from outside, typewriter, carbon paper etc. Thirty copies of Mark Time came out each week, all pictures traced and hand- finished by Sid using tracing paper which was a 'very fine tough Japanese tissue', Chinese ink sticks and calligraphy brushes (cat's hair in bamboo). In the magazine one week Sid explained, 'now you know why we get so annoyed when we hear of people using our handiwork for cigarettes.'

These magazines were a tremendous morale-raiser for the troops. Alex Jardine writes:

'I think of Sid as a remarkable person in many ways. I don't remember much about him doing his drawings. He never stood around so everybody could see him doing it; he just quietly got on with it.'

Regarding the Japanese guards' cartoons, Sid writes:

'I used to make quick doodles of the Jap types that were worth doing – head shapes – mouth formations and teeth – facial expressions. I'd use those as reference and eventually get the likeness I wanted. Then I'd redraw it several times, commit it to memory and then destroy it. Fortunately I never got spotted.'

That could have meant decapitation for Sid. After the first 'golden year' at Bandoeng, things suddenly changed, and a severe regime was introduced as in other camps till the end of the war. Alex writes:

'There was the odd clandestine radio about. Two Australians had made a radio that was carried in wooden clubs. One of our chaps, in our kitchen, had designed one which could be buried in the sink. On special occasions he was able, through skill and earphones, to listen to the BBC. If the radio had been found out, the man might have been killed, decapitated. So we were able to hear how the war was going. It didn't help us very much, because the news wasn't very good.'

Food, as time went on, became scarcer. Alex was Senior RAF officer, responsible for discipline, a difficult job which he did well. Here also officers' quarters fared no better than the men's. He says:

'We would have a duck's egg once in a while, and if there were four of us, would divide the egg very carefully and each have a bit. Sometimes the rice came with a blob of chilli or garlic about an inch in diameter and a little bit of ground-up what we were told was intestines of an animal rather than the actual meat.'

The American hair cut by Sid Scales. (Courtesy S. Scales OBE.)

Sid Scales remembers clearly one incident:

'It was during the "bad times" when we were hungry. A bunch of us decided to augment our meagre rations by catching some Java sparrows. To do this we used the old children's trick of a container of some sort poised upside down on a stick, with a string attached. In one case it was a tin helmet. Bait, of carefully saved rice grains and breadcrumbs, was laid up to the trap. Eager POWs on the other ends of the strings would pull the sticks away when the birds were under the container. My vivid recollection of this is of a dozen or more little Java sparrows, all plucked and gutted, strung on a wire, ready to be made into a stew (beaks, legs and all).'

'[Alex adds:] I don't think the Japanese were prepared to deal with prisoners of war; I don't think they really knew what to do with us. Their creed was that it was an absolute disgrace to be a prisoner of war, that you should die for the Emperor rather than let yourself be captured. I feel that they had not been prepared to arrange for prisoners. Keeping us alive, I think was just a matter of economics; they didn't want to waste all their ammunition on a bunch of people that were sitting around doing nothing. Keeping us in camps was the easiest thing to do.'

BRITISH SUBMARINES AT WAR

Along with other factors bringing the Axis submarine onslaught to an end, a tremendous part was played by the flotillas of British submarines, with one Dutch sub, the *Zvaardvis*, which we have seen. They were based on Ceylon, at Trincomalee. Twenty-six of them were there up to September 1944. In 1945 they began to range more widely, some with the British Pacific Fleet. Their story is covered in John Winton's book[4].

1944 began with the sinking of the Japanese cruiser *Kuma* on 11 January, followed by the ex-Italian UIT/23 on 23 February, both by Lt/Cdr Bennington in HMS *Tally-Ho*. The next came on 17 July when HMS *Telemachus* sank I/166 in the Malacca Strait. In the autumn success came faster, as DS *Zvaardvis* sank not only U/168 (many of Pich's crew being saved) but also a minesweeper, the *Itsukushima*, on 17 October. At a minelaying period, this was a good thing to achieve. The pressure by British and American submarines caused a retreat. Germany gave up the Penang base and the U-boats moved to Batavia on 25 October 1944.

On 9 November 1944 the US submarine *Flounder* sank yet another of the 65 Far East U-boats, U/537, while four days later HMS *Taurus* sent I/34 plunging down. The USN *Besugo* submarine sank U/183 in the Java Sea while *Trenchant's* Lt/Cdr Hezlett, sank the U/859. He is now Vice Admiral Sir Arthur Hezlett KBE, CB, DSO and Bar, DSC and Bar. During this time three British submarines were lost. They were HMS *Stonehenge*, sunk on 22 March 1944, HMS *Stratagem* lost on 22 April 1944 and HMS *Porpoise* the following year on 19 January 1945.

MERIT AWARDS

One DFC in 1943 was given to F/Sgt, later F/Lt, David Pitkeathly, a pilot of Dundee. For part of his time in East Africa with 259 Squadron he was a Flight Sergeant Captain of a non-commissioned crew. He became Flying Officer in 1943. With an example of the various outstanding operations he carried out, the *Dundee Courier* in April 1944 quotes the citation: 'This officer has proved himself to possess a high degree of operational skill and outstanding courage during a long tour as captain of aircraft.'

An incident quoted in the citation is one which David finds it 'hair-raising to recall'. In the Seychelles area

'We were nearing the end of an escort to a convoy and on the return to base ran into the foulest of weather with 10/10 heavy cloud and intermittent electric storms. Our W/OP could get no fixes at all and astro-navigation – to which my navigator, F/Lt George Curtis, and myself were addicted – was out of the question. To crown everything we had an experience "enjoyed" never before or since. Suddenly the propellers were two giant Catherine Wheels – a tremendous firework display which I recognised as St Elmo's Fire.

'We still could get no radio assistance, but with the fuel running out (pardon the Engineer's plaintive cry) "Jesus Christ, skipper, you should see the shit that's coming through the fuel pipe!" It was obvious we were going to have to ditch, so instructions were given to send out an S-O-S and the crew to have the dinghies ready and all seat harnesses fixed. It was pitch dark and one could only hope the altimeter was not too far out.

'When the engines spluttered and died I could only put us into as shallow a glide as possible and guess when to switch on the landing lights and fire off a flare. Our luck was in for we got close to the water and I was able to make a full stall landing. There was a fair swell but we stayed put. The W/OP sent out "mayday" (S-O-S) as long as possible while the rest of the crew threw out sea anchors. I cannot speak too highly of my crew who behaved splendidly in what must have been a somewhat devastating experience.'

Next day they were towed in to harbour.

Things did not turn out so well for another Cat, 'M' (FP 115), the Ferry Flight which, like the April mystery Cat, was carrying an extra crew going on leave, on 8 July 1945. It also crashed on landing with a glassy surface on Lake Victoria at Kisumu, which an inexperienced pilot may not have judged well. F/Sgt Deans, the Flight Engineer, and five others, F/O S.W. Ives, P/O D.C.W. Churchill, F/Sgt Noel Wilks, F/Sgt L.R. McIntosh and F/Sgt G.T. Thomas. were killed. F/Lt Ken Grainger, the Captain, was not piloting, and had broken bones but survived as did the rest.

My M.T. driver friend, LAC Ron Smith, having 'found the Lord', through Nairobi hospitality with the Hacking family, knew Ken Grainger who attended our weekly Bible Study in the camp chapel at Dar-es-Salaam. Ron's diary therefore records the fact there was a memorial service in the camp on 17 July for the six airmen killed in the crash. This was because, as Desmond Scherr recorded with his camera, they were buried at Kisumu. Des, a 259 Sq Flight Engineer. would have been in that crash if he hadn't been playing cricket for the AOC Sir Brian Baker's team against the Aga Khan's XI that day in Dar-es-Salaam.

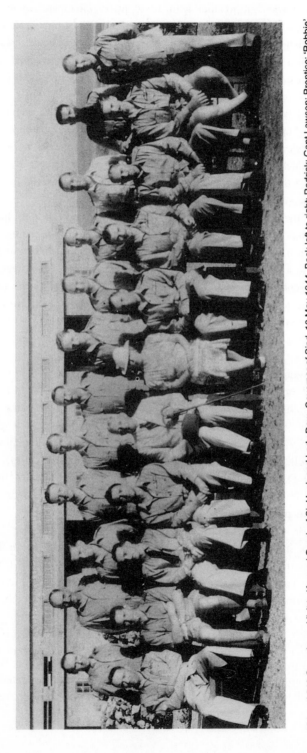

191 and 212 Squadrons. Visit to Korangi Creek of Sir Hugh and Lady Dow, Governor of Sind, 10 May 1944. Back left to right: Rodrick; Capt Lawson; Prentice; 'Robbie' Robotham (Adjutant); Windaler; Barton; Wilson; Flynn; Stagg; Welsby; Morgan; McHardy. Front left to right: Stafford; Langham; Birchenough; Brown; Cornabe; Sir Hugh Dow; Lady Dow; Slater; Porteous; Major Smythe; Slade. *(courtesy Mrs Robotham)*

A DESK JOB

Awards were only rarely given to ground staff but here is a 'recommendation' for one which was well deserved. A Mention in Dispatches was an award not worn as a medal, or in letters after your name but F/Lt Clifford Robotham was recommended for this in a lengthy tribute by his Commanding Officer, W/Cdr R.A. Phillips of 191 Squadron near Karachi. He was known by all as Robbie, and his widow, Mrs Dorothy Robotham, near Leamington Spa, has supplied me with much 'gen' about him. In June 1943 he joined the newly formed 191 Catalina Squadron as Adjutant. RAF Korangi Creek (shared with 212 Sq) was a huddle of tents in the wide Sind desert.

The Squadron was large with separate Marine Craft and Motor Transport Sections, both officer-less so Robbie had a triple job. The unit was isolated and far from back-up facilities, needing much initiative by Robbie. 'In spite of these difficulties,' wrote his CO, 'F/Lt Robotham by dint of great perseverance succeeded in getting this unit on a sound administrative basis.' At the age of 32, Robbie used to say, he felt like a grandfather to these young men of 19 and 20 who came to 191. It almost broke his heart when he had to tell parents or wife that their son or husband had died in action.

In 1944 he supervised the move of the whole Squadron 1,500 miles southward to RAF Redhills Lake, near Madras, and got through 'mountains of work' in the last few days. The recommendation ends:

'During his time with the unit F/Lt Robotham has shown great tact and initiative, and unstinting efforts have resulted in an efficient administrative side to this unit. Recognition recommended: Mention in Dispatches'.

It was never awarded.

WOMEN IN THE SERVICES

Wrens and WAAFs and nurses rarely appear in war histories, perhaps because their extremely valuable work, as clerks or signallers, goes on behind the scenes. The Navy certainly relied on large numbers of the Women's Royal Naval Service in the naval bases at Kilindini, Mombasa, at Colombo and even (as we have seen, in the *Khedive Ismail* tragedy) at the Fleet Air Arm base, RNAS Tanga, south of Mombasa, when 58 Wrens were among the 1,500 drowned.

Colin Stones, of 205 Sq, in a long article for me, showed that Wrens' company was appreciated by the RAF. This despite having officially to 'book' a blind date collectively. Arthur Davies, of 212 Sq, Karachi, sums it up.

Upper left: 'Passion Wagon', RAF lorry provided for shopping trips from Koggala into Galle, Ceylon. LACW Irene Collins, Nancy's friend, is standing in foreground on right. *(Courtesy Mrs N. Worrall)*

Upper right: L.A.C.W. Nancy Barnett, WAAF Teleprinter operator at Koggala, with billets in background. *(Courtesy Mrs N. Worrall)*

Lower: Assistant Section Officer Doreen Guthrie with Canadian personnel at Seychelles. She and ASO, Heather Leake were WAAF Cipher Officers there in 1944. 3rd from left in group is F/Lt A.F. Joplin RCAF and 4th is F/Lt V.C. 'Flash' Johnson, his navigator. *(Courtesy of F. Joplin)*

'212 escorted the convoy into Bombay which carried on board the first Wrens to serve in India. This paid a few dividends as the crews were invited to an open house at their Wrennery. It enabled some of the smoother ones to get a date with some of the Wrens. It wasn't quite like a normal date as one had to sign them out and in and explain what you intended to do and where you were going. This naturally caused the truth to be bent a little . . .'

Turning to the WAAFs I was kindly given a small glimpse into their daily life at Koggala, by an LACW (Leading Aircraftwoman) who was 'out there'. In early 1945, in Ceylon at least, the WAAF contingent was sent to work in Koggala alongside the men, roughing it in the dripping heat. LACW Nancy Barnett, later Mrs Worrall, who had come from Newcastle-upon-Tyne, sailed for Ceylon in a Dutch troopship, the *Johan van Olden Barneveldt*, out of convoy.

> 'This led a handful of WAAFS to a sumptuous style of life from the one we had left. Real food on real tables and so much we usually took Gateau, wrapped in our serviettes, to the boys on board. We were full of apprehension when we were told there was a sub in the area . . . but nothing happened.'

Courtenay Elliot, who had been an agriculture student near Guildford and was then a Pilot Flying Officer, adds to the tale:

> 'I believe it was Christmas Eve and we had an emergency Boat Drill. I was put in charge of a group of WAAFS who were formed up on the starboard side of the open Boat Deck. It was nearly pitch dark as we waited for further instructions. The WAAFS sang carols – and how they sang. Since that night fifty Christmases have come and gone, and on each one, without fail, whenever I have heard or sung Silent Night . . . it has reminded me of that dark Christmas night in the Med and those WAAFS.'

In January 1945 Nancy volunteered with two friends, Jennie and Irene, to work on the teleprinter in the Koggala signals section. On their first day in camp amid the tall gloomy palm trees, where lived enormous monitor-type lizards called Kobragoyas,

'There, there, did those WAAFs frighten you?' A pair of Kobragoyas at Koggala.
(Courtesy of W.H. Davies)

'we three girls were startled out of our wits by the sudden slow emergence of 'the daddy of them all' which honestly was easily about 15 feet from nose to tail tip. We simply froze until it passed into the undergrowth about 10 yards ahead of us. We had been warned they could slice the legs off people. I was centre and Jennie and Irene almost climbed aboard me in shock; three shivering bits of khaki.'

Other WAAFS were in ciphers, or were WAAF nurses, even a WAAF hairdresser. As a small group of 40 in a station of 2,000 men, there was a stern warning to the 'brutal and licentious soldiery' that these women were here to do a job – even 'wolf whistles' would not be acceptable. This was adhered to and the WAAFs got on with the job.

Nancy and two colleagues had to maintain a three-shift cover on the teleprinter for 24 hours a day, seven days a week. They suffered fevers with everyone else, and tended to get run down. in the high humidity, but the main relaxation was keeping cool in the water at the beach nearby and the occasional run into Galle in the 'passion wagon' which belied its name. It was a relief to go on leave up in the hills at Nuwara Eliya, in a cool English-type atmosphere and enjoy the luxury of guest-houses run like a country house with log fires in the grate and other comforts. Then back to the damp heat of the palm plantations, the snakes and the minor dragons at Koggala, backing up the flying boats out on patrol. 'The Sunderlands and Catalinas looked a fine sight on the lagoon – how I would have liked a trip in one, but never did – we just sent out messages.' Nancy later married in Ceylon.

MORE ENEMY ACTION

Now that there was little anti-submarine work for the maritime squadrons, they were given the job of backing up the gradual re-occupation by SEAC of Burma and the other South East Asian countries under, yes you have guessed it, W/Cdr John Stacey in charge of 'Special Ops', mostly landing our agents behind the enemy lines. This is not really part of the remit of this book but three examples can be given of what the eastern squadrons moved on to, before the end of the Japanese war.

292 SQUADRON

Meantime this Air Sea Rescue squadron was doing wonders across the Bay of Bengal and down the Burma coast, to Singapore. It was equipped with little Sea Otters, which were very like Walruses with a propeller at the front; (see the plate in the Appendix with "British Aircraft") also Vickers Warwicks (related to Wellingtons) and Liberator Sixes. Later it was split into a number of flights.

There are many thrilling stories of rescues, some in the teeth of Japanese fighters, too lengthy for this final chapter. A glimpse must suffice of what it was like to crash into a hostile sea, 1,000 miles away from some of the rescue bases. Flying Officer Dave Bockus RCAF, from 99 Sq, was flying his Spitfire VIII on 11 January 1945. He and another pilot were

Fort McLeod

UPPER: The Liberty Ship SS *Fort McLeod's* 230 Sq rescue. Ship drawn by Len Sales, who was rescued through P/230, Black Peter. *(Courtesy of W/Cdr. D. Bednall)*

LOWER LEFT: F/Lt Alan Pedley DFC. *(Courtesy of A. Pedley DFC)*

LOWER RIGHT: 'Gert' (Q/230) disembarking Chindits at Dibrugarh after the Gert and Daisy rescue. *(Courtesy of J. Foxon)*

doing a recce on the Burma coast when Dave's engine failed and to avoid being sliced up by the Japs in the jungle he headed for the sea. As he went into a spin, Dave only just managed to get out in time with parachute and one-man dinghy. He writes:

'Many a pilot has drowned because he released the compressed air into the dinghy too quickly, as a twist could form and blow a hole in the dinghy. It is

347

not so easy to think about these things when dangling in the water and thinking about sharks. Those dinghies are difficult to get into. Once in, I started paddling out to sea.

'As I sat there drifting I watched a formation of B24s bombing the Myebon area. Had an uneasy moment when two unidentified aircraft were flying along the beach so kept paddling out to sea. Another sinking feeling when I realised that the covering Spits were looking too far North. You realise what a tiny speck you are on a large ocean.

'That evening a Sea Otter of 292 Squadron, with S/L Bob Day the Squadron CO aboard, picked me up.'

This was often a dangerous business for 292 Sq, with Jap fighters about, as when W/O John Horan RNZAF, rear gunner in F/Lt J.P. Almack's Sea Otter, was shot up in a brave fight, on 1 January 1945, a story with a sequel told in Saga magazine.[5] Also 212 Squadron Catalinas were picking up American crews of the B29 Superfortresses, a famous rescue being one by F/Lt C.R. Bradford RCAF of Winnipeg.

GERT AND DAISY

This pair of well-loved Cockney charladies (played by Elsie and Doris Waters) from the stage and radio had their names given to a couple of Sunderlands from 230 Squadron at Koggala. Their feats in rescuing 537 sick and wounded Chindit fighters in Burma from Jap-held Lake Indawgyi across the mountains have been told by more than one writer including the 230 Squadron CO W/Cdr Dundas Bednall.[6]

Bednall deputed S/Ldr J.L. Middleton of Folkestone to lead the detachment of two Sunderlands, 'Q' for Queenie under a New Zealander, F/Lt Jack Rand and 'O' for Orange under F/O K.V. 'Ted' Garside with F/O Noel Verney RAAF as Chief Navigator.

With Garside was F/Lt A.J. 'Jack' Norton of Ingersoll, Ontario, the only Canadian in 230 Squadron, who gave me a personal view of the operation. Although the journey was not long (a three and a half hour round trip) starting from the fast-flowing Brahmaputra River at Dibrugahr, the Chin Hills which the aircraft had to cross, through the Ledo Pass, were at this period always covered in thick cloud. The Japanese held the lower part of the lake but did not interfere till the end when a Jap fighter – too late – strafed the lake.

'The problem was that the Sunderland engines were not supercharged and the only height you could fly at was 11,000 to 12,000 feet and the pass we were going through was 8,500 to 9,000 feet. Doesn't leave much room for error. The maps we were provided with were not especially accurate- one day I was surprised to see the height of land above us that wasn't supposed to be there. When there were thunderclouds we got thrown about quite a bit.

'The approach to Lake Indawgyi was a relatively easy one and the lake was good for landings. The Army arranged for getting the men from shore to boat (in unwieldy American DUKW amphibious vehicles). We carried about 50 at a time. I was astonished at their condition, riddled with dysentery.'

When most of the Chindits were out, 'O' for Orange who was Daisy, had her float broken off by a 'DUCK' that had been swung against her by the tide on the Brahmaputra and she sank.(It was not a monsoon storm, as stated in one version.) Gert ('Q' for Queenie) carried out a few more runs so that all 537 Chindits were out, and then took the other crew back to Koggala. It was a magnificent feat and DFCs were given to Middleton, Garside, Rand and Verney while Jack Norton collected an MID. The episode boosted 230 Squadron morale. After the liberation in South-East Asia the real Gert and Daisy, with Leslie Henson, did come out to cheer up the POWs and during their long Sunderland flight insisted on cooking all the meals for a delighted crew.

One sad event occurred after W/Cdr Bednall had left Koggala. He had painted his own Sunderland III, P/230 (JM 673) with black camouflage, experimentally. She had taken part in the rescue of survivors from SS *Fort McLeod*. Again I have a pages-long description of the survivors' rescue, by one of the seamen, Len Sales. He remembers their fear of being massacred by the submarine crew if they were Japs, and of being nudged by sharks which were longer than the lifeboat. They were ever grateful to the Sunderland which found them. S/Ldr K.V. Ingham RAAF was her new Captain with crew named as in the Chapter Notes[7] Peter Swaine, of the Wirral, tells me that his mother, then Hilda Haines, a Wren Telephonist was engaged to Reg Williams. Another Wren, called Paula, was engaged to Crawford, and Walliker, then married, was to be Best Man. Mrs Walliker visited Sri Lanka in 1992 for the anniversary celebrations of Birchall's flight. 'P'-Peter was the only aircraft painted black.

However, on 28 November 1944, Black Peter set out on an anti-submarine patrol from Koggala into the Bay of Bengal where there was 'cyclonic weather'. We heard from someone watching the radar at base that they followed the blip of Ingham's plane going towards this cyclone on the screen. The two marks met and after that there was no more blip. I believe this was the only 230 crew lost at Koggala.

Over the next few days an enormous search was mounted, involving three of 230's own aircraft; four Cats from 205 Sq; two Cats from 413 and one Cat from China Bay (321?). Nothing was seen.

PEDLEY AT WORK

Another series of exploits was carried out by Fl/Lt Alan Pedley DFC of 230 Squadron. What brought him a decoration was, again, not a single attack, but a number of sorties, best summarised by a Leeds newspaper (where Alan later became Lord Mayor).

'LEEDS PILOT'S DARING – F/Lt A.S. Pedley captained Sunderland flying boats which have again flown across the Indo-Burma frontier and over the Chin Hills to take heavy equipment to the British Armies in Burma.

It was a 1,210-mile flight and most of it was over jungle where there was nowhere to land if things went wrong. F/Lt Pedley was returning from the Chindwin River when two engines failed as he was over the Chin Hills at a height of 14,000 feet but he got back to Calcutta.'

S/Ldr Deller, F/Lt Potter and F/Lt Levy- Haarscher and their crews made similar hazardous trips.

Another episode is best told in Pedley's own words:

'I was briefed to do a photo-reconnaissance of Singora in the South China Sea, round about the Malay- Thailand border, so I was flying behind Jap Lines. I went down the coast of Malaya, got down below the height of the palm-trees and did the last 150 miles at virtually sea level, getting over Singora undetected.

'We flew round at about 400 feet taking photographs. On the third circuit we opened up from the turrets on anything that looked Japanese but by then the Japs had found where they had hidden their guns and started firing back. I got a few holes in the back of the plane and a lump out of the tail plane. Having dropped our depth charges we set off back through Malaya and finally got back to Rangoon. We were debriefed, turned in our photographs and about four days later, in the SEAC Times, we saw that Bomber Command from India had done a night raid on Singora. They had blitzed the town from about 5,000 feet.

'That was the end of the story till I was coming home on the *Mauretania* in November 1945. When chatting on the deck with various other aircrew, one skipper said he'd been in Bomber Command and his last trip had been a beauty. He said; "We did a night raid on Singora. We didn't only have target maps, we had a complete photo-montage of the entire town! You could see the names on the shops and the faces in the streets," he

said," Some silly beggar with a Sunderland had been in at about 300 feet!"
"Oh yes? " I said.'

SUGAR DOGS

The maritime war in the Bay of Bengal changed in character during 1945.

The Japanese troops strung out in Burma, and Siam (Thailand) had to be kept supplied somehow. F/Lt George McKendrick, DFC, a 209 pilot, explains:

'Japanese convoys supplying their armies in Burma began to be harried increasingly. The ever resourceful Japanese conceived the idea of small shallow-draught vessels creeping up the islet-studded coast, too close in to be threatened by normal naval activity. They built large numbers of these motorised barges. One would carry enough rice etc to feed 100 soldiers for a month. We called them Sugar Dogs (S meaning targets and D small merchant ships in SEAC nomenclature).'

The Allies then modified Sunderlands to act like Beaufighters at long range, for attacking these barges, which were often disguised as tree-covered islets that would stop moving when aircraft were detected. They had anti-aircraft guns which could fire if their disguise was penetrated. Other sampans were like local fishing vessels but the pilots were told anything motorised was bound to be enemy. Fishing sampans were told to go straight out to sea.

On one such sortie George and his crew were going up the coast. He explains:

'When I resumed my seat my attention was caught by a couple of small wooded islets which seemed to have wind or current marks on the sea leading up to them. Through the binoculars I could see nothing but bushes. My suspicions were almost assuaged but not entirely, so I asked the waist gunner on the intercom to fire a short burst into each. The effect was instantaneous; the "islands" both started into motion and began to circle at speed.'

W/O John Smith, McKendrick's Second Pilot, who was in the cabin, after describing the attack, says :

'One vessel disintegrated after a huge explosion; the other vessel was damaged and beached. Both sugar dog crews returned fire and, showing great courage, continued firing right to the end. Our starboard aileron control was lost, and F/Sgt Tom Galliford, the Flight Engineer, discovered inside the wing that the control cables had been severed.'

George knew that they had to go back through the turbulence of the Inter-Tropical Front, and was afraid they might be flipped over. He says:

'Our Flight Engineer was a small man with great courage. He volunteered to crawl into the wing and attempt a repair job if he could reach the broken ends. To do so he had to creep into the confined space behind the fire wall of the starboard inner engine where it was like an oven and then make the repair at full stretch.'

With John Smith holding on to him, after an hour in great danger, Tom succeeded and they got home safely. As well as George McKendrick's DFC, F/Sgt Galliford and F/Sgt Norman Thorpe, the front gunner were awarded DFMs.

'Sampan-bashing', however, was not popular in 209 Squadron and seemed an unfair contest against these brave little boats. Sunderland Q/209 (PP 159), a Mark GR V, was captained by F/Lt Eric Yeomans with 2nd Pilot, F/O Norman Wilson who was formerly of Coventry, but now lives in Danbury, Essex.

Norman described to me the series of coastal attacks they made, on several days between 1 and 11 August 1945. Such were two Sugar Dogs in the South China Sea; five on another day; a tug towing two barges probably carrying torpedoes from Japan. Much flak. Many sunk with bombs or machine-gun fire. Yeomans was awarded a DFC but wouldn't wear it and had to be ordered to, in the end.

THE WAR ENDS

Gp/Capt Alex Jardine, by now with Laurens van der Post in one of the worst POW camps in Java, comments.

'A lot of people say what a horrible thing the atom bomb was. Most of us were in such a poor physical condition that if the war had continued for another three months we would all have been dead from starvation. I have to say that if it hadn't been for the bomb, many, many more millions of people would have been killed, because the Japanese would never have given in under normal circumstances.'

I am told there was a British POW in Nagasaki on the day of the Atom

Bomb, but he escaped injury as he was down in a mine on forced labour. There may have been others. The Naval Base of Penang was one of the first places to be liberated, W/O Ernie Hopkinson, a WOP/AG/ASV Operator of 240 Squadron being on Sunderland PP 131. This was flown by the Squadron CO, Wing Commander Ruston, and it brought the British envoys to accept the surrender of the Japanese on Penang Island. Ernie had the privilege of flashing D on his Aldis lamp to the *King George V* battleship (he thinks it was) as the signal to enter harbour with her large contingent of Royal Marines, who would take over the Island. He also was the one to pull down the Japanese flag and received a sword, later 'nicked' from him by the refueller crew. He says:

> 'I remember all the Japs lined up and their rifles were stacked. Then they were marched on to the jetty and loaded into four barges towed by a tug to take them to the mainland.'

Penang must have rejoiced.

PLOWSHARES AT LAST

Apart from the men and women leaving the Indian Ocean, people wondered what might happen to the weapons of war, in particular the flying boats in which some had spent the last two or three years. Was there any peaceful purpose they could be used for? Sadly, for many, no. In East Africa some of 259 and 209 Cat Squadrons, men and machines, came into the Cat Ferry Flight, which did a useful transport and communications job.

Sunderland squadrons such as 230 and 209, performed valuable functions in the Far East up to the Korean War, but Cats were often under American Lend-Lease agreements and had either to be returned to the US – too costly – or destroyed wherever they were.

CATS METAMORPHOSE

Meantime, after the war, BOAC air services and East African Airways were expanding all over East Africa. Staff were becoming available with a skilled, ex-Army African work-force, but equipment for the many Radio Stations was in short supply, as were spare engines for aircraft. The late Stan 'Dolly' Gray was in charge of Signals both for EAA and BOAC, and in the latter's magazine Touchdown recalled what happened. At Kisumu, Kenya, on Lake Victoria about 1947 there were six new Catalinas of 209 or 259 Squadron still sitting on the banks of the lake, unattached. The Air

Ministry in London sent an request that they were to be towed out into the middle of the lake and sunk.

Dolly Gray and Cliff Gowdy, the engineer, were both horrified that such new equipment should be wasted. They set to work removing the engines and all the radio equipment before towing the empty aircraft out into Kavirondo Gulf and opening the sea cocks in the haunt of crocodiles. Gray adds: 'It was a sad ending for such magnificent aircraft.'

However, one peacetime use soon emerged. BOAC wanted to set up an alighting area for its Empire boats near Nairobi, on Lake Naivasha, home of hippos and flamingoes. 'Some of the ex-Catalina equipment was used to build a small radio station there,' Gray informs us.

Flight Lieutenant Don Bleach, of 209 Sq, now Wing Commander, was with the Cat Ferry Flight after the war and had much more trouble at Mombasa towing *his* redundant Catalinas out to sea for scuttling. Another peacetime use for Cats occurred in 1946 when an East African Airways Corporation passenger biplane, a Rapide, flown by Capt T. C. Stack, crash-landed in remote and inaccessible bush in north-east Kenya. The pilot had five passengers including Mrs Pauline Edmonds and her two-month old baby Tricia, now Mrs John Carr of Aberfoyle. A 30,000-square-mile search by aircraft included 13 from the RAF. A Martin Baltimore bomber crew found them after 48 hours and dropped water, a rifle and torch, baby food etc. The five passengers were unhurt and the baby was held aloft to show she was OK. The Baltimore, captained by F/Lt Ginger Lamb, could not stay, so Don Bleach's Catalina did a quick dash from Tanga area and with more food drops, stayed as long as possible before they were relieved by a second Cat flown by F/O Geoff Kirkland. The baby was no worse for the ordeal. A 1945 sketch by the author at Entebbe of a de Havilland Rapide may be seen in the plate "British Aircraft" in the Appendix.

Dai Thomas, of 259 Squadron, Dar and Mombasa, penned his own requiem for a rusting flying boat, 'S' for Sugar.

Where are you now, old silver bird
Gone to a great hangar in the sky,
Your Pratt and Whitneys silent, no longer heard
Shadows from the past both you and I.
Yet when a tropic moon was on the rise,
Or the hot sun burnt the morning mist away,
We travelled far across the burnished skies,
On routes together, day by day.
Towns and villages saw us come and go,
Your engines hauled us across the sea and plains,

We saw miles of turquoise sea pass by below,
And often battled the Monsoon's endless rains.
Weeping oil, faded paint, leaking astrodome
Not for us the crisply suited VIP,
But non-comms, and sometimes, someone going home.
Our lot was a mixture in a wide diversity,
Who felt the bite of Diego Suarez dust,
Who watched red dawns break over Indian Sea,
Who hangs beneath those velvet nights,
Who sees the thousand things we saw,
As now you rot in rust.

SUNDERLAND MERCY FLIGHTS

From being the terror of the Burma coast, when the end of war came, Sunderlands proved to be ideal for the role of rescuers to the Far East POWs. Thousands of the sick, battered and emaciated prisoners had died in the months leading up to Japan's capitulation. Thousands more would die within sight of freedom unless they could be given food and then rapidly evacuated from the remote jungle camps or concentrations along the coast. One of the things that infuriated the prisoners was that when their guards surrendered, they brought out Red Cross medical supplies and parcels which had been stored up over the years and could have saved many lives.

W/O John Smith of 209 Sq says their aircraft were modified to take stretcher cases.

> 'They were the first into Singapore to bring back to Ceylon our prisoners of war from Changi Gaol. Lady Edwina Mountbatten had made arrangements for the men to be cared for by the Ceylon tea-planters up- country so that they could recuperate before going off to the UK.'

The Squadron then moved to Hong Kong and the first batch of internees from Stanley prison camp left in one of the Squadron's aircraft, adds John Smith. Actually 240 Squadron had beaten them to it, as two of their Catalinas had transported the military contingent there, to accept the surrender of the Japanese.

Lord Louis Mountbatten's wife, Lady Edwina, was the moving spirit in organising care for the prisoners, all the way from the dreaded camps to convalescence in the hills of India and Ceylon. As Head of the International Red Cross she tirelessly toured the hospitals where the sick POWs were being gathered. Steve Cairns, now National Welfare Officer for Far East POWs in this country, but then a Royal Artillery Bombadier, says the troops were very fond of her. The 52nd Indian-British General Hospital, which had the intake from all Thailand, was her favourite, and Steve remembers her sitting on the bed next to his, and writing a letter home for a young POW who was in a bad way. Lord Louis in his energetic tours was always missing her by days and would say to the lads: 'I've still not caught up with that bloody wife of mine!' The main means of travel then was by Dakota aircraft, hospital trains, and ships, including RN and American destroyers.

Vice-Admiral Lord Louis Mountbatten, Supreme Allied Commander in S.E. Asia, inspecting 413 Squadron and talking to S/Ldr G.H.U. Bayly DFC. (Courtesy of 'Terk' Bayly)

F/O Les Bennett RAF, now in Victoria, Australia, was Navigator on F/O Les George's 209 Sq Sunderland. His memory is that

> 'during our return from Singapore to Koggala, we were much touched by the gratitude of the British ex-prisoners for the slightest action that it was our privilege to carry out for them. The vileness and savagery of their imprisonment had not quelled their superb courage, and they were self-effacing about their sufferings.'

Les George is described by his Navigator, Les Bennett, as:

> 'the finest type of English gentleman, beloved by every one of his crew . . . impressively cool in emergencies.'

One included an unplanned flight under Sydney Harbour Bridge on 14 January 1946 while carrying troops home. Les also gave a telling-off to a Queen Alexandra nursing sister who was late getting on to his Sunderland, which was bound for Hong Kong. Despite this, Sister Elizabeth Paddon married him in Hong Kong Cathedral. They went on honeymoon to Macao in a Sea Otter, escorted off by six Sunderlands (see the wedding photographs in Chapter 7).

DUTCH WOMEN IN JAVA

1980s UK television series *Tenko*, about women interned by the Japanese in the Far East, has been one of the few reminders of the fate of internees in South East Asia, apart from one or two books. Before telling another Sunderland story, with a happy ending, we need to look at the unhappy beginning for one Dutch girl, Cornelia van Gennep, known as Cory, now Mrs Bradford in Berkshire.

When the Japanese forces made their grab for Dutch East Indies oil which was so vital to their war effort, they took Java and other Indonesian islands and found themselves with thousands of Dutch women and children on their hands. They set up internment camps for most of them. Some families were allowed to stay on in their country homes as did the van Genneps, mother, son and 18-year-old Cory. Father had been taken away and once he reached Singapore they heard no more.

They and many other Dutch families lived near a large women's camp next door to a POW camp, mainly for defeated Dutch soldiers, badly treated like other POWs. Mrs van Gennep helped run three safe houses for escapees, using the space under their garage roof to hide two or three men.

Cory, at 18, looked 14, and with her bicycle and friends on cycles, she would carry messages for the 'underground', throwing vital scraps of screwed-up paper over the prison walls, and risking capital punishment from the Japanese if she were caught. The girls used to cycle alongside the weary lines of soldiers, and give drinks of water when they could, while the Jap guards chased them off.

To annoy and tire the guards at the Kamp Baros gate groups of girls then would bow to the sentry all day long, as the illustration shows. By Japanese custom the man was obliged to bow back. Then the van Genneps were betrayed by the Javanese to the Japs and Cory and her mother finished up inside the camp. There they met an older lady known just as "Auntie" who used to draw pictures of what went on inside or outside the camp. Cory can't recall her name but she was given many of

357

these pictures which she used to hide in her bedding roll – again at risk of death, if they were found.

The Dutch women discovered that they were next door to the Japanese Cavalry stables, where the prisoners had to muck out the horses,

UPPER: Sketch by 'Auntie', before Dutch women were interned, where the girls offered help to the POWs in Java, 1942.

LOWER: Dutch internees in a Java camp pestering the Jap Guard by forcing him to bow back all day. *(both courtesy of Mrs Cory Bradford)*

so they would shout through the jute sacking and play gramophone music, rumbas etc, all faithfully recorded in colour by Auntie. A kind Japanese guard might turn a blind eye, but others jumped on the walls to threaten them with guns. The Japs were annoyed because Dutch women would never give up resisting.

Trading with the local population through the fence was forbidden. Corry remembers the punishment when girls were caught for Dedekking (bartering across the wire). The Jap guards would clip all their hair then cram them into small wire cages and put them out in the blazing sun all day. For lesser crimes they had to wear placards around their necks on which their crimes were written and they were denied food.

The guards were brutal or they might beat you up, but at least here, they wouldn't rape you. When one woman did complain about a rapist, he was shot at once. The guards had their own women or else internees who wanted to collaborate to get better food for their children. However, for many women things were as bad as the POW camps and some died.

When liberation came Cory became a Red Cross nurse and in Singapore supervised groups of women and children who were being transported home to Holland, This is how she came to be on F/Lt Sid Lane's Sunderland R-230 (PP 149) when it was returning to Seletar in January 1946. Among the crew, listed at the end of the chapter[8] was F/Lt Peter (P.R.C.) Bradford, the Navigator. By now Cory was no longer skinny but had put on weight and her photo in Singapore looks very attractive. She, on the other hand, found Peter a bit like Tyrone Power (see the wedding photographs in Chpater 7). She recalled:

'Peter coming down from the Upper Deck and going for the biscuit tin. He kept staring at me and munching biscuits. I was invited by the Captain to the Flight Deck -Peter was sitting by the table with all his maps on it, navigating. I thought he had a lovely window, with a view, so I pushed his maps out of the way and said " May I? "'

This was how the romance began but when the crew returned to Singapore Peter had no idea where she was staying. One day, after her long-lost father had been discovered, in a bad way in Changi Gaol, she says,

'I was in the cinema when I suddenly saw on the screen WILL MISS VAN GENNEP PLEASE COME TO THE FOYER. I thought some relapse must have happened to my father. Outside I felt a tap on my shoulder and it was Johnny, the Air Gunner.'

Peter had been sending the rest of the crew everywhere to look for her – he subsequently proposed and they were married in England in June 1946. Her father said it was like the story of Cinderella.

GOING HOME

All over Asia and Africa servicemen and women were saying or thinking 'Roll on that boat' and putting up with boring Education Classes to fit them for civvy life and for 'the Vote' in the post-war elections back in Britain. To airmen 'stuck out in the Far East', demobilisation after a three-and-a-half year tour was too slow, and, as the then CO of 230 Squadron at Singapore says, there was much unrest at bases as far back as Palestine. The final 'straw' for the airmen at Seletar came when the Japanese prisoners, working at the RAF base there, were moved out of their tents as the rains came; they were put into hangars and barracks while the airmen occupying them were shifted into the tents. After a widespread downing of tools, in January 1946, it was agreed to reduce the tour to three years – but 230 Squadron's work of repatriating from the Netherlands East Indies continued throughout the troubles.

One airman in 209 Squadron, Mombasa, LAC Cyril Johnson of Merthyr Vale, tried putting his thoughts into words, at which he was a bit of a Welsh wizard. Once again, a long masterpiece was produced, out of which one can only cull a few phrases. After some sad reflections on leaving, and the ones who never returned, Cyril turns to the Empire we had been fighting to defend. Should it continue? He writes:

'Engaged, as we were, in fighting dictatorship, it became blatantly ironic to impose our will upon another. And so, as we flew home that December day, there were seeds in our minds expecting a fruitful germination.

This opportunity arrived at the 1945 General Election when our desires were recorded as Servicemen, almost *en bloc*. Desires requiring no return to the *status quo* of 1939 where it conflicted with the ideology of a world-wide brotherhood. Terms such as "Bwana, Effendi and Sahib" could be bundled away in some dusty museum of anachronisms.' [Winston Churchill, it may be recalled, was voted out of office in that election].

'Goodbye to the Indian Ocean, that vast tract of powerful water, broken only by its intriguing variety of islands – Seychelles, Mauritius, Pamanzi and Madagascar – islands which magically afforded treasured and traumatic memories of "detachments" spent among them. As the powerful engines of our Sunderland pulled us away from this land, so the pages of a new book were being prepared to replace the old one we were just leaving.'

One twenty-year-old navigator would not be leaving Africa. Tom Clucas of 621 Wellington Squadron had been with the crew of 'E' after the episode of U/852 in Chapter 9. Moving to North Africa he had been killed in a crash there and his old crew, Oliver Gomersal and Wally Stevenson with others, hoped there would be room to include this poem he had written. In shortened form, then, as a tribute to those who didn't make it home, here are:

THE THOUGHTS OF YOUTH

Oh, that I could the power be given
To write a prayer of thanks to heaven
To sing to God a psalm of praise,
For reaching me in such wondrous ways
The beauty of this our life,
Still so glorious in a world of strife.

Why I write, I know not why,
Except perhaps when I should die,
These words to a talented youth be given,
And he in apology to heaven,
Will take his pen, and tear asunder
My effort of praise in its pitiful wonder.

Thank you God, for the sky so blue,
For the wispy clouds and the great ones too;
For the planets and stars and heavens of space,
For the sun and all its gleaming grace,
For the silvery moon riding at night,
Across a silent world of white.

And by Your word the sea was born,
And the gracefully bending golden corn,
The orchids with their stately splendour,
Contrasting with daisies simple grandeur;
These all cry out in fervent prayer;
'Thank God, you fools,' but do we hear?

Alas: we humans have little time,
We have our dance and a spot of wine;
And in our world of such a skirmish
We forget our God and in our wormish
And humanly ungrateful way,
We only live just day by day.

When soon our judgement day has come,
We will regret all that was done,
And with head bowed, knee humbly bent,
We will want only to repent.
Teach us God, before that dawn,
To live a life of thanks, and be reborn.

This is all I ask in life,
So cool and cutting as the tempered knife,
That I some day a man may be,
Like the one who walked o'er Galilee;
And help in just some little way,
To sing God's praises day by day.

Some of the 25 maritime RAF squadrons stayed on to serve in the Far East or India and Africa. Others were disbanded or like 621 were relocated and the RAF returned to its peacetime role.

TO SUM UP

As an RAF history writer I seem to have worked the Air Marshals quite hard, from the preface onward. It is only fair, then, to give one of them the last word. AVM Ted Hawkins writes that he had, by 6 December 1944, moved on to be Wing Commander Operations at HQ 222 Group, Bangalore.

'By this time, operational activity had greatly increased, and included support for RN Task Forces, Anti-submarine sweeps, and mining by RAF Liberators. Cooperation with the Royal Navy was very good and by then we had the benefit of ULTRA.

'Now to answer your question "Who made the major contribution to the winning of the Battle for the Indian Ocean?" In my view neither the Royal Navy nor the Royal Air Force can claim predominance. It was the combined effort of air, surface and submarine forces acting in close co-ordination that eventually achieved success.

'When our flying boat squadrons went out in 1942 they were the only long-range "eyes" and undoubtedly limited the freedom of U-Boats to operate. Outside Intelligence was minimal. Admittedly the "kill" rate was very low when measured against the effort expended, but there is ample evidence to show that our patrols were effective. It was the flexibility of Allied maritime aircraft and the flying boat in particular (with the Royal Navy), that enabled the "thin blue line" to be held during the difficult earlier period.

'However, with the build-up of RN Task Forces and Hunter Killer groups and the introduction of RAF Long-range Liberators, more combined offensive action was possible and victory was in sight by the end of 1944. So eventual success must be shared.'

NOTES

[1] *Savior of Ceylon*, A/Cdre L.J. Birchall OBE DFC CD (personal memoir)

[2] *The Cocos Islands*, W/Cdr Derek Martin OBE, article in *Flight* magazine 17.2.1949

[3] The writings of Gp/Capt Alex Jardine AFC RCAF and F/O Scales RNZAF – both 205 Sq

[4] *The Forgotten Fleet*, John Winton (Michael Joseph), London 1969.

[5] *A Hero finally Laid to Rest*, article and letter in *Saga* magazine – November/December 1995

[6] *Sun on my Wings*, Dundas Bednall (Paternoster Press), Pembroke Dock 1988

[7] Crew of P/230 F/Lt A.B. Gilbert, 2nd Pilot; W/O Walliker, Navigator; F/Sgt E.R.J. (Reg) Williams, Flight Engineer; F/Sgt N.D. Crawford; F/Sgt A.J. Bonner; F/Sgt R.F. Juffs; F/O S.L. Cary; Sgt D.W. Underwood.

[8] Crew of R/230 (PP 149): F/O Sid Lane Capt.; F/O 'Russ' Crisp, 2nd Pilot; F/Lt Peter Bradford, Navigator; F/Sgt 'Rocky' Rockett, WOP/AG; F/Sgt Frank Hart, WOP/AG; W/O 'Jock' Aitken, F/Engineer; W/O 'Taff' Jones, F/Engineer; F/Sgt 'Tommy' Taylor A/G; F/Sgt 'Johnny' Crank, WOP/AG.

British, allied and neutral merchant shipping lost from enemy action
1939 to 1945

Adapted from Roskill S.W. "The War at Sea. Vols I-III

INDIAN OCEAN
Monthly Tonnage with Ship Numbers sunk in brackets.

	1939	1940	1941	1942	1943	1944	1945
Jan	-	-	10,298 (2)	46,062 (13)	-	56,213 (8)	-
Feb	-	-	26,291 (5)	38,151 (18)	15,787 (3)	64,169 (10)	7,176 (1)
Mar	-	-	-	68,539 (65)[1]	62,303 (10)	75,498 (12)	-
Apr	-	-	14,094 (2)	153,930 (31)	43,007 (6)	-	-
May	-	-	3,663 (1)	22,049 (4)	28,058 (6)	-	-
June	-	15,445 (2)	7,625 (2)	90,322 (18)	67,929 (12)	19,319 (3)	-
July	-	15,275 (2)	-	47,012 (9)	97,214 (17)	30,176 (5)	-
Aug	-	31,001 (5)	-	5,237 (1)	46,401 (7)	57,732 (9)	-
Sep	-	39,409 (6)	10,347 (3)	30,052 (6)	39,471 (6)	5,670 (1)	-
Oct	-	14,621 (2)	-	63,552 (11)	25,833 (6)	-	-
Nov	706 (1)	57,665 (7)	-	131,071 (23)	29,148 (4)	14,025 (2)	-
Dec	-	-	837 (5)	28,508 (6)	31,173 (5)	-	-
date not known							1,806 (2)
Yearly totals	706 (1)	173,416 (24)	73,155 (20)	724,485 (205)	486,324 (82)	320,802 (50)	8,982 (3)
TOTAL FOR 1939 TO 1945 SUNK. 385 SHIPS 1,787,870 TONS.							

N O T E S

[1] Careful readers may wonder why such a small tonnage (68,539) is given for 65 ships sunk in March 1942. These were a host of small vessels sunk by the Japanese around S. E. Asia during their invasion.

Anti-submarine Squadrons in the Indian Ocean
1939 to 1945

F = Flying boat   L = Landplane

SQUAD-RON	MAIN BASES (see Map of Indian Ocean)	FIRST TIME OUT OR REFORMED	YEARS IN INDIAN OCEAN SUB PATROLS	REPRESENTATIVE AIRCRAFT USED	NOTES
8	KHORMAKSAR L	May 1942	1942 to 1945	Blenheim *Va* Wellington XIII	General Reconnaissance. Assisted capture of Italian sub *Galileo* 1940. Shared the destruction of U/852 off the Horn of Africa, 2.5.1944
22	RATMLANA L VAVUYINA	May 1942	1942 to 1945	Beaufort I Beaufighter X	Mainly Anti-shipping but some convoy escort and ASR. (Air-Sea-Rescue)
36	SELETAR L TANJORE	Oct 1942	1942 to 1943	Wellington Ic, VIII X, XI,XII,XIII,XIV	Squadron wiped out 1942 in S.E. Asia. Re-formed 1942 for maritime work with Wellingtons. Moved on to North Africa June 1943.
160	RATMALANA L SIGIRIYA KANKESANTURAI	Feb 1943	1943 to 1945	Liberator III,IIIa V and VI	A/S (Anti-sub) Patrols. 1943 fights with Jap Zeros. W/C Cohen's crew lost. 2 sub attacks. Feb 1945 Mine-laying ops (operations).

No.	Bases		Date	Period	Aircraft	Remarks
191	KORANGI REDHILLS KOGGALA	F	May 1943	1943 to 1945	Catalina Ib and Ivb	A/S Patrols, no enemy contacts. In April 1945 Cat landed mid-ocean to pick up Liberator crew.
200	ST THOMAS MOUNT JESSORE	L	Mar 1944	1944 to 1945	Liberator V and VI	Came from W.Africa, where Trigg won posthumous VC sinking U/468, 11.8.43. A/S Patrols with one sub attack, by F/O Smith Dec 1944.
203	KHORMAKSAR SANTA CRUZ MADURA	L	Nov 1943	1940 to 1944	Blenheim IV Wellington XIII Liberator VI	Helped capture of *Galileo* sub by RN 1940. A/S Patrols 1944 one sub attack 12.7.44 by F/O McKay unsuccessful
205	SELETAR KOGGALA	F	Sep 1939 Jul 1942	1939 to 1945	Singapore III Catalina I,Ib,IVb Sunderland GR V	Squadron decimated by Japs 1942 in defence of Singapore. Re-formed for A/S Patrols Koggala, S/L Melville attacks sub 3.3.1944. Sabang 'raid'
209	KIPEVU KOGGALA	F	Jun 1942	1942 to 1945	Catalina I and Iia Sunderland GR V	A/S Patrols till 1945. Took part in sinking of supply ship by RN 12.2.1944 and in anti-shipping work off Burma.
212	KORANGI REDHILLS	F	Oct 1942	1942 to 1945	Catalina Ib and Ivb	A/S Patrols from Korangi and two submarine contacts in 1944 but no result. One by F/L Gallagher. In July 1945 re-numbered as 240 Sq.
217	MINNERIYA VAVUYINA		Jul 1942	1942 to 1945	Beaufort I, II Hudson IIIA, VI	Anti-shipping and anti-submarine patrols but no submarine contacts.
230	CHINA BAY DAR-ES-SALAAM KOGGALA AKYAB	F	Jan 1943	1939 to 1945	Sunderland Mk III and MK GR V	Short stay Ceylon en route Middle East. Dar-es-Salaam A/S patrols 1943-1944. Koggala 1944 evacuated 500 casualties Lake Indawgyi A/Sub and then anti-shipping 1945.
240	REDHILLS	F	Jun 1942	1942 to 1945	Catalinas I,II & IV Sunderland GR V	1942, Defence of Ceylon then A/S patrols till 1944. Jan 1944 F/L Groves attacked sub, possibly sank it.

Sqn	Bases	L/F	Formed	Period	Aircraft	Notes
244	SHAIBAH MASIRAH	L	Nov 1940	1940 to 1945	Vincents, Blenheims Mk.I,IV and V. Welldington XIII	Mainly land bombing role till 1942 then A/S patrols until end of war. On 25.10.1942 Sgt Chapman DFM sank U/533. (K/L Hennig)
259	KIPEVU CONGELLA DAR-ES-SALAAM	F	Feb 1943	1943 to 1945	Catalina Ib Sunderland GR V	A/S patrols. F/L Barnett DFC (C259 and F/Lt Robin DFC of 265 Sq sank U/197, (K/L Bartels) Sgt Caligari given DFM.. Took part in sinking of supply ship and hunt for U/198 1944.
262	CONGELLA	F	Nov 1942	1942 to 1945	Catalina Ib and IVb	A/S patrols. 1943 F/L Grant attacked sub. F/L E.S.S. Nash 1944 sank UIT 22, assisted by F/L F. Roddick RCAF DFC and F/L A.H. Surridge. Sq transferred to SAAF as 35 Squadron 1944/5.
265	DIEGO SUAREZ	F	Mar 1943	1943 to 1945	Catalina Ib	A/S patrols. 20.08.1943 F/O F. Robin DFC RCAF sank U-197, after 259 Sq damaged it. Took part in sinking of the supply ship and U/198.
292	JESSORE AGARTALA	F	Feb 1944	1944 to 1945	Walrus II Warwick I Sea Otter II Liberator VI	ASR duties in the Bay of Bengal with rescue of American Liberator and other bomber crews.
321 (Dutch)	N.E.I. (Netherlands East Indies) CHINA BAY	F	Aug 1942 under RAF	1941 to 1945 as Royal Netherlands Naval Air Service (RNNAS)	Catalina II and III (Amphibian Cansos) Liberator VI	Re-formed 1942 from crews and aircraft escaped from N.E.I. A/S patrols in detachments from Langebaan to the Cocos Islands. 2 sub attacks (Lt Vonk 24.05.1943 and Lt Haman 22.01.1944).
353	DUMDUM TANJORE PALAM	L	June 1942	1942 to 1945	Hudson III and VI Dakota and Anson	Shipping reconnaissance and A/S patrols. P/O Smith 18.08.1942 attacked Japanese flying boat. Began Burma invasion support but transferred to transport.

354	CUTTACK MINNERIYA	L	July 1943	1943 to 1944	Liberators III,V and VI	Mainly anti-shipping role but occasionally Anti/submarine patrols.
413 Canada	KOGGALA	F	Apl 1942 RCAF	1942 to 1945	Catalina I and IV	Squadron began with the famous flight of S/L L.J. Birchall OBE DFC spotting the Japanese Fleet heading for Ceylon, on 04.04.1942. F/L Rae Thomas DFC also shot down then. Continued with eventful ASRs and 2 sub attacks (F/O Gowans and P/O Grandin - 1943)
621	PORT REITZ MOGADISHU KHORMAKSAR	L	Sep 1943	1943 to 1945	Wellington XIII and XIV	Convoy operations off Eastern Africa, followed by similar A/S patrols based on Aden. On 01.05.1944 squadron attacked U/852 off Somaliland coast and with later help from 8 Squadron destroyed it. F/O Mitchell won DFC and Sgt. Stevenson the DFM
628	REDHILLS	F	Mar 1944	1944	Catalina Ib and IV	Formed from B Flight of 327 Sq for Met. Flights and Air-Sea Rescues, for six months operating.

357 Sq. did fly Catalinas from Redhills, but was used for dropping secret agents in Burma.

In the Indian Ocean much maritime anti-submarine work was performed by the South African Air Force, by the Fleet Air Arm, by the Indian Air Force's 'Coastal Defence Flights' and occasional forces co-operating with the Royal Navy's Eastern Fleet and other naval forces. Details may be found in the books recommended in the Bibliography.

Sources for this table are mainly "COASTAL, SUPPORT AND SPECIAL SQUADRONS of the RAF and their aircraft" by John Rawlings (Jane's) London 1982; also Operation Record Books of RAF Squadrons at the Public Record Office, Kew and personal communications to the author.

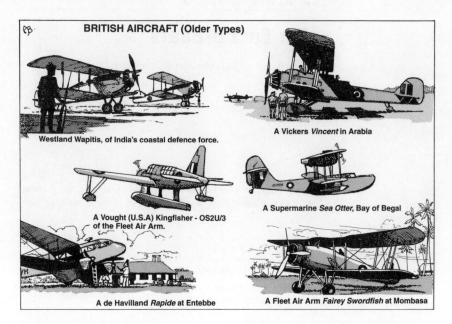

BRITISH AIRCRAFT (Older Types)

Westland Wapitis, of India's coastal defence force.

A Vickers *Vincent* in Arabia

A Vought (U.S.A) Kingfisher - OS2U/3 of the Fleet Air Arm.

A Supermarine *Sea Otter*, Bay of Begal

A de Havilland *Rapide* at Entebbe

A Fleet Air Arm *Fairey Swordfish* at Mombasa

UPPER LEFT *(courtesy D. W. Warne)*

MIDDLE LEFT *(courtesy Chris Ashworth)*

LOWER LEFT *(author's sketch in 1945)*

UPPER RIGHT: *(courtesy Chris Ashworth)*

MIDDLE RIGHT *(courtesy Bob Ferguson)*

LOWER RIGHT: *(courtesy Mrs Seymour)*

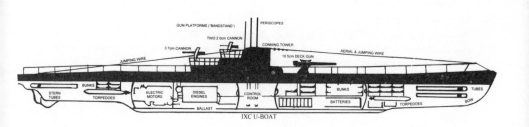

IXC U-BOAT

Far East U-Boats

This table, compiled with the help of Christopher Lowe, describes the 66 German submarines intended for Indian Ocean operations, with the number of ships sunk by them in all oceans.

(NS) = not sunk by enemy action.

Dates as given by Lowe (alternative dates in brackets).

'Type' has Roman numerals first (e.g. IXC is Type Nine-C).

RN and RAF as in glossary.

Sq = Squadron, implies RAF, unless stated.

DC = Depth charge.

IJN = Imperial Japanese Navy.

USN = United States Navy.

USAAF = United States Army Air Force.

EC = Escort Carrier).

a/c = aircraft

c = circa, approximately

Commandant's rank (K/K etc) as at end of glossary.

Some details are incomplete, but where sources are contradictory the most likely is chosen. Other facts, such as date of commissioning, may be found in the sources referred to. American Navy squadron letters indicate the type of squadron, V meaning Fixed-wing Aircraft.

VB = bombers.

VC = composite squadron (say mixed Wildcat fighters and Avenger TBF Torpedo-bombers)

VF = Fighters

VP = Patrol aircraft

VS = Search or reconnaissance

VT = Torpedo bombers.

US Army Air Force air-craft (USAAF) were all land-based, like the Liberators of the USN, especially those on Ascension Island. Most strike aircraft in the Middle Atlantic were based on Escort Carriers in the hunter-killer groups.

U-BOAT	TYPE	COMMANDANT	PERIOD including I.O.Ops	SHIPS SUNK totals for Captains	SEQUELS (Dates as given by Chrisopher Lowe, others in brackets)	SUR-VIVORS (killed)
68	IX C	K/K Herten O/L Lauzemis O/L Seehausen	1941 - 1942	33 27 Merten 6 Lauzemis	Sunk NW of Madeira 10.04.1944 by a/c of EC USS *Guadalcanal* (V.C.58)	None (56)
156	IX C	K/K Hartenstein	1942	19 (including the 'Laconia')	Sunk E of Barbados 08.03.1943 by USN a/c (VP 53)	None (52)
159	IX C	K/L **Helmut** Witte O/L Beckmann	1942-1943	23 23 H. Witte	Sunk S of Haiti 15.07.1943 by USN a/c (VP 32)	None (53)
160	IX C	K/L Lassen O/L von Pommer-Esch	1942-1943	26 26 Lassen	Sunk W of Azores 14.07.1943 by a/c from EC USS *Santee* (V.C.29)	None (57)
168	IX C	K/L Pich	1943-1944	3	Sunk off Batavia 06.10.1944 by RNNS (Dutch) submarine *Zwaardvis* (Commander H.A.W. Goossens)	22 (23)
172	IX C	K/L Emmermann (Hoffmann ?)	1942	27	Sunk NW of Cape Verde Is. by a/c from USS *Bogue* (VC 19) on 13.12.43 assisted by 4 escorts, USS *Du Pont, Clemson, George W. Ingram,* and *George E. Badger.*	c.?40 (13)
177	IX D2	K/L Schulze K/K Gysae K/K Bucholz	1942-1944	14 14 Gysae	Sunk off Ascension Is on 06.02.1944 by USN Liberators (VB 107) Sank *Alice F. Palmer* 1943 (see Ch.3)	10 (50)

No.	Type	Commander(s)	Dates	Ships sunk	Fate	Survivors
178 N.S. (not sunk)	IX D2	KzS Ibbeken K/K Dommes K/L Spahr	1942-1944	13 6 Ibbeken 6 Dommes 1 Spahr	Decommissioned Bordeaux 19.08.1944. Scuttled 20.08.1944	All
179	IX D2	K/K Sobe	1942	1	Sunk NW of Capetown 08.10.1942 by RN Destroyer HMS *Active*	None (61)
180	IX D1	F/K Musenberg O/L Lange O/L Riesen	1943	2 2 Musenberg	Sunk off Gironde Estuary 22.08.1944 by RAF-laid mine (had, on 26.04.1942 transferred Indian leader BOSE to Japanese sub I/29 (Commander Zyniti-Isu)	None (56)
181 N.S.	IX D2	K/K Lüth KzS Freiwald	1942 -	27 22 Lüth 5 Freiwald	Transferred to IJN 08.05.1945 (15.07.1945) and re-named I-501. Surrendered Singapore 16.08.1945 and scuttled off Singapore 12.02.1946. Lüth killed by accident 14.5.45	All
182	IXD2	K/L Clausen	1942-1943	5	Sunk 250 miles West of Madeira on 15 or 16.05 1943 by USN Destroyer *"Mackenzie"*	None
183	IX C40	K/K Schäfer K/K Schneewind	1943-1945	5 2 Schäfer 3 Schneewind	Sunk off Java 23.04.1945 by USN submarine *Besugo* (U.183 sank *Fort McLeod* and *British Loyalty* mentioned in text).	c.5 (54)
188 N.S	IX C40	K/L Lüdden	1942-1944	9 including 1943 HMS *Beverley*	Scuttled Bordeaux 20.08.1944. Crew later captured by the Maquis, but their lives were spared.	All
195 N.S.	IX D2	K/K Bucholz O/L Steinfeldt	1943-1945	3 2 Bucholz 1 Steinfeldt	Transferred to IJN 15.07.1945 and became I-506. Surrendered to Dutch at Soerabaya 10.08.1945. Scrapped 1947.	All

No.	Type	Commander	Years	Ships sunk	Fate	
196	IX D2	K/K Kentrat K/L Striegler	1943-1944	2	Sunk between Java and Sumatra (Sundar Strait) 12.11.1944 possibly by a mine.	None
197	IX D2	K/L Bartels	1943	3	Sunk S of Madagascar on 20.08.1943 by RAF 259 Sq (F/Lt L.O. Barnett DFC) and 265 Sq (F/O C.E. Robin DFC RCAF)	None (67)
198	IX D2	KzS (F/K) Hartmann O/L von Waldegg	1943-1944	11 7 Hartmann 4 von Waldegg	Sunk N of Seychelles 12.08.1944 by RN Frigate HMS *Findborn* with HMIS *Godavari* and HMS *Parrett*; FAA a/c from EC HMS *Shab* (851 Sq) and EC HMS *Begum* (FAA 832 Sq) plus RAF Catalina squadrons, 209, 259 and 265.	None (66)
199	IX D2	K/L Kraus	1942-1943	1 + 1 Allied a/c	Sunk E of Rio de Janeiro 31.07.1943 by one USN a/c of VP 74 and two Brazilian a/c.	12 (49)
200	IX D2	K/K Schonder	1943-1945	None	Sunk SW of Iceland en route Far East by US Catalina of VP 84 squadron on 24.06.1943	None (62)
219 N.S.	X B (Cargo type)	K/K Burghagen	1943-	None (supply boats had no tubes)	Transferred to IJN 08.05.1944 becoming I/505. Surrendered at Djakarta 16.08.1945	All
234 N.S.	X B	K/L Fehler	1945	None	Surrendered at Portsmouth USA 16.05.45 en route Tokyo (was carrying Uranium 234 and $ 5 million of mercury)	All
459	XIV (U-tanker)	K/K von Wilamowitz-Möllendorf	1942-1943	None (tankers also did not torpedo ships)	Sunk off Corunna by Wellington Q of RAF Sq 172 (F/O W.H.T. Jennings) on 24.07.1943. She was supplying U-boats en route to the Far East.	41 (19)
462	XIV	O/L Voew (Voes)	1942-1943	None	Sunk off Corunna 30.07.1943 by Halifaxes of 502 Sq.	64 (1)

No.	Type	Commander	Years	Ships sunk	Fate	Survivors (casualties)
487	XIV	O/L Metz	1943	None	Sunk midway between Florida and W. Africa on 13.07.1943 by a/c from EC USS *Core* (VC 13)	32 (31)
488	XIV	O/L Bartke	1944	None	Sunk NW of Cape Verde Is by 4 USN destroyers, USS *Huse, Barber, Frost, Snowden* on 26.04.1944.	None (64)
490	XIV	O/L Gerlach	1944	None	Sunk NW of Azores on 12.06.1944. Bombed by a/c from EC USS *Croatan* (VC 25). Sunk by gunfire from USN destroyers USS *Frost, Huse* and *Inch*	All
504	IX C	K/K Poske K/L Luis	1942-1943	16 16 Poske	Sunk off Corunna, 30.07.1943 by RN sloops, HMS *Kite, Wildgoose, Woodpecker,* and *Wren*.	None (53)
506	IX C	K/L Würdemann	1942	15	Sunk West of Vigo on 12.07.43 by US Army Air Force Anti-submarine Squadron no. 1	6 (48)
509	IX C	K/K Wolfe K/L **Werner** Witte	1943-1943	7 7 Witte	Sunk SE of Azores 15.07.1943 by a/c from EC USS *Santee* (VC 29)	None (54)
510 N.S.	IX C	F/K Neitzel K/L Eick	1942-1945	14 5 Neitzel 9 Eick	Taken over by the French at Bordeaux 12.05.1945 (or 24.04.1945) and became U-BOUAN till 1960	All
511 N.S.	IX C	K/L Steinhoff K/L Schneewind	1942-1945	5 2 Steinhoff 3 Schneewind	Given to IJN after 4 patrols, on 07.08.1943 becoming RO/500. Crew remained spare at Penang. Surrendered to USN at Maizuru Gulf August 1945.	All
514	IX C	K/L Auffermann	1942-1943	6	Sunk off Cap Finisterre 08.07.1943 by Liberator R of 224 Sq RAF, piloted by Coastal Command ace, S/Ldr T.M. Bulloch DSO DFC	None (54)
515	IX C	K/L Henke	1942-1944	24 12.11.42 damaged HMS *Marne*	Sunk N of Madeira on 09.04.1944 by a/c of EC USS *Guadalcanal* (VC 58) with escorts USS *Chatelain, Flaherty* and *Pillsbury*.	44 (16)

No.	Type	Commander(s)	Years	Ships Sunk	Fate	Losses
516	IX C	K/K Wiebe K/L Kuppisch K/L Tillesen O/L Petran	1942–1943	16 9 Wiebe 7 Tillesen	Refuelled two on Far East route then was diverted to the Caribbean and returned to Europe. Surrendered at Lough Foyle 14.08.1945.	All
532 N.S.	IX C40	F/K Junker	1943–1945	7	Surrendered Liverpool 10.05.1945. Sunk Opn. Deadlight. Successful blockade runner.	All
533	IX C40	K/L Hennig	1943	None	Sunk in Gulf of Oman 16.10.1943 by 244 Sq RAF Bisley. (Sergeant L. Chapman DFM)	1 (52)
537	IX C40	K/L Schrewe	1943–1944	None	Sunk E of Sourabaya on 09.11.1944 by USN submarine *Flounder*. Captain J.E. Stevens)	None (58)
549	IX C40	K/L Krankenhagen	1943–1944	Sank EC USS *Block Island*	Sunk SW of Madeira on 29.05.1944 by USS warships, USS *Abrens* and USS *Eugene E. Elmore*	None (57)
801	IX C40	K/L Brans	1944	None	Sunk W of Cape Verde Is. on 16.03.1944 (06.03.1944) by a/c of USS *Block Island* (VC 6) with USS *Cory* and USS *Bronstein*	c.40 (10)
843	IX C40	K/L Herwartz	1943–1944	1	Sunk in the Kattegat (Denmark) on 09.04.1945 after a long voyage home, by RAF Mosquito rocket fire (F/O A.J. Randall of 235 Sq with 143 and 245 Sqq) Sub was raised by Sweden in 1958.	10 (44)
847	IX D2	K/L Guggenberger K/L Metzler K/L Kuppisch	1943	None	Sunk in the Saragossa Sea (28.19N/37.58W) by USN a/c of EC USS *Card* (VC 1) on 27.08.1943	None (62)
848	IX D2	K/K Rollmann	1943	1	Sunk W of Congo Delta on 05.11.1943 by Liberators of the USAAF (1st Compron) and USN (VB 107)	None (62)

No.	Type	Commander	Year		Fate	Survivors
849	IX D2	K/L Schulze	1943	None	Sunk W of Congo Delta on 25.11.1943 by two USN Liberators (VB 107) based on Ascension Island.	None (63)
850	IX D2	F/K Ewerth	1943	None	Sunk W of Madeira on 20.12.1943 by USN a/c from EC USS *Bogue* (VC 19)	None (66)
851	IX D2	K/K Weingärtner	1944	None	Sunk south of Iceland towards Newfoundland through unknown cause. Last message 27.03.1944	None (70)
852	IX D2	K/L Eck	1944	2	Destroyed off Somaliland on 3-5.05.1944 by Wellington bombers of RAF 621 Sq (F/O Roy H. Michell DFC) and 8 Squadron. Eck and 2 others received death penalty for shooting of survivors of Greek ship *Peleus* 13.03.1944	c. 40 (6)
859	IX D2	K/L Jebsen	1944	3	Sunk off Penang 23.09.1944 by torpedoes of RN submarine HMS/M *Trenchant* (Commander A.R. Hezlett DSO DSC)	20
860	IX D2	F/K Büchel	1944	None	Sunk SSE of St. Helena Is. on 15.06.1944 by DCs of USN Avengers from USS *Solomons* (also given as 04.07.1944) (VC 9)	20 (44)
861 N.S.	IX D2	K/K Oesten	1944-1945	5	Surrendered at Trondheim 06.05.1945. Contraband cargo unloaded Pembroke Dock. Sunk at Lisahally by gunfire in Operation Deadlight.	All
862 N.S.	IX D2	K/K Timm	1944-	7 (2 off Australia)	Transferred to IJN at VE Day, re-named I-502. Surrendered at Singapore 16.08.1945 and scuttled there 13.02.1946. Shot down 1 USAAF Lightning and 1 RAF Catalina II-265. (see Chapter 11)	All
863	IX D2	K/L von der Esch	1944	None	Sunk SW of Pernambuco, Brazil, 29.09.1944 by USN Liberators, land-based, (VB 107)	None (69)
864	IX D2	K/K Wolfram	1945	None	Sunk W of Bergen 09.02.1945 (02.02.1945) by RN Submarine HMS/M *Venturer*. Norwegian sub *Utstra* mentioned in another source.	None (73)

No.	Type	Commander	Year		Fate	Casualties
867	IX C	KzS von Mühlendahl	1944	None	Sunk NW of Shetland Is 19.09.1944 en route Far East by RAF Liberator Q of 224 Sq (F/Lt H.J. Rayner)	10 (60)
871	IX D2	K/L Ganzer	1944	None	Sunk NW of Azores on 26.09.1944 by RAF Flying Fortress P of 220 Squadron (F/Lt A.F. Wallace)	None (69)
957	VII C41	O/L Saar / O/L Schaar	1943-1944	4 including HMS *Hardy*	Collided off Norway with supply ship on 19.10.1944 and decommissioned. (Crew went to U/1060 which was sunk on 27.10.1944.) After VE Day sunk at Loch Ryan 29.05.45.	26 (2 in U/1060)
1059	VII F (transport only)	O/L Brünninghaus / O/L Leupold	1944	None (No torpedo tubes)	Sunk N of Brazil on 19.03.1944 by Avengers of USS *Block Island* (VC 6). Was carrying a cargo of torpedoes	Some (47)
1060	VII F	O/L Brammer (Brunner)	1944	None	Sunk off Trondheim, with crew of U/957 on 27.10.1944. First damaged by FAA Firefly a/c of 1771 Sq. HMS *Implacable*. Then sunk by 2 Liberators of 311 (Czech) Sq and 2 Halifax a/c of 502 Sq	43 (12 and 2 from U/957)
1061 N.S.	VII F (transport only)	O/L Hinrichs / O/L Jäger	1944	None (no torpedo tubes)	Surrendered Bergen 05.05.1945 (30.05.1945) and sunk in Operation Deadlight at Loch Ryan.	All
1062	VII F	O/L Albrecht	1944	None	Sunk SW of Cape Verde Is on 30.09.1944 by USN Destroyer *Fessenden*. She was carrying 25 torpedoes	None (55)
1224	IX C	K/L Preuss (? Japanese Captain later)	1944	None	Sunk by USN Destroyer USS *Francis M. Robinson* on 13.05.1944 NW of Cape Verde Is. Had been transferred to IJN on 28.02.1944 and re-named Ro 501	None (All Japanese crew)

UIT 21 N.S.	Calvi	C/C Giudice T/V Rosetto O/L Steinfeld	1944	None	Scuttled in Bordeaux 25.08.1944. After transfer from Italian Navy she had so many defects she never operated. Formerly ITN *Finzi*. UIT means *Unterseeboot Italienisch*.	All
UIT 22	Luzzi	C/F Toson-Pittoni C/C Chialamberto T/V Tei O/L Wunderlich	1943-1944	None	Sunk S of Capetown on 11.03.1944 by 3 Catalinas of RAF 262 Squadron. (S/Ldr 'Gar' Nash DFC AFC, F/L Roddick DFC RCAF.) Not sunk by SAAF squadrons 226 or 279 as in some sources (See chapter 8) Formerly ITN *Bagnolini*	None (43)
UIT 23	Luzzi	C/F Bruno K/K Schäfer O/L Striegler	1944	None	Sunk in the Straits of Malacca 15.02.1944 by RN submarine HMS/M *TallyHo* (Lt/Cdr L.W.A. Bennington DSO DSC). This submarine was former ITN *Giuliani*.	15 (31)
UIT 24 N.S.	Marcello	C/C Todaro T/V Lenzi T/V Reveden K/L Pahls	1944	None	Surrendered to USN at Kobe, Japan on 02.09.1945 and scuttled. Had been transferred to IJN on 10.05.1945 and re-named I 503. Formerly ITN *Capellini*.	All
UIT 25	Marconi	C/F Longobardo C/C di Giacomo O/L Striegler K/L Schrein O/L Meier	1944	None	Surrendered to USN at Kobe on 10./05.1945 (02.09.1945). Had been transferred to IJN and re-named I-504 (10.05.1945). Former Italian name was *Luigi Torelli*.	All

A. CHRISTOPHER LOWE'S SOURCES

Die Deutschen Kriegschiffe 1815 – 1945, Volume 3 (8 volume set), Editors Gröner, Jung and Maass, Bernard and Graefe Verlag, Koblenz, 1983-93

The U-boat War in the Atlantic 1939 – 1945, Günther Hessler, Editor, HMSO publications, London, 1939

Embleme, Wappen. Malings. Deutscher U-boote 1939 – 1945, Georg Högel, Koehlers Verlag, Herford, 1987

Die Deutsche Kriegsmarine 1939 – 1945, Lohmann and Hildebrand, (Podzum-Pallas-Verlag), Bad Nauheim 1956 – 1964

Records relating to U-boat Warfare 1939 – 1945, Kathleen Quigley, Editor, (National Archives and Records Administration – NARES), Washington DC, 1956 – 1964

The U-boat, Eberhard Rössler, Arms and Armour Press, London, 1981

Axis Submarine Successes 1939 – 1945, Jürgen Rohwer, Patrick Stephens Ltd, Cambridge, 1983

Chronology of the War at Sea 1939 – 1945, Rohwer and Hümmelchen, Greenhill Books, London, 1992

Search, Find and Kill. Coastal Command's U-boat Successes, Norman L.R. Franks (Aston Publications) Bourne End, Bucks 1990

B. AUTHOR'S SOURCES

German Submarines in Eastern Waters 1943 – 1945. Extracted from C.B. 4523 (3) *The War in the Atlantic, Volume III* (translated from the German)

U-boat Files, Herr Horst Bredow, *Stiftung Traditionsarchiv Unterseeboote*, U-boat Museum, Cuxhaven

Far East U-boats, Article by Günther Schomaekers (untraced)

German Warships of World War II, J.C. TayLor, Ian Allan, London 1966

The Penang Submarines, Dennis Gunton, George Town City Council, Penang 1970

Personal Communications, *Korvettenkapitän* Jürgen Oesten (Commandant U/861) and other German submariners

Most sources have been used for cross-checking only.

Japanese Submarines based on Penang

(from "The Penang Submarines", Gunton)

No.	SUNK	DATE
I-8	Off Okinawa by U.S. destroyers	4.7.1944
I-10	Marianas by U.S. destroyers	31.4.1945
I-16	Solomons by U.S. destroyer-escort	19.5.1944
I-18	Solomons by U.S. destroyer and aircraft	11.2.1943
I-20	Solomons by U.S. destroyers	1.10.1943
I-26	West Pacific Unknown causes	Oct. 1944
I-27	Maldives by R.N. escorts	12.2.1944
I-29	S.Formosa by U.S. submarine	26.7.1944
I-30	Singapore by R.N. mine	13.10.1942
I-34	Penang by R.N. submarine	12.11.1943
I-37	Palau by U.S. destroyers	19.11.1944
I-52	W. of Cape Verde by U.S.N. aircraft	23.6.1944
I-162	Ran aground in S. Korea	26.6.1945
I-165	Central Pacific by U.S.N. aircraft	27.6.1945
I-166	Malacca Straits by R.N. submarine	17.7.1944
RO 110	E. Indian coast by R.N. escorts	11.2.1944
RO 111	Admiralty Islands by U.S. destroyer	11.6.1944
RO 113	Luzon by U.S. submarine	13.2.1945
RO 115	Philippines by U.S. destroyers	31.1.1945

Quoted by kind permission of the Municipal Council of Penang, where copies of the book are still obtainable.

THE PENANG BASE

After the invasion of South East Asia by the Japanese, Penang became, in February 1942, the base for the Imperial Japanese Navy's 11th Submarine Flotilla. Then in April 1943 it was chosen for the 8th Submarine Squadron headquarters. It also began to provide facilities for the 33rd U-boat Flotilla.

For U-boat men who had survived the long, hazardous journeys from Europe, with months of malodorous, claustrophobic life, Penang was a breath of beautiful fresh air. They looked forward to their tropical paradise, with its rich food and trips to Penang Hill, Frasers Hill and the Cameron Highlands. Many sports and recreations were also on hand, with the unwilling co-operation of the local populations.

Repair facilities were not adequate and skilled labour not easily available. Both Japanese and Germans were afraid of Penang islanders carrying out sabotage and therefore avoided giving them any chance. Major repairs were carried out in the dry dock at Singapore (re-named Shonan). U-boats and Japanese submarines continued to use the base till the last of them, U/843, left Swettenham Pier on 1st December 1944. The lack of anti-aircraft protection, the sinking of Penang submarines by RN submarines (and one Dutch sub) and the minelaying round the island by RAF Liberator bombers all hastened the end of Penang's enforced service as an Axis base.

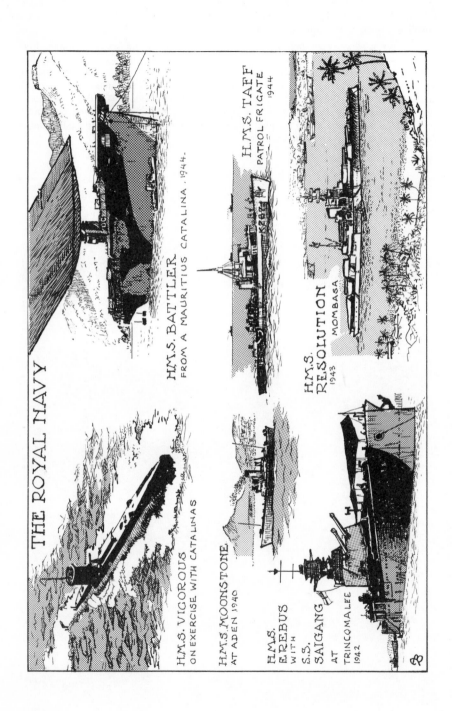

THE ROYAL NAVY

H.M.S. BATTLER
FROM A MAURITIUS CATALINA, 1944.

H.M.S. TAFF
PATROL FRIGATE
1944

H.M.S. VIGOROUS
ON EXERCISE WITH CATALINAS

H.M.S. MOONSTONE
AT ADEN 1940

H.M.S.
EREBUS
WITH
S.S.
SAIGANG
AT
TRINCOMALEE
1942

H.M.S.
RESOLUTION
1943
MOMBASA

Glossary

This does not include some slang words which are in common use and can be found in a modern English dictionary such as *The Oxford Handy Dictionary*.

A/A	Anti-aircraft
abeam	to the side of a ship, at 90° to the direction of travel
a/c	aircraft
AC	Aircraft Carrier
ack-ack	anti-aircraft
AFC	Air Force Cross
AG	Air Gunner
AHQ	Air Headquarters
Aldis Lamp	lamp to send Morse Code
Allies	Alliance of European, American and Commonweath nations to fight Facism
AMC	Armed Merchant Cruiser
AOC	Air Officer Commanding
AOC-in-C	Air Officer Commanding-in-Chief
APU	Auxiliary Power Unit (small petrol engine)
A/S	Anti-submarine
Asdic	hydrophone for detecting submarines
ASP	Anti-submarine patrol
ASR	Air-sea Rescue
Astro	Astro-navigation
ASV	Air-to-Surface-Vessel (radar contact)
Axis	the alliance of Germany, Italy and Japan in the fight against the 'Allies'
bale out	to leap from plane in flight, preferably with parachute
bandit	enemy aircraft (RAF slang)
BdU	*Befehlshaber der U-boote*, U-boat Command or Admiral Dönitz' own HQ
beaching	hauling a flying boat out of the water for repairs
beam	area to the side of a ship or aircraft
beat up	to fly low as if attacking, usually lightheartedly
BEM	British Empire Medal

bilge	the space at the bottom of a boat or flying boat – bilge-water had to be pumped out when present
blip	the mark on a radar screen showing a ship or solid object, e.g. whale or hill
blister	perspex cupola on a Cat housing the guns, or at a Sunderland's wingtips housing centimetric radar
BOAC	British Overseas Airways Corporation
Bofors	40 mm Swedish anti-aircraft gun equivalent to the 37 mm German A-A gun
bomb scow	large boat for carrying bombs or ammunition for an armourer to load up in aircraft
bulk heads	strong walls dividing a ship or aircraft into watertight compartments
Cat	Catalina flying boat
CD	Canadian Forces Decoration
C-in-C	Commander-in-Chief
Chiefy	Ground Staff Flight Sergeant (RAF slang, derived from RNAS days when a F/Sgt was a Chief Petty Officer)
circuits and bumps	practice landings and take-offs of aircraft
CO	Commanding Officer
Coxswain (Cox'n)	Marine craft airman in charge of a boat
CRNR	Ceylon Royal Naval Reserve
cu-nim	cumulo-nimbus cloud, anvil or tower-shaped (thundery)
DC	Depth-charge – cylindrical bomb from ship or aircraft to blow up underwater vessels
D/F	(Radio) Direction Finding used in radar
DFC	Distinguished Flying Cross
DFC and Bar	awarded twice
DFM	Distinguished Flying Medal
DI	Daily Inspection, different sections being signed for before an aircraft could take off
dinghy	the marine tender used for ferrying personnel to or from a moored aircraft
ditch	to make a forced landing at sea
dogsbody	drudge (slang)
DR	Dead Reckoning (navigation by calculations without help of radio or sun or star 'fixes')
drink	the sea (RAF slang)
DSC	Distinguished Service Cross
DSM	Distinguished Service Medal
DSO	Distinguished Service Order
elevator	mobile section of tail-plane for vertical control
ETA	estimated time of arrival
F	Flight, e.g. F/Sergeant

FB	Flying Boat. Its hull alights on the water, unlike a sea-plane where only the floats touch the water
Flight	Unit of three or six aircraft
Flight deck	cabin or cockpit in a flying boat
FAA	Fleet Air Arm
feathering	altering a propeller's pitch
fin	tail-fin, the fixed upright section of the tail unit
fire tender	marine equivalent of fire engine
Fitter	the trade of one who fixes engines or electricals
Fitter 2(E)	Fitter (Second class) Electrical
fix	the position of a sub, etc.., obtained by the intersection of two or three direction lines usually on radar or the position of sun and stars in the sky determined by the navigator.
flak	anti-aircraft fire
flare	rocket fired to illuminate night scene, e.g. sub or as a distress signal from a boat for rescue.
flare-path	Three or more flares or lamps set at night for the landing or take-off path of a flying boat or any aircraft
floats	boat-shaped attachments usually to a flying boat's wings to stabilise it on water
FMA	Flight Mechanic (Airframe)
FME	Flight Mechanic (Engines)
fo'cs'le	Forecastle – crew quarters under fore part of deck
forward	(pronounced 'forrard') the front part of a ship or its direction forward
gate	frame limiting the throttles (emergency gate could allow even further power) in an aircraft
gen	information (RAF slang); also 'pukka'gen (correct) or 'duff' gen (incorrect)
George	Automatic Pilot (RAF slang)
GM	George Medal awarded for heroism not on enemy operations
GR	General Reconnaissance as in Sunderland Mark GR V(five)
HMAS	His Majesty's Australian Ship
HMS	His Majesty's Ship
HMIS	His Majesty's Indian Ship
HMS/M	HM Submarine
HMT	His Majesty's Troopship
HQ	Headquarters
hull	the fuselage of a flying boat, that rests on water
ibid	*ibidem*, from the same book, passage, etc.
i/c	in charge (of)
IFF	Identification Friend or Foe radio transmitter in RAF aircraft to be switched on when approaching an unknown vessel
IJN	Imperial Japanese Navy
It.N	Italian Navy
kite	aircraft (RAF slang)

knot	one nautical mile per hour (6,080 feet)
Kriegsmarine	German Navy
Lascar	Asiatic seaman (usually Indian)
Lib	Consolidated Liberator, 4-engined long-range bomber
lineshooting	shooting a line means bragging or telling a tall story
Mae West	life jacket (orange, inflatable) named after the busty American actress
Mamba	Venomous African snake, up to 10 feet long, fast as a galloping horse
Med	Mediterranean Sea
Met	Meteorological (e.g. Met Report or Met Observer)
Met Flight	Meteorological Flight used to make weather observations at various altitudes up to say 30,000 feet
Met Observer	RAF Weather clerk
MCS	Marine Craft Service
Marine tender	often known as 'dinghy', motor launch to convey personnel or goods to and from aircraft
MBE	Member of the Order of the British Empire
MID	Mention in Despatches, a decoration just lesser than medals like DFC
Milch Cow	Also *Milch Kuh*, a U-boat acting as refueller for other U-boats or a tanker acting as a mother ship to a group of U-boats
MOD	Ministry of Defence
NAAFI	Navy, Army, Air Force Institute (canteens for servicemen)
nautical mile	6,080 feet (statute mile 5,280 feet), see 'knot'
NCO	Non-commisioned officer, Warrant Officer, Flight Sergeant or Sergeant
Neutrals	those countries and ships which did not join either Axis or Allied side but still lost many ships
Nip	Nipponese or Japanese (Forces slang)
OC	Officer Commanding
OKM	*Oberkommando der Marine,* High Command, German Navy
OBE	Order of the British Empire
Oerlikon	20 mm anti-aircraft cannon (Swiss) rapid-firing like the German equivalent
Op	Operator
ops	operations
PD	Pembroke Dock, the flying boat base in South West Wales
pistol	Device on Depth Charge to enable detonation to take place at a certain depth, e.g. 25 feet by water pressure
poop	area at stern of the ship
port	left-hand side of ship or aircraft, looking forward
POW	Prisoner of War
prop	propeller
quarter	the area round a ship (or direction) between astern and abeam (e.g. on the port quarter)
q.v.	*quod vide,* which see (i.e. look up the reference mentioned)
RAAF	Royal Australian Air Force

radar	a system for ascertaining the presence of objects such as ships by means of reflected short-wave radio waves
RAN	Royal Australian Navy
Radial Engine	where the cylinders are set like spokes in a wheel
Rating	non-commissioned sailor
recce	slang for Reconnaissance
Reconnaissanc	the search for enemy units or the aerial survey of any designated areas
RCAF	Royal Canadian Air Force
refueller	large boat for pumping fuel into aircraft's tanks
RFC	Royal Flying Corps – WW1 forerunner of today's RAF
Rigger	a crew member who has the care of the airframe of an aircraft
RIN	Royal Indian Navy
RN	Royal Navy
RNAS	Royal Naval Air Service, which preceded the Fleet Air Arm and partly the RAF
RNNAS	Royal Netherlands Naval Air Service
RNNS	Royal Netherlands Naval Service
RNVR	Royal Naval Volunteer Reserve
R/T	Radio Telephony – Communication by voice and not Morse Code (W/T)
rudder	the mobile section attached behind the tail fin for turning laterally, as in a ship's rudder
SAAF	South African Air Force
SANF	South African Naval Forces
SEAC	South East Asia Command, the war machine which under Lord Louis Mountbatten won back South East Asia from the Japanese
Second Dicky	Co-pilot (RAF but originally RNAS slang)
shoot up	to dive over object below the aircraft, to shoot it or as if shooting *vide* beat up
sinker	weight, often concrete, for sinking line attached to buoy or to a flare-path light
SKL	*Seekriegsleitung* (operational staff of OKW)
Skipper	Captain of aircraft or ship
Slip	Slipway or concrete ramp sloping down to the sea for hauling flying boats out of the water and parking them
SNO	Senior Naval Officer, e.g. of a convoy
Snorkel	*schnorchel,* German device for supplying air to a submerged U-boat
sortie	operational flight
Spam	Spiced ham, US tinned processed ham
sprung rivet	Loosened rivet, sometimes due to a heavy landing on the hull
Sq	Squadron, RAF unit of 12 to 18 aircraft formed for various purposes
Sqq	Squadrons
SS	Steamship
stall	when an aircraft loses speed so much that there is no lift for the wings and it falls out of control

stall landing	when a flying boat is put into a controlled stall to land on water in a tight situation, *vide* 3-point landing on land
starboard	right-hand side of a ship or aircraft looking forward
step	the place under the hull of a flying boat where a right-angled or curved break in continuity enables it to break the suction effect of the water on take-off
stick	(or cluster) of depth charges when dropped
straddle	the spread of bombs or DCs on a target at a fine angle equally on both sides of it.
sweep	aircraft's various methods of sweeping an area in the detection of vessels or objects on the sea
swell	heaving of the sea with waves even 30 feet high that do not break but can smash an aircraft landing
tail-trolley	the 2-wheeled trolley to support the tail of a flying boat when on the slipway
taxi	to move along the ground or water with an aircraft before take-off or after landing
throttles	levers to increase engine power, four in a 'gate' (q.v.)
T/O	Take-off (aircraft leaving the ground or water)
trim-tabs	or trimmimg tabs. Small flaps in the rudder and elsewhere for finer control of the aircraft
trots	Line of mooring buoys – a moored flying boat may be 'on the trots'
U-cruiser	Long-range U-boat, e.g. IXD2
U-tanker	U-boat used to supply fuel to other U-boats
UIT	Unterseeboot Italienisch (German ex-Italian U-boat)
USAAF	United States Army Air Force
USN	United States Navy
Very light	Flare projected from a pistol in emergencies or to light up the scene in darkness
vide	see, or look up something
VIP	Very Important Person. In the Indian Ocean such passengers would be Governors, top Army, Navy or Air Force personnel
WAAF	Women's Auxiliary Air Force, now WRAF (Women's Royal Air Force) a member being commonly known as a WAAF
Wardroom	Central room on the lower deck of a Sunderland, originally designated for officers, as in the Royal Navy
Winter-garden	U-boat gun platform(s) known in RN submarines as a Bandstand; in USN-subs as the Cigarette deck
WOM	Wireless Operator Mechanic
WOP	or W/Op – Wireless Operator
WOP/AG	Wireless Operator/Air Gunner
W/T	Wireless Telegraphy, using Morse Code as opposed to R/T Radio Telephony (speech)
WRNS	Women's Royal Naval Service, a member being a Wren
WW1	World War One, 1914 to 1919
WW2	World War Two, 1939 to 1945

SOME GERMAN NAVAL RANKS OR POSTS

with British Equivalents
which differ from American

Matrose	Ordinary Seaman
Matrosen-Ober-gefreiter	Leading Seaman
Ober-maat	Chief Petty Officer
Oberbootsmann	Chief Boatswain
Oberfahnrich(O/F) zur See	Sub-Lieutenant
Leutnant (L)	Lieutenant (Junior)
Leitender Ingenieur(LI)	Chief Engineer (not a rank)
Oberleutnant(O/L) zur See	Lieutenant (Senior)
Doktor (med)	Medical Officer
Kapitänleutnant (K/L)	Lieutenant Commander
Korvettenkapitän (K/K)	Commander
Fregattenkapitän (F/K)	Captain (Junior Grade)
Kapitän zur See (KzS)	Captain
Kommodore	Commodore
Vizeadmiral	Vice-Admiral
Admiral	Admiral
Generaladmiral	Admiral of the Fleet
Grossadmiral	(Grand Admiral – not in RN use)

THREE ITALIAN RANKS

Teniente di Vascello (TV)	Lieutenant
Capitano di Corvetta (CC)	Lieutenant
Capitano di Fregatta (CF)	Commander

BRITISH RANKS IN WORLD WAR TWO

In the three services the ranks are not exactly equivalent and these are only main ranks – about which some books differ. The term 'rating' can be applied to various ranks of non-commissioned seamen. The Army ranks are a rough comparison.

ROYAL AIR FORCE	Abbrev.	ROYAL NAVY	ARMY
Aircraftman 2nd Class	AC2	Ordinary Seaman O.S.	Private
Aircraftman 1st Class	AC1	Able Seaman A.B.	
Leading Aircraftman	LAC	Leading Seaman L.S.	Lance- corporal
Corporal	Cpl		Corporal

Sergeant	Sgt	Petty Officer P.O.	Sergeant
Flight Sergeant	F/Sgt	Chief Petty Officer C.P.O.	Staff Sergeant
Warrant Officer	WO	Fleet Chief F.C.P.O. Petty Officer	Warrant Officer 2 Warrant Officer 1
Pilot Officer	P/O	Midshipman	Second Lieutenant
Flying Officer	F/O	Sub-Lieutenant Sub-Lt	Lieutenant
Flight Lieutenant	F/Lt	Lieutenant Lt	Captain
Squadron Leader	S/Ldr	Lieutenant-Commander Lt-Cdr	Major
Wing Commander	W/Cdr	Commander Cdr	Lieutenant- Colonel
Group Captain	G/Cpt	Captain Capt	Colonel
Air Commodore	A/Cdre	Commodore Cdre	Brigadier
Air Vice Marshal	AVM	Rear-Admiral R.Adml	Major- General
Air Marshal	AM	Vice-Admiral V.Adml	Lieutenant- General
Air Chief Marshal	ACM	Admiral	General
Marshal of the Royal Air Force	MRAF	Admiral of the Fleet	Field Marshal

SOME WAAF RANKS REFERRED TO

WAAF		RAF EQUIVALENT	
Aircraftwoman 2	ACW2	Aircraftman 2	AC2
Aircraftwoman 1	ACW1	Aircraftman 1	AC1
Leading Aircraftwoman	LACW	Leading Aircraftman	LAC
Corporal	Cpl	Corporal	Cpl
Assistant Section Officer	AS/O	Pilot Officer	P/O
Section Officer	S/O	Flying Officer	F/O
Flight Officer	F/O	Flight Lieutenant	F/Lt

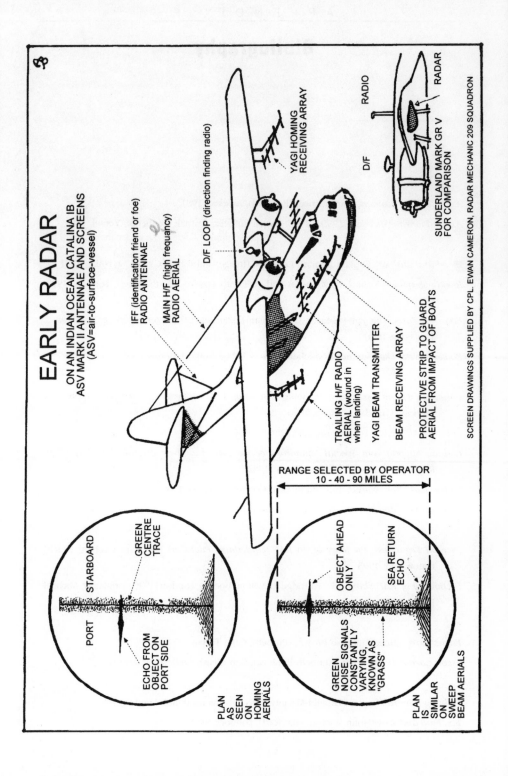

EARLY RADAR

ON AN INDIAN OCEAN CATALINA IB ASV MARK II ANTENNAE AND SCREENS
(ASV=air-to-surface-vessel)

IFF (identification friend or foe) RADIO ANTENNAE

MAIN H/F (high frequency) RADIO AERIAL

D/F LOOP (direction finding radio)

YAGI HOMING RECEIVING ARRAY

TRAILING H/F RADIO AERIAL (wound in when landing)

YAGI BEAM TRANSMITTER

BEAM RECEIVING ARRAY

PROTECTIVE STRIP TO GUARD AERIAL FROM IMPACT OF BOATS

RADIO

D/F

RADAR

SUNDERLAND MARK GR V FOR COMPARISON

SCREEN DRAWINGS SUPPLIED BY CPL. EWAN CAMERON, RADAR MECHANIC 209 SQUADRON

RANGE SELECTED BY OPERATOR
10 - 40 - 90 MILES

STARBOARD

GREEN CENTRE TRACE

PORT

ECHO FROM OBJECT ON PORT SIDE

PLAN AS SEEN ON HOMING AERIALS

OBJECT AHEAD ONLY

SEA RETURN ECHO

GREEN NOISE SIGNALS CONSTANTLY VARYING, KNOWN AS "GRASS"

PLAN IS SIMILAR ON SWEEP BEAM AERIALS

Bibliography

Axis Blockade Runners, Martin Brice, (Batsford), London, 1981

Axis Submarine Successes 1939 – 1945, Jürgen Rohwer, (Patrick Stephens), Yeovil, 1983

Blood and Bushido, Captain Bernard Edwards, (Images Publishing), Worcestershire, 1991

Bloody Shambles, Volumes 1,2 Shores and Cull with Ozawa, (Grub Street), London, 1992, 1993

Boarding Party, The, James Leasor, (Heinemann), London, 1978 (later called *The Sea Wolves,* as was the film)

Boote im Netz, Die, Günther Böddeker, (Gustav Lübbe Verlag), Bergisch Gladbach, 1983

Canadian Flying Operations in South-East Asia, T.W. Melnyk, (Ministry of Supply and Services, Canada), Ottawa, 1976

Cats, G.H.U. Bayly, (Graphic Images), Ontario, 1993

Coastal, Support and Special Squadrons of the RAF and their Aircraft, Rev John D.R. Rawlings, (Janes), Coulsdon, Surrey, 1982

Coffin Boats, The, Warner and Senoo, (Leo Cooper), London, 1988

Concise Encyclopaedia of British Military Aircraft, The, Chaz Bowyer, (Bison Books), 1982

Dice on Regardless, the Story of an RAF Sunderland Pilot Ken Robinson (Richard Leach) Ditton Kent 1993

Dictionary of RAF Slang Eric Partridge (Pavilion Books) London 1990 (originally Michael Joseph 1945)

Eagles Strike, James Ambrose Brown, (Purnell), Cape Town, 1974

Escort Carrier 1941 – 1945, Kenneth Poolman, (Ian Allan), Addlestone, Surrey, 1972

Fighting Admiral, Captain Donald Macintyre RN, (Evans Brothers), London, 1961

Fix, Find and Strike, John Winton, (Batsford), London, 1980

Flying Cats, Andrew Hendrie, (Airlife), Shrewsbury, 1988

Forgotten Air Force, The, Air/Cdre H.A. Probert, (Brassey's (UK) Ltd), London, 1995

Forgotten Fleet, The, John Winton, (Michael Joseph), London, 1969

Forgotten Ones, The, Shirley Fenton Huie, (Angus and Robertson), Australia, 1992

Forgotten Skies, The Story of the Air Forces in India and Burma, W/Cdr W.W. Russell, Hutchinson, London, 1945

Gathering of the Clans – A history of the Clan Line, N.L. Middlemiss, (Shield Publications), Newcastle-on-Tyne, 1988

German Warships of World War II, J.C. Taylor, (Ian Allan), London, 1966

Haie im Paradies, Der Deutsche U-Boot-Krieg in Asiens gewässern 1943 –1945, Jochen Brennecke, (Wilhelm Heyne Verlag), Munich 1983

Hunters and the Hunted, The, Jochen Brennecke, (Elmfield Press), Morley, Yorkshire, 1973, German original known as *Jäger – Gejagte*

Hunting of Force Z, The, Richard Hough, (Collins), London, 1963

It's Really Quite Safe, Lt/Cdr G.A. Rotherham, (Hangar Books), Ontario, 1985

Knights of Bushido, The, Lord Russell of Liverpool, (Cassell), 1958

Lesser known Squadrons (22,36,191,200,203,209,212,244,259, 262,265,621), F/Lt Andrew Thomas RAF, articles – *Aviation News*, Berkhamsted

Most Dangerous Moment, The, Michael Tomlinson, (Kimber), Wellingborough, 1976

Night of the New Moon, The, Sir Laurens van der Post, (Hogarth Press), London, 1970

Penang Submarines, The, Dennis Gunton, (George Town City Council), Penang, 1970

PBY Catalina in Action, Captain W.E. Scarborough USN, (Squadron/Signal Publications Inc), Carrollton, Texas, 1983

PBY: The Catalina Flying Boat Roscoe Creed, (The Naval Institute Press), Annapolis, Maryland, 1985

Royal Air Force, The Aircraft in Service since 1918, Michael Turner (paintings), Chaz Bowyer (text), (Temple Press), 1981

Royal Indian Navy, The, Cdr D.J. Hastings RINVR, (McFarlane and Co Inc), Jefferson USA, 1988

Scourge of the Swastika, The, Lord Russell of Liverpool, (Cassell), London, 1954

Sea War 1939– 1945, Janus Piekalkiewicz, (Blandford Press), Poole, 1987 – translated from the German *Seekrieg 1939– 1945*

Sea Wolves, The (see *The Boarding Party*)

Search, Find and Kill, Norman Fanks, (Grub Street), London, 1995 (new edition)

Second World War, The Volumes I-VI, W.S. Churchill, (Cassell), London, 1948 – 1954

Short Sunderland, Chaz Bowyer, (Aston), Tonbridge, 1984

S.O.E. in the Far East, Charles Cruickshank, (Oxford University Press), Oxford, 1983

South Africa at War – Vol 7, South African Forces WW2, Henry J. Martin, (Purnell), Cape Town, 1979

Squadrons of the Fleet Air Arm, Ray Sturtivant, (Air Britain), 1984

Sunderland at War, Chaz Bowyer, (Ian Allan), 1978

Sun on my Wings, W/Cdr D. Bednall, (Paterchurch Publications), Pembroke Dock, 1989

Sunk, The Story of the Japanese Fleet 1942– 1945, M. Hashimoto, (Cassell), London, 1955

Submarines Versus U-Boats, Geoffrey Jones, (Kimber), 1986

Submarines. An illustrated History. Richard Humble (Basinghall) 1981

Submarines with Wings: Past, present and future of Aircraft carrying Submaines Terry Treadwell (Maritime) 1985

Tankmotorschiff Charlotte Schliemann, Otto Mielke, (Moewig), Munich, 1955

Ultra at Sea, John Winton, (Leo Cooper), 1988

Ultra Goes to War, Ronald Lewin, (Hutchinson), London, 1978

Underwater War, The, Richard Compton-Hall, (Blandford Press), 1982

Unsolved Murders and Mysteries, John Canning, Editor, (Treasure Press), 1990 – for the *Fort Stikine* disaster, 1944

Verdammter Atlantik, Hans Herlin, (Econ Verlag GmbH), Düsseldorf, 1959

War at Sea, The, Vols I-III, Captain S.W. Roskill DSC RN (HMSO), 1954 –61

War at Sea, The, Gordon Smith, (Ian Allan), Shepperton, 1989

War in the Southern Oceans, Turner, Gordon-Cumming and Bezler, (Oxford University Press), Cape Town, 1961

Wings at Sea Gerard, A. Woods, (Conway), London, 1985

Yashimoto's Last Dive, Antony Trew, (Collins), Glasgow 1986 – a novel which gives an authentic Indian Ocean and naval angle

OFFICIAL, UNPUBLISHED OR OTHER SOURCES

Air Historical Branch, Ministry of Defence, London. AHB Narrative, *The RAF in Maritime War,* Volume VII, Part 3, August 1945, Indian Ocean Narrative

Birchall, Air Commodore L.J. OBE DFC CD, Unpublished writings

British Vessels Lost at Sea 1939-1945, (Her Majesty's Stationery Office), 1947 London

Far East U-boats, Günther Schomaekers, article untraced.

Fitzpatrick, Air Commodore D.B., CB OBE DFC – Notes for future autobiography

German Submarines in the Far East, A.M. Saville, US Naval Proceedings, August 1961

German Submarines in Eastern Waters 1943 – 1945, Extracted from C.B. 4523 (3), *The War in the Atlantic, Volume III* (translated from the German)

La Marina Italiana nella Seconda Guerra Mondiale Volume X *Le Operazione in Africa Orientale,* Chapter 5 Italian Navy Historical Office, Rome.

Monthly Anti-Submarine Report Naval Historical Branch, Ministry of Defence, London.

RAF Mediterranean Review, Number 7 and others.

RAF Squadron Records, ORBs or Operation Record Books, Public Record Office, Kew

205 Squadron Records, courtesy of Group Captain Alec Jardine AFC RCAF, British Columbia

413 Squadron Records, courtesy of Commanding Officer, 413 Transport and Rescue Squadron RCAF Greenwood, N.S. Canada

Stiftung Traditionsarchiv Unterseeboote (Horst Bredow), U-Boat Museum, Cuxhaven – sundry files

U-boat Summaries, Christopher Lowe, Nottingham

U-boat Logbooks – various private sources, in German only; also Documentation Service, Chief of the South African Defence Force, with translations

War Diary of Third (Fast Battleship) Squadron, (Japanese National Institute for Defence Studies), Tokyo

As with all other history authors, my research has depended on the labours of these previous researchers to whom I am very grateful.

THE NATIONAL INSTITUTE FOR DEFENSE STUDIES

2 - 2 - 1, Nakameguro, Meguro - ku, Tokyo 153
JAPAN

14 February 1992

Air Commodore L.J. Birchall,RCAF(Ret.)
128 Welborne Ave.,
Kingston, Ontario K7M 4E9
CANADA

Dear Commodore Birchall,

This replies to your letter of 4 February, in which you requested informations concerning IJN destroyer Isokaze, especiaaly if she had picked you up on 4 April, 1942 in the Indian Ocean.

It was her that did pick you up on that date. Some details in the documents in our Archive are as follows, and I enclose copies of their relevant portions;

a. "IJN Offensive Operations in the Dutch East Indies and Bay of Bengal", an Official War History,
b. "War Diary of the Third Squadron (Fast Battleships) in April, 1942",
c. "Isokaze, in the Record of IJN Ship Movements,
d. a picture of Isokaze in a publication.

I just do not have time to translate all of them for you, however, the marked part of the copy-a (p.643) will read by my poor English;

(On 4 April) at 1855(I:-9), as Hiei(FBB) detected an enemy amphibious plane northward, immediately commenced A/A fire against him with an alert purpose(to the entire force) as well. By this, all(four) of our aircraft-carriers launched the ready Zero fighters(3 each except 6 from Hiryu, total 18) and they made the enemy ditched on the water. In the meantime, (the Task Fleet) intercepted his radio transmmision in plain, "3 BBs and 1 CV are sighted, course 305 degrees ····". As he ditched in flame at 1922, Isokaze, one of the Early Warning Unit ships, closed to the spot, picked up the aircrews and had them POWed. While the enemy plane shadowed us for 27 minutes, reported our formation which was received by Radio Stations Colombo, Bombay and Aden who at once relayed(broadcast) it. At 1945 all of Zeroes were recovered by CVs. The enemy patrol plane had been destroyed, however, it was so apparent for the enemy to acknowledge our situation that the considerable enemy counterattacks were inevitable. But the decision was made for the air-raids against Colombo (next morning) as previously planned.

As you mentioned, Isokaze was one of the three DDs escorted CV Shina-no. She was finally sunken with that giant BB Yamato at south of Kyushu by the U.S.carrier-aircraft attacks on 7 April, 1945. I also enclose a (ℓ), copy of page 383, in our official war history,"IJN Operations in Okinawa Area".

I hope I have thus answered to you except those English translation of the documents enclosed, for which I beg your pardon.

Sincerely yours,

Taro Nagae

Taro Nagae
LtCol,JGSDF(Ret.)
Special Military Archivist
Military History Department

Ranks where known are given as final ones; otherwise they are those of that time. For contributors' names see Acknowledgements in Appendix. For lists of RAF Squadrons and Axis submarines see Appendix (German Knights Cross [KC] etc. stated where known).

A German list of the 67 crew of u-197 is on page 186.

401

Foxon P/O John 101, 133

Free Sgt K.G. 266

Fry F/Lt F.A. 328

Gallagher F/Lt J. 92, 148

Galliford F/Sgt Tom DFM 352

Gardner S/Ldr C.J.T. OBE 62

Garside F/O Ted DFC 348-49

Gattrell Sgt A 301-04

Gay F/O C.W. 328

Gee Sgt Alan 156

Gething W/O 270

Gething W/Cdr R.T. AFC 92

Gilbert F/Lt A.B. 363

Ginn LAC J. 78, 96, 149, 151, 294

Gleaves Sgt W. 130

Glynn F/Sgt C. 299-310

Gomersal F/Sgt O. 325-27

Goodey F/O 361

Goolden F/O 68

Graham F/Lt J. 62

Grainger F/Lt Ken 327, 341

Grant Sgt (205 Sq) 37

Grant F/Lt DFC 146

Green Charles, Intell. Officer 226

Green W/Cdr P. 250-56

Greenwood W/O Reg 275

Groves F/Lt Jack 111

Grundy Sgt (F. Eug. 160 sq) 318

Gurman F/Sgt F. 328

Gurney F/Sgt C.C. 49

Guy W/O G. 92

Hackett Capt J. (BOAC) 94, 109, 217

Hall P/O (160 Sq) 135

Hallas Sgt E. 167

Halstead LAC (265) 299-310

Hamill F/Sgt 'Charley' 200

Hamilton F/O 194

Hammond F/Sgt H.L. 177

Hanson F/O (later F/Lt) S.B. 224-40

Hardiker Sgt J. 266

Hawkins AVM D.E. CB CBE DFC 259-62, 362

Haywood F/O 26

Head AC1 Ginger 151

Henzell Sgt J. 49

Herman (205 Sq) 37

Hibberd F/O W. 273

Hill P/O (160 Sq) 115

Hill F/Sgt Bill 240

Hitchcock Sgt. S. 132

Holder F/Sgt. (262) 177

Hodoul Cpl P. 299-310

Hopkins F/Sgt G.A. 328

Hopkinson W/O E. 353

Housely Sgt D.L. 49

Hudson Sgt N. 118-22

Hugger F/O H.T. 224-40

Hughes LAC H. 77

Hughes Cpl 78

Hull Sgt C. 266

Hunt Sgt. 'Spike' 156

Inglis F/Lt J. 84-90, 166

Instrell F/Sgt Roy 291

Irvine F/Lt J.F. 136

Ives F/O S.W. 341

James F/O (621) 253

James W/O Don 209

Jillings W/Cdr Tony 30

Johnson LAC C. 77-78

Jones Sgt A.L. 266

Jones LAC "Pamanzi" 77

Jones W/O 'Taff' (230) 363

Jones AC1 Glyndwr 140

Jones F/Sgt (262) 240

Jones F/Sgt (262) 240

Jones AC2 151

Jones LAC J. 107

Juffs F/Sgt R.F. 363

Kendall (205 Sq) 24

Kenny F/O P.N. 49

Kerby AVM H.S CB DSC AFC 206

King Sgt A. 103

Kirkland F/O Geoff 354

Kirkup W/O W.R. 200

Knight Sgt Eric 132

Laister F/Lt H. 207

Lamb F/Lt Ginger 354

Lane F/O Sid 363

Lapsley Sgt W.C. 264

Lauper W/O E. 328

Lawson F/O Jim 278, 282, 299

Ladd LAC Tom 153

Lee Sgt Ben 147

Leece F/O Norman 273, 289, 325-27

Levy-Haarscher F/Lt 350

Linsley Cpl Steve 264

Lindley Sgt 153

Little F/Sgt Bill 177

Lock P/O Willie 146, 177

Lough F/Lt J.S. 299-310

Louw Gp/Capt J. DFC OBE 30, 219-20

Lowe F/Lt (205 Sq) 146

Lucy Sgt (621) 251, 266

Lumsden F/O 108, 164

Lynam Sgt D.R. 162

Lynn Sgt G. 179

Lywood W/Cdr Alan DFC 30

Maclean Sgt 'Snowy' 169

MacRae F/O L. 96

Mallon Sgt E. 167

Martin P/O Bill 273

Martin Sgt 'Dickie' 172

Martin W/Cdr D. OBE 335

Maxwell-Hudson F/Lt T. DFC 122

McCallum F/Lt (RAF) 156

McCreadie F/O Bob BEM 328

McDougal AC1 151

McIntosh F/Sgt L.R. 341

McKay F/O (203 Sq) 289

McKay Sgt Jock 147

McKay Sgt (212 Sq) 93

McKendrick F/Lt G.DFC. 152, 156

Mclean Sgt 200

McNamara Air Vice Marshal VC 258

McNichol F/O I.W. DFC 103

McPhail F/O C.D. 327

Macpherson F/O 270

MacRae F/O Lewis 96

McVicker P/O 45

Meecher Cpl 77

Meadows F/Sgt 157

Meiklejohn Sgt I.R.E. 137

Mellersh AVM F.J.W. 311

Melville-Jackson S/Ldr 194

Middleton S/Ldr J.L. DFC 348-49

Miles F/Sgt.45

Miller F/Sgt J.C. 242

Miller F/Sgt N 266

Millom Sgt G. 84-86

Mills Sgt 148

Misset Sgt Cliff 68

Mitchell F/O (262) 147

Mitchell F/O R.H. DFC 246

Mobley Sgt G. 84-86

Mole Cpl Pete 77

Moore Cpl (209 Sq) 278

Morgan W/O W. 301-02

Morris Sgt 45

Mosely Sgt P. 295

Moxley Sgt F. 266

Mudd F/Sgt Neville 138-40

Murray F/Lt K. DFC 75

Murray Sgt N. 132

Murrell Sgt (244) 210

Nash W/Cdr E.S.S. DFC AFC 224, 240

Nelson LAC George Medal 291

Newstead Cpl (MID) 291

Nobes Sgt D. 84-86

O'Leary Sgt A.W. 167

Osborne Sgt. Ron 67

Qxley Sgt Stan MID 179-81

Pack F/O J. 91, 197

Palmer Sgt (621), 261-66

Palmer F/Sgt Fred 200

Pamment AC1 'Pam of Pamanzi' 151

Parker Sgt 84

Parker P/O (36 Sq.) 262

Peacock F/Sgt Bert 177

Pearce Sgt Norman 172-82

Peattie Sgt. A. 132

Pedley F/Lt A.DFC 108, 350

Peel Sgt 'Bobby' 172-87

Pierse, ACM Sir Richard, KCB DSO DFC 333

Piteathly F/Lt D. DFC 178, 280, 340-41

Philip Sgt A.R. 246

Phillips W/O F. C. 49

Phillips W/Cdr R.A. 343

Platts W/O Gus 108, 152

Popple (205 Sq.) 37

Popple Sgt M.S. 299-310

Potter F/Lt 343

Pountain Sgt Ken 68

Pow Sgt Bob 156

Preston Sgt. A. A. 132

Probert Air Cdre Henry 310

Pulford AVM C.W.H. CB OBE AFC 40

Reace AC1 Taffy 151

Read F/O E.E. 248

Riddell W/O H. 246

Roberts F/O O.G.E. 48

Robothan F/O Clifford 243

Rockett F/Sgt 'Rocky' 363

Royle Sgt 200

Russell W/Cdr W.W. 64

Rutter F/Sgt Dennis 240

Ryan W/O A. 328

Scherr F/Sgt Des 341

Scannell F/Sgt Jack. 137

Schroeder F/O G. 132

Seymour Air/Cdre T.P CBE 90

Shaw Sgt Bernard 84

Cpl. Slater 278

Sheppee F/Sgt R. 118

Skinner F/Sgt E.J. 328

Small D. (CD Flight) 64

Smith Sgt 45

Smith F/Sgt Frank 328

Smith F/O (265 Sq) 197

Smith F/Lt A.H. 282

Smith Sgt 'Ginger' 68

Smith F/Sgt Harold 159, 162

Smith F/Sgt Henry 142, 228, 232

Smith W/O John 351, 355

Smith LAC R.W. 96, 291, 341

Smith Sgt W.R. 162

Smith W.W.W. 167

Smythe Sgt 147

Snowden Sgt J.M. 167

Snape F/Sgt Vew 240

Spencer Cpl Joe 290

Spry Sgt 102

Stacey AVM J.N. CBE DSO DFC 112, 122, 194, 311

Stait Cpl (209 Sq) 278

Staniforth Sgt 84

Stanyon Sgt F.J. 271

Sibley F/Sgt R.W. 266

Statham LAC Joe 299-310, 327

Stevenson Sgt W.R. DFM 246-361

Stewart F/Sgt 200

Stones F/Sgt Colin 343

Stratford W/O H.F. 328

Street F/Sgt DFM 167

Surridge F/Lt 240

Sweet F/Sgt 240

Taylor W/O M. 102, 291

Taylor G/Capt R. OBE 102, 153

Taylor F/S Tommy (230)

Temple-Murray F/O 91

Thomas Sgt Dai, 77, 94

Thomas F/Sgt G.T 341

Thomas Sgt R. 90, 299

Thomas F/Lt Rae DFC 48, 252

Thomson F/O A.J. 132

Thorpe F/Sgt Norman DFM 352

Thunder W/Cdr M.D. 132

Todd F/Lt A.M. 164

Tromans F/Sgt T. 224-40

Tucker P/O S.A. 42

Tugwell Sgt 45

Turner F/O I.J. 328

Underwood Sgt D.W. 363

Wade F/Lt (621) 248

Wadsworth Sgt F. 132

Walker F/Sgt E. 'Ted' 224-40

Wallace W/Cdr G.E. 88, 166

Walliker W/O 363

411

(Y)

Y-Service (Sigint) 173, 192, 272

(Z)

Zimbabwe 27

AVM H.S. Kerby CB, DSC, AFC; G/C A.F. Johnson DFC; W/C H. Duke-Woolley DFC, W/C;
L.C. Dennis; G/C Lord Nigel Douglas-Hamilton OBE, AFC; W/C H.F. Brushwood OBE;
Cpl Tyler WAAF; S/L S.W. Fitt. (Courtesy Air/Cdre P. Seyman)